R. E. Olds

A self-assured R. E. Olds at the peak of his career as an industrial leader (1905-1910)

R. E. Olds

Auto Industry Pioneer

by

George S. May

William B. Eerdmans Publishing Company

To Timothy George
and Rebecca Ann
and to their grandmother

Library of Congress Cataloging in Publication Data

May, George Smith, 1924–
  R. E. Olds, auto industry pioneer.

  1. Olds, Ransom Eli, 1864–1950. 2. Automobile
industry and trade—United States—History.
3. Businessmen—United States—Biography. I. Title.
HD9710.U520435   338.7'62'920924 [B]   77-7988
ISBN 0-8028-7028-7

Contents

List of Illustrations

Prologue

FOR THE AUTOMOBILE BUFF—indeed, for anyone interested in what has been going on in the United States in the twentieth century—the photograph spread across two pages of the June 17, 1946 issue of *Life* magazine is nostalgia incarnate. Almost swallowed up by an enormous collage of car names and insignias in the background and by a cloth-covered banquet table in the foreground, are twelve aging, well-dressed, rather tired-looking figures who were assembled for the photograph in Detroit on May 31, 1946. Old and tired they may have been, but what figures they had been! Third from the right, looking straight into the camera, one hand in an inside pocket, is Henry Ford—Henry Ford the *first*. A few chairs away is Barney Oldfield, the one and only. Further along the table is Charles W. Nash, who, unlike Ford, was still the active in 1946 as chairman of the board of the Wisconsin automobile firm bearing his name. Down at Ford's end of the table are J. Frank Duryea and Edgar L. Apperson: both had successfully built and manufactured gasoline-powered automobiles before Ford had been able to, though by 1946 no new Duryeas or Appersons had appeared for many years. Also near Ford in the picture is an old acquaintance of his, Charles B. King, still hale and hearty at seventy-eight and still actively experimenting and inventing as he had been in the mid-1890s. He was the first experimenter in Detroit—possibly in the entire state of Michigan—to build and operate a primitive version of the kind of vehicle powered by a gasoline, internal-combustion engine which by 1946 had long since become an everyday

1

part of the lives of tens of millions of families and individuals.

In fact, it was partly the realization that the fiftieth anniversary of King's historic public debut in his motor vehicle on March 6, 1896 had already passed that inspired George W. Romney, the managing director of the Automobile Manufacturers Association, to take the lead in arranging a spectacular celebration in Detroit from May 29 to June 9, 1946, an event hailed as the Automotive Golden Jubilee. The title reflected the extent to which Detroit felt it dominated the automobile industry: although the celebration coincided with the fiftieth anniversary of the test of Henry Ford's first car in Detroit on June 4, 1896, it smugly ignored the work of others elsewhere in Michigan, the United States, and Europe, which had predated that of Detroiters Ford and King by several years and even decades.

A highlight of the festivities was the induction of Ford and King and the other old-timers at their table into the Automotive Hall of Fame, which was created for the occasion but, curiously, not developed further by Detroit thereafter.[1]

Among the non-Detroiters present that May night—besides Frank Duryea and Edgar Apperson—was the bespectacled figure of Ransom E. Olds of Lansing, Michigan. Olds, who would turn eighty-two a few days after this banquet, was relatively inactive in 1946, but he had also been busily engaged in producing gasoline engines fifty years earlier. In fact, he built one of them to power a vehicle which he successfully tested two months after Ford operated his first motor vehicle. But this accomplishment came almost a decade after Olds had completed and operated the first of two steam-powered carriages. Within less than a decade after 1896, it was Olds more than anyone else, including Ford, whose manufacturing of automobiles made Detroit the center of the new auto industry. Inducting the originator of the Oldsmobile and Reo—two motor vehicles still in production in 1946—into the Automotive Hall of Fame was the least the industry could do for this great pioneer.

The Automotive Golden Jubilee was the last hurrah for most of the surviving members of the auto industry's first generation of leaders. Before long, despite a tendency among these automobile pioneers to live to an unusually old age, nearly all of the twelve men at the table were dead. The first to go was Barney Oldfield, youngest of the group, in the autumn of 1946. The following spring, Henry Ford, with whose name Oldfield's would always be coupled for their brief but illustrious association in the field of auto racing, breathed his last in the candle-lit surroundings of his flooded Dearborn estate. Nash died in 1948, and the car named for him vanished from dealers' showrooms a decade later. King died in 1957, Apperson in 1959, and Frank Duryea not until 1967, when he was in his ninety-seventh year.

Ransom Olds died at his Lansing home on August 26, 1950, at the age of eighty-six. In the southwestern part of that city and at six other assembly plants elsewhere in the country, the Oldsmobile Division of General Motors produced 396,757 automobiles that year, eighty times as many as were produced a half century earlier by all of the automobile manufacturers in the country, including Detroit's Olds Motor Works. Only a short distance down South Washington Avenue from the Olds home, Reo Motors, though beset by perennial financial difficulties, produced in 1950 a respectable total of 9,368 trucks whose name was an acronym derived from R. E. Olds' initials. But at the time of his death, Olds had had no managerial connection with Oldsmobile in over forty-six years, and he had played no active part in the affairs of the Reo company since his resignation as a director and chairman of the board in 1936. For this reason, news of his death perhaps came as something of a surprise to many outside his own community, who probably assumed that Olds had died years before. Even in Lansing, which during his lifetime had continued to regard Olds as its most prominent citizen, his name seemed on its way to forgotten annals only a few years after his death. The Olds name was taken off the tallest building in town and off the city's leading hotel, whose construction in both instances had symbolized Olds' important nonautomotive business interests. And in the late sixties, despite last-minute efforts to save the historic if somewhat unattractive Olds mansion at South Washington and Main, it was demolished as part of an expressway project that was designed to speed the passage of automotive traffic through the area.

Before the opening of the Automotive Golden Jubilee, George W. Stark, Detroit historian and veteran member of the *Detroit News* staff, interviewed Olds at his office in Lansing's Olds Tower. Stark wrote that Olds "earnestly believes that he is fairly entitled to rank legitimately as the father of the industry, for while others may have preceded him in bringing the horseless carriage to the highway ... still it was he who brought to the fledgling enterprise the miracle of quantity production."[2] However, the details of Olds' career were so poorly recorded that a colleague of Stark, writing in the same issue of the *News,* managed in one brief biographical sketch to get his facts wrong on every aspect of Olds' automotive career that he covered.[2]

Although Olds, rather characteristically, raised no great hue and cry about his failure to receive the kind of recognition that he obviously thought was his due, he did devote a considerable amount of time in the last years of his life to making available a more satisfactory account of his long career. He may have been motivated in part by his induction into the Automotive Hall of Fame; but there was also great interest in him at a community-sponsored celebration of his eightieth birthday in June 1944. Interviews with Olds became an annual feature in the Lansing *State Journal* on the occasion of his subsequent birthdays. Even beyond encouraging such efforts, Olds was working on a book-length study; although he did not specify, it was to be either an autobiography or—as seems more likely—a biography written with Olds' full cooperation.[3] Brief biographical sketches of Olds had appeared as early as 1900 in a Detroit publication entitled *Men of Progress,* with one of the longest of those that followed being a twelve-page account in *Automotive Giants of America,* put out in 1926 by the B. C. Forbes Publishing Company. But no full-length biography had ever been published. This same neglect was the lot of many of the automotive pioneers, but Olds would not have been human had he not felt a certain amount of envy, a twinge of bitterness perhaps, as he witnessed the steady stream of books and articles on Henry Ford that had been appearing since before World War I and continued to make Ford front-page news almost to the time of his death. By the 1940s there were also well-publicized autobiographies of Walter P. Chrysler and Alfred P. Sloan, Jr., two men who had entered the auto industry even later than Ford, a relative latecomer from the perspective of Olds' career beginnings.

A book-length biography of Olds finally did appear in 1949, the year before his death; but it was unfortunately of little help in promoting any meaningful appreciation of Olds' achievements and their importance. Published, copy-righted, and—one daughter asserts—virtually ghost-written by Olds, *Auto Pioneering: The Remarkable Story of R. E. Olds* is apparently based on little other than Olds' memory, which was quite obviously failing him by that time. Whether the author, Duane Yarnell, approached Olds with the idea of the book first, as he claimed, or whether Olds hired Yarnell to write the book which Olds himself had indicated in 1946 he was trying to get out, the choice was an un-fortunate one. Yarnell's previous experience as a writer of books for boys did not provide him with the background that might have enabled him to spot some of the errors and inaccuracies in what Olds narrated to him. Nor did Yarnell apparently have any inclination to check Olds' recollections against information that was available in newspaper files or in Olds' own surviving records.[4]

Those records, though far from complete, did exist and some years after Olds' death were deposited by the family at Michigan State University. They formed the basis for a second—and considerably better—biography of Olds, writ-ten by Glenn A. Niemeyer originally as a doctoral disserta-tion at Michigan State and then published in 1963 by his alma mater with the title *The Automotive Career of Ransom E. Olds*. Despite his use of the Olds papers, his interviews with over a dozen individuals who had known Olds well, and his more scholarly and more objective approach to the sub-ject than Yarnell's, Niemeyer's work is weakened by a certain shortsightedness which largely fails to view Olds within the broader context of what was occurring in the automotive world of his time. An equally serious defect is his uncritical acceptance of too many of the earlier interpretations and stories about Olds. Some of these could have been corrected by additional research into newspapers and trade journal files and by the use of such governmental records as state corporation reports and U.S. Patent Office files. In other cases, however, Niemeyer's errors were unavoidable, because many of the mistakes of previous writers and interpreters have only become evident with the deposit at Michigan State since 1963 of additional Olds manuscripts, not available when Niemeyer was engaged in his research.

Perhaps the most common assessment of Ransom Olds' career, viewed in its entirety, is summarized in a review of Niemeyer's book by Frank Ernest Hill, himself the collaborator with Allan Nevins on a three-volume biography of Henry Ford. The story of Olds, Hill declared, "was in a sense a tragic story, for Olds had greater capacity than he showed. Somewhere between 1905 and 1920 he faltered, and Henry Ford, whose gifts were similar, became a world-word for automotive and social progress, while Olds remained merely an interesting contemporary."[5] This is essentially the view of all who have attempted to assess the importance of Olds' life work. He was, it has been assumed, a man who reached the peak of his career and of his chosen profession by the time he was forty, but who then dropped out and watched while others passed him by.

Now, however, interest in Olds seems to be reviving in Lansing: the once-familiar name again appears on the hotel across from the State Capitol; it also now designates the portion of the I-696 expressway that slices through the area where Olds' home once stood; and there seems to be a growing interest in serious appraisals of automobiles and the industry that produces them. The time has arrived for a fresh look at the Ransom Olds image. What is the correct measure of the man? As an industrialist, was he nothing but a flash-in-the-pan, a pioneer somehow lacking in the strength and stamina needed to stay on top? Is it fair to view him only in terms of his "automotive career"? What other careers and interests did he have?

Primary as a knowledge of Olds' work as an automobile manufacturer must and does remain in this biography, a greater awareness of his life's total activities is provided to show that he was not "merely an interesting contemporary" of other, hardier competitors in the toughest of all business worlds. Here instead was a man who seems to have consciously decided that the gain was not necessarily worth the game, and who chose a fuller, more fulfilling life. He was, in a sense, one of those businessmen, perhaps not as atypical as the prevailing view would have us believe, who saw that there is more to life than the counting room or—in Olds' case—the assembly line. And he meant to find it before it was too late.

CHAPTER ONE

P. F. Olds & Son

IN A SENSE, the 1860s could be called the decade in which the automobile industry in the United States had its origins, because it was amid the tragedy and conflict that gripped the nation during those years that the foremost figures in the early development of the automobile were born. That generation of men grew up during the climax of the experimental phase in the development of the means necessary to propel an automobile. Inspired by new ideas and unencumbered by a strong commitment to earlier ways, these pioneers were seeking to make their mark in the business world by the time they reached their thirties. They realized the importance of the horseless carriage experiments and, while most of their contemporaries of an older generation were too wedded to other ways of life and most of those of a later generation were too young to take advantage of the available knowledge of this transportation revolution, those born in the 1860s saw that the time had arrived for the commercial production of motorized vehicles.

Among the future automotive leaders born during the Civil War years was Charles E. Duryea (1861), who, with his younger brother Frank, was the first American to achieve success—limited though it was—in manufacturing gasoline cars. Born the same year as Charles Duryea was Elmer Apperson, who with his younger brother Edgar collaborated with Elwood Haynes, four years older than Elmer, in the production of another of the gasoline cars to originate in the nineties. Other famous names in automotive annals who were born in the 1860s include Alexander Winton, who in

9

1897 began producing one of the best known of the earlier makes; Charles B. King, the first to attract attention to Detroit as a city involved in automotive developments; Henry B. Joy, also of Detroit, who made the Packard that city's first major entry in the luxury-car field; Jonathan Maxwell and Benjamin Briscoe, who joined forces to found the company that later became the Chrysler Corporation; John and Horace Dodge, parts manufacturers who finally went on to develop their own car; Charles Nash, like the Dodges a latecomer in the production of his own car; and Windsor White, eldest of the three brothers who developed the technically successful White steam car before switching to gasoline vehicles and establishing the firm that survives today as White Motors.

Towering over these and other names that might be cited are those of the three giants of the industry, all born that same decade: William C. Durant (1861), best remembered as the founder of General Motors; Henry Ford, born in 1863; and Ransom Olds, born on June 3, 1864. Three and a half decades later Olds would emerge as the most influential early leader in determining the course which the auto industry in the United States would follow in the twentieth century.

Like most people who came to be associated with Michigan during the nineteenth century, Olds was not a native Michiganian. He was born in Geneva, a town in northeastern Ohio with a population of about eighteen hundred. Since 1854, Olds' father had been operating in Geneva what is variously described as a blacksmith shop and a machine shop. Although Ransom would be the only member of his Geneva household to achieve widespread fame, some of the other Oldses should not be overlooked.

The Olds name in America dates back to about 1670, when Robert Old (or Ould, as the family then spelled its name) came from England to Connecticut, where he had received a grant of fifty acres of land. His great-great-grandson, Jason Olds (the form that the family name had by then assumed), moved from Massachusetts to the West in the early nineteenth century to serve as a Congregational missionary. He settled in Ohio, where his son Pliny was born in 1828. Twenty years later Pliny Olds married Sarah Whipple, a young woman from New York, and the couple settled in Geneva shortly thereafter.

Ransom Eli Olds, who as a boy was called Ranny and Ranse by his family—but who as an adult disliked both his Christian names and preferred to be called simply R.E.—was the youngest of five children born to Sarah Whipple Olds and Pliny Fisk Olds. The oldest child, Wilbur Jason Olds, born in 1850, struck out on his own while Ransom was still a child, moving somewhere to the West. Although he lived until 1913, Wilbur seems to have had little further contact with his youngest brother. Emory Whipple Olds, born in 1853, also struck out on his own after marrying in 1875. However, he had fallen on difficult times by the early 1900s and was helped out by his more successful brother, Ransom, for whom Emory acted as a kind of private secretary and manager of some real estate holdings during the decade before his death in 1914.

The only daughter in the family, Sarah Eliza Olds, nicknamed Sadie, was five years older than Ransom. She was at home while her younger brother was growing up; even after her marriage in 1887 she continued to be close to her parents and brothers—both in geographical proximity and in family relationships. This was also true for a time with the third brother, Wallace Samuel Olds, eight years Ransom's senior, who, unlike the other children, was directly and also somewhat controversially involved in the early business ventures of R. E. Olds.[1]

However, from a historical standpoint, the most important member of this family other than Ransom himself was his father, who has been rather shamefully slighted by earlier Ransom Olds biographers and other writers on automotive history. Pliny Olds deserves more attention not only because he was the father of R. E. Olds but because he was the founder of the business that eventually evolved into today's giant Oldsmobile division of General Motors.

Pliny did not follow his father Jason into the Congrega-

Pliny and Sarah Olds during their years of retirement in San Diego

tional ministry; in fact, he did not even remain a member of that church, becoming a Spiritualist instead. Details regarding his early life before marriage are almost entirely missing. Presumably he had apprenticed or had been otherwise trained as a blacksmith and machinist and was doing sufficiently well by the time he was twenty to feel that he could support a wife and family. Six years later he opened his own shop in Geneva. Although he carried on that business for sixteen years, it is doubtful that it was ever very profitable. At any rate, Ransom Olds later recalled that the family always seemed to lack a sense of real economic security during those years. Thus it was perhaps no surprise to the family and the community when in 1870 Pliny Olds traded the shop for a house and lot in Cleveland, where he had received the job of superintendent of the Variety Iron Works.

Four years later Pliny resigned from this position, reportedly for reasons of health. However, the economic depression which followed the Panic of 1873 could well have forced the iron works to reduce its staff, and may have had something to do with Olds' departure. This time Pliny Olds was able to exchange his Cleveland property for a farm at Parma, nine miles south of Cleveland. The outdoor life appears to have disposed of any health problems that had plagued Pliny Olds in the city, but he failed as a farmer. Though he may well have acquired the knowledge a successful farmer needed, the depression years of the mid-seventies were a time during which even established farmers in an agricultural state found the going rough. In 1878, therefore, Olds jumped at the chance to return to Cleveland for a job as a pattern-maker at the Garden and Price Printing Press Company. However, he was unable to dispose of his farm and was thus forced to leave the family behind and take a room in the city. Sarah Olds soon joined her husband, apparently leaving the farm in the care of Wallace, now twenty-two and still living at home with nineteen-year-old Sadie and fourteen-year-old Ransom. There is some evidence that Ransom was later brought to Cleveland so that he could be enrolled in school there.[2]

Actually, it is by no means clear who went to live in Cleveland with Pliny Olds in 1878, which simply illustrates the gaps and contradictions that abound in the surviving information about Ransom Olds' early years. All of the information is based on recollections and reminiscences that were recorded, in most cases, many years later. An unpublished typewritten manuscript entitled "That Boy Ranny," prepared under Olds' direction for the benefit of his children and grandchildren, provides what seems to be the best and most complete account of his childhood.

The picture of young Ransom that emerges from this and other sources is of a rather shy boy who was looked after by his older brothers; they made toys for him or helped him make them in their father's shop. These were, he later declared, the only toys he had, perhaps another indication of the family's limited financial resources in those years (though it should be noted that Henry Ford, whose family was admittedly prosperous by the standards of the time, also recalled that the only toys he had "were handmade"). It was Ransom's sister Sadie, however, who took him by the hand and helped him through that painful, even terrifying, moment of initiation in any child's life—the first day in school. Fortunately, Olds' first teacher was a short, plump, kindly woman who took a liking to the boy and gave him a book as a gift at the end of the term.

Although these experiences probably occurred in Cleveland, where the family lived during the years when he would have been old enough to start school, his most vivid recollections were of the country schoolhouse near Parma, which he attended later in the seventies when the family had left Cleveland for the farm. At noontime Ransom played in the schoolhouse yard, a mile from home, after eating the lunch that his mother had packed for him. The boys played too rough for him, and he thus preferred to play games with the girls. According to his family, Ransom Olds never did develop a liking for vigorous athletic activities, nor did he develop much of an interest in strictly male social activities as an adult, though he did find membership in organizations such as Rotary valuable for business reasons.

Like some of the mature R. E. Olds' social predilections,

From Duane Yarnell, Auto Pioneering

Four-year-old Ranny Olds of Geneva, Ohio, spruced up for the photographer

his fascination with machines, which would be the most obvious element running throughout his business career, had already become quite clear in this period. When the family moved to Cleveland in 1870, the six-year-old boy delighted in visiting his father at the iron works to observe the many wondrous goings-on in the shop. Later, on the farm, Pliny Olds built a small blacksmith shop for the repair of his tools, and the boy enjoyed helping his father. Young Ransom found in farm life much to occupy his attention and to satisfy his interest in things mechanical. On a stream that ran through the property he discovered an old dam, broken and useless, which had once been used to provide power for a small sawmill. Since one of his chores was to maintain a supply of wood for the house, Ransom thought that he could make the job easier if he could repair the dam and thereby create a mechanical means of cutting up the firewood. After much hard labor, he filled the break in the dam and succeeded in making the desired use of the water power. When a heavy rain, lasting several days, threatened to wash out the dam, the boy, who could not have been more than twelve or thirteen, went out in the pouring rain to buttress the weakened dam structure. His father found him there, soaked to the skin; apparently not realizing how much the dam meant to his son, Pliny upbraided him: "Don't you know better than to work in the rain?" He then seized the boy, shook him, brought him back to the house, and gave him a whipping that Ransom Olds, decades later, declared he had "remembered all his life." When the rain had stopped, the boy went out and found that the dam had been washed away and with it all his work.

Although Olds recalled in considerable detail this experience and the harshness of the punishment meted out by his father, it does not appear to have left a permanent scar on the relationship between him and his father, whom Ransom seems always to have regarded with respect and affection. In any event, the Olds father-son relationship was certainly much closer to normal than that of his two great automobile contemporaries. William C. Durant's adult personality was deeply affected by his alcoholic father's desertion of the family; and the strained relationships that seem to have developed between Henry Ford and his father, whether their cause was real or imagined by the son, are thought by at least one recent Ford biographer to provide the psychological key to an understanding of the adult Ford's often baffling behavior.[3]

On the whole, Olds' memories of his boyhood years on the farm were happy ones, but these experiences did not inspire in the youth any desire to become a farmer. On the contrary, like Henry Ford, who spent his first sixteen years on his family's farm near Dearborn, Michigan, Olds developed an active dislike for farm life, a feeling which had a distinct effect on the course of his later actions. Ford grew up with an aversion to the hard physical labor that was the lot of the farmer in the mid-nineteenth century and as a result, he claimed, was moved to become not a farmer but one who devised and manufactured machines intended to ease and improve the work of farmers and others. Olds declared on more than one occasion in later years: "I didn't like the smell of horses on the farm." This distaste, he claimed, had had the salutary effect of leading him to develop machines that would reduce man's dependence on these animals. While this cannot be the only—or even major—explanation for Olds' subsequent interest in automobiles, it is true that in discussing and advertising his early vehicles he constantly emphasized their superiority to horsedrawn vehicles, pointing to the prospect of greatly improved transportation conditions when horseless carriages such as his had banished the horse from the highway.[4]

* * * * *

In September 1880, Pliny Olds reunited his family again in one home, but in a new location and a new state—Lansing, Michigan. The details of the move are not clear. One granddaughter believes that he had read about a machine shop in Lansing which was up for sale. Eager to be in business for himself once again and by now skilled in the techniques of barter, Pliny traded his Ohio farm for a house and two lots in Lansing. It appears that he then sold one of the lots in order to purchase equipment for the shop, which he opened later that fall. Some accounts indicate that he may have used that lot money to build the shop itself, though his granddaughter's version of these events would indicate that he took over an existing business.[5]

Lansing in 1880 was a town of about eight thousand people, far more than were found in the rural surroundings to which the Olds family had become accustomed. One publication of that period described Lansing as "a beautiful site, well elevated above the stream, moderately undulating, with broad streets and avenues crossing each other at right angles, nearly all of which are graded, and many of which are lined on either side with forest trees, now of sufficient size to afford a luxurious shade in summer." Most of the city was tucked into a great horseshoe bend of the Grand River, which made for good ice-skating opportunities in the winter and boating in the summer, while furnishing an excellent source of water power. "The city," the report concluded, "boasts many fine public and private buildings, enjoys a prosperous trade with the flourishing surrounding country, and is rapidly increasing in wealth, trade and population."

However, conditions were not quite as idyllic as this and other contemporary reports would suggest. In terms of public improvements, most of Lansing's streets in 1880 were unpaved, and those which had been paved—beginning with Washington Avenue in 1878—were paved with cedar blocks laid down the center of the roadway and cobblestones along the side, scarcely an ideal surface after the wood had begun to wear. The first brick pavement would not be laid until 1893, and it would be many years before all the cedar paving would be replaced. Later it was said that the inadequate nature of Lansing's streets, in contrast to Detroit's relatively extensive network of paved thoroughfares, was one of the main reasons Ransom Olds favored moving his automobile operations to Detroit in 1899, the conditions there being far better for testing and demonstrating motor vehicles.

Lansing did have gas lighting as a result of the establishment of the Lansing Gas Light Company in 1873 by Eugene

F. Cooley and Frederick Thoman, both of whom would later become important investors in the Olds automobile companies. However, residents still pumped their water from wells until 1885, when a city waterworks was established; electricity also first became available at that time. Seven railroad lines served the city, yet Lansing's links to the main trunk lines of the nation were not as direct as those of Michigan communities to the south, which lay along the main routes of the Michigan Central or the Lake Shore and Michigan Southern.

Within the city, those who did not walk traveled by horse, until the middle of the 1880s, when bicycles became popular and the first horsedrawn streetcar lines were built. Still, although Lansing was one of the youngest cities in the state, it was as advanced in such matters as most communities in Michigan. The decision of the Michigan legislature in 1847 to convert what was then virtually a virgin wilderness into the state's capital was responsible not only for Lansing's origin but also for much of its growth and importance from that time on. The dominance of politics in the life of the city had been underscored the year before the Olds family arrived with the dedication of a new state capitol. The dome of this million-and-a-half-dollar structure was for many decades the city's chief landmark, until Ransom Olds reshaped the city's skyline a half-century later with an eight-story hotel and a skyscraping, twenty-six-floor office building which he constructed just across the street from the capitol.

Already by 1880, however, it was clear that politics was not all there was to Lansing. In 1873 the Lansing Improvement Association published a booster book which claimed that Lansing was becoming the commercial and financial—as well as the political—capital of Michigan. Few non-Lansingites would have agreed, but the association went on to cite Lansing's "natural and acquired" advantages that would interest the manufacturer. Its foremost assets were the timber resources that were still plentiful and an agricultural development in the surrounding area which was still far from its peak and which created a ready market for many kinds of manufactured goods.

This publication of 1873 is an early indication of the efforts various community groups conducted during the seventies to promote the growth in Lansing of new business activities. The one greatest product of these activities was to come in 1901 with the location of the Oldsmobile operations in the city. It is not known whether the Lansing Improvement Association had anything to do with Pliny Olds' decision to locate in the state capital in 1880, but the promotional efforts of the 1870s had doubtless had something to do with the development of a surprising number of relatively small but diversified Lansing industries by the time the Olds family arrived in town.

The availability of timber in the area accounted for a small sawmill operation; for five planing mills, which turned out a variety of wood products; and for a barrel manufacturing company, which with its shop in Lansing and three branches elsewhere in the state employed three hundred workers. Agriculture accounted for five flour and grist mills, and indirectly for E. Bement and Sons, the largest manufacturing firm in the city, which in 1880 added a substantial new main building to its already extensive plant. The firm's one hundred employees manufactured agricultural implements and stoves, which Bement sold from New York to the Dakotas. There were also two small iron works and two carriage works, the most important being A. Clark and Company. This company manufactured light carriages that were distributed throughout the northern states, and it would build the body for Ransom Olds' first gasoline car sixteen years later. Among other local industrial establishments in Lansing in 1880 were several breweries and furniture makers, a marble works, a brickyard, a pottery, and a tannery that had burned down a few weeks before the Olds family arrived.[6]

None of these enterprises cast much of a shadow in national business circles, but their presence helps to explain the decision of Pliny Olds to move from northern Ohio, where the opportunities for a man of his skills might appear to have been more numerous than in central Michigan. The growth of Lansing's manufacturing economy and the increasingly

P. F. OLDS & SON,

PRACTICAL MACHINISTS.

MANUFACTURERS OF

STEAM YACHTS

VERTICAL

STEAM ENGINES

OF 3, 5 AND 10 HORSE POWER.

ALSO

IRON and BRASS CASTINGS.

Special Attention given to

JOB WORK.

All Work Warranted.   LANSING, MICH.

This early advertisement for P. F. Olds & Son, appearing in the *Michigan State Gazetteer* only three years after the company had been established, gives greatest emphasis to its engines; but it includes perhaps the first printed association of the Olds name with the transportation field.

mechanized operations of the nearby farms created a need for expert repair services for the large number of machines that were in use. Pliny Olds proposed both to offer such services and to turn out additional machinery, particularly steam engines, which had replaced water power as the main source of power in the city's factories and on the farms. Therefore, with his son Wallace as his partner, Pliny Olds opened the doors of an eighteen-by-twenty-six-foot shop on River Street in the fall of 1880, under the name P. F. Olds & Son.

The shop may have been, as has usually been recorded, mostly concerned with repair work, but advertisements indicate that Pliny and Wallace Olds were soon trying to build up a business in manufactured products, which seems quite appropriate for a firm which was the ancestor of a division of General Motors. In an advertisement in the 1883 *Michigan State Gazetteer,* P. F. Olds & Son, "practical machinists," called attention to their "vertical steam engines of 3, 5 and 10 horsepower." They also made castings and gave "special attention" to job work. The same ad appeared in the next biennial number of the *Gazetteer,* with the added information that twelve and twenty-five horsepower steam engines were newly available.[7]

At the outset, Ransom Olds, who was sixteen years old when the family settled in Lansing, had only a part-time role in the family business, where he and his father and brother initially constituted the entire work force. Ransom is said to have attended the city's high school, located in a new building that stood on land now occupied by Lansing Community College, but records of the Lansing school district fail to show that Olds was ever enrolled in the city's schools. His youngest daughter, however, declares that he did complete the tenth grade before dropping out of school when he felt— and his father apparently agreed—that it was more important for him to work in the shop than continue in school. Failure to finish high school was common at that time, particularly for young men, and was viewed in a much less unfavorable light by that society than by a later one. Few of Olds' fellow automotive pioneers had much more or even as much of a formal education as he had. William C. Durant, for example, dropped out of school in his senior year in high school, while Henry Ford's public school experience was limited to the ungraded country school near his home, which at best provided the equivalent of an elementary school education in a city school system.[8]

If young Ransom did attend school in Lansing during the autumn of 1880, he was among 1,232 students enrolled at that time in the city's public schools, which, despite a relatively large building program in the seventies, were still quite crowded. This was a mild foretaste of what lay ahead within a few years: a flood of new residents, drawn by the boom in industry, would render existing city facilities totally inadequate in the burgeoning urban areas throughout southern Michigan.

* * * * *

During the school year, according to Olds' recollections, his job was to get up at five in the morning, build the fires in the Olds home on Cherry Street, then go to the nearby River Street shop and fire up the boiler, come home, eat breakfast, and hurry off to school. He worked in the shop after class in the afternoons, on Saturdays, and during school vacations. In one account, Olds said that during the first two years his father paid him nothing, and after two years he paid the youth only fifty cents a day during vacations. In another interview, however, Olds remembered his father as more generous, paying him fifty cents a day at the outset and after a year or two raising that to two dollars a day. This would have been a very high wage for a workman in the eighties and no doubt reflected Pliny's satisfaction with his son, whom he had trained as a machinist and in such skills as pattern-making and molding. Although Ransom Olds' formal education reportedly included several months during 1882–83 at the Lansing Business College, in addition to his years in public schools in Ohio and Lansing, he frequently remarked that the most valuable training he had received in preparing him for his business career was that given him by his father.[9]

By 1883 Ransom was apparently employed full-time at P. F. Olds & Son both as a machinist and bookkeeper, the latter position presumably resulting from the courses he had taken from Professor H. P. Bartlett, founder and principal instructor at the local business school. When he reached the age of twenty-one in 1885, Ransom bought out his brother Wallace's interest in the company and became his father's partner—the son in P. F. Olds & Son. To pay for Wallace's half interest in the business, he could come up with only $300 in cash. Thus he gave his father a personal note—at eight per cent interest—for the remaining $800 (although

the exact amount of money involved in the transaction dif-
fers slightly in some sources), which he owed for Wallace's
share in the firm.[10]

Wallace Olds had married in 1883 (though the Lansing
City Directory listed him as still boarding in his parents'
home as late as 1887), and he and his wife had their first child
in 1884. Thus, when he sold out to his younger brother the
next year it may have been because he needed the money. He
continued to work in the shop but without the authority he
had had over the affairs of the company in earlier years.
Wallace seems to have inherited from his father much the
same aptitude for mechanics as had his brother, but he apparently lacked the ambition to get ahead that drove Ransom during this period.[11]

The young man who had now assumed his older brother's
position in the family business and thus the full responsibilities of adulthood was not one who would have stood out
physically in a crowd as a figure destined for greatness. He
was of about average height for his day—five feet, nine
inches; his weight, as recorded in the diaries that survived
(from the time he was in his forties), was always within a
rather steady range of 175 to 180 pounds, and photographs
that date from the 1890s would indicate that that would be a
reasonable estimate of his weight in those earlier years as
well. By 1885, or shortly thereafter, he had grown a mustache that he would wear the rest of his life. Although mus-
taches were very much in fashion in the late nineteenth
century, Ransom Olds may have grown one not only to be
stylish but to add a touch of maturity and strength to his still
youthful appearance. Without the mustache Olds' round,
almost cherubic face, with the frequent twinkle in the eyes,
accurately reflected his friendly, essentially kind personality, and this good-natured image may not have been what
Olds wanted to present in his new role as a businessman. But
no mustache could disguise Olds' relatively humble
working-class origins, which were reflected throughout his
life in folksy, down-to-earth manners and speech characterized by simple, basic vocabulary and inflections that carried more than a hint of his New England ancestry. Olds

might have appeared ordinary in contrast to a contemporary like Henry Ford, whose handsome, stylish looks projected an image of enormous self-assurance, one of Ford's greatest assets in his business dealings. However, Ransom Olds' appearance may well have been deceptive, for he possessed a keen, shrewd mind that was fully capable of tough-minded, decisive action, as the events of the second twenty-one-year period in his life were to reveal.[12]

* * * * *

Despite his youth and his limited experience—not to mention his all too slim financial resources—Ransom Olds quickly established himself as the dominant partner in P. F. Olds & Son. He soon expressed an interest in plans for a more vigorous development of the company than his father had been willing to undertake, perhaps because of the latter's age or his health, which had not been good a decade earlier and would be one cause of his retirement a few years later. In 1885 the firm had an income of about $7,000, but it was beset by financial problems. In order to pay their seven employees at that time, the Oldses "had to borrow many times," Ransom said in 1921, and he had "done without money myself in order to pay them." In one specific instance, when there was no money to pay the workers at week's end, Ransom Olds took the train to nearby Charlotte, hoping to collect twenty-five dollars from one of P. F. Olds & Son's customers there. However, the best he could do was raise five dollars, which he divided among the employees late Saturday, with a promise that he would get an outside job himself in order to pay them the remainder. Pliny then reportedly saved the company by securing a loan of $1,500 from Professor Robert C. Kedzie of Michigan Agricultural College in return for a mortgage on everything the family owned. After two years, during which Ransom Olds claimed to have taken only fifty dollars a year as his salary, the firm was back on its feet and was paying the interest and some of the principal on the loan.[13]

The difficulties that this small Lansing business experienced in the mid-eighties were due partially, if not entirely, according to Ransom, to the unsatisfactory development of sales of the steam engines which it had been producing for several years. Yet this was the side of the business that interested him the most. "Engines were the one thing I could never get out of my head," he told the business writer O. D. Foster forty years later. "I wanted to manufacture and it seemed to me that we could create a demand for small engines." The result was the development of what the company was soon referring to as its "celebrated one-horse-power Gasoline Engine." The terminology was misleading and would be the source of much confusion in later years regarding the nature of Olds' first horseless carriage powered by this engine. It was not a gasoline engine as that term is usually defined, but rather a steam engine in which a gasoline burner was used to heat the water. The burner's ability to achieve the desired steam pressure in a matter of only five minutes, plus the economy and ease with which it could be operated, made it especially attractive, the company asserted, in shops "where light power is needed."

The company continued to offer the earlier vertical, balanced steam engines, by then available in sizes from three to sixty horsepower, along with such articles as pulleys, shafting, and hinges. Even in the nineties, when P. F. Olds & Son had become nationally known for its engines, it was still advertising locally such products as "Iron Building Material, Columns, Lintels, Etc.," and "Iron Work in all Branches." Nevertheless, the little "gasoline" steam engine quickly became the mainstay of the Olds line and the one product that was promoted to the exclusion of all others when the Lansing firm began advertising in such important national publications as *Scientific American*.[14]

Although the new engine may have been produced as early as 1885, large-scale production was delayed by the Oldses' money problems, meager plant facilities, and small staff, which made it possible for them to produce only about a dozen engines a year. (Ransom Olds' statement in 1905 that the company was producing from one hundred to two hundred engines a year during that period was clearly mis-

OLDS' GASOLINE ENGINE.

Best small power in the world.

One or Two Horse Power.

DON'T fail to write for a descriptive catalogue of this

ENGINE.

If in need of power of any kind, write to us.

P. F. OLDS & SON,

218 River St., Lansing, Mich.

This advertisement, here enlarged from the original small notice appearing in the May 2, 1891 issue of *Scientific American*, was one of the first attempts to make the Olds engines, which R. E. insisted on calling "gasoline engines," known beyond the southern Michigan region.

taken; perhaps it reflects his recollection of the firm's increased production later in the decade, after they had acquired enlarged facilities.) By 1887, probably as a result of the loan from Professor Kedzie, P. F. Olds & Son was able to move out of its original shop into a new two-story building across the street, twenty-five by one hundred feet in dimension, with additions by 1890 increasing its overall size to fifty-five by 135 feet. In that year the plant was said to have an annual production capacity of four hundred engines, but because the firm was still "clear behind on orders," additional plant expansion was being planned. A picture of the factory in the mid-nineties depicts a substantial brick structure with what appear to be two large wings extending straight back from the original two-story building that occupied the space between 218 and 224 River Street. The company boasted "one of the best equipped plants for the manufacture of light engines that can be found anywhere"; furthermore, it operated "on the principle that the best is the cheapest and they do nothing but strictly first-class work, and sell at prices as low as are often quoted for second or third class products."

Between 1887 and 1892, P. F. Olds & Son is reported to have produced 2,000 of the small steam engines, and *Scientific American* noted that in 1893 fifty-three more orders for engines were received than in any previous year. The work force, which had grown from the original crew of Pliny Olds and his two sons in 1880 to seven by 1885 and twelve by 1887, had risen to twenty-three by 1893, as sales in that year reached $24,148.25. In spite of the severe depression that followed the Panic of 1893, with its disastrous consequences for many businesses in Lansing and throughout the country, the market for the Olds engines held up. Sales continued to rise, though at a slower rate, reaching $29,179.73 for the year 1896. Indeed, as the Lansing *State Republican* had observed in 1890, "the star of prosperity" shone down with favor on the Olds company during those years.[15]

The rapid growth of the Olds business led to its incorporation on July 31, 1890, still under the name of P. F. Olds & Son, for the stated "purpose or purposes" of "the manufacturing of engines, boilers, and machinery and general foundry & machine work." The capitalization of the new firm was $30,000, with $15,000 paid in, representing half the par value of the three thousand shares of stock that were issued. Several writers, including Olds' most recent biographer, Glenn Niemeyer, have claimed that the Olds partners incorporated in order to secure outside financial support. They have asserted in particular that Edward W. Sparrow and Samuel L. Smith, two Michigan capitalists with strong Lansing business ties, invested in the Olds company at the time of its incorporation. However, although Sparrow and Smith would later become the most important backers of the early Olds automobile ventures, neither the state corporation records nor the local newspaper coverage support the conclusion that they were investors in P. F. Olds & Son in 1890. The Lansing *State Republican,* in reporting the incorporation of the company, indicated that the only stockholders were members of the Olds family. This is borne out in the articles of association filed with the state on July 31, which listed Pliny and Ransom Olds as holding 1450 shares of stock each, and Wallace Olds, who was still active in the business, though no longer as a partner, as owning the remaining hundred shares. An Ingham County justice of the peace certified that Pliny, Ransom, and Wallace Olds, and no one else, had acknowledged before him on July 31 that they had "freely and for the intents and purposes therein mentioned" executed the articles of association.

Later, in the first annual report that the new corporation filed with the secretary of state, P. F. Olds & Son certified that as of January 2, 1892 all the stock was still held by the three members of the Olds family. Not until 1897 is any of the stock shown to have been owned by anyone outside the family. It seems most unlikely that either Sparrow or Smith would have put any money into the company between 1890 and 1897 without receiving stock in return. It is possible, of course, that they loaned the corporation money without becoming stockholders, but there is no evidence to suggest that such loans were in fact made. The annual reports of P. F. Olds & Son during the 1890s never show a very high level of indebtedness, and the debts that are recorded are no more than one would expect in the normal day-to-day operations of such a business. In short, the evidence indicates that from 1890 to 1897 the Olds family retained complete control of both the ownership and the operation of this increasingly successful business.[16]

Pliny Olds had the title of president of the newly incorporated firm, and he retained this title through the following years, with Ransom Olds holding the apparently subordinate offices of secretary and treasurer. However, there is no doubt that the son was the dominant figure in the company: he claimed in 1904 that his duties made his position comparable to that of a general manager from 1885 on. Pliny, who was sixty-two in 1890, was too easy-going to suit his ambitious son. The older man loved to stop and chat with the workmen in the shop, to the annoyance of Ransom, who was too busy to engage in such socializing on company time and who fretted at the production delays caused by his father's congenial nature. Of more basic concern to the son, however, was his belief that his father was far too conservative in his thinking regarding company policy; and this finally led Ransom to attempt tactful ways of convincing his father to turn over full control of the business to him.

One day, as Olds recalled the occasion many years later, Pliny said to him: "Son, are you trying to tell me that I'm not a very good businessman?" Before Ransom had a chance to reply, his father went on to say: "Perhaps, you're right. I guess you can't teach an old dog new tricks, at that. Maybe, in the past, I've been upset at some of the things you've tried. But I've lived to see a lot of those things work out for you. If I've never said it before, I'd like to say it now—you're a good mechanic, R. E., and I've got great faith in you. Now tell me, son, just what you've got in mind." According to Ransom, this was his father's graceful and amicable accession to his taking full control of the company which Pliny had founded a decade or so earlier.

Whether or not the change occurred quite as easily as Ransom Olds remembered, it does appear that Pliny, though still officially the president, had withdrawn from any active role in the business by 1894. At that time his stockholdings were reduced to 1,150 shares: he sold or transferred 150 shares to both Wallace and Ransom, giving the latter 1600 shares and a majority of the stock. By January 1897, Pliny's holdings were reduced to a mere fifty shares, while Ransom had 2,600 and Wallace 200, fifty shares less than he had held in 1894. Madison F. Bates, an employee of the firm, bought the first 150 shares to go outside the Olds family.

In November 1898, shortly after a reorganization of the Olds business, with which P. F. Olds probably had little connection, Ransom gave a farewell dinner party for his parents, who were departing for the west coast. Pliny Olds, then in poor health, was to begin spending much of the year with his wife in San Diego. Later, in 1905, they moved to what became Daytona Beach, Florida, where Ransom Olds bought them a house. It became the first unit of what developed into the Olds family's winter home, where Ransom Olds would go annually until his death. Pliny and Sarah Olds would return for a few weeks to Michigan during the summers, as they did in mid-June 1908. There, in Lansing, Olds noted in his diary on June 21, he and his wife Metta and their two daughters went to his brother Emory's house "for Dinner with Pa & Ma." It was the last such family gathering, for ten days later, on July 1, 1908, Pliny Olds died. The funeral was on July 2, and on the following day Ransom Olds accompanied his father's body into Detroit for the cremation which apparently could not at that time be taken care of in Lansing. Pliny's ashes, along with those of his wife, who died in 1910, would eventually repose in a family mausoleum in Lansing. The parents had lived to see their youngest child become a wealthy man and one of the recognized leaders in an industry that had been unknown thirty years earlier when they had settled in Michigan's capital city.[17]

Just how much credit is due R. E. Olds for the sharp rise in the family's business fortunes after 1885 is difficult to determine; family and business records are generally missing for that period. At the time of Pliny Olds' death, the Lansing *Journal,* no doubt on the basis of information supplied by the family, credited him with having developed the small steam engine which was the original basis for the company's success. It seems probable also that others, like Wallace Olds, who was an able mechanic, and some of the employees, had a hand in the development. But the fact remains that the first engine-related patent—and apparently the first patent of any kind awarded to a member of the Olds family or assigned to the company—was issued to Ransom Olds on July 28, 1891 for a governor on steam engines. In applying for this patent Olds swore before a local notary public on March 6, 1890 that to the best of his knowledge he was the "original, first and sole inventor" of this mechanical device. This declaration is also consistent with Olds' sworn statement in a deposition in 1905 that he personally designed and was responsible for the company's engine "from the drafting room until it was completed and in operation."

The object of his 1890 invention, as Ransom explained it in his application, was in keeping with the stated objectives of the Olds steam engines and nearly all of Olds' later developments: to achieve increased simplicity and efficiency, in this case by the use of a device controlling the speed of a

Courtesy of Gladys Olds Anderson

This photo of Olds and his family emerging from a very early carport was used as a promotional piece by the Olds Motor Works (discovered by the Oldsmobile researcher Charles E. Hulse). The accompanying statement remarked on the ease of attaching such a "housed porte cochere" to one's home, as Olds had done.

steam engine. The patent, No. 456,837, was the first of thirty-four patents awarded to Olds during the following half-century. The last one, No. 2,230,308, a patent on an internal combustion engine, came on February 4, 1941, when Olds was in his seventy-seventh year, and very nearly fifty years after his first patent. In only four instances is Olds listed as co-inventor with someone else. In all other cases his is the only name appearing on the application and the only one listed on the final Letters Patent as the inventor of the patented item. The available evidence, therefore, would indicate that Ransom Olds was, at the very least, "a good mechanic," as his father put it, with the talents that were necessary for him to make a major contribution to the design of the small, gasoline-heated steam engine, if he was not indeed principally responsible for this crucial development in his company's success.[18]

In addition to his mechanical talents, however, it was apparently Ransom Olds who had the business sense to size up correctly the most likely market for this engine and to proceed to circularize some two thousand weekly newspapers with a sales pitch that made those small shops the best customers for the Olds engine. One Charlotte, Michigan newsman recalled that Ransom Olds even came over and "personally installed" one of the engines in the shop of the Charlotte *Tribune*, "and he treated the machine with almost parental care and attention."[19]

By the end of his first decade in Lansing, Ransom Olds was being referred to by a local paper as "one of Lansing's most deserving young men." Feeling more secure financially, the successful young businessman married Metta Ursula Woodward on June 5, 1889. She was almost exactly the same age as her husband, having been born on June 6, 1864 (three days after Olds' birth) in Pinckney, Michigan. Her father, Joseph D. Woodward, a transplanted New Yorker, was a cooper in Pinckney. Miss Woodward had lived there and for a time in Fowlerville before coming to Lansing, where she was clerking in a gift shop when she first met Olds. She attracted the attention of her future husband when she rode as a passenger on a launch powered by an Olds steam engine, on which the enterprising Ransom provided Sunday afternoon excursions on the Grand River as a means of supplementing the family's income. The two were married in the Lansing home of the bride's aunt and uncle, with whom she was living. They then took the train to Grand Rapids for a weekend honeymoon and returned to Lansing to live in a house that Olds and one of his employees had built in their spare time. Olds, in fact, was still shingling the roof of this house on the morning of his wedding day.

Here, on East Kalamazoo Street, a short distance from the Olds shop and the home of his parents, the couple lived until 1896, when—with two daughters to look after—they moved into a larger house at the corner of Grand and Kalamazoo. The changes that were occurring in Olds' life were apparent

not only by the increased space that he needed for his growing family. Within a few months he had built on to his new
residence what must have been one of America's first attached garages, in order to house the gasoline-driven carriage that he had developed and was driving. For the manager of P. F. Olds & Son a new and far greater business
career lay ahead.[20]

CHAPTER TWO

Horseless Carriage Experiments

THROUGHOUT HIS ADULT YEARS, Ransom Olds' business activities, important as they were, never seem to have meant everything to him. The fact that his name became almost synonymous with automobiles should not lead one to the mistaken assumption that automobiles were all he thought of. This was far from the truth.

Among Olds' foremost interests was his family. Besides his parents, his sister, and one or two of his brothers, with whom he had had and would continue to have close relationships, his marriage in 1889 gave him more immediate family responsibilities and interests. Four children would be born to Metta and Ransom Olds. The third and fourth children, a girl and a boy, died in infancy. The first two children, Gladys, born in 1892, and Bernice, born two years later, lived to become part of what was obviously a closely knit family circle. Although some of the daughters' earliest recollections are of their father in his study going over plans for one of his mechanical devices, they also recall his participation in family life which revealed at this early stage the love of social activities, travel, and other leisure occupations for which Olds would become famous in later years.[1]

Metta Olds had a personality clearly unlike her husband's. A quiet, almost retiring woman, particularly as she grew older, she nonetheless provided the cement that held the family together, according to a grandson. The source of her strength and authority within the family was based on strong religious convictions. At the time of her marriage in 1889, and until her death in 1950, Metta Olds was an active

Baptist, although it was apparently not until 1903 that she actually joined the First Baptist Church of Lansing. Her husband, on the other hand, had not been a churchgoer when they were married; in fact, he once declared that he "hardly knew what the inside of a church looked like."

Both of Ransom's parents were Spiritualists. During the 1880s, Pliny Olds served as president of the Namoka Spiritual Camp Meeting Association, which held property on Pine Lake (now Lake Lansing), a few miles northeast of Lansing. There the Spiritualists held summer gatherings, and various families, including the Oldses, had cottages there. Ransom Olds, however, did not share his parents' interest in Spiritualism. His break with them on this issue was publicly proclaimed at one memorable meeting when, to the extreme dismay of his mother, the youthful Ransom yanked on a sheet and succeeded in exposing an individual who was engaged in undercover manipulations designed to create an impression that spirits were present at the assembly. This experience may well have led Olds to a certain skeptical stance toward religion in general. As a result, Olds has usually been depicted as resistant to the efforts of his wife over many years to get him to join her church. He finally agreed to join, it is said, when it came time for his daughters to become members. However, though Olds did not formally join the First Baptist Church of Lansing until July 1912, his diaries show that he had been attending church services with increasing frequency for a number of years before 1912, and as early as 1891 the young people of the church were meeting at Olds' residence for "a literary and musical entertainment," presumably with the head of the household's approval. Once he officially joined the church, Olds took an active and even enthusiastic interest in church activities, particularly those connected with the business operation of the institution.[2]

In addition to his family and eventually his church, Olds also developed a strong interest in community activities. As his fame and importance in the business world grew, this would lead to his becoming the most influential individual in his hometown. For many years—up to Olds' death in

Courtesy of Gladys Olds Anderson

Metta Woodward Olds

1950—a word from him was said to be enough to assure the success or defeat of any major civic proposal in Lansing. The first tangible sign of Olds' emergence as a civic leader came in March 1893, when the caucus held in the Sixth Ward to select candidates for the Lansing school board nominated Olds, a ward resident, for one of the two positions from that ward. The Lansing *Journal* reported that the Republicans at the meeting split their support between two candidates, which "resulted in the selection of a Populist, Ransom E. Olds, to fill the vacancy." The association of Olds with that era's radical third party is startling indeed in view of Olds' later espousal of conservative political ideas and staunch support of the Republican party. If the local paper was correct in labeling him a Populist in 1893, one might conclude that Olds' business success was still not great enough by that time to wipe out the bitter taste of the earlier hard times through which he and his family had struggled on the Ohio farm and in the Lansing shop. These struggles may have given the partially socialistic economic programs of the Populists a magnetic attraction for Olds, as they had for many other farmers, workers, and small businessmen of that day.

Nomination at the ward caucus was tantamount to election, and when the school board election itself was held in April 1893, Olds and Frank G. Clark of the local carriage company were the only candidates on the ballot for the two positions from the Sixth Ward. Clark, who was an incumbent running for another two-year term on the board, received 254 votes, compared with only 180 for Olds. Despite this early apparent lack of enthusiasm among some of the electorate for an alleged Populist, in a ward where less than five per cent of the votes cast in the 1892 General Election were for Populist candidates, Olds succeeded in winning re-election to the board, continuing to serve there until September 1899, when his business interests compelled him to resign his seat as he prepared to move his residence to Detroit. Olds served as board treasurer from 1895 to 1898, when he took over the position of clerk. He served on committees that dealt with supplies, the library, and textbooks and courses of study. In addition to Frank Clark, other prominent individuals on the school board with Olds in the years 1893 to 1899 included Orlando F. Barnes, a member of one of Lansing's wealthiest and best-known families, Clarence Bement of the farm equipment and stove manufacturing firm, and Harris E. Thomas, a successful attorney.

The school board position, the only elected public office Olds ever held, demanded a considerable amount of time and involved a myriad of rather small, vexing details. How effective Olds was on this board is open to some doubt. On one occasion, as chairman of the committee on supplies, he introduced a salesman who was promoting a new kind of window shade; but Olds could get no support for his motion that the board buy two hundred of the shades. On another occasion Harris Thomas indirectly criticized Olds, who was serving as treasurer at the time, for the manner in which bills were submitted to the board for approval. Thomas complained that there was no indication in some cases that the work had been completed or that it had ever been duly authorized. However, offsetting the headaches that came with the job was the added prestige that it brought Olds in the community. And he no doubt regarded the opportunity to become better acquainted with the other board members as potentially beneficial to the advancement of his business interests.[3]

In activities more directly connected with his business career, Olds showed an early tendency to develop wide-ranging interests that would ultimately lead him into such nonautomotive fields as lawnmowers, refrigeration, banking, and land development. In July 1895, for example, just a month before filing applications with the United States Patent Office for important new engine patents, Ransom Olds, in company with George E. DeVore of Lansing, was applying for a patent on a totally unrelated product—an elevator gate.[4] Although it is safe to say that engines, not elevator gates, were foremost in Olds' thoughts and the conduct of his business affairs, it would be incorrect to assume that his mind turned first and always to vehicular utility when he

contemplated ways in which his engines might be employed.
Beyond the industrial applications suggested in early ads for
the steam engines, Olds experimented in the eighties with
the use of the engines in various crafts which he and his
family operated on the Grand River. This led to an emphasis
on the engine's usefulness in powering boats, especially
yachts, which began an association of the Olds name with
the marine engine field for which it became especially well
known in the nineties. On a more personal note, this also
marked the beginning for Ransom Olds of a love affair with
boating that would become his principal leisure activity in
later years.[5]

By the mid-1880s steam power had been used to propel
vessels on the Great Lakes for well over sixty years, and it
was on a lake steamer that the Olds family had covered the
first leg of the trip from Ohio to their new Michigan home in
1880. Arriving at Detroit, they had then gone on to Lansing
by train, another form of steam transportation that had been
used in Michigan since the late 1830s, only a decade after it
had been introduced in the East. Olds later claimed that
traveling on these two kinds of steam-powered modes of
transportation in 1880 had started him dreaming about
building a steam-powered road vehicle that would take the
place of the horsedrawn conveyances he had disliked ever
since he had been assigned what was to him the disagreeable
task of caring for the family horse.[6]

The idea of a self-propelled steam road vehicle was hardly
a new one by the eighties. As early as the 1850s, in Jefferson
County, Ohio, about a hundred miles south of Ransom Olds'
birthplace, Joseph McCune, a farmer who used a steam engine in threshing operations, had connected this engine by a
chain to the rear wheels to enable the machinery to be
moved about under its own power. In 1858 he drove this
vehicle to the Cadiz Fair, twenty-three miles from his home.
In subsequent years such ponderous self-propelled machines
became fairly common sights on the roads of the Midwest.
Henry Ford credited an 1876 encounter with such a vehicle
on a road into Detroit as a determining factor in turning
his thoughts toward road transportation. It would seem a

safe assumption that Olds also must have seen one or more of these steam vehicles operating in rural Ohio during that period and that the experience influenced his dreams just as it had those of young Ford.[7]

With the interest he had acquired in steam machines from working with his father and brother to design and produce the engines, Olds would certainly have had some knowledge by the mid-eighties of the efforts of other Americans who had been trying to develop practical steam passenger vehicles for a century, since the pioneering work of Oliver Evans in Pennsylvania during the late eighteenth century. The most persistent of these experimenters was Sylvester H. Roper of Roxbury, Massachusetts, who built ten such vehicles between 1859 and 1895. These had received considerable publicity, especially through the efforts of "Professor" W. W. Austen, who displayed and demonstrated some of Roper's machines at county fairs and circuses as far west as Indiana. Since Olds said in 1905 that, aside from vehicles that he himself had built, the first horseless carriages he had actually seen were those at the Chicago World's Fair in 1893, it may be assumed that he never witnessed one of Austen's performances in the 1860s and 1870s. But Olds may well have heard of them. There is a stronger possibility that by the mid-eighties he would have heard about and quite possibly read about the work of another experimenter, Lucius D. Copeland, whose success in building and operating both a steam-powered bicycle and a three-wheeled steam vehicle had received considerable publicity. Copeland's three-wheeler was advertised for sale by a Philadelphia firm in the spring of 1886—though apparently without takers.[8]

Much closer to home was the example of John Clegg and his son Thomas: in their machine shop in the eastern Michigan country town of Memphis they constructed a four-passenger vehicle with a one-cylinder steam engine during the winter of 1884–85. In 1885, Thomas Clegg is said to have driven this horseless carriage for several hundred miles in and around Memphis at speeds of up to twelve miles an hour, including an appearance in the Fourth of July parade in Emmet, eighteen miles away. Many years later, an old man who had known the Cleggs asserted that Thomas Clegg had been an acquaintance of Ransom Olds and had, in fact, worked with Olds on the steam vehicle which the latter subsequently built. This unsubstantiated story is intriguing because, if it is true, it would help to dispel the myth—in Olds' case, at least—of the automobile pioneer laboring away in total ignorance of the work of other like-minded experimenters. The fact that P. F. Olds & Son soon began advertising in *Scientific American* would also seem to dissolve such a myth about Ransom Olds: he clearly had close familiarity with this journal, which in the eighties and nineties reported frequently on the progress of horseless carriage developments both in Europe and in America. It was perhaps from this magazine that Olds had acquired the fairly extensive knowledge of the work of earlier automotive experimenters which he displayed in a paper given before the Michigan Engineering Society in 1897.[9]

Exactly when Ransom Olds completed his first steam carriage is uncertain, mainly because Olds, like Henry Ford, Charles King, the Duryea brothers, and others, had great difficulty in remembering dates in later years. One account of Olds' career, published during the Automotive Golden Jubilee in 1946, claimed that he had begun work on his first car in 1883 but that it was not until the end of 1886 that he "completed the engine." This may have meant that the vehicle itself was not operating until the next year. However, a full-page article on Olds in the Jackson *Citizen-Patriot* of July 7, 1929 reported that the vehicle itself had been completed by 1885. Olds himself eventually settled on 1886 as the year in which he built and tested his first motor vehicle, and it is this date which most commonly appears in stories published during Olds' later years; this is also the year that appears on the monument which the family erected in 1953 on River Street in Lansing to commemorate his work.

However, in a biographical sketch published in 1900, in articles in trade journals during that period, and in Olds' own testimony in the Selden Patent case of 1905, the original Olds horseless carriage is said to have been "invented and constructed" by Olds in 1887 and tested by him in the latter part of that year. As late as 1915 the automotive writer David Beecroft, in an authoritative series of articles on the early development of the automobile, used the 1887 date; but by 1925, O. D. Foster, in his sketch of Ransom Olds, was giving 1886 as the year in which Olds built his first motorized vehicle, the date which by that time Olds had apparently decided to use. The year 1887 would appear most likely to be correct because of its common usage in the early literature and patent notices. But it is also likely that Olds, who in 1905 claimed that he had "always wanted a self propelled vehicle" since he was a boy and that he had "studied on it a great deal while in school," had prepared some preliminary plans and perhaps had even begun to build this vehicle before 1887.[10]

Ten years later, in his first recorded recollections of this development, Olds declared that he had given much thought to this motor carriage, designing "several in my head ... in fact, I could almost see myself flying down the street." Finally, he settled on a design which was, like Lucius Copeland's invention and a good many of the early horseless carriages, a three-wheeled affair. Olds placed two wheels in the back and a smaller one—mounted in a fork—in front, just the reverse of the vehicle Copeland constructed at that same time. Olds' wheel arrangement made steering the vehicle a simple operation, as he noted, comparable to steering a child's tricycle today.

By later standards this first Olds motorized vehicle was, as even he confessed, pretty crude. The one-horsepower, gasoline-heated steam engine was enclosed in a box, eighteen inches high, which was part of the body of the carriage and was located behind the single seat. He said in 1897 that he had thought that he must "get the machinery out of sight, never thinking that we do not try to get the horse or locomotive out of sight." Although the motive power for Olds' second steamer in the early 1890s was highly visible, the gasoline cars he built from 1896 to 1904 again followed the "invisibility" principle. Indeed, most American automakers of that period placed the engine underneath the body as if to try to hide its presence, rather than placing it boldly out in front under a hood, as French designers had begun to do in the early 1890s.

With the exception of the engine for his 1887 machine, which Ransom and his men could produce, outside suppliers provided most if not all of the other materials for the carriage, with Olds somehow managing to pay for these parts from his limited cash reserve. The steel-tired buggy wheels, the body built of whitewood, and the oak frame apparently came from local sources, as did some of the metal parts. However, the steel gears—"the finest cut gears made"—were ordered from a company in Providence, Rhode Island, probably the Brown & Sharpe Manufacturing Company, which was nationally known for its precision work. The Midwestern representative of Brown & Sharpe was Henry M. Leland, who would later become one of the early parts suppliers for the Oldsmobile after he opened his own shop in Detroit.

Sometime during the summer of 1887, Olds, who had worked sixteen to eighteen hours a day, and toward the end even longer hours, to complete the vehicle, gave the machine

An artist's sketch of Olds' three-wheeled steamer of 1887

From Duane Yarnell, Auto Pioneering

its first road test. He reported that considerable interest in what he was doing had developed among local residents, and on the day that the final touches were put on the vehicle a crowd had assembled at the shop. They were hoping to see Olds test the strange machine then and there, but they were to be disappointed. Olds told them that he was going to wait until the next day, "not saying about my intentions of being up before the birds, as I realized that I had a colt on my hands, and did not care to have too many spectators." Like many of his fellow auto pioneers, including Henry Ford and Charles King, Olds was not entirely sure that his initial experimental vehicle would work or, if it worked, how well or over what distance. Hence the inventor desired to conduct the first tests at a time when there would be little likelihood of the presence of spectators to embarrass him if the tests were less than successful. Therefore, Olds fired up the boiler of his three-wheeled steamer the following morning at three o'clock. In spite of the fast five-minute build-up time which was one of the advertised virtues of the Olds steam engine, it was not until ninety minutes later that Olds was ready to go, and the door of the shop was opened.

> I mounted to the seat and pulled the lever; she moved slowly, but speed was increased as it went down the platform out of the shop; there was a slight raise, however, before crossing the sidewalk and she refused to ascend the grade, so I at once dismounted, and going behind, gave it a push to be remembered, which did the business, and it reached the sidewalk in safety; I again mounted to the seat; there was yet a descent to the street in my favor, so that I had but little trouble in reaching the road and running a block without a stop; at this point the efforts of the engine were exhausted, and an assistant was necessary, as it was getting quite light and there was no more time to be lost; I secured two pushers behind, and together with the engine, got it back without an accident, which ended my first trip in a horseless carriage.[11]

As the years passed the story of this historic predawn ride was considerably embellished with additional and sometimes contradictory details. In later accounts the machine was described as producing an unearthly loud noise, the result of the steel gears Olds was using in the transmission, though he had secured the finest gears possible specifically "to avoid the noise." "Unfortunately," Olds told O. D. Foster, "there was no transmission case, and when the car was run the wood supports for the gears magnified the noise, like a sounding board." This racket was said to have caused windows in the neighborhood to be thrown open as residents were awakened by the demonstration. Many came outside to gape at the spectacle of a horseless vehicle proceeding along River Street. According to one story, a horse pulling a milk wagon became frightened at the sight of the steamer and bolted, causing the loss of nine quarts of milk and a quart of buttermilk before the driver—with the help of Olds— managed to get the horse under control. Even though these revised versions recorded that Olds was able to get the machine back into his shop under its own steam, without the manual assistance his account of 1897 declared had been required, the net impression left by all accounts—as well as the conclusion Olds himself obviously reached following this and further experiments—was that this venerable ancestor of the modern Oldsmobile had flunked its tests.[12]

Some obituaries of Olds in 1950 referred to his 1887 steamer as the "first really practical automobile," echoing the sentimental view Olds himself sometimes expressed in his old age. It was, of course, nothing of the kind; neither was it "the first three-wheeled 'horseless carriage,'" nor even the first horseless carriage in Michigan, as other obituaries stated.[13] However, Olds' experiences in 1887, though they duplicated the earlier work of such experimenters as Roper, Copeland, and the Cleggs—none of whom went on to become successful manufacturers of their vehicles—did give him a head start on most of those contemporaries who would become major figures in the subsequent development of the American auto industry. For example, the Duryeas, Elwood Haynes, and Alexander Winton were in 1887 years away from building their first automobiles, and only in the case of the Duryeas is there much evidence that they were then even thinking along such lines. In Michigan at the time, Henry Ford had worked with steam engines, and he would later claim to have built a self-propelled piece of farm equipment; but even Ford did not claim to have duplicated Olds' steam-powered road vehicle. In 1887, Charles King was a student at Cornell University pursuing studies in mechanical and engineering problems other than automotive, with which he would not become concerned until 1893. William C. Durant was thinking of new ways to promote the sales of the horsedrawn—not motorized—carriages which he and his partner J. Dallas Dort had begun to manufacture in Flint in 1886. Thus, the knowledge Ransom Olds had begun to acquire in the summer of 1887 helps to explain his ability, some fourteen years later, to seize the lead in manufacturing automobiles from others who lacked his years of experience in the development of these vehicles.

Olds' opinion of his initial creation of 1887 became clear when, after tinkering with it for three or four years, he tore it apart and started over again. Pliny Olds had been less than enthusiastic concerning his son's project, remarking to one customer: "Ranse thinks he can put an engine in a buggy and make the contraption carry him over the roads. If he doesn't get killed at his fool undertaking, I will be satisfied." However, when Olds spoke to Duane Yarnell about it in 1949, he certainly exaggerated the degree to which his efforts to build this steamer were opposed or ridiculed by his father, the workmen in the shop, or the townspeople. Actually, the public had long ago become accustomed to the use of steam engines in the transportation field and was much more likely to accept steam-powered road vehicles than they were those powered by the new—and as yet unfamiliar—gasoline internal combustion engine. This was one reason many experimenters and manufacturers would stick with the steam car well into the following century.[14]

Whether Ransom Olds in 1887 contemplated manufacturing steam vehicles or, as seems more likely, he was just experimenting with a different use of the engines he and his father were producing, he recognized that the major fault of his steam carriage was its lack of sufficient power. When he was making his plans, he "used to watch the wheels of our carriage, and often get into the shafts myself to see how much power it would require." He decided finally "that a 1 H. P. motor would make it hum." What he had failed to realize, however, as he explained to Arthur Lauder sixty years later, was that his calculations had not included as part of the overall weight of the buggy the weight of the engine that would be replacing the horse. After he replaced the one-horsepower engine with one twice as powerful, however, the vehicle was still unsatisfactory. In his second steamer, therefore, he again doubled the power, installing a rear platform on which he placed two two-horsepower steam engines which were joined to form one power unit. These were directly connected to the driving wheels, eliminating the transmission and gears that had proved so bothersome in the first steamer. For greater stability he used four wheels, although with the two front wheels placed close together and of greater diameter than the rear wheels the completed vehicle still looked somewhat like a tricycle. A photograph of this machine, which was completed by at least early 1892, shows Olds and one passenger seated over the front wheels, with a fringed canopy over their heads and extending back over the engines that loom up in the rear.[15]

Olds demonstrated the steamer for a reporter from *Scientific American* magazine, whose story in the May 21, 1892 issue of that widely circulated and influential New York journal was a follow-up of a few news stories that are said to have appeared about the Olds steam carriage. It was probably the first indication to the outside world of any significant automotive developments in Michigan. Equally important from a publicity standpoint, the *Scientific American* story was reprinted a few weeks later in the July issue of *The Hub,* one of the most important trade journals in the carriage industry. Although he later professed to have been surprised that a New York magazine would be interested in what he was doing in Lansing, Michigan, it seems likely that Olds, whose company had been advertising its engines in *Scientific American* for some time, was responsible for calling his work to the attention of the editor and urging him to send out a reporter to take a look. The editor may have been especially willing to grant the request because of the ads that P. F. Olds

This woodcut, showing R. E. Olds (left) and an unidentified companion in the second Olds steam carriage, accompanied an article describing the fringe-covered vehicle in the May 21, 1892 *Scientific American*.

& Son had bought in the past and the increasing advertising revenue they might well supply in the future if favorable attention were given to their vehicle.[16]

The twelve-hundred-pound vehicle operated much more quietly than the earlier machine of 1887. Its "usual" speed of fifteen miles an hour also marked a decided improvement over the ten miles an hour which was the top speed of Olds' first effort. Olds was quoted as saying that the "great advantages" of his horseless carriage were "that it never kicks or bites, never tires out on long runs, and during hot weather [the driver] can ride fast enough to make a breeze without sweating the horse. It does not require care in the stable, and only eats while it is on the road, which is no more than at the rate of 1 cent per mile." However, there were certain disadvantages which Olds, understandably, did not dwell on. Although the gasoline tank supplying the burner was enough for a forty-mile trip, the water had to be replaced every ten or fifteen miles. In addition, this vehicle, like its predecessor, could not be put into reverse—a common failing among early horseless carriages. And, though Olds assured the reporter that the vehicle "will ascend any ordinary grade," he admitted in 1897 that when he was driving, "I dreaded the sight of a hill." Not only was the steamer's ability to climb a hill in question, but if it stalled there was apparently some doubt that the brakes would be able to hold the machine in place.[17]

It is probable that Olds saw the story in *Scientific American* primarily as just another means of calling attention to the efficiency of the Olds steam engine, which was advertised elsewhere in that same issue of May 21. However, the article—either in its original form or as reprinted in *The Hub* or elsewhere—led to an offer from a patent medicine firm, the Francis Times Company of London, England, to purchase the steam vehicle from Olds. After some correspondence, a price of $400 was agreed upon, and in the spring of 1893 the Olds machine was shipped from Lansing to the English company's branch office in Bombay, India. Olds claimed on another occasion that the vehicle had been sold to an Indian potentate and it is not certain whether the steam carriage ever arrived in India. One report has it that the ship carrying the steamer sank at sea, and as a result, Olds said, his "reputation was saved." Another report, however, maintains that the Michigan-made vehicle arrived safely at its destination and gave satisfactory service to its owner for several years. It is interesting to note that because gasoline was so difficult to purchase in India, and even when available it sold at a prohibitively high price of about nine dollars a gallon, steam vehicles were much preferred over gasoline-powered vehicles when automobiles first began to appear in any numbers on that subcontinent in the early twentieth century. However, the amount of gasoline consumed in the Olds steamer to heat the boilers was comparable to that used in the early cars powered by gasoline internal combustion engines, and it would not have made the Lansing vehicle a desirable buy from the standpoint of gas economy.[18]

-The sale of that Olds vehicle in 1893 appears to be the first purchase of a Michigan-made self-propelled passenger road vehicle. It may also have been the first horseless carriage made anywhere in the United States to be shipped abroad to a foreign buyer. However, it was clearly not the first sale of an American-made automobile to anyone, as many writers have asserted. The Olds steamer was strictly an experimental vehicle, and there are reports of sales of other such experimental or demonstration models long before 1893, such as W. W. Austen's purchase of a Roper steamer in 1868. In any event, these sales should not be confused with the beginning of real commercial automobile production, which dates from about 1890 in Europe and 1896 in the United States, when the Duryea Motor Wagon Company of Springfield, Massachusetts produced and marketed thirteen vehicles of a standard design.[19]

Although Ransom Olds declared that he had fully intended to go on to build a third steam-powered vehicle, his company's decision to develop a gasoline engine led Olds to abandon steam power in favor of the internal combustion engine as a far more suitable method of propelling a road vehicle. The White brothers of Cleveland and the Stanley brothers of Massachusetts would in a few years achieve fame with their advanced steam cars, but Ransom Olds and all other major Michigan automotive pioneers after 1893 concentrated almost all their efforts on gasoline-powered motor vehicles. Since that was the kind of vehicle to ultimately capture the public's fancy, this switch helps to explain the rise of Michigan automobile companies to leadership in the industry. Important segments of the industry elsewhere stayed with steam or electricity until it was too late for most of them to catch up with the gasoline car producers, when the popularity of the latter's automobile made a change from steamers or electrics virtually essential for continued business survival.

Again, just as with the date of Olds' first horseless carriage, there is much confusion about exactly when Olds decided to work on the development of a gasoline engine. Olds is responsible for at least some of this confusion: for example, when he was in his eighties he identified one of the surviving Olds gasoline engines as one he had built in 1888, predating the engine by probably ten years. The evidence seems to indicate that Olds and his associates and staff were not engaged in very serious work on a gasoline engine until 1894. Of course, this kind of engine originated many years before, in the mid-nineteenth century in Europe. At the Philadelphia Centennial Exposition of 1876, six Otto-type gasoline engines were exhibited, manufactured by the firm of Otto and Langen of Germany. This show was instrumental in awakening American engineers and mechanics to the advantages of such engines over the steam engine. Within a decade and a half about 18,500 of these Otto engines were in use in the United States. A Detroit shipbuilding company is said to have purchased one of the first two of these engines imported into the country, and by the nineties several Michigan companies were engaged in manufacturing gasoline engines, particularly for the marine trade.[20]

At least one of these firms, the Sintz company of Grand Rapids, exhibited its engines at the World's Columbian Exposition in Chicago in 1893, and an examination of the one-cylinder Sintz at that time was instrumental in spurring on such auto pioneers as Elwood Haynes and Charles King to proceed with their plans for a gasoline-powered horseless carriage. The very large number of gasoline engines displayed by many companies at Chicago in 1893, in contrast to the handful exhibited at Philadelphia seventeen years earlier, was itself a dramatic illustration of the rapid strides this new source of power had made in capturing the market in America. There is little doubt that this had an important influence on Ransom Olds, who visited the fair in June 1893. He must have concluded from what he saw there and from what he knew was happening generally in the engine industry in the United States that his company's fortunes were certain to descend if it did not join the parade and move into this field.

It appears that for a time he searched for a way of combining the old with the new, because on August 13, 1895 he applied for a patent on "a combined gas and steam engine." But eleven days later a clearer indication of a new direction for P. F. Olds & Son came when Olds and Madison F. Bates, a member of Olds' staff who assigned patent rights to the company, applied for a patent on a "gas or vapor engine," a patent that was awarded one year later, on August 11, 1896.[21]

Until the spring of 1896, P. F. Olds & Son continued to advertise only the steam engine, on which its reputation had been built for a decade. But that March the first announcements regarding the new Olds Safety Gas and Vapor engines appeared. An article in the March 14 issue of *Scientific American,* that dependable Olds promotional medium, emphasized the simplicity, efficiency, and safety of this "improved" engine, features that were emphasized in other advertisements the company began placing elsewhere that same month. The success of the new engine was quickly established: sales rose from $29,179.73 in 1896 to $42,208.25 in 1897, the increase attributable largely, if not entirely, to the popularity of the Olds gas and vapor engines. An ad in May 1897 referred to this new product as "The Engine that Built a 10,000 square ft. addition last year." The new engine added greater luster to the national reputation P. F. Olds & Son had already earned with its steam engine. By March of

1897 the company claimed that its engines were found in 144 Michigan communities and in nearly all of the states across the nation. To provide the additional space that was still required to keep up with manufacturing demand, the company was reorganized in November 1897, with its capitalization raised from $30,000 to $50,000 and its name changed to Olds Gasoline Engine Works.

Initially, there was no suggestion that the new engine, which was produced in various sizes up to fifty horsepower and came in both horizontal and vertical models, might be used in a road vehicle. The first use Ransom Olds made of the engine was reportedly to power launches on the Grand River; and it is significant that this was the only kind of use specifically mentioned not only in *Scientific American* but in an article on the engine in the March 1896 issue of the automotive journal *Horseless Age*. As Ransom knew from past experience and from other Michigan engine manufacturers, there was good money to be made in producing marine engines.[22]

A considerable amount of unnecessary confusion has resulted from an attempt to establish the date on which Ransom Olds first used his new gasoline engine in a horseless carriage. The earliest date given is found in the 1949 biography by Duane Yarnell, in which the author, repeating what Olds had told him, states that Olds built his "first usable gasoline vehicle" in 1893, implying that he may have constructed some less practical vehicles of this type prior to that year. If true, this would put Olds in close competition with the Duryea brothers, whose motor wagon was tested in September 1893 and has been most commonly cited as America's first successful gasoline-powered car. But in December 1905, in sworn testimony which he gave to the attorneys in the Selden Patent case, Olds declared that he had built his first gasoline-powered vehicle in 1894–95, although just when he was successful in operating it is not clear (at one point in his testimony he indicated that the vehicle was not driven until 1895, while at another point he recalled having driven it in the latter part of 1894).

The patent records, which indicate that Olds had not completed work on his gasoline engine until 1895, are sufficient to disprove the accuracy of the 1893 or 1894 dates for his first gasoline carriage. These records seem to lend credence to the more persistent claim by Olds and others that he completed his first gasoline motor vehicle in 1895. However, in later life, when Olds mentioned that year or the earlier years of 1893 and 1894, he had obviously forgotten that in 1897, when his memory of these events was fresher, he had told a public gathering that after he sold his second steamer in 1893, "the immense demand" created by his company's switch to gasoline engines had prevented him from returning to his experiments with horseless carriages "till 1896, when I realized that I ought to make a move at once in this direction, or all my former experience would be fruitless; I at once set about my present carriage, which was completed in June, 1896." Contemporary newspaper accounts confirm the general accuracy of this account, thus removing any reason to believe various claims that the first Olds gasoline vehicle was completed at any time prior to 1896.[23]

It is clear enough why Olds would have thought at that time that immediate action was necessary in order to avoid wasting the experience and knowledge he had gained earlier in building motorized vehicles. In June 1893, when he visited the Chicago World's Fair, he saw a Benz, a gasoline automobile of European origins. He even had a brief ride in it, although he recalled in 1905: "I was with a large party taking in the Fair and had very little time to examine it." Horseless carriages were still such a rarity in the United States at that time that Olds reported that this Benz, plus an electric vehicle he also saw on exhibit at the fair, were the first such self-propelled vehicles—aside from the steamers he had built—that he had seen. However, within two years horseless carriages, which had been the subject of much speculation but little action up to that time, suddenly seemed about to become a much more commonplace sight, and the development of a full-scale industry to manufacture these vehicles appeared imminent.

In 1895, when the Chicago *Times-Herald* sponsored

Charles King and Oliver Barthel in the first public test of King's experimental "horseless carriage," March 6, 1896

America's first real horseless carriage competition, the scores of entries the paper received provided the first substantial evidence of the large number of experimenters around the country who had been working on the problem of developing practical motor vehicles. Although only six such vehicles actually took part in the race on Thanksgiving Day, and only two managed to complete the snow-covered course, the victory of an American-made Duryea over an imported Benz indicated the rapid strides American experimenters had made in catching up with the Europeans, who had been manufacturing and selling automobiles for several years. It was this race, incidentally, which has been cited as the inspiration for Olds to complete his gasoline vehicle in 1895. Although Olds did not—by his own admission in 1897—build the vehicle until the following year, there are indications that he was tempted to enter the Chicago race but abandoned the idea when he realized he could not spare the time required to build the vehicle during a period in which he was completing work on the Olds Safety Gas and Vapor Engine and overseeing the complicated task of putting that engine into production.

In addition to the Duryeas, who capitalized on their success in winning the Chicago race by proceeding to manufacture their motor wagon in 1896, Elwood Haynes and the Apperson brothers of Kokomo, Indiana were working on plans to manufacture a vehicle, following their successful test in 1894 of a carriage powered by a Sintz engine. By 1895 newspaper articles were reporting several horseless carriage projects underway in Michigan alone. Considerable attention at the end of the year focused on a machine that was to be manufactured by the Benton Harbor Motor Carriage Company; but the vehicle was never successfully tested and the company failed to materialize. However, in March 1896 newspapers again carried stories of a horseless carriage, this one built by Charles B. King. King's vehicle was tested with undoubted success on Woodward Avenue in Detroit on the night of March 6, and King told reporters that this success signalled his intention of manufacturing these automobiles.

Through newspapers and such journals as *Scientific American* and *Horseless Age,* Ransom Olds would have been well aware of these and many other developments of horseless carriages that were being reported by 1896. Of course, it would be many years before competition from established manufacturers in the auto industry would be developed to the point where newcomers in the field would have difficulty staying in business. But one can appreciate Olds' view in 1896 of the urgent need for action on his part if he was not to fall hopelessly behind those who had already developed successful motor cars. "The gasoline engines were our bread-and-butter business, and most people thought the car was just a toy," Olds recalled in the 1920s, "but I knew that the car was my big venture."[25]

Olds had some important advantages over many of his fellow automotive pioneers. It is true, for example, that both Charles King and Henry Ford were ahead of Olds in building and testing a gasoline car; but they were handicapped in their further progress by lack of manufacturing experience, facilities, and staff. As the manager of a thriving business, Olds had these advantages at his command and was able to draw on them not only in his continuing experimental work but also in his subsequent production and sale of automobiles long before King and Ford were able to reach that goal.

Olds was also a step ahead of other businessmen and manufacturers who possessed resources equal or superior to his and now sought to use these resources to enter the new and promising field of automobile manufacturing. The knowledge of engines which he and his staff had gained over the years was such that they did not have to waste time familiarizing themselves with the intricacies of the gasoline engine, as was the case with some of the early manufacturers of gasoline automobiles whose previous experience had not been with motors. "Ninety-five percent of our gasoline motor carriages are experiencing trouble for want of a proper motor, the vital point," Olds declared in 1897. "Most of the horseless carriage inventors are without gasoline-engine experience, which is the cause of a great deal of trouble in getting a proper motor. . . . A carriage is a very poor place to experiment with a motor."[26] Furthermore, some of Olds' contemporaries, such as bicycle manufacturer Colonel Albert Pope, who concentrated on electric cars when he first entered the automotive field, or the White brothers, who used the resources of the White Sewing Machine Company to put out steam cars, had yet to learn what Olds had already concluded by the mid-nineties: the future was not in electrics or steamers but in the gasoline-driven vehicle.

When Olds first tackled the job of building such a vehicle in 1896, he realized, just as he had in 1887, that he and his men could take care of the engine and certain other mechanical features but lacked the training to build a body of the same quality for the vehicle. Nine years earlier Olds seems to have purchased the various parts he needed from outside suppliers and then put them together in the Olds company shop. In 1896 he arranged with his school board colleague Frank G. Clark to have the carriage manufacturing firm of Clark and Son, of which Frank Clark was the assistant superintendent, provide the carriage while Olds would provide the means of making the carriage horseless in its operation. The two men and their respective crews of workmen completed their job sometime during the summer, and by early August their preliminary tests on the vehicle had been satisfactorily completed.

On August 11, 1896, coincidentally the very day on which the patent for the Olds-Bates gasoline engine was awarded by the patent office—more than five months after King's test of his vehicle and two months after Ford's relatively unheralded test of his "quadricycle"—Lansing's first gasoline-powered carriage was demonstrated by Olds for the benefit of a local newspaper reporter. The newsman was impressed, reporting the following day: "There is no doubt that the much mooted question of the horseless carriage has been successfully solved by Messrs. Olds & Clark."

The excellence of Clark's work was evident in "the beauty of the vehicle," with its dark green body and "dainty red trimmings" and its "leather furnishings of the latest pattern." There were two seats, with the rear seat adjustable so that passengers could face backward, if they desired—the dos-a-dos arrangement. The back seat could also be folded up if the front seat alone was required. Beneath the body was a one-cylinder, five-horsepower Olds gasoline engine which was not attached directly to the body, a feature which, when combined with the vehicle's suspension system, gave the passengers a more vibration-free ride than was customary in horseless carriages of that period.

Among other features, ball bearings were used throughout, and the wheels were fitted with cushion tires. These were very likely supplied by the Michigan Wheel Company of Lansing, founded several years earlier by William K. Prudden, a harness-racing buff who had built a rubber-tired sulky and then began to manufacture and sell the wheels he had developed for the sulky. In the spring of 1896, Prudden's firm was advertising the superiority of its cushion-tired wheels to solid rubber tires. A later version of this Olds car (now in the Smithsonian Institution), which dates from 1897–98, used solid rubber tires; but these too could have been furnished by Prudden, who by 1898 was advertising that he supplied both solid and cushion tires for "all kinds of carriages," including "Motor Wagons." Prudden had thus already begun a career that would make his company one of the major suppliers for the early automobiles, including Ransom Olds' Oldsmobile.[27]

When he was in his eighties Olds apparently told Duane Yarnell that he had started the engine of this 1896 car by using the primitive hot-tube method to ignite the gasoline. He said that later, however, an electrician at Sing Sing Prison in New York sent him a crude version of a spark plug, which—the prison employee told him—could be used to ignite the gasoline with an electric spark. Thus, by chance, Olds and his men were led to install an electric ignition system in the vehicle. This is an interesting story, with just the right touch added when Olds pointed out that among the electrician's duties was "keeping the electric chair in working order." But it is only a story, its chronological inaccuracy apparently being the result of confusion either on the part of Yarnell or the aging industrialist. Electric ignition had been used by some automobile pioneers at least since the early 1880s, and by 1896 scarcely any American experimenters in this field were still using the hot-tube technique, which *Motocycle* magazine characterized as "dangerous" in a November 1895 article that spelled out the advantages of the electric ignition method. Olds was obviously aware of these advantages, since it was the electric spark method that he specified as the one used when he applied for a patent on his gasoline vehicle in September 1896. Describing the vehicle at that time, Olds said:

> I preferably use a body which affords convenient room underneath the seat to store away therein the electric ignitor for the engine, the latter being of any preferred known construction of the type in which the speed is controlled by an automat-

ic governor, as that after starting the engine by hand when the vehicle is first started it is kept running during all the contingencies of travel.

Electric ignition was likewise the method Olds referred to in his discussion of how his vehicle operated at the 1897 meeting of the Michigan Engineering Society.

The Sing Sing story, if it has any basis in fact (and it seems unlikely that Olds would have intentionally invented the tale), probably had its origins in some earlier communication from the prison electrician regarding the method of starting the Olds Safety Gas and Vapor Engine. As it was described in March 1896, this engine could be started either by the hot-tube or the electric method. In fact, this seems to be the instance Olds had in mind when he discussed these distant events with Arthur Lauder, who reported them in his book *Lansing Unlimited,* published in 1947. In any event, in the mid-nineties Olds had clearly given considerable thought to the method by which gasoline engines could best be started, and in 1898 he was to apply for a patent on an improved electric starter. Yarnell's suggestion that Olds was so poorly informed at the time he built his first gasoline automobile that he needed the chance advice of a total stranger to apprise him of a mechanical development that had long been common knowledge among horseless-carriage experimenters of the period is a characteristic instance of the manner in which peculiar and unverified stories have sprung up about Olds and his work. Many of these stories—with or without Olds' assistance—have tended to diminish the true nature and importance of his pioneering efforts.[28]

After cranking up the motor and starting the engine on that August day in 1896, Olds climbed up into the driver's seat. As in almost all horseless carriages of that day, the driver sat on the right. With his right hand Olds moved a lever which enabled him to shift from low to high gear, to reverse, or back to stopping position. Steering was done with a tiller, located to the driver's left. The top speed of the thousand-pound vehicle (a weight Olds said he could reduce by at least twenty per cent) was variously reported between eighteen and twenty-five miles per hour; but Olds indicated that, as a practical matter, road conditions dictated a maximum speed of no more than nine to twelve miles per hour. The three gallons of "common stove gasoline" that were carried in the tank would last from twenty-five to fifty miles, again depending on road conditions. This gas mileage record was later markedly improved in Olds' one-cylinder curved-dash Oldsmobile, which on one long and grueling trip in 1901 had a respectable average of twenty-seven miles to the gallon, in contrast to the top figure of about sixteen mpg quoted for the pioneer Olds gasoline vehicle.[29]

Exclaiming "Eureka," Olds expressed his complete satisfaction with the performance of his new machine on the occasion of its first publicized outing. The reporter who witnessed the tests was also impressed with the manner in which the vehicle demonstrated its ability to climb hills and pass the other tests to which it was subjected.

Following the August 12 appearance of the story about Olds' demonstration in the Lansing *State Republican,* news of this latest horseless carriage spread rapidly to the outside world. On August 13 the *Detroit News* reported that the vehicle, which could go twenty-five miles an hour—faster than the top figure that had earlier been reported in the Lansing *State Republican*—was the result of six years' experimentation by Olds. The *Detroit Free Press,* while giving the more conservative estimate of twelve miles an hour as the speed at which the motor carriage could be operated "on any kind of roads," lavishly praised it as "probably the most successful vehicle of its kind ever turned out." The *Grand Rapids Democrat* of August 14 reported that Olds' vehicle "is said to work to perfection and his friends predict that it will come into general use."

In less than a week news of Olds' achievement had spread into Canada, where the horseless carriage enthusiast W. G. Walton of Hamilton, Ontario wrote to his friend Charles King, requesting more details. King, who was busily engaged in new horseless carriage tests of his own at this same time, wrote to Walton on August 20: "In reference to the

Old's [*sic*] vehicle: I can only state that I have not seen his carriage or the motor, but know that the Old's Company experimented five or six years ago with a steam carriage. This, however, proved to be too bulky, and upon taking up the manufacture of the gasoline engine which they have done recently they have experimented further with the horseless carriage problem." Other than that, King said, he knew no more than the information that had appeared in the papers.

A communication from P. F. Olds & Son and a photograph of the Olds vehicle appeared in the September issue of *Motocycle,* and a similar story and picture appeared in *Horseless Age* the following month. Olds' company advised the readers of these automotive journals that after working on the project "for some months . . . they have finally reduced

The Smithsonian Institution's 1897 version of Olds' — and Lansing's — first gasoline-powered carriage, with a one-cylinder, five-horsepower gasoline engine, "leather furnishings of the latest pattern," and solid rubber tires

Courtesy of Oldsmobile Division, General Motors

their ideas to tangible shape and find the result quite satisfactory." Finally, late in November another illustrated article in *Scientific American* reported that the "compact and well proportioned vehicle . . . has been giving good service during the past few weeks on the country roads of Michigan. . . . The machinery is simple in construction and is practically noiseless."[30]

Although the original story in the Lansing *State Republican* had emphasized that this was a joint venture of Ransom Olds and Frank Clark, the stories elsewhere, most of which clearly emanated from the Olds company, do not mention Clark. Instead, they refer to the vehicle as the "Olds Motor Carriage" which had been "invented by Mr. R. E. Olds." When Clark was interviewed a quarter of a century later, he said that Olds and he had worked together on this project for some two years, "chiefly after their regular hours of labor." (The time span mentioned by Clark might indicate that preliminary work on the motor carriage had begun in 1895; or it might mean only that Clark continued to be involved with Olds in the modifications that were made in the carriage in the year following the August 1896 demonstration.) Clark claimed that he not only built the body, with which he is generally credited, but that he was also involved in the development—with Olds—of the suspension system and the drive train. Arthur Pound later checked Olds' reactions to Clark's recollections and reported: "The correctness of this narrative at all points is questioned by Mr. Olds."[31]

Whatever the nature of Clark's role may have been, the evidence seems to point to Olds as the one deserving major credit for the 1896 vehicle's development. In fact, on September 5, 1896, Olds took an oath before Charles F. Hammond, an Ingham County notary public, and Harris Thomas, who was personally acquainted with both Clark and Olds from his service with them on the school board, that he, R. E. Olds, "verily believes himself to be the original, first and sole inventor of the improvements in Motor Carriage described and claimed" in the patent application that he had had prepared at that time. This application, which was recorded at the patent office in Washington, D. C. on September 18, had been prepared by the Detroit patent law firm of Thomas S. Sprague & Son, which described the invention in its casebook as one on an "auto-mobile carriage," an interesting and very early use of a term that would not be commonly used in the United States until about 1899.

Olds had been doing business with Sprague & Son since November, 1891, when he sought a patent on an invention relating to bearings, an application which he either subsequently withdrew or which was rejected by the patent office, since the patent was never issued to him. The Detroit firm was at this time actually owned by Adolph Barthel and James Whittemore, who had bought out the earlier owners but had retained the original name of the business established in 1865. The work Barthel and Whittemore did for Olds led them into an association with the automobile industry that proved to be most profitable for both men and is one of the first examples of the wide-ranging impact that Olds' automotive activities had on other individuals and companies. Later in the nineties Barthel left the firm, forming the new firm of Barthel and Barthel with his nephew Otto, who had been an office boy for Sprague & Son. Whittemore retained control of Sprague & Son, which survives today under the name of Whittemore, Hulbert & Belknap. Between the two of them, Whittemore and Barthel virtually monopolized the lucrative automobile patent business in the Detroit area for many years, until the larger automobile companies created their own patent law staffs to handle this work. As late as 1941, however, Whittemore, Hulbert & Belknap was still handling the patents of Ransom Olds.[32]

In November 1896 the patent office examiner questioned one of the thirteen claims that Olds made for his vehicle, declaring that it was covered by two earlier patents issued in 1894. Through his attorneys, Olds continued to uphold the patentable character of the questioned claim in February 1897. However, when the examiner again rejected the claim the next month, citing "as a further reference" a Duryea patent of 1896, Olds agreed to strike the disputed item from his application. On October 30, 1897 the patent office notified Olds that the amended application had been

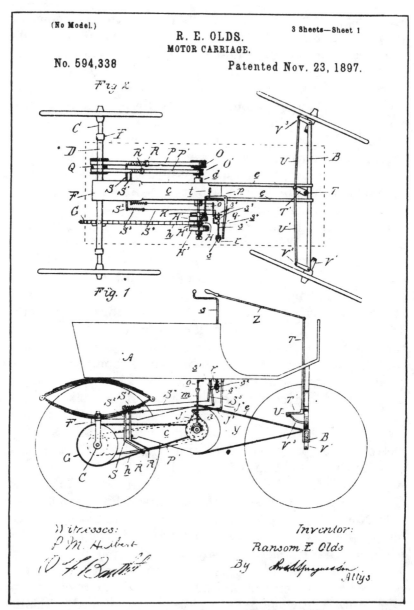

One of three sheets of drawings of Olds' 1896 motor carriage that accompanied his application for patent and were printed with a detailed account of the mechanism when the patent was awarded in 1897

allowed, and after Sprague & Son had forwarded the final fee of twenty dollars, patent No. 594,338 was awarded to Olds, dated November 23, 1897.[33]

Olds' application of September 1896, which, with the elimination of the one claim and some other minor changes in punctuation and spelling, became a part of the official published records of the United States Patent Office has been inexplicably either overlooked or ignored by all previous writers on Olds. It is, however, a most revealing document, for in it Olds not only sets forth the purposes he had in mind in building this "motor carriage," but he also presents the first reasonably complete statement of what would become the basic motivation of most of the successful Michigan automobile manufacturers in later years.

> My invention relates to that type of motor carriage in which the motive power is produced by a gasoline motor, and the object of my invention is to produce a road vehicle that will meet most of the requirements for the ordinary uses on the road without complicated gear or requiring engine of great power, and to avoid all unnecessary weight.[34]

Here is an emphasis on a simple, uncomplicated mechanism, similar to what Olds had been striving for earlier in his steam and gasoline engines and which he would again return to with his curved-dash Oldsmobile. He would advertise that later vehicle as simple enough for a child to operate. This objective was important in the early stage of the automobile's development, when many of the vehicles on the market were too complicated for the inexperienced drivers of that day to handle. In addition to this objective, Olds was seeking to build a lightweight car with just enough power to meet the average driver's needs and one that would thus be also relatively inexpensive. These were goals that Henry Ford was to achieve with spectacular success with his introduction of the immortal Model T in 1908. However, Ford at that time was merely solidifying the position of the low-priced, utilitarian, mass-produced automobile as the backbone of the Michigan auto industry. Ransom Olds had set these goals for himself twelve years earlier; and the success he would have in achieving these objectives when he introduced the low-priced curved-dash Oldsmobile in 1900 soon convinced others in Michigan that this was the path to follow, paving the way for Ford's great breakthrough with his "universal car" eight years later.

In addition, in the nineties Olds had more general ideas about the automobile which he set forth in a remarkable paper that he read to the Michigan Engineering Society, meeting in Port Huron in December 1897. This paper is notable not so much for its contents, illuminating as they are, as for the fact that this was one of the rare recorded instances in the early history of the automobile industry when one of its major figures stood before an audience to express his views and to answer questions relating to his activities. After briefly referring to the earlier efforts of others to develop "horseless carriages" (as the automobile was still most commonly called in the United States in 1897), Olds elaborated on the reasons why he was convinced that the gasoline car was certain to become the popular choice of the public. His experience with steam engines in his first two experimental vehicles had led him to confine his attention mainly to the two other types—"electricity and gasoline"—which were, he declared, the "two means of propelling the carriage, which is occupying the attention of the people." He correctly forecast that the excessive weight of the storage batteries required to operate the electric car was its main drawback, "and while they will be used to some extent, they will not come into general use, unless some improvements are made in storage batteries over what we have at present." It was, therefore, not the battery nor the steam engine but, in his opinion, "the gasoline vapor motor . . . which has come to the rescue of the horseless carriage." Olds felt the reasons behind its present and future widespread adoption were clear.

> It is always ready on a moment's notice; instead of hitching up a horse in the ordinary way, all one has to do is turn the motor over to draw in a mixture of gasoline and air, which is ignited inside the cylinder by an electric spark, and the engine at once starts and runs continuously, so that the operator has only to throw the lever to different points to back, stop, or

This advertisement in the spring of 1903 answered those who questioned the automobile's safety with a contrast between the strong, "instantly responsive" mechanism of the runabout and the uncertainty and dangers of the horsedrawn carriage.

start the carriage without any reference to the motor or mercy on the horse; especially when it is ninety in the shade, when flies and dust are unbearable, you have only to turn on a little more speed to secure a breeze and leave the dust behind. When through using, you have only to throw out the electric switch and the horse is taken care of till needed again.

Olds could "see no reason" why this kind of motor car would not "come into general use." He conceded that at first the place of the horseless carriage was in the cities, and he foresaw a time when city dwellings would "be designed with a horseless carriage room in the house" (following his own example of the garage he added to his Lansing residence). But as soon as these vehicles were widely used in the city, those living in the country would come to want them, "which will cause better roads and will practically dispense with the dust, which is to be credited to steel tires and the horse."

Again and again Olds gave evidence of his dislike for the horse and his fervent conviction that the automobile would be a blessing to society if for no other reason than that it would rid the city of the horse and all its attendant evils. A few weeks before Olds' death in 1950 an interviewer asked him if the early automobile manufacturers had had any idea that their product would replace the horse. "I don't think so," Olds replied. "They felt as though the horse was here to stay." But if such was indeed the view of the industry as a whole in the 1890s, Olds himself certainly hoped that the horse would not survive as the backbone of man's transportation needs. He enthusiastically welcomed the prospect of the horse's replacement by the motor vehicle. "Did you ever stop to think," he asked the engineers in 1897, "what a grand thing it would be to dispense with the clanking of the horses' hooves on the city pavements, how much cleaner our streets would be, and that with rubber tires, a city may become a veritable beehive without the deafening noise of today, as well as the cracking of the whip, in order to force the poor horse over the pavements?" Someone in the audience asked if the presence of a large number of motor carriages on the street would not result in many collisions. "There would be less opportunity for a collision in crowded streets," Olds replied, "as the carriage is under perfect control, not like a horse which might get frightened or shy at some passing object." What about the danger to pedestrians, he was asked. Olds responded that horseless carriages would present less danger than the horsedrawn vehicles, "as the horse obstructs the view in front of the driver to a certain extent, besides the driver often depends on the horse to turn out."[35]

Had he desired, Olds could have elaborated on the rate of horse-related accidents, which was quite high judging from the frequency with which such accidents were reported in the newspapers of the day. Just the previous August in Lansing, Mrs. Reuben Shettler, wife of a local businessman who was soon to become a close business associate of Olds, had had her carriage horse bolt when it became frightened by a streetcar, damaging the carriage, though Mrs. Shettler was only shaken up. A few days earlier, Olds' brother Wallace had been knocked down and badly bruised by a runaway horse at nearby Pine Lake.[36]

Surprisingly, Olds is one of the few automotive pioneers who had much to say about the automobile's superior qualities compared with those of any of the existing forms of transportation. For the most part, these early manufacturers and enthusiasts seem to have been chiefly absorbed with the problems of developing satisfactory motor vehicles and of explaining to a somewhat skeptical public how the machines operated, without attempting to contrast this radically new type of transportation with more familiar types. In point of fact, they might have had a difficult time convincing even themselves of the superiority of their crude contraptions to the railroads, interurbans, streetcars, or even perhaps bicycles. Of course, the horsedrawn vehicle was a much easier mark.

To those of a later generation who have come to regard the gasoline automobile as the main polluter of the atmosphere, a cause of the urban crisis, and a deadly menace on the highways, Olds' views of the beneficial conditions that would result from the automobile's adoption may seem peculiar indeed. But one of the most telling and persistent arguments

used to win support for the automobile at the turn of the
century was the very one Olds had used in 1892 in *Scientific
American* and which he expanded on in 1897: that the cities
in particular would become cleaner, healthier, safer, and
more pleasant places in which to live after the stench, the
filth, and the hordes of flies associated with the horse barns
and found in every street horses frequented had been eliminated.

It was further argued that the equine species would be
much better off when motor-driven vehicles had relieved the
workhorse of its cruel burden. Olds and his contemporaries
had seen horses fall and break their legs pulling drays and
hacks over icy streets, or bolt and run panic-stricken down
the street and over sidewalks, or drop dead in their tracks in
hot weather, by the thousands some years in large cities—
their carcasses often lying on the streets for days until they
could be dragged away. To people disturbed by these conditions the horse-and-buggy era held no attraction. It was
something from which they wished to escape. Today's concerned citizens who would condemn Olds and his colleagues
for the means they used to effect this escape and the problems which the automobile has brought to society should not
allow their criticisms to prevent them from recognizing that
the evils men like Olds were attacking and were successful
in banishing were considered as real and serious in the 1890s
as the ecological problems with which society has become
concerned in the 1970s.

CHAPTER THREE

The Olds Motor Vehicle Company

In August 1896, when Ransom Olds was asked if he intended to manufacture the motor carriage that he had just demonstrated, he replied without hesitation, "Certainly." He readily admitted that he had no illusions that the sale of his horseless carriages would present any immediate threat to the market for horsedrawn carriages. It was, after all, only six months earlier that Frank Duryea had sold the first two Duryea Motor Wagons at the Mechanics Fair in Boston, thereby kicking off the beginning of the commercial phase of the automobile industry's development in the United States. Only thirteen Duryeas were produced in 1896, and there were few other American-made cars sold that year. Olds probably had little awareness of the actual number of cars that were being sold, poorly publicized as this information was at that time; but he certainly would have known from his reading of the trade literature that the full-scale exploitation of the market for horseless carriages was a development whose time was yet to come. Nevertheless, he expressed confidence that there were "a great many persons in this country and Europe" who would want to buy a motorized vehicle that was a proven success. "There is no trouble about selling them after you once get the article that class of customers want," Olds maintained. He left no doubt that his vehicle was, in his estimation, precisely that kind of article.[1]

The first advertisement for the Olds gasoline vehicle is said to have appeared later in 1896. According to Glenn Niemeyer, it contained an invitation to the public to call at

73

the Olds factory where they could inspect the "Motor-Cycle," and for a thousand dollars could place their orders for future delivery of one of the machines.[2] The Olds vehicle was referred to both as a "Motor-Cycle," a generic term for horseless carriages which failed to win widespread acceptance—at least for the four-wheel variety—and as a "trap," which identified the body style. A trap was a common horsedrawn carriage style, just as were the stanhope, brougham, phaeton, and runabout, terms used for other early American automobile models which also simply copied existing carriage designs.

In fact, it was a carriage industry journal, *The Hub,* that provided one of the most detailed descriptions of the Olds gasoline-powered trap. The vehicle, the magazine reported in 1897, was "arranged to make either a one or two seated rig." Olds' objective was "to produce a practical motor cycle, one which will combine simplicity, economy and durability, with as little confusion to the operator as possible." The vehicle was still priced at $1,000, about a dollar a pound, although there are conflicting reports of the carriage's weight. A statement in August 1897 placed it at twelve-hundred pounds, while other accounts stuck with the thousand-pound figure given at the time of the test run on August 11, 1896. Since so few American-made horseless carriages were being offered for sale at any price and so few individuals were seriously thinking of buying one, the price of these novelties was not yet a major competitive factor. However, comparison shoppers in 1896–97 would have found the Olds price tag of $1,000 equal to that of the first production models produced by Alexander Winton in Cleveland a year or so later. A story that appeared in 1904—and had obviously come from the Olds company—declared that one of the three vehicles that it credited Olds with having built in this early period had been sold for only $900. This was, according to the account, Olds' only sale at that time, although other accounts raise doubts about whether he succeeded in selling and delivering any vehicles in the remaining months of 1896 and early months of 1897. Like so many other automobile pioneers, Ransom Olds was to discover that manufacturing horseless carriages was far more difficult to accomplish than it was to construct one experimental model. It was to be five years from the time that he tested his first gasoline vehicle before these difficulties were fully overcome.[3]

*　*　*　*　*

Olds had thought that he could handle the construction of vehicles in the existing factory of P. F. Olds & Son, where in the latter part of 1896 efforts were being made to fill the several orders for the car that had reportedly been received. The Olds employees were not to build the entire vehicle. Instead, the body and wheels would come from outside suppliers, to be assembled in the Olds shop with the engine and certain other mechanical parts that Olds felt he and his men would be able to produce. But the brisk demand for the Olds gasoline engines, which for several years would continue to be, in Olds' words, the "bread-and-butter business" of the company, required the energies of the entire staff. In January 1897, P. F. Olds & Son was reported "obliged to run their factory day and night because of a press of orders [for engines] received since January 1." That same month the firm informed readers of *Horseless Age* that it had been impossible as yet to complete any motor vehicles, although it expressed the intention "to do so soon."

At that time Olds may have thought that the completion of an addition to the plant then under construction, which was to double their production capacity, would relieve the pressure sufficiently to allow a few vehicles to be turned out along with the engines. Yet, when the company moved into the new facilities on March 30, the news story reporting the move did not mention any plans for the production of automobiles, although it did report that Olds "has just put upon the market a pumping outfit, which will be a great rival to the windmill," another example of the diversity of Olds' manufacturing interests. By summer *The Hub* was reporting that Olds & Son was still so swamped with orders for engines that it could not promise to fill orders for its motorized rig with any promptness, as those customers who were waiting for the vehicles they had ordered the previous fall could readily have told the magazine's editor.[4]

Although the horseless carriage was what Olds would come to regard as his "big venture," he apparently felt in 1896–97 that the continued success of his company's proven money-maker, the gasoline engine, would be jeopardized by any attempt on his part to divert the amount of company funds and personnel that would have been required to produce any significant number of the vehicles. This was, in fact, the explanation that he gave in 1905 for the long delay in filling the early orders for his horseless carriage. It had become apparent that to produce these carriages an entirely separate manufacturing operation would have to be established. And Olds seems to have felt that this was beyond his or his family's financial capabilities. The capital stock of P. F. Olds & Son, still owned almost entirely by Pliny, Ransom, and Wallace Olds, had not been increased from the original capitalization of $30,000, established when the firm was first incorporated in 1890. The resources of the Olds family were apparently stretched to their limits. The new capital that Olds realized he would need for the horseless carriage venture would have to be sought elsewhere.

Economic conditions in 1896 would not have favored such efforts, if Olds indeed made any preliminary search for the needed financial backing at that time. The economy was still recovering from the severe dislocation of the depression into which the nation had been plunged in 1893, and in the summer and fall of 1896 a new source of instability arose from the fears created in financial and business circles by the presidential campaign of William Jennings Bryan, the radical-sounding "Boy Orator of the Platte." In August the Detroiter Charles King, who had hoped to raise money to finance his own automobile manufacturing venture, observed pessimistically: "The times are too hard at present for any development in the motor industry. I can see no other alternate except to wait until the clouds pass over and the people have money enough to enter into this new field."[5]

As business conditions began to improve following William McKinley's victory over Bryan in November of

1896, Ransom Olds was forced to face up to his need for financial help. He had essentially three alternatives: he could seek to borrow money from Lansing's banks; he could try to interest local individuals in investing in the company; or he could seek greener pastures in other communities with greater financial resources than those available in Lansing. In each case he could present a strong argument in favor of the advancement of the funds he sought. Under his management P. F. Olds & Son had shown a steady growth, based largely on the great success of the steam engine the company had introduced in the mid-eighties and on the even greater success of the gasoline engine it had begun to market early in 1896. Although Pliny and Wallace Olds, as well as Madison Bates and other employees, had made important contributions that helped to account for the firm's prosperous condition, Ransom Olds was the one actually in charge of operations during these years, and he had certainly emerged with a solid reputation for both the technical knowledge and the administrative ability that were required to transform a small local machine shop into a nationally known engine manufacturer.

Lansing bankers, one suspects, might have been interested in loaning money to finance an expansion of the engine plant, given the well-established, profitable nature of the product involved. But bank officials would have justifiably regarded any suggestion of a loan for a horseless carriage venture in 1897 far too risky and speculative a use of the bank's funds. Bankers in Lansing would have tended to be especially cautious regarding any loans at this time because of the earlier failure of three local banks during the depression, failures that had given the city, in the words of the Lansing *State Republican,* a "terrible black eye."[6] Banks in Detroit and elsewhere in southern Michigan would later become notorious for their liberality in extending credit to Michigan auto companies, but only after a few pioneers, notably Olds, had proved that there was money to be made in this new business. In 1897, therefore, Ransom Olds got money not from banks but from individuals, several of whom were indeed officers in banks but who presumably put up

Edward W. Sparrow, the personification of the successful Irish immigrant, in a photograph taken some years after he encouraged the development of Olds' automobile plans in 1897

their own funds, not those of the financial institutions they headed.

Olds drew attention to himself and his horseless carriage by continuing to drive it around town and out into the surrounding countryside in the weeks and months after its public debut in August 1896. A year later, the *State Republican* declared that "nearly every citizen of Lansing is doubtless familiar" with the Olds horseless carriage because of the frequency with which it had appeared on the streets. Apparently the machine had performed reasonably well, well enough at least to convince some local residents and others elsewhere that Olds had once again come up with a product that had potential market value. Sometime during the summer of 1897, therefore, a group of Lansing businessmen became interested in gambling a few dollars on the chance that the Olds motor carriage would enjoy the same success the Olds engines had.[7]

The leader of this group was Edward W. Sparrow, the first outsider to exert a decisive influence on the development of Ransom Olds' business interests. Sparrow was born in 1846—eighteen years before Olds' birth—in County Wexford, Ireland, the son of a landed proprietor. At the age of twelve, Sparrow, like so many of the Irish during that period, came to the United States with members of his family, who then settled in Lansing. There he held a variety of jobs before following his father's inclinations and concentrating on land-buying. He became one of Lansing's largest landowners, at one time controlling sixteen blocks of the city's business district. He was also a land developer, building over two hundred residential structures in Lansing in the early part of his career.

By the 1870s Sparrow was expanding his activities into northern Michigan, picking up large tracts of timber and mineral lands, before moving on to holdings in Minnesota's fabulously iron-rich Mesabi Range, in Idaho, Oregon, Alabama, Florida, and, before his death in 1913, in Canada and Brazil. Throughout all this financial expansion, however, he maintained his home base in Lansing, where he was highly successful personally and in helping to boost the economic fortunes of the city. In the 1870s Sparrow was an officer in the Lansing Improvement Association. The following decade he helped to organize and was the long-time president of the City National Bank. He also served as president of one of the city's largest manufacturers, the Lansing Wheelbarrow Company, as well as being an officer with several other local businesses.[8]

The summer of 1897 was a very busy time for Sparrow. For one thing, the Michigan Land and Lumber Company, a speculative land venture organized some years earlier by Sparrow, Samuel L. Smith, and Judge Isaac Marston, had become involved in a complicated series of legal actions that were developing in a manner unwelcome to Sparrow and his associates. Meanwhile, Sparrow, who was still a bachelor at fifty, was now preparing for his marriage, late that summer, to the daughter of Michigan Supreme Court Justice Claudius B. Grant. Then in the third week of August, the land speculator and prospective bridegroom donned his banker's hat and was off to Detroit for the annual convention of the American Bankers Association. When Sparrow returned to Lansing on Thursday evening, August 19, he was highly optimistic about the economic outlook. He told a reporter that he had talked with bankers from all over the nation and found that "they were unanimous in reporting the long looked for return of prosperity." Their unanimity no doubt encouraged him to proceed two days later with the organization of the first company ever formed to produce Olds-designed automobiles.[9]

One report of the relationship preceding this development states that Sparrow became interested in Ransom Olds' newest invention when he happened one day to see Olds driving his motor carriage. This story has it that Sparrow asked Olds to drop around to his office to discuss the possibility of the former's investing in the manufacture of this vehicle. Such an investment would have fit with his past business activities, since he had earlier served as a director of the Anderson Road Cart Company. Another account, however, indicates that Olds made the first approach to Sparrow, and this would seem the more likely of the two stories. The first version, it is true, is more in keeping with the popular image of Olds that past writers have promoted—one whose success was determined not so much by his own efforts as by a lucky break here and a chance encounter there. But this is a false image. Olds was no passive receiver of beneficence, and in the summer of 1897 he needed the assistance which Sparrow—perhaps more than anyone else in Lansing—was in a position to provide. Olds, who had not hesitated to go out and seek the cash his financially distressed company needed in the mid-eighties, would certainly have shown equal initiative in dealing with the company's greater financial needs in 1897.[10]

In any event, Sparrow was not the only one who had become interested in the manufacturing possibilities of the Olds carriage. Pursuing prospective aid elsewhere, Olds had succeeded in receiving by the summer of 1897 "several offers from parties in Detroit and Chicago who were anxious to put money into a company for the manufacture of the carriage." The Lansing *State Republican,* in reporting these offers, provided no names or other details except to indicate that had Olds accepted any of them he would apparently have had to relocate his company in the city from which the offer had come. This is a tantalizing piece of information; if the offers were genuine, and if we knew more about them, some fascinating theories and speculations could be advanced. Chicago was the center of considerable automotive activity in the nineties, particularly after the excitement generated by the *Times-Herald* competition in 1895. However, most of the manufacturing efforts that started there centered around the electric car, and this helps to explain why the Windy City never developed into an important center of the auto industry once the gasoline-powered vehicles came to dominate the scene. A more vigorous bid by Chicago investors for Olds' services in 1897, therefore, might have affected that city's industrial growth by starting it off on a more fruitful path than that of electric vehicles. Since Detroit, the other outside bidder for Olds' company in 1897, did become the Motor City, it would be even more important to know the identity of the individuals involved in the one or more offers that Olds re-

ceived from that city. Although Charles King had had no
luck in 1896 securing money for the manufacture of his
motor vehicle from any of his fellow Detroiters, he had reported to Charles Duryea in April of that year that several
Detroit businessmen, "representing considerable capital,"
had expressed to him an interest in investing in an
activity—the exact nature of which is not clear—related to
the manufacture of the Duryea, "if the wagon was as represented." King provided no further details, but his report,
together with the offers to Olds in 1897, whether or not any
of the same individuals were concerned, indicates the early
emergence of an interest in automobile manufacturing
among Detroit capitalists which would be one of the major
causes of the full flowering of that industry in the City of the
Straits a few years later.[11]

Ransom Olds "preferred to remain in Lansing" in 1897,
and thus the main value of the offers he had received from
Detroit and Chicago was his ability to tell Sparrow that he
might be forced to accept one of the offers and leave Lansing
if local support did not develop. This may well have had a
decisive effect on Sparrow: since his days as secretary of the
Lansing Improvement Association a quarter of a century
earlier, he had been committed to the expansion, not the
contraction, of business activity in Lansing. At any rate, the
meeting that was convened in Sparrow's office on Saturday
afternoon, August 21, 1897, resulted in the organization of
the Olds Motor Vehicle Company for the stated purpose of
"manufacturing and selling motor vehicles," with the company to be located in the River Street factory of Olds & Son
until separate quarters could be obtained.[12]

The Olds Motor Vehicle Company was, at the time of its
organization, probably the first automobile company to have
been officially formed in Michigan. The Benton Harbor
Motor Carriage Company, which was clearly no longer in
business in 1897, had reportedly been formed in November
1895; but it appears not to have gone beyond the talking
stage after the vehicle it was to manufacture could not be
successfully tested, thus killing any further interest in the
company's organization. In point of fact, the Olds Motor Ve-

E.F.COOLEY our
handsome Director
Has appointed
himself an Inspector
Dont have any fear
if there's a lady in
here
You may wager your
life he'll detect her.

Courtesy of Michigan Historical Collections

A rare and light-hearted depiction of Eugene Cooley in his role as a company director

hicle Company itself did not survive long. The Oldsmobile division celebrations in 1972 on the occasion of what it called its seventy-fifth anniversary were actually premature, since its birth was not the founding of the Olds Motor Vehicle Company in 1897 but the organization of the Olds Motor Works two years later.

The Olds Motor Vehicle Company was capitalized at $50,000, which, according to the local news report, would "be paid in as fast as it is required." At the outset, only $10,000 in cash was forthcoming from Sparrow and his group of investors. They included, the *State Republican* noted, some of the city's "most prominent business men and capitalists . . . and the mere mention of the officers of the new concern . . . is sufficient to show that it will add one more to Lansing's list of sound business firms."[13]

Heading the list of officers, naturally, was Edward Sparrow, who was listed as owning a tenth of the five thousand shares of stock and who had been selected as the president of the company. The vice president, though he owned the absolute minimum of stock—one share—was Eugene F. Cooley, son of Thomas M. Cooley of Ann Arbor, one of the leading nineteenth-century jurists not only of Michigan but the nation. Rather than following his father into the law profession, young Cooley had entered the business world and had made good on his own. In 1872 he had come to Lansing to build and manage the gas works; subsequently, he established a separate company that handled the installation of gas service; and after that he added to his growing list of enterprises a plumbing and heating company. Later, when electricity began to compete with Cooley's gas works, he helped to acquire control of the electric company and then managed it. He found the time to devote still more of his managerial talents to the Lansing Wagon Works. This business, organized by the two Cooleys, Arthur Bement, Orlando M. Barnes, Fred Thoman, and others, became, under the younger Cooley's direction, the second largest manufacturing establishment in Lansing.

Important as Cooley's experience in the manufacture of horsedrawn vehicles may have been in convincing him of the possibilities of Olds' horseless vehicles, however, it is probable that his friendship and business associations with Edward Sparrow were responsible for his early involvement in the Olds Motor Vehicle Company. That relationship dated back to at least 1876, when the two men had joined the Lansing Rod and Gun Club. In May and June of 1884 they had taken a combined business and pleasure trip together to the Dakotas and Montana; two years later they were among the organizers of the City National Bank. As president and vice president, respectively, of the latter institution, Sparrow and Cooley had long since become familiar with the roles they now assumed in the Olds company.[14]

Two other investors, each of whom acquired five hundred shares of stock—equal to the number assigned Sparrow— had close business ties with Sparrow. Arthur C. Stebbins, secretary of Sparrow's Lansing Wheelbarrow Company, now assumed the same title in the Olds vehicle company; Fred M. Seibly was the wheelbarrow company's assistant secretary. Another investor, Alfred Beamer, who had been the manager of the local telephone office since it opened in 1880, as well as the Lansing agent of the American Express Company, does not seem to have been a business associate of Sparrow, but he was one of Sparrow's closest friends. James Beamer, another stockholder, was no doubt related to Alfred Beamer, while the 125 shares acquired by Frank Clark were undoubtedly due to the role he had played in constructing the Olds motor vehicle, whether or not he also had some association with Sparrow.[15]

There was one other investor in for five hundred shares: Samuel L. Smith, formerly of Lansing but by 1897 a resident of Detroit. Like Cooley, Stebbins, and Seibly, Smith had direct business connections with Sparrow and was one of the organizers of the City National Bank in the 1880s. Although he had moved to Detroit in the nineties, Smith had kept in close contact with Lansing, was a frequent visitor in the capital, and his Lansing acquaintances could count on a cordial welcome at his mansion in Detroit. He had also continued his business association with Sparrow in the Michigan Land and Lumber Company, but this was an association in which Smith was the dominant figure: he served as chairman of the company, Sparrow as secretary-treasurer. Sparrow had very likely talked Smith into making his initial investment in the Olds company, but by so doing the Lansing-ite had brought into the firm a shrewd businessman who would, within a year and a half, gain undisputed financial mastery of the entire Olds business operations, and who was instrumental in relocating their main offices in Detroit.

Samuel Latta Smith was sixteen years older than Edward Sparrow, nearly the age of Ransom Olds' father. He was born in 1830 in Algonac, Michigan, where his business career began twenty years later and where he was elected to represent St. Clair County in the Michigan House of Representatives in the late fifties. (A Democrat, Smith was twice his party's unsuccessful candidate for state-wide office during the sixties.) In 1859, Smith left southern Michigan and went to the Copper Country in Michigan's Upper Peninsula, where he would make his fortune. He began modestly enough as a merchant in Houghton, but soon went on to participate in the organization of several copper mining companies, including the Copper Range Company, the major Michigan copper producer still operating in the 1970s. Perhaps of more direct bearing on his interest in Olds' work of developing a new form of transportation was Smith's success in bringing to completion the Portage Lake and Lake Superior Ship Canal, and in organizing two railroads, the Marquette, Houghton & Ontonagon and the Copper Range. All of these transportation projects were vital links in the economical shipment of copper. It is probable that with this background, Smith—though now in semi-retirement—did not require too much urging from Edward Sparrow to be persuaded to risk a small amount of money in what would turn out to be the most important investment of his long business career.[16]

Indeed, it is likely that most of the investors in the Olds Motor Vehicle Company that summer of 1897 regarded this venture as a relatively minor speculation on their part. Their interest may have been stimulated not only by viewing Olds' machine in motion but also by reading (as they could have in a Lansing newspaper the previous winter, for example) of the great future that was being predicted for the motor vehicle and the impact that its manufacture would have on the economy. But Eugene Cooley accurately reflected his thinking in August 1897, and probably that of his colleagues, when he recalled later:

> Here was a contrivance that would run on the roads by means of power developed within itself. I did not see any great possibilities for it, but nevertheless any contrivance that would do that I felt was worthy of some encouragement. I am sure I did not see any great future for the invention, and I do not think others did, but we felt that if developed the power vehicle would have some sale and that a business possibly could be developed which would show a profit. I am free to say that I had not the faintest vision of what has eventuated in the automobile business.[17]

Frank Clark's mere 125 shares in a company that would manufacture a vehicle in whose development he had had a major role may indicate that he had no more money to invest; or it may be an early sign of his misgivings about the venture, misgivings which would lead him in a few months to dispose of his stock. However, there can be no doubt of the confidence that Ransom Olds placed in the new company. He quickly added Clark's holdings to those he already controlled, which amounted to exactly half of the five thousand shares of stock. Olds apparently did not put any of his own money into the company at the time it was organized. Instead, the other stockholders awarded him a quarter interest—1,250 shares—in return for his professional services as manager of the company. In addition, Olds served as trustee for another 1,250 shares, which were awarded to the firm of P. F. Olds & Son. This was a logical distribution since any Olds motor vehicles that might be produced at the outset would have to come out of the P. F. Olds & Son shop.

It is not difficult to perceive the desire of Sparrow and his colleagues to establish a solid link between the nascent automobile firm and the healthy, well-established engine company. These ties were greatly strengthened three months later when P. F. Olds & Son was reorganized as the Olds Gasoline Engine Works and its capitalization increased to

$50,000 from the initial figure of $30,000. Eugene Cooley acquired a thousand shares of the new stock and was promptly named vice president of the engine works, and another Lansing businessman, James P. Edmonds, became the company's secretary. Ransom Olds continued as manager as well as assuming the title of president that had previously been held by his father, but the infusion of significant amounts of outside capital changed the entire character of the company that Pliny Olds had established seventeen years earlier. Automobiles were an interesting speculation, but gasoline engines had become one of the most desirable investment opportunities of the day. Ransom Olds' appeal for funds to finance his automobile may well have been regarded by some of those who responded as simply a means of worming their way into the profit-making engine works.[18]

In retrospect, it would seem that Ransom Olds exercised poor financial judgment in the last half of 1897. He gave up too much and received too little in return. The sum of $10,000 acquired by the capitalization of the Olds Motor Vehicle Company was simply not enough money to launch a separate automobile manufacturing establishment, even at that early stage in the industry's development. Perhaps Olds thought it could be done with that amount of money, or perhaps that was all Sparrow and his associates were willing to risk, although they had apparently agreed to supply additional amounts up to the par value of their stockholdings as these funds might be required. However, even $25,000, which would have represented the face value of the stock that was not initially controlled by Olds, would have been insufficient to make the motor vehicle company a viable, independent firm. This insufficiency was demonstrated by the fact that the separate factory announced as part of the new firm's plans was never acquired during the lifetime of the Olds Motor Vehicle Company. As a result, Olds found himself still faced with the impossible task of manufacturing automobiles in the engine factory while engine production was continued at full capacity.

A more serious problem for Olds in the long run was created by the incorporation: he no longer had the kind of

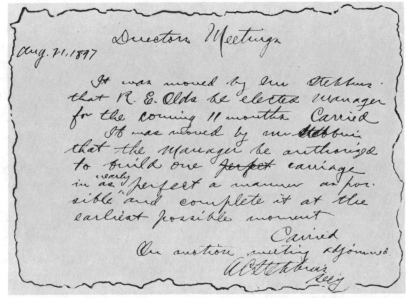

Courtesy of Oldsmobile Division, General Motors

The minutes of the Olds Motor Vehicle Company's board meeting of August 21, 1897

control he had exercised earlier over his family-owned business. He did control half the stock in the Olds Motor Vehicle Company and at the first meeting of the directors on August 21 was elected manager "for the coming 11 months"; he was also given the job of treasurer. But in managing the company Olds was no longer dealing with his father and brother, with whom he had grown up in the engine business and who knew and understood the product. Instead, he now had to deal with outsiders who wanted to make money from a product about which they knew little or nothing. The problems that could result for Olds were brought out in that first board meeting when President Sparrow is reported to have said: "Olds, we want you to make one perfect horseless carriage." Ransom Olds, who a year before had boasted to a newspaperman that his vehicle was "noiseless and light running, yet perfect in every detail as regards wear, stability and carrying capacity," now out of earshot of the public, told Sparrow that his request was impossible to carry out. Sparrow "shouldn't even expect" him to build a perfect horseless carriage at a time when so much remained to be learned about these vehicles, Olds contended. He managed to win approval for his viewpoint, and Secretary Stebbins, in the minutes of the meeting (a copy of which hung in Olds' office up to the time of his death), crossed out the word "perfect" and inserted the words "nearly perfect" in the motion as finally adopted. With men of the stature and ambition of Sparrow and Samuel Smith involved in the company's direction, however, Ransom Olds could not be sure that his judgment would always prevail. Even in the Olds Gasoline Engine Works, where under the reorganization completed that November Olds retained control of a substantial majority of the stock, he could not afford to ignore the wishes of his fellow officers, who had put up the money which Olds apparently believed was necessary for further expansion of the engine factory.[19]

One can envision a more imaginative, free-wheeling entrepreneur like William C. Durant acting in a much different fashion than did Olds in 1897. Such a promoter might very well have used the engine company's excellent record of earnings as a more direct means of raising the funds needed to launch the automobile venture. This could have been accomplished by recapitalizing the engine company at a much larger figure than $50,000, an increase that could easily have been justified. While retaining control of a majority of the new stock, Olds could then have offered the public enough of the new stock issue to raise the funds that would have enabled him to develop the manufacture of automobiles as a subsidiary of a going concern. This was approximately the arrangement that finally had to be made before Olds automobiles became a reality, but by that time only under conditions that resulted in Ransom Olds' losing all financial control of the company. However, it must be pointed out in Olds' defense that he learned a valuable lesson from this experience, as he demonstrated brilliantly in organizing his second automobile venture in 1904. Moreover, a final accounting of the financial rewards he reaped during his entire business career, conservative as his methods may have been, showed him far ahead of such high-flying promoters as Durant and Benjamin Briscoe.

After the organizational meeting of the Olds Motor Vehicle Company in August 1897, Olds' new business associates returned to their normal day-to-day occupations—except for President Edward Sparrow. Following a bachelor dinner given for him by Vice President Cooley and several other long-time colleagues in the rod and gun club, he was married at noon on September 15 to Helen Grant. Sparrow and his bride then immediately departed on a honeymoon trip that took them out of the country to Europe for the remainder of the year, leaving on the shoulders of Manager Olds the responsibility of making a go of Sparrow's newest business venture. However, Sparrow was by now too much the inveterate businessman to be distracted for long by the romance of a honeymoon. Thus, while he and his young bride were touring France, he took the opportunity to make "a very careful study" of that country's booming automobile industry. He came away convinced, as he later told Olds, of the bright future that awaited the industry in the United States, as well as the company they had organized.[20]

During the autumn of 1897, Ransom Olds devoted his main energies to the development of the motor vehicle company, delegating to his brother Wallace the task of supervising the engine company. The younger brother soon demonstrated the same talent in creating interest in his motor vehicle that he had shown earlier in promoting his engines. On the Sunday following the organization of the vehicle company, he drove the company's one motor vehicle from Lansing to nearby Grand Ledge and back, making the twelve-mile return trip in one hour and fifteen minutes, at a cost of four cents worth of gas, or a third of a cent per mile (although a standard claim made in 1896–97 was that fuel to operate the machine cost only a quarter of a cent per mile). "No trouble whatever was experienced in climbing or descending the steep hill about half way to Grand Ledge," Olds informed the *State Republican*.[21]

Olds seized upon any opportunity he saw to demonstrate his vehicle before large crowds. He recalled in 1950 that he "hired out to several fairs as an attraction and would run [his motor carriage] around in front of the grandstand between races." Such publicity techniques followed the promotional lead taken in 1896 by the manufacturers of the Duryea Motor Wagon, one of whose vehicles was a featured attraction of the Barnum and Bailey Circus, and actually much earlier by W. W. Austen in his exhibition of the Roper steamer at county fairs in the 1860s. In June 1897, Olds was scheduled to give a demonstration run as a special feature of a horse-racing program at the Lansing Driving Club's track; but at the last minute he withdrew because—ostensibly, at least—he had found it "impossible to arrange his business affairs so he could be present." In fact, it was not until two years later, during the summer of 1899, that a public gathering in Lansing would be treated to a formal demonstration of the capabilities of the Olds vehicle, although by that time Olds was driving it around town almost daily. On August 11, 1899 the opening of the Lansing horse-racing season included a test run by Olds in his "automobile" (this being one of the first recorded uses of the term by the local press), cryptically referred to as "one of the most interesting features" of the afternoon. Ten days later the "Olds' Horseless Carriage" was part of the manufacturers' parade that opened a street fair and carnival in Lansing, and three days after that, Olds, accompanied by his daughters Gladys and Bernice and his sister Sadie (Metta Olds was awaiting the birth of their third child), drove his car, decorated with the national colors, in a floral parade during the same fair.[22]

During the intervening two years Olds made similar appearances in a number of nearby communities, beginning in late September and early October 1897, at the Barry County Fair in Hastings and the Eaton County Fair in Charlotte. The crowd of 20,000 at the latter was the largest Olds had ever seen at such an event. His trip to these communities is apparently the trip of "about 50 miles" that he declared in 1905 was the longest drive he took in this first Olds gasoline vehicle. Strangely enough, Olds and his machine apparently did not create a sensation at either of these central Michigan county seats. In its coverage of the Barry County Fair, the Hastings *Banner* gave no indication that Olds had been on the program, although one news item which clearly referred to Olds' vehicle reported that "a horseless carriage" had been in town at that time, giving "the noble horse" further "cause to mourn the various devices that are being used to cheat him out of an honest occupation." The Charlotte *Tribune*, whose city editor, Harry T. McGrath, would later recall in some detail Olds' appearance at the Eaton County Fair, contained only one rather enigmatic reference to a "Brother Sherman," who rode out to the fair in "no ordinary turnout" but in "the horseless carriage of which he speaks very highly, although he won't buy one just yet." Olds managed to obtain more adequate press coverage of these out-of-town appearances in his hometown papers, where it was reported that he was especially pleased at being able to make the thirty-mile trip from Hastings to Charlotte in only three and a half hours and on one and a half gallons of gasoline, despite the fact that "the roads were very poor and no end of hills and sand."[23]

Ransom Olds had good reason to be pleased with the results of those tests, the most far-ranging he had yet conducted of his motor vehicle. For the motorist of the latter part of the twentieth century, accustomed for decades to driving on paved roads, it is next to impossible to imagine the problems faced by pioneer motorists driving primitive vehicles in a state such as Michigan in the 1890s, where professionally built and maintained dirt roads—let alone paved highways—were virtually unknown. And among the Michigan automobile pioneers, Olds was the first driver to traverse the miserable roads of central Michigan. The Charlotte *Tribune* did not have to be more specific in referring to "the horseless carriage." In 1897, Olds' was the only such carriage in the area; he had the roads to himself. His only concern, he later recalled, was the possibility of an encounter with a horsedrawn rig, in which case a runaway was likely to occur, followed by some unpleasantness with the horse's owner.

In addition to his trips out of Lansing, Olds continued to test and demonstrate his vehicle in town. On October 5, 1897, he was accompanied on "a tour of the town" by Walter D. Gregory, the treasurer of a firm which published *The Hub*. The report of this demonstration, which appeared in that magazine's October issue, was a particularly important one for Olds: this was no company publicity handout, as was obviously the case with many of the glowing notices that Olds and other auto pioneers received in the trade journals of the period. Instead, like the report on Olds' steam vehicle in *Scientific American* in 1892, this was a testimonial from an outside observer of his firsthand experience with the vehicle. In addition, *The Hub*, as might be expected of a journal representing the carriage industry, had been more skeptical of the claims made for the early horseless carriages than had been such automotive journals as *Horseless Age*. Thus, Gregory's uniformly favorable comments on his ride in the Olds vehicle, appearing where they did, gave Olds added publicity value among a select and knowledgeable national clientele.

Gregory declared that it had taken "but a few moments" to start the motor carriage, which was parked outside Olds' office. When they got underway, "hills were climbed and descended with as much ease as the level road was traversed, and the speed was regulated from zero to 12 miles per hour with the utmost ease and safety." Vibration, Gregory found, was "scarcely perceptible," and he could detect no noticeable odor while the vehicle was in use. These were significant points to bring out, because in early 1897 *The Hub* had dismissed all the horseless carriages then in use as unacceptable because they all lacked "the essentials of success." These had to include, the editor declared, reliability, simplicity, light weight, "an absence from the annoyance of the vibration and grating incident to machinery, . . . the use of some method devoid of obnoxious fumes," and "the ability to make progress over all kinds of roads and through snow and mud." With the exception of its ability to handle snow and mud, which could not have been tested at the time, the Olds motor vehicle measured up reasonably well to all of *The Hub*'s standards of success, according to Gregory's report.

This included its thousand-pound weight, relatively low for that period, though it was not the lightest motor vehicle yet produced, as Olds had claimed in August.[24]

By the end of 1897, however, the editor of *The Hub* had either forgotten what he had published in October or had not been as impressed with Olds' work as Gregory had been. He reiterated his earlier contention that none of the gasoline cars built up to that time had satisfactorily overcome the problems of odor and vibration. To these criticisms he added another: the initial cost of purchasing such a vehicle, he said, would be a serious impediment to the widespread adoption of motorized transportation until it could be reduced. Olds was more vulnerable to this last criticism than he may have been to the editor's others. By the first part of October he had raised the price of his vehicle from the figure of $1,000, which he had quoted earlier, to $1,200 for the one-seat carriage model and $1,400 for the two-seat model. The price increase, attributable perhaps to the claim that "more attention" would be "paid to the upholstering and to finishing various parts of the machinery" in the production models than had been the case in the prototype vehicle, marked the beginning of an Olds move away from the concept of a utilitarian, inexpensive machine to a fancier, more expensive type. Not until he returned to that earlier concept in the fall of 1900, with the $600 to $650 Oldsmobile runabout, would he become a successful automobile producer.[25]

Nevertheless, in the fall of 1897 Olds professed to be—and probably was—confident that his vehicle would enjoy "a large demand." Ten orders were reported to have been received by October, although some of these orders apparently dated back to the fall of 1896. Specific details are lacking that would enable us to identify these patient pioneer customers for a Michigan-made car. Olds said that while he was at the fairs in Hastings and Charlotte in September he received orders from a doctor in North Branch, a town in Michigan's Thumb area, and from "a Chicago party." In November Olds reported another sale of one of his "improved vehicles" to an unnamed "gentleman from Grand Rapids," who had spent several days in Lansing "inspecting the workings of the carriage and was very much pleased with it." This buyer intended to take the vehicle with him to Florida that winter, and it was apparently this sale that Olds recalled in 1905 as the first of his gasoline vehicles to be shipped out of Lansing. This may also have been the car that Olds had in mind decades later when he said that the first Oldsmobile he sold was purchased to carry passengers along the coast of Florida between Ormond and Daytona Beach, although it should be added that the Oldsmobile trade name was not used until 1900.[26]

Exactly how many vehicles the Olds Motor Vehicle Company succeeded in making and selling is uncertain. The lowest estimate appeared in the *Detroit News* in April 1899, stating that up to that time Olds had produced no "more than two or three motor vehicles." Later reports placed the number as high as six, but in 1942 James P. Edmonds, who was secretary of the Olds Gasoline Engine Works during this period, could list only four sales of which he had any definite recollection. The four included a vehicle sold to a Grand Rapids buyer, presumably the cautious soul who had required several days in November 1897 to be convinced of the wisdom of purchasing a horseless carriage; a vehicle which was shipped to Chattanooga; another which was shipped to Florida (although this may have been the vehicle purchased by the Grand Rapids buyer for shipment to Florida); and a fourth, which was eventually donated by the Olds Motor Works to the Smithsonian Institution in 1915. Since it is not clear who had owned this last car before 1915, however, it may have been one of the other three Olds cars of which Edmonds recalls the sale.[27] It was the only one of the early Olds-built automobiles to survive.

At first, Smithsonian officials believed that they had received Olds' original gasoline model of 1896, until they learned—as Olds testified in 1905—that that vehicle had been destroyed in the 1901 fire at the Olds company's Detroit factory where it was being exhibited. Although the Smithsonian's model closely resembles the Olds 1896 vehicle in many of its features, when they are compared with those visible in photographs of the earlier model, the height of the

dash is not the same, and the four-passenger seating arrangement, which was *dos-à-dos* in 1896, is of the more conventional type in the Smithsonian's carriage—both seats facing forward. The Smithsonian clearly has one of the $1400
four-passenger cars supposedly produced in the Olds shop in
the fall of 1897, and the institution has therefore attached
that date to the vehicle in its possession.[28]

Had the plans of the Olds Motor Vehicle Company as outlined at the time of the company's formation been carried
out, there would be no reason to doubt that several vehicles,
including the Smithsonian's, could have been produced during the later months of 1897. In August of that year the
board stated that "a number of men" would "be put to work
at once" on vehicle production and that it was hoped that the
first vehicle would be completed within sixty days. More
than two and a half months later, however, the best the
company could report was that it had "a number of carriages
in process of construction" and that it expected to complete at
least some of its orders "within a short time." But by the end
of December, when he was asked at the Michigan Engineering Society's meeting how soon the machine would be on the
market, Olds could still only reply: "We are now manufacturing the carriages, and will have a large number ready for
spring delivery." The wording of the question and of Olds'
response would seem to indicate that at the end of 1897 he
and his men had not yet completed any production models.
Even by the following spring the Olds Motor Vehicle Company was still complaining that its "greatest problem" was
in producing vehicles "fast enough to supply the demand.
They have quite a number under way, but could sell an unlimited number of them if they could get them made fast
enough." If any of the vehicles that had been "in process of
construction" the previous November were completed and
sold by the spring of 1898, there was no mention of such an
accomplishment.[29]

There are several explanations for the slow progress that
plagued Olds in manufacturing the motor vehicles. The
twenty to forty per cent increase in the price of the vehicle,
which was announced in the fall of 1897, resulting presum-

ably from a re-evaluation of the costs involved in manufacturing the product, suggests that part of the explanation for the delay lay in Olds' inexperience in manufacturing such a product. Unlike Henry Ford, whose problems with the Detroit Automobile Company in 1899 and the Henry Ford Company in 1901 were partially the result of his lack of any real manufacturing background, Olds had had a dozen years or more of general manufacturing experience by 1897. However, knowing how to manufacture engines and pumps would not necessarily have prepared him for the more complex task of manufacturing automobiles.

There is also the possibility that mechanical imperfections were another reason for Olds' failure to market a significant number of his first models. Although most contemporary reports indicated that the vehicle operated acceptably, there are hints of problems that may not have been immediately apparent to casual observers who had been, after all, rarely exposed to the sight of an automobile in operation. Thus, whereas the Hastings *Banner* reported in September 1897 that the vehicle "runs easily, noiselessly and at small expense," Harry T. McGrath of Charlotte, recalling Olds' appearance at the Eaton County Fair, said that the latter admitted that he had had to stop eight times to add oil during the eighteen-mile trip from Lansing to Charlotte. Furthermore, after Olds made "his slow but successful drive" around the track at the fairgrounds, he stopped at McGrath's home to take on water for the return trip to Lansing. The vehicle's high rate of water, and particularly oil, consumption may have been symptoms of mechanical problems that Olds would have wanted to correct before producing large numbers of the cars. In fact, there are said to have been rumors in Lansing at the time that Olds' machine "would not run with a sufficient degree of enthusiasm to warrant great expectations of it on the part of all concerned."[30]

Still another cause of production delays certainly must have been the labor problems that beset the Olds engine plant for several months in early 1898. These followed a drive conducted by the machinists' union to recruit members from the previously non-union Olds shop. Although Ransom

Olds, like nearly all of the automobile pioneers, would later take a strong stand against any unions in the auto industry, he seems to have retained his father's good relations with the employees and was reportedly willing to sit down and talk with the machinists' union in 1898, when it sought to bargain on behalf of the members it had acquired among the Olds work force. However, when he discovered that his brother Wallace was supporting the union and not upholding the management's point of view in the negotiations, Ransom fired his brother. To replace the latter as manager of the engine works in March 1898, he hired Richard H. Scott, a twenty-eight-year-old native of Canada who was the factory manager of the Toledo Machine and Tool Company. In April, Wallace's remaining link with the company which he had once co-owned was severed when his $2,000 stock interest was transferred to Ransom. However, Wallace Olds was popular with the Olds workers. This had been shown the previous Christmas, when the company—as was "the usual custom"—had given each of its forty employees a silver dollar. In return, the men of the foundry "presented W. S. Olds with a very handsome solid oak writing desk, as a Christmas gift." The newspaper report of this holiday exchange of gifts contained no reference to any the workers may have presented to Wallace's younger brother. Therefore, when Ransom Olds removed his brother from his job, Wallace's supporters in the plant went out on strike, demanding Scott's removal and Wallace's reinstatement. For several months production in the factory was hampered by these labor problems. Ransom Olds refused to give in to the strikers' demands, and eventually Scott gained control of the situation.[31]

Thus began a long period of close association between Ransom Olds and Richard Scott. In a few years Scott was to acquire an importance in the operation of the Olds manufacturing business that equalled—some said surpassed—that of Olds himself. Still later, however, conflicts over business policies would lead to a permanent rupture of the friendship between the two men. Meanwhile, in May 1899, Wallace Olds joined a former Olds patternmaker, David M. Hough, to take over the operation of a St. Louis, Michigan machine shop, "with gratifying success," it was soon reported. The following year a patent on a carburetor was awarded to the two men. By 1902, however, Wallace seems to have rejoined his brother in some kind of capacity, perhaps as a consultant on engines. At the time of their father's death six years later, Wallace was connected with an engine company that seems to have been unrelated to his brother's business interests; but the events of 1898 apparently did not cause more than a temporary division between the brothers. For example, in the summer of 1928, a year before Wallace's death, he was listed in Ransom's diary as among a group of guests whom Olds entertained for a week at his lodge in northern Michigan.[32]

In spite of the labor unrest that plagued the Olds Gasoline Engine Works early in 1898, its remarkable growth record was not noticeably slowed. Sales for the year totalled nearly $72,000, up about $30,000 from the figures for the previous year. These sales, when combined with a large backlog of orders still to be filled for the Olds engines, led to yet another reorganization of the Olds manufacturing operations in the fall of 1898. It was hoped that the new reorganization would lead not only to a great expansion of the engine production capacity but would also enable the Olds horseless carriage to finally be produced in discernible numbers.[33]

In the summer of 1898 preliminary arrangements for a large-scale refinancing of the Olds businesses were worked out between Ransom Olds and a Detroit group headed by John T. Holmes, secretary-treasurer of the Michigan Portland Cement Company, and John M. Nicol, whose occupation was listed simply as the "investment business." There is some evidence that the talks leading up to these arrangements were initiated by Olds and not by the Detroiters, though some of them may have been among those residents of that city who had expressed an interest in the Olds motor vehicle in 1897. The interest of the Holmes-Nicol group, however, was obviously aroused more by the splendid record of the Olds Gasoline Engine Works than by the as yet unproven market for the products of the Olds Motor Vehicle Company. As Samuel Smith's son later recalled, it was "the sure field for the gas engine" that appealed to the "cold-nosed wealthy."[34] As a result, the Detroiters came up with a proposal, which was put in the form of a contract that was signed by Olds, Holmes, and Nicol on July 28. On its face it was the most favorable offer that Olds had yet received. It called for the combination of the engine works and the motor vehicle company into a one-million-dollar corporation to be based in Detroit. The relative importance placed on each company was indicated by the proposal to acquire control of the motor vehicle company for $40,000 in cash and stock, while $75,000 in cash and $125,000 in stock was the price to be paid for the engine works. The agreement also called for $350,000 in cash to be pumped into the new corporation, presumably to be raised through the sale of company stock, which the three contracting individuals would control. Backing it up, however, would be a $500,000 mortgage on the property of the engine and motor vehicle companies, secured by negotiable bonds that would be payable in ten years. It was this last aspect of the deal that Olds later declared he had found objectionable, and he decided not to go ahead with the plan. His reasons are not entirely clear, but he apparently felt that the planned method of financing the new corporation would not have proved sufficiently worthwhile for him to throw in with the Detroiters. But their offer, like those he had reportedly received in 1897 from other Detroit and Chicago businessmen, became useful to Olds in approaching Lansing backers and asking them to increase their investment if they wished to keep him from moving his manufacturing activities elsewhere.[35]

On September 30, 1898, therefore, revised articles of incorporation were filed that raised the authorized capitalization of the Olds Gasoline Engine Works to $150,000, with the paid-in capital boosted to $95,500, an increase of $54,500 over the amount previously available. The action, according to the *Detroit News,* was a direct response by Lansing capitalists—headed by Edward Sparrow—to the offer that Olds had received earlier that summer to move his operations to Detroit. The Lansing *State Republican* reported that several other "very large cities" in addition to Detroit had been trying to get the Olds Motor Vehicle Company "to locate in their midst.... But to all these offers the Olds people have turned a deaf ear, preferring to give Lansing ... the benefit of any good that might accrue from the employment of labor in the manufacture of the vehicle."[36]

Under the new arrangement, Ransom Olds retained control of a majority of the outstanding stock, 5,000 of the 9,550 shares, but Eugene Cooley increased his holdings to 2,200 shares, more than double his previous holdings. New investors, with 500 shares each, included Frederick Thoman, Cooley's long-time business associate, and Reuben Shettler, who was reported to have been one of the principal figures in these negotiations and who would be one of Ransom Olds' most influential backers during the next twelve years. Pliny Olds, Madison Bates, Richard Scott, and R. E. Hardy, another Olds employee, held from 100 to 300 shares of the new stock. But in the long run the most important of the new investors was to be Samuel Smith's son Frederick (sometimes spelled Frederic), the only non-Lansingite in the group, with 500 shares of Olds Gasoline Engine stock. The younger Smith was born in 1870 and had been active in his father's mineral land and lumber business operations for some years. His investment in the Olds engine stock was an early sign that for this aggressive and ambitious Detroiter, as for many others of his generation in that city, a career in manufacturing held greater attraction than did the forms of economic activity with which his father and his contemporaries had been associated. The zeal with which Fred Smith was to pursue his new business interest would ultimately have fateful consequences for R. E. Olds.[37]

With the more than $50,000 in new money coming from the recapitalization of the Olds Gasoline Engine company, additional properties adjacent to the existing engine plant were purchased, including the land and shops of the old Anderson Road Cart Company, in which Edward Sparrow had had an interest. Plans for two "immense brick buildings" to

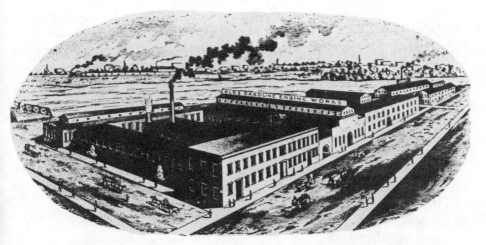

A bird's-eye view, no doubt somewhat idealized, of the Olds Gasoline
Engine Works factory as it had developed by the late 1890s

be constructed on the new site had already been drawn in
September by the local architect Edwin A. Bowd. The contracts were awarded on September 30, with the work
scheduled for completion within sixty days.[38]

The expansion was intended to enable the company not
only to produce more engines, the demand for which had
completely outstripped the capacity of the existing plant, but
also to permit the manufacture of the Olds horseless carriage
on "an extensive scale." At the end of September 1898, Olds
admitted that manufacturing delays had prevented him and
his associates from making an effort "to in any way push the
business" of selling the Olds gasoline carriages. However,
when asked what he thought were the prospects for developing sales of this product, he replied: "There is not the shadow
of a doubt that it will be a great success, and we are confident, both from personal knowledge and a close study of the
different makes of motor vehicles, that we have the simplest,
most practical wagons yet invented." Olds reported that his
company had received the astounding total of "over 3,000
letters" inquiring about his vehicle. Regrettably, these letters, which would constitute an immensely valuable source

for any study of the emerging interest in the automobile in the late nineties, have not survived; they were probably destroyed in the fire that gutted the Olds Detroit offices and plant in 1901. In any case, Olds left no doubt in 1898 that the sheer volume of mail the company had received had encouraged him to believe in the commercial possibilities of his vehicle. He made specific reference to the contents of only one letter, from a correspondent in Paris, then the leading automobile manufacturing center in the world, who claimed that he could sell all the automobiles Olds could make. "Possibilities? Why, there is no limit to them," was Olds' enthusiastic conclusion.[39]

It is unclear what happened to the Olds Motor Vehicle Company at this time. Press reports of the three-fold increase in the stock of the Olds Gasoline Engine Works at the end of September 1898 declared that the engine works had "absorbed" the vehicle company. This may be an accurate description of what happened to the motor vehicle firm; in any event, it had always depended on the facilities and labor force of the engine works for whatever it had been able to produce. But legally the Olds Motor Vehicle Company continued to exist. It filed an annual report with the state on January 31, 1899, noting that as of the previous August 2, Ransom Olds was acting as trustee of all but five of the 5,000 shares of company stock, the remaining five shares being held by the directors, who now consisted of Olds, Eugene Cooley, Richard Scott, and R. E. Hardy. Hardy had succeeded Arthur Stebbins as secretary, and Olds had apparently moved up to the position of president, previously held by Edward Sparrow. Olds' position as trustee of virtually all the motor vehicle stock seems to have been an arrangement Sparrow and the other stockholders agreed on to enable Olds to speak with complete authority in any negotiations that contemplated the merger of the company with or sale to other interests.[40]

The newspaper reports seem to indicate that Olds thought the recapitalization of the engine works would solve the problems that had been delaying the production of his vehicles. But in a very few weeks he was once again searching for more capital. Actually, the events of the next eight months make it appear quite possible that the reorganization on September 30, 1898 was never regarded as anything but a temporary step by some—if not all—of those involved. The suspicion arises that more was going on in 1898 and 1899 than simply a search for more money to finance the construction of the facilities needed to manufacture the Olds automobile. If that alone was the case, one cannot but feel that Olds and his associates were being too cautious. The capital invested in the Olds business by the fall of 1898 and the expansion of the Lansing plant that was to be completed by the end of the year, when combined with the manifestly great interest in the vehicle, would seem to have been enough to persuade them to launch a determined effort to manufacture and market these machines, even if it meant curtailing further expansion of engine production. However, it was not until 1901 that any significant number of Olds automobiles were produced, despite the increased capital investment and plant facilities in 1898 and the far greater increases that followed in 1899. Lack of money, equipment, and manpower does not appear to have been the main cause of the delays that kept Olds vehicles off the market for so long. Olds' own uncertainty about the kind of automobile to produce and the best way of going about it was certainly part of the problem. However, it seems plausible that the delays in 1898 and 1899 were also due to a struggle between the Lansing-based backers of the Olds enterprises and groups elsewhere to gain financial dominance over the operations— plus the maneuvering of Olds to secure the most advantageous terms from these competing groups.

CHAPTER FOUR

The Olds Motor Works

ON THE MORNING OF NOVEMBER 23, 1898, Ransom Olds left Lansing on a trip to Boston and New York that was expected to last about ten days, on what the Lansing *State Republican* termed "business connected with the Horseless Carriage Co." Writing in the 1930s, Arthur Pound stated that Lansing bankers, who are not named but were said to have been aware of Olds' financial needs, had "pulled wires" to secure an offer to Olds from New York capitalists who had an interest in establishing a large automobile company in the East. Such an interest was widespread in eastern financial circles at this time, as a sudden awareness developed of the speculative possibilities in the manufacturing of automobiles. For example, in January 1899, Ellery I. Garfield of Boston, who was seeking to form a company to produce the automobile Henry Ford was developing, wrote a letter to William Maybury, the mayor of Detroit, who shared the same ambition. Garfield urged the latter to get Ford to complete his work so that they might take advantage of the bullish feeling among easterners towards automobile investments. "I think you cannot have any true idea of the number of Motor Wagon Co.'s that are starting up," Garfield wrote. "A week does not pass but that I do not learn of two or three companies." Several months later, in an article in *McClure's* magazine, Ray Stannard Baker (who was, incidentally, a native of Lansing and still a frequent visitor there) reported that during the first four months of 1899 automobile companies with a total capitalization of over $388,000,000 had been formed in the United States.[1]

It is not surprising, therefore, that Olds would have received a proposal from some of these eastern capitalists who were interested in automobile investments in the late nineties. Specific details about the proposal are lacking, including even the date when it was made. Olds' only recorded trip to the East in late 1898 and early 1899 was the one beginning in late November. Late in March 1899, the Lansing *State Republican* did report the return from the East of George Olds, whose kinship to Ransom Olds, if any, is not known but who was described as a representative of the Olds Gasoline Engine Works; he had spent seven weeks visiting the company's eastern agencies. But, unless the latter's trip was somehow connected with the eastern bid for the Olds automotive enterprise, it would appear that Ransom Olds held the discussions with eastern investors mentioned by Arthur Pound and others around Thanksgiving of 1898. Olds is said to have been intrigued by the possibilities not only of manufacturing his vehicles on a large scale, as the easterners indicated they would want him to do, but also of producing them in a location near the large centers of population, where the prospect of marketing the product would be far simpler than what he faced operating out of Lansing. He is even said to have picked a site for the factory in Newark, New Jersey. But then the promised financial backing failed to materialize, and Olds had to abandon this effort and return to Michigan.[2]

Much has been made of this incident, about which so little is actually known. It has been cited as an example of the cautiousness of the eastern moneymen toward automobile investments, which may have been a reason for that region's loss of the auto industry to the more venturesome Midwest. Had Olds located his plant in the East, it has been asserted, the history of the industry might have been entirely different, with the New York area—not Detroit—developing into the center of automobile manufacturing. This is pure speculation, of course, and considering the track record of the multi-million-dollar automobile stock companies that were formed in the East in the late nineties, none of which survived for long or got very far into manufacturing operations, it was perhaps just as well for Ransom Olds' future success in auto production that the New York deal fell through.

Unproductive as his trip to Boston, New York, and Newark turned out to be, it at least enabled Olds once again to point out to his current backers that they were not the only ones who were interested in his work. This, in turn, may have stimulated them to make additional investments in order to strengthen their hold on the Olds companies and to ward off—as they had in 1897 and 1898—the threat of a takeover by outsiders and the removal of the Olds enterprises to other locations.

There are two conflicting accounts of what happened when Olds returned from the East. According to a questionnaire that Olds himself filled out in 1924, he met John T. Holmes in the Michigan Central train station in Detroit, where Olds had to change trains to get back to Lansing. Holmes renewed his proposition of the previous summer when he learned of the collapse of the eastern financing proposal. However, Olds again turned down Holmes' offer. Another account, which appeared in print several years before Olds' version of 1924, declared that Olds was met at the station not by Holmes but by Samuel L. Smith, whose investments in the Olds Motor Vehicle Company and those of his son in the Olds Gasoline Engine Works certainly made him familiar with the problems Olds faced. After discussing the matter with Olds, Smith is said to have agreed to provide the funds that were needed to make a go of the automobile venture. But in 1924 Olds said that it was not until later that he had this particular talk with Smith. In view of the amount of time that elapsed between Olds' eastern trip late in 1898 and the date of the announcement of the changes accompanying Smith's increased investment in the Olds business four months later, Olds' 1924 version of these events seems the more likely one. In any event, both accounts agree on the result: Smith would back Olds to the tune of about $200,000, which offer—though apparently a less remunerative offer than Holmes'—Olds accepted.[3]

Samuel Smith deserves a sizable share of the credit that is

usually given to Olds for fostering the automobile industry in Detroit, since it was Smith's money and contacts that finally put the Olds horseless carriage operation on its feet and in a new location, the future Motor City. Edward Sparrow was responsible for securing Smith's initial investment in 1897, but it was the older man's shrewd analysis of the prospects of Olds' enterprises that accounts for his 1899 decision to make his large, life-giving transfusion of money. His decision has often been pictured as a wealthy father's desire to acquire control of a company in which his sons, Fred and Angus, could become involved. Both sons did become officers in the Olds company; in fact, a story in the *Detroit Free Press* in 1905 even credited Fred Smith with responsibility for "forming" the new firm. However, it is more likely that the popularity of the Olds engines, not family sentiment, lay behind Samuel Smith's decision to back this venture. The terms of his offer called for the merger of the engine and motor vehicle operations into one company—the same merger contemplated in the reorganization of the Olds Gasoline Engine Works the previous year but not yet legally completed. Whatever Smith's interest in the Olds automobile may have been, he knew that with the Olds gasoline engine under the control of his new firm he was not likely to lose his investment.[4]

On April 6, 1899, both Edward Sparrow and Eugene Cooley were in Detroit to wrap up the negotiations with Samuel Smith, their business associate of many years' standing, on his proposal to refinance the Olds enterprises. The very next day the announcement was made that the Olds Gasoline Engine Works had been sold. The names of those who had purchased the company were not given, nor was the residence of the purchasers made clear at that time. The Lansing *State Republican* reported that the local firm had been sold to a group of "Detroit and Lansing capitalists." That news release, which probably came from Olds' office, would seem to have been part of a conscious effort by Olds over the next several months to disguise the real implications of what had happened and leave the impression in

Samuel Latta Smith, the shrewd old investor whose money put the Olds automotive venture on the sound financial footing that it needed to succeed

Lansing that that city would continue to play a more important role in the operations of the reorganized company than was actually the case.

The Detroit papers gave a markedly different—and more accurate—picture of what had happened. In April neither the *News* nor the *Free Press* indicated that any Lansing capitalists were involved in the takeover: the *News* reported that the engine company had been sold to "Detroit parties," while the *Free Press* dispatch from Lansing described the transaction in rather unusual terms, stating that "a controlling interest in the Olds Gasoline Engine Works . . . has been foreclosed by Detroit capitalists." Since the word "foreclose," as that term is usually employed, does not seem to fit this situation, it could mean that in his discussions with Olds that winter Samuel Smith had been given an option to purchase control of the engine company, an option which he now exercised, or "foreclosed." But in April 1899, Samuel Smith's connection with the Olds transaction was not known. It was rumored in Lansing that the "Detroit parties" who had purchased the company were the Holmes-Nicol group that was known to have had talks with Olds the previous year, but when contacted, one of the members of this group denied any involvement in the purchase or any knowledge of which Detroiters were involved.[5]

The mystery was cleared up on May 8, when incorporation papers for the Olds Motor Works were filed with the secretary of state, and the names of those involved in the latest reorganization were made public. The new company was capitalized at $500,000, a modest figure in a day when the speculative interest in automobiles was leading to the incorporation of firms with far larger capitalizations; for example, the grandiosely named Anglo-American Rapid Vehicle Company planned to issue $75,000,000 in stock. Furthermore, only $350,000 of the Olds stock, with a par value of ten dollars a share, was initially issued. Of this total, Samuel Smith received all but forty of the first twenty thousand shares. The forty shares that he did not take were equally divided among Ransom Olds, Edward Sparrow, Fred Smith, and James H. Seager of Hancock, Michigan, the four individuals who, with Smith, signed the incorporation papers.[6]

Seager was the only new figure. A resident of the Copper Country, where Samuel Smith had spent so many productive years of his life, Seager had ties with Smith which suggest how the former came to make the first of several investments; within five years he and other members of his family would have control of more stock in the Olds Motor Works than any other stockholders except the Smiths. To begin with, Seager was Smith's brother-in-law. He had come to the Copper Country in 1871 to serve as Smith's business associate, and the two had been involved in many of the same ventures. When Smith moved back to the lower peninsula, Seager had stayed on to become one of the more prominent businessmen of the Copper Country, with interests in railroads, banks, hotels, newspapers, and other activities in addition to copper mines.[7]

There was probably never any intention that Samuel Smith would retain control of his huge block of 19,960 shares of Olds stock. According to Fred Smith, one quarter of the money his father put into the Olds Motor Works was distributed to the stockholders in the engine works and the Olds Motor Vehicle Company. The remainder ($150,000) was put in the company's treasury. In addition to the cash they received, the stockholders in the two earlier companies received a total of $150,000 in the stock of the new firm, the figure of $200,000 (Smith's $50,000 plus the $150,000 in stock) being the value at which the assets of the two absorbed businesses had been pegged. Upon this distribution, the shares held by Olds, Sparrow, and Fred Smith, as well as the holdings of the other stockholders in the merged firms, reached more respectable totals when compared with those of Samuel Smith. Furthermore, Smith almost immediately sold or otherwise disposed of many of his shares to others, enabling him to get back some of his initial investment as well as broadening the base of support for the company. By the early part of 1900, Smith's holdings were down to 12,085, a sharp decline from the 19,960 shares he had received in the initial distribution plus the additional shares he would have received later as a shareholder in the Olds Motor Vehicle Company. Still, he retained a commanding lead over Ransom Olds, who with 7,500 had the second largest number of shares by the beginning of 1900.[8]

Among the investors not previously represented among the stockholders in either of the earlier companies was one Lansingite, Schuyler Seager Olds, who was now the fourth largest stockholder in the Olds Motor Works with 1,500 shares. "Sky" Olds, as this corporation lawyer and Republican political leader was familiarly known, was not related to Ransom Olds. He had been well known for many years in Lansing, where his family had settled in 1863, particularly after he became secretary to United States Senator Francis B. Stockbridge in the late 1880s. His activities were constantly being recorded in the Lansing papers at a time when many months would slip by without a word in print about the city's other Olds family. S. S. Olds had some business links with the Sparrow-Cooley group, but it is clear that in 1899, he, like the other important new investors in the Olds Motor Works, came in because of his close associations with the Detroit group, who now completely overshadowed the Lansing element. Sky Olds was related by marriage to both Samuel Smith and James Seager. His father and Seager's father, Schuyler Seager, were such close friends that the Reverend Carmi Olds had named his son after his friend. Subsequently, Olds and Smith married sisters of James Seager, making all three men brothers-in-law of one another.[9]

Sky Olds, who was once described by the Lansing *State Republican* as "a slick piece of goods . . . but a gentleman who is . . . true to his friends," was also the chief lobbyist in Lansing for the railroads (another paper dubbed him "The Lobby King of the Senate Cloak Room"). This probably helps to account for the presence among the new investors of the Detroiter Henry Russel, long-time general counsel of the Michigan Central Railroad, for whom Olds had done legal work. Russel in turn brought in his brother, George Russel, prominent Detroit banker and the immediate past president of the American Bankers Association; Henry Ledyard, president for many years of Michigan Central and grandson of Michigan's foremost political figure of the nineteenth century, Lewis Cass; and Henry M. Campbell, Henry Russel's law partner, whose father was almost as highly regarded a jurist as Eugene Cooley's father.[10]

It was an impressive and distinguished group of men that Samuel Smith had added to the roster of Olds stockholders. The holdovers along with Smith and Ransom Olds included Cooley, with the third largest block of shares; Edward Sparrow, now tied with Henry Russel and behind S. S. Olds in the number of shares; Fred Smith, Fred Thoman, Reuben Shettler, Arthur Stebbins; and at the bottom of the list the venerable Pliny Olds, with 125 shares in a company that was the successor of the firm he had founded.

Of the 35,000 shares of stock in the Olds Motor Works, Ransom Olds and his father controlled only 7,625. Thus, financial control of the business that only two years earlier had still been an almost exclusively family-owned affair, had passed out of Olds' hands. And yet the Olds Motor Works in 1899 was still in an important sense Ransom Olds' company. He had the mechanical knowledge and background needed to make a go of the new company, and the stockholders recognized his importance. Initial reports in April stated that Olds would continue as president and general manager under the new management. In May, however, when official details of the Olds Motor Works were unveiled, Samuel Smith was listed as president, with Olds serving as vice president and general manager. That was changed again, however, on January 9, 1900, when the earlier reports in automotive trade publications that the company would be headed by Olds were confirmed. In a meeting of the directors at that time, Samuel Smith moved that Olds be elected president in his place. The motion was seconded by Henry Russel and was adopted; whereupon Olds, with equal success, moved that Smith be elected vice president. Fred Smith continued as secretary-treasurer of the company, whose five-man board consisted of the two Smiths, Olds, Russel, and Eugene Cooley.[11]

The Detroit orientation of the majority of the officers of the Olds Motor Works, as well as of those who controlled the majority of the stock, may have been—as some have assumed—responsible for the decision to move the firm's main operations from Lansing to Detroit. Although the Olds Motor Works had reportedly been offered factory sites by the cities of Chicago, Toledo, Cleveland, Indianapolis, Muskegon, and Buffalo, with the cheap source of power provided by Niagara Falls thrown in as an added inducement by the last city, there is no doubt that Detroit was the only location that was ever seriously considered. On April 8, when the first reports of the formation of the company appeared in print, the construction of a large new plant in Detroit was noted as a project that was to commence at once. Negotiations for a factory site had begun some weeks earlier with Walter S. Campbell, secretary of Detroit's Merchants and Manufacturers Exchange, and Edward I. Stimson, a Detroit realtor who specialized in manufacturing properties. These were completed, and on May 13 the announcement was made that the Olds Motor Works had purchased nearly five acres of land formerly occupied by an iron works, on Jefferson Avenue in Detroit, at a reported cost of $40,000, although the exact purchase price was not officially revealed.[12]

In Lansing, Ransom Olds continued to reassure the local citizenry that there was no intention of abandoning the Lansing plant. "We shall move some of the machinery we have in the Lansing plant," he admitted, but they had "too much money invested in it to let it remain idle." In fact, Olds said, the Lansing plant would be expanded to meet the increasing demand for the Olds engines. When he was asked in May how a recent increase in gasoline prices had affected the sales of engines, Olds replied: "Oh, it has increased our trade, as, when gasoline is high every one is more particular to get the most economical engine on the market, and we have it. In fact the present high price of gasoline has turned a great many orders our way." Later in the summer, when rumors circulated in Lansing that the Olds Motor Works had underway a massive movement of equipment from the Lansing plant to the new Detroit plant, which would result in the closing of the Lansing factory, Olds firmly denied the accuracy of those reports. "We couldn't stop this plant if we wanted to," he told a Lansing reporter. "Business is crowding in on us and we are forced to run the factory to its fullest capacity."[13]

Actually, however, the rumors were not unfounded. The articles of association of the Olds Motor Works clearly specified that the offices of the firm were to be located in Detroit and that manufacturing operations were also to be conducted in that area. The Lansing plant was to continue in use in the production of engines for the time being; but by the summer of 1899 trade journals—if not the local Lansing press—were predicting that, with the full completion of the new Detroit facility, manufacturing would be entirely centered in Detroit. The articles of association certainly foresaw that development. And references in the Lansing papers to the "Big Branch" plant that was to be built in Detroit could not for long disguise the fact that the Lansing plant would shortly be the branch of a Detroit company and that it would be only a matter of time before it would be phased out entirely.[14]

The articles of association in May 1899 were not as clear on the matter of the product that was to be emphasized. The Olds Motor Works was being formed, the document stated, for the purpose of manufacturing and selling "all kinds of machinery, Engines, Motors, Motor carriages and all appliances and equipments connected therewith or appurtenant thereto." The order in which these objectives were listed, together with the failure to mention carriages or vehicles in the name of the company, would seem to confirm the suspicion that the Smiths and their fellow investors were more interested in Olds' engines than they were in his motorized vehicles. However, although the reports of the formation of the new firm in April and May 1899 indicated that one reason for the reorganization was to permit the expansion of engine production at both the Lansing and Detroit plants, the main objective, these reports indicated, was "to manufacture the motor vehicles under the Olds patents, and also the motor trucks, for which the patents are now pending." The experimental work in which Ransom Olds had been engaged over the past several years was now at an end, the *Detroit Free Press* reported on May 14, and when the new Detroit plant was in full operation, "manufacture of automobiles will be a specialty."[15]

Thus, from the inception of the plan to build a new factory in Detroit, Olds and his associates envisioned it as the long-delayed plant where Olds' motor vehicles would be produced. This was a momentous decision, since the result of it was to make Detroit, within a matter of no more than five years, the

Three views of the Olds trap, which the newly formed Olds Motor Works planned to produce, accompanied a story that appeared in the pages of *The Hub* in June 1899.

Courtesy of University of Michigan Transportation Library

THE OLDS TRAP.

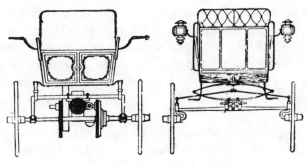

FRONT AND REAR VIEWS.

recognized leader of the automobile industry in the United States. Of course, it is unlikely that anyone in the spring of 1899 recognized anything like the real significance of this action. The manufacturing advantages of a city the size of Detroit over one as small as Lansing were sufficiently obvious to explain the move to most people's satisfaction. The control that the Smiths, Russels, and their fellow Detroiters had obtained over the conduct of the company no doubt predisposed them to locate the company in their own city. Yet, two years later these same men readily accepted an offer that led them to move much of the company's operations back to Lansing and transfer all remaining activities to the capital city in 1905. Thus, hometown sentiment would seem to have had little lasting influence over the business decisions of these Detroiters.

The same can be said of Ransom Olds and his attachment to the town where he had lived for nearly two decades and which had nurtured the Olds business enterprise from its infancy to the lusty status it had achieved by the late nineties. Despite his protestations in 1897 and 1898 to the effect that he wished to keep his company in Lansing, Olds was perfectly willing to move his operations to the East in the winter of 1898–99 had the right kind of financial arrangements been worked out. There is thus no reason to think that he raised any objections to the later proposals to make the move to Detroit. Arthur Pound declared that Olds had realized that Lansing lacked the number of skilled workers the automobile plant would need; at the same time it lacked the housing that would be required for any large number of workers who might be brought in from elsewhere. Detroit, on the other hand, had a large resident pool of experienced workmen which could be drawn upon. In addition, Olds claimed that he suggested a move to Detroit because of the superiority of that city's streets to those found in Lansing, which had hampered the development of his automobile work.[16]

The transportation facilities at the Detroit site were certainly among its foremost assets. With 195 feet fronting on Jefferson Avenue, the Olds factory would have access to one of Detroit's main thoroughfares, along which were located some of the city's major industries. Furthermore, though Detroit's streets would be important both as testing grounds for automobiles and as avenues for conveying materials into the plant, other means of transportation to which Olds would have similar access were of even greater importance in the selection of this site. In 1897 the Anderson Manufacturing Company, which manufactured the closely related product of carriages, explained a similar decision to move its factory from Port Huron to Detroit: "railroad facilities, together with unsurpassed opportunities for receipt and shipment by water, give Detroit advantages over almost any other Western city in all manufactories that involve the handling of bulky freight." The property which the Olds Motor Works acquired extended back more than one thousand feet from Jefferson Avenue to the Detroit River, where the 195 feet of river frontage, which the company planned to develop, gave it direct access to Great Lakes shipping. This water transportation advantage of the Detroit site had been, of course, nonexistent at the Lansing plant.

Some writers have regarded Detroit's position on the Great Lakes waterways as a major reason for its emergence as the center of the auto industry and would regard this feature as the key to Olds' decision to locate in Detroit. Of far greater importance, however, was a sidetrack running into the Detroit site, which connected it with the Belt Line system of Henry Russel's and Henry Ledyard's Michigan Central Railroad. The Belt Line, in turn, tied the shipper into the city's entire network of railroads. The water and street connections provided at the Jefferson Avenue site were undoubtedly taken into consideration; but the determining factor in the board's decision must have been their recognition that adequate rail connections were a necessity, since most of the incoming and outgoing freight shipments would be moved by rail. Waterborne freight would occasionally figure in the operation of the Detroit Olds plant, but the very fact that within six years the company would be operating entirely out of Lansing is an indication of the relatively slight importance attached to a location on the Great Lakes.[17]

Courtesy of Gladys Olds Anderson

Ransom and Metta Olds with their daughters Gladys (left) and Bernice at the time when business developments made it necessary for them to move to Detroit

On the morning of April 13, 1899, Ransom Olds went into Detroit on the first of many trips that he would make in the following weeks to direct the development of his company's new Detroit operations. According to the initial reports, it had been anticipated that he could continue to manage both plants by commuting between Lansing and Detroit, and it may have been thought he could retain his residence in Lansing. But by that summer the demands of the Detroit operation were taking more and more of his time. With the approaching completion of the Jefferson Avenue plant, which would provide the office facilities for the company as well as space for manufacturing activities, it became inevitable that Olds would move his family to Detroit.

On September 11, therefore, Olds resigned from the Lansing school board, "because of his prospective removal to Detroit." Several weeks later Olds purchased a house at 106 Edmund Place in Detroit, about a mile out Woodward Avenue from the downtown area and some three miles from the new plant. It was by far the largest house the family had owned and was chosen, one daughter believes, in part because it was an easy walk to two of Detroit's main streetcar lines, which Olds could use to get to work. Later he would also adopt the practice of driving one of his horseless carriages to the office, pioneering a practice that would eventually have a devastating effect on the maintenance of a viable public transportation system in the Motor City.[18]

On November 9, 1899, with little fanfare, the Olds family left Lansing for its new home in Detroit. It must have been a difficult period for the family: in addition to the turmoil that normally accompanies the preparations for a move to a new city, there was the added excitement of the birth in September of Metta and Ransom's third child, Mildred— excitement that ended quickly and tragically in the baby's death only twelve days later. Nevertheless, by the end of the year Ransom, Metta, and their two daughters, aged five and seven, were settled in their Detroit home. There, on New Year's Eve, Olds awakened the two girls "just before midnight," Gladys recalled years later, and explained "that we would not have the chance ever again to see a new century born and he didn't want us to miss it." For Olds it must have been a satisfying moment. Since 1896 he had persistently sought to find a way to manufacture his automobile. Now a new year and a new century dawned with success finally within his grasp.[19]

CHAPTER FIVE

The Curved-dash Oldsmobile

THE PERIOD during which Ransom Olds and his family resided in Detroit was to be a brief but eventful one in his life. At the time of his arrival his name meant nothing to most Detroit residents, and even in 1901, by which time his business activities were attracting increasing attention, the *Detroit News* carelessly referred to him on one occasion as R. F. Olds and on another as C. Olds.[1] The fact was that motor vehicles were not yet big news in Michigan's largest city. About one-seventh of its citizens worked in factories that had long since given Detroit a reputation as a center for the manufacturing of railroad cars, stoves, pharmaceuticals, tobacco products, chemicals, paints and varnishes, ships, and carriages. Next to Olds' Jefferson Avenue plant, in fact, was one of Detroit's best-known companies, the Detroit Stove Works, whose Jewel brand stoves provided stiff competition for the Garland stove, produced by the Michigan Stove Company, also located on Jefferson. Both companies claimed at various times to be the biggest stove manufacturer in the world.

As recently as 1897, Charles B. King, Detroit's pioneer gasoline automobile builder, had known of only four automobiles that were in use in the city. King's efforts to interest backers in financing the manufacture of the car he had developed met with so little enthusiasm that he had turned instead to the production of marine engines, a safer field and one in which Detroiters were already interested. Another Detroit automobile experimenter, Barton Peck, son of a wealthy and indulgent father, had built a couple of gasoline vehicles by 1898; in fact, at one point he had announced that he was forming an automobile manufacturing company. But Peck also dropped the idea, probably not so much because of financial problems but because, as he explained in the summer of 1899, he had been unable to eliminate the disagreeable smell and noise associated with the gasoline-powered machine.[2]

Meanwhile, Henry Ford, a third Detroiter to have built gasoline motor vehicles during this period (he tested his first one in June 1896), had been more successful than his friend Charles King in securing financial support for his experiments. These experiments had encouraged his backers, nearly all of them from Detroit, to form the Detroit Automobile Company. The organization was announced in August 1899, three months after the incorporation papers of the Olds Motor Works had been filed. Such developments led a writer for *Motor Age* to make the bold prediction in September 1899 that Detroit "promises to become a center of motor vehicle manufacture."[3]

The events of the months that followed did nothing to bear out the accuracy of this forecast. The Detroit Automobile Company, with Ford as its production head, repeatedly failed to live up to the promises of its officers that the company would soon be turning out large numbers of the Ford "motor wagons." Instead, by the spring of 1900 the company's failure to produce much of anything—largely the fault of Henry Ford himself—was foretelling the demise of the firm by the end of the year. A similar promising beginning was made by Charles Annesley, a Detroit electrician who had purchased Ford's original 1896 car and had gone on to build a reported total of four electrics and three gasoline vehicles by 1899. But these failed to lead to the permanent manufacturing enterprise in Detroit that some expected. Instead, by 1900 Annesley had left Detroit for a job with a Buffalo engine manufacturing company.

It was against this background of unsuccessful efforts to get an automobile industry underway in a city far more absorbed with other economic interests that Ransom Olds and his associates arrived in 1899. That was the year, a *Detroit*

Courtesy of Eastern Michigan University Library

A youthful Ransom Olds, in this photograph dating from the 1890s, appeared with a full-page biographical sketch in *Men of Progress*, a 1900 Michigan publication. Olds was the only person treated in the 528-page book who was listed as a manufacturer of automobiles.

News publication declared two years later, in which automobiles first became at all noticeable on the streets of the city. The failures of King, Ford, Peck, Annesley, and others to manufacture automobiles in the late nineties only add increased significance to the success Olds would have within two years in moving Detroit toward establishing itself as the world's automotive capital.[4]

The rapid manner in which the Olds Jefferson Avenue plant took shape in the last half of 1899 seemed to bode well for the company's future. Plans for the factory complex had already been drafted by Fred Thoman, Jr., son of the Lansing capitalist and stockholder in the Olds Gasoline Engine Works, when the Detroit site was acquired in May. At that time it was announced that the new plant was expected to be completed by the following August, but these expectations were impossible to fulfill. It was not until June 10 that Ransom Olds went into Detroit with the intention of letting the construction contracts. However, the bids were much higher than the preliminary estimates. "They thought we were in a hurry and they could force us to pay most any price," Olds reported. "So I just came home and we've been making $1,000 a day by waiting. The bidders are just tumbling over themselves now to get it." The contracts were awarded later in June, and by early July construction work had begun, with a completion date scheduled within sixty days. These estimates again proved to be overly optimistic; nevertheless, by October the machinery was being installed and by the beginning of 1900 manufacturing operations were underway, with a staff of one hundred at work by March 1900.

The completed factory was, superficially at least, an impressive establishment. The plant consisted of four buildings, set well back on the property towards the river, with a total of two and a half acres of floor space. Facing the street was a three-story, "L"-shaped brick structure, about 150 feet wide by fifty feet deep. The first floor was divided between offices and a showroom, with the engine room in the basement, automobile finishing work on the second floor, and the paint shop on the top floor. To the rear, a connecting two-story building, measuring seventy by 280 feet, contained the machine shop and storage facilities, while two other nearby buildings housed the foundry and the forging departments.[5]

The claim was soon made that this Jefferson Avenue factory was the first manufacturing establishment ever built for the purpose of producing automobiles, and subsequently the Olds Motor Works erected a lighted sign calling it "The Largest Automobile Factory in the World." Whatever may have been the validity of either of these claims, it is a fact that at the outset, though the plant was designed primarily for automobile production, gasoline engines were also manufactured here, as well as at the existing plant in Lansing. Engines continued to be regarded as the staple product of the company until the latter part of 1901. Future plans for the Detroit site called for the building of a separate plant near the river for the production of marine engines. These particular plans were not carried out, but in February 1900 the Olds company acquired Charles King's marine engine business and hired King to direct the production of these engines, which now received special emphasis in company advertising. Without the profits that came from the steady sales of engines, the Olds Motor Works would probably not have been able to survive the losses its automotive department suffered in the first two years of operation. All accounts, including those of Ransom Olds and Fred Smith, agree that these losses were in excess of $80,000. Once again, the anticipated large volume production and sales of Olds motor vehicles was failing to develop.[6]

The unprofitable nature of Olds' automotive endeavors in 1899 and 1900 would seem to be explained not so much by the problems of financing, factory space, and manpower that had plagued his earlier efforts, but by the uncertainty Ransom Olds showed in deciding on what kind of motor vehicle to produce. In the late nineties he strayed from the traditional goals of the Olds businesses, which had always been to produce simple, practical, relatively inexpensive machines. In 1899 and 1900, Olds and his staff came up with about eleven different automobile models, ranging in price from $1,200 for the two-passenger trap on up to $2,750 for a four-passenger brougham. Nearly all the models were differentiated by their body style and not by their mechanical elements, which featured a two-cylinder, seven-horsepower engine. In fact, this was one of the advantages claimed for the Olds vehicles, because as a result of its patented method of construction, whereby the engine was not attached to the body, the builders could use "any style of carriage body which will best suit the trade." Thus from its formation the Olds Motor Works indicated plans for a wide-ranging line of vehicles, including "pleasure carriages, delivery wagons, park carriages and motor trucks."[7]

Olds was not content, however, with the patent on the construction of his carriage, which he had received in 1897, or his earlier patent on the Olds engine. In 1898 and 1899 he also applied for patents on an electric ignitor for gas engines, a mixing and controlling device for gas engines, a pneumatic cushion tire, and a clutch mechanism, all of which were awarded to him by the patent office. (Other patents may have been applied for but rejected by the patent office.) "We thought we had quite a car," Olds said in later years, as he recalled how he and his staff had used the various Olds patents to design a vehicle "with some very up-to-the-minute improvements—pneumatic clutch, cushion tires, and electric push-button starter."[8]

In view of the difficulties and even hazards early motorists faced when trying to start their engines with a crank, this last Olds invention would seem to have guaranteed the success of the Olds models equipped with it; but this was not to be the case. The Olds starting device was actually designed to begin operating when the driver shut off the engine. At that time, relief cams automatically left one of the pistons off center, so that this piston would retain a "proper mixture." When the driver wanted to get underway again, he simply pushed a button at the side of the seat, producing a spark which ignited this mixture, thus starting the engine. In practice, however, the system was no more reliable than the many self-starting methods others tried to popularize in the years before Charles F. Kettering and his staff developed a truly successful self-starter in 1910–11. The major drawback in the Olds method probably resulted from the fact that if the engine remained idle for any length of time, leakage would cause the mixture in the piston to deteriorate so that it would no longer ignite. At any rate, Olds abandoned the use of his self-starter after 1900 in favor of the crank; but since he located this crank at the side of the vehicle within reach of the seated driver, he could still claim that his car could be "started from the seat."[9]

Such dubious "improvements" as a self-starter that could not be depended on to function properly made the Olds gasoline models of 1899–1900 more difficult to operate than the machines for which the Olds name had become famous earlier, when the major selling point of the Olds steam and gasoline engines had been their simplicity in operation. Looking back on this period, Olds declared that "we soon found that [these cars were] too complicated for the public."[10] This, plus the prices of the models, which made most of them more expensive than such better known and well-respected cars as the Winton, may have accounted for the lack of interest the public showed in any of these early Olds vehicles.

Late in 1900 the Olds Motor Works adopted the Oldsmobile trade name, although it did not register the term as a trademark until 1902.[11] Oldsmobile is today the oldest surviving American automobile marque. (Autocar predates the use of Oldsmobile, but, though it was originally applied to automobiles, it has referred only to trucks since 1911.) It followed such earlier names as Gasmobile, Locomobile, Mobile, and Steamobile, which had appeared since 1898, with the term "automobile" used increasingly in preference to the earlier favorite "horseless carriage." Initially, however, an Oldsmobile did not necessarily refer to the gasoline-consuming machines that later generations would automatically associate with the name; for, although his earlier thinking had led him to dismiss the electric vehicle in 1897 as impractical compared with the gasoline-powered carriage, in 1899 and 1900 Ransom Olds devoted considerable time to the development of electric automobiles.

It is not difficult to discern the reasons for Olds' changing assessment of the electric car's importance. The electric was the last of the three major types of motorized vehicles to be developed: its development in Europe dated only from the 1880s, while what is usually thought to have been the first successful electric road vehicle in the United States was developed by William Morrison of Des Moines, Iowa and tested as recently as 1891. Even so, by the time the Olds automotive activities were being relocated in Detroit in 1899, it appeared to many observers that the battery-powered vehicle had moved to the forefront in the United States horseless-carriage competition. One writer, comparing the motor vehicle progress that had been made in Europe with that in the United States, declared in September 1899 that, whereas the dominant motive power of automobiles in European countries was "oil," in America "it is principally electricity." No doubt this was in part due to the willingness of the American public, accustomed by the nineties to both seeing and using electrically-operated streetcars and interurbans, to accept the electric automobile more readily than it would a vehicle powered by the noisy, noxious, unfamiliar—and to some rather frightening—internal combustion engine. In addition, engineers and mechanics had found the problems of building reasonably good electric vehicles far more easily and quickly resolved than were those connected with designing a similarly satisfactory gasoline car.

A sizable percentage—perhaps a majority—of the automotive pioneers still undoubtedly shared Olds' preference for the gasoline-powered vehicle, and many of them may have shared the view of the editor of *Horseless Age,* whose dislike of electrics was so intense that another editor reported that he was seized with "a fit of lead colic every time he sees an electromobile." However, the opposing view was also apparently widespread. Although dubious of the future of any automobile, *The Hub* declared at the beginning of 1898: "We pin what faith we have on the electric motor."[12]

While the advantages of the electric—instant starting, safety, little or no odor, noise, and vibration—were publicized at the time, its disadvantages were also brought out. The latter included the problems created by the heavy batteries and the resulting excessive weight of the vehicle, and by the fact that the electrics could not be driven more than a few score miles at most before the batteries needed recharging. This eliminated them from consideration for long-distance travel. However, since road conditions in the United States at this time were on the whole so bad that they severely limited a motorist's opportunities for straying very far beyond the city's limits, the advantages of the electric as a vehicle for town use seemed more important to most people than its disadvantages as a touring car. It was true that the electrics also developed a reputation as slow-moving vehicles, although specially designed electrics were capable of attaining high speeds for short distances. But this reputation again arose from the vehicle's limitation to use in the cities, where recharging stations were readily available and where the speed limits still reflected the slow pace of horsedrawn traffic. There was thus little incentive for engineers to design commercial electric models to perform at speeds that the driver would rarely if ever use.

Although completely trustworthy records are not available, it would appear that by 1899 there were more electric automobiles operating in the United States than there were steamers, which ranked second, and gasoline vehicles, which lagged behind in third place. Numerous companies had been formed to produce electrics, with the Electric Vehicle Company, formed in 1899 by a group of well-known and powerful New York businessmen and financiers, leading the way. By the beginning of the twentieth century it threatened to dominate not only the field of electrics but the entire American auto industry in a manner that later generations would associate with General Motors. In keeping with the electric auto's limited sphere of use, the Electric Vehicle Company's main goal at the outset was to develop and control a network of electric cab companies in the cities across the country. According to announcements made late in 1900, Detroit was on the list of communities for which such service was scheduled. By that time the use of the electric as a town car was gaining increasing favor in Detroit as elsewhere, especially among wealthy women who were attracted by the simplicity of operation of these cars. An estimated twenty such machines were being driven in Detroit in October 1900, including a Baker, manufactured in Cleveland, which was driven by Mrs. Henry B. Joy, who "makes her social calls and does her shopping in a much more satisfactory way than the horse and carriage or street car method of transportation would afford." Although Henry Joy would for many years be the president of the Packard gasoline automobile firm, his wife continued to drive an electric almost up to the time of her death in the late 1950s.[13]

Ransom Olds was not the first or only Detroit-based automaker to work on the development of electrics in a city that would become world-famous for its gas-guzzling buggies. In 1897, at the same time that Henry Ford, Charles King, and others in Detroit were experimenting with gasoline-powered vehicles, H. W. Koehler, a local carriagemaker, was working on "an improved electric motor horseless carriage, which he considers far ahead of anything seen in that line." Koehler never produced this vehicle, though he may have been involved with the abortive attempt of Charles Annesley to put out an electric later in the decade. Among several electrics that were eventually manufactured in Detroit, the Detroit Electric, which was being produced in limited quantities as late as the 1930s, still ranks as the best-selling electric passenger car ever produced in the United States.[14]

By July 1900, Olds, obviously attempting to capitalize on the public's interest in the electrics, was far enough along on the development of his own electric car to place an order with the Cleveland firm of Sipe & Sigler for a large number of batteries, in anticipation of full-scale production the following winter. That September, Olds unveiled this new vehicle at the "First International Automobile Exhibition and Tournament," held in Chicago's Washington Park, one of the earliest auto shows in the United States and certainly the first one at which Olds was an exhibitor. Although the attendance at the show was reported as "rather light," those who came out saw a small but fairly representative sampling of the companies and the cars which then comprised the infant American automobile industry. From the city of Chicago itself, about twenty electric vehicles were exhibited by the

Woods Motor Vehicle Company, probably the chief competitor of the Electric Vehicle Company in the production of this type of automobile; five electrics were displayed by the Hewitt-Lindstrom Electric Company; while the Chicago Motor Vehicle Company exhibited one or more of its gasoline-powered commercial vehicles, named after their designer, William O. Worth. The latter had earlier been associated with the ill-fated Benton Harbor Motor Carriage venture in 1895–96. The Milwaukee Steamer, produced by the Milwaukee Automobile Company, and the far more successful Locomobile from Bridgeport, Connecticut, as well as the Mobile from Tarrytown, New York, represented the steam vehicles that were available in 1900. Gasoline-powered passenger cars on exhibit, besides William Worth's, included one from the St. Louis Motor Carriage Company; a Packard, produced at that time in Warren, Ohio; and the tiny DeDion-Bouton Motorette, a car of French origins distributed in the United States by a firm in Brooklyn, New York.[15]

Ransom Olds and his company made their debut in an industry show with what the Chicago trade journal *Motor Age* called "one of the most tastefully arranged exhibits... albeit it contained but one vehicle, a handsome electric stanhope." Advertisements from this period priced the Olds electric stanhope at $1,650, with an electric phaeton selling for a hundred dollars more. Olds thus had become the only major automotive designer to explore all the options open to him at that time—electricity, steam, and gasoline—and actually produce and sell all three kinds of cars (if one counts the one-time-only sale of his experimental steamer in 1893). When Olds was in his seventies he was experimenting with and securing patents on still a fourth source of power, the diesel engine.[16]

Olds thought of his electric as a town car which would be a sideline to his gasoline auto, which he was certainly as convinced in 1900 as he had been in 1897 would become the most popular type of vehicle. However, of the eleven models that he had available, the number of vehicles—gasoline or electric—that Olds actually produced and sold in 1899-1900 is not known. It would appear to have been very small. One automotive historian, writing in 1941, put the number sold between mid-1899 and the end of 1900 at 400. He does not specify how he arrived at this number, but it seems an unlikely total on the face of it.* In terms of the known production figures of other companies at that time, the production of 400 cars in a year and a half would have made Olds' Detroit firm one of the leading automakers in the country and would have given Olds and his associates little grounds for the concern they obviously came to share concerning the future of their automotive division.

References that appeared in print during these years give the same impression as do those of the earlier 1896–98 period—that very few vehicles were coming out of the Olds factory. In the spring of 1899, an ad for the Olds Gasoline Engine Works declared that "owing to the great demand for these vehicles we cannot fill additional orders before October 1st." At the time of the formation of the Olds Motor Works, the company said that it would "not receive orders on vehicles for delivery before September, as they have all the orders that they can fill for some time to come." But in June 1899, a more extended discussion of the new company reported that after several years of work "the experimental stage is passed, and it is prepared to manufacture motor carriages." This would seem to imply that no actual production had yet occurred. The same inference can be drawn from a story in *Horseless Age* as late as October 1900, which described the important features of the Olds electric and gasoline cars and reported that the company had published "a catalogue of various styles of vehicles they intend to build." Perhaps the final verdict on the Oldsmobiles of 1899–1900, as expressed in an article in *Automobile Review* in 1904, was that most of the models "were really fine vehicles. Some, however, were too expensive, and all were open to

---

*Even less credible are the production figures given in an article in the Silver Anniversary issue of the *Automobile Trade Journal*, which listed car production of the Olds Motor Works as 1400 vehicles in 1900, with figures for the following years likewise at variance with all other available production data. (*Automobile Trade Journal*, XXIX:71 [Dec., 1924])

one objection or another which made it impractical for a wide market."[17]

Sometime in the summer or early fall of 1900, therefore, Ransom Olds, "after a long sleepless night," decided to turn from the kinds of cars he had been developing over the preceding two or three years and to return to the model he had originally had in mind in 1896. The following morning he left his home on Edmund Place, went downtown to the Jefferson Avenue plant—perhaps driving to work in one of the 1900 models—and went into the office of one of his young engineers, Horace Loomis. He drew for Loomis some rough sketches of the automobile he had in mind. At a later date Loomis recalled that Olds had told him: "What we want to build is a small low down runabout that will have a shop cost around $300.00 and will sell for $650.00," which would have been half the price of the lowest-priced Olds vehicle then available. Olds' ideas were fleshed out by Loomis, Milton Beck, and Jonathan Maxwell. Beck was a Canadian who seems to have gone to work for Olds the previous year and is credited by Loomis with designing the engine for the new car. According to Loomis, Maxwell developed part of the mechanism for the transmission, although others would later claim that Maxwell deserved the primary credit for the design of the entire vehicle. By October the Olds staff had completed and tested the prototype of what would become one of the most famous automobiles of all time, the curved-dash Oldsmobile, a tiny one-cylinder vehicle that became the inspiration for the song "My Merry Oldsmobile" ("Come away with me, Lucille") and—of greater importance—captured the public's fancy to such an extent that the Detroit firm soon became the volume leader in the entire industry.[18]

* * * * *

There is no greater source of frustration to the student of Ransom Olds' life than the discovery of the woeful incompleteness of available materials relating to the most important decision of Olds' career—the decision to concentrate on the production of the Oldsmobile runabout. However, if this development is studied within the broader context of the time, one point becomes clear from the outset: the idea behind the type of vehicle Olds decided to build in 1900 was not original with him. The commonly expressed view that Ransom Olds broke with precedent by offering the public a small, inexpensive car at a time when all there was to choose from were big, expensive automobiles is not true at all, as a reading of the automotive trade journals in the latter part of the nineties proves beyond any question.

The real pioneer in small automobiles seems to have been the French firm of DeDion, Bouton et Cie, which experimented with lightweight motor cars in the nineties. It finally enjoyed great success with its one-cylinder DeDion-Bouton Voiturette, introduced in 1899. By April 1901 it had sold about 1,500 of these cars. The vehicle was imported to the United States, where it was referred to as a Motorette, weighed as little as 450 pounds, and sold for about $850, much less than Olds' early models of 1899 and 1900. Exhibits at the Paris Exposition of 1899 indicated that the French auto industry was following the lead of DeDion-Bouton, turning from the heavier to more lightweight automobiles, whose price in some cases was less than that of the DeDion-Bouton Voiturette. A similar trend was evident among other European manufacturers by the summer of 1899, when one Belgian company was offering not a one-cylinder but a two-cylinder gasoline car for the equivalent of only $700.[19]

During the early months of 1899 numerous lightweight models were being unveiled by American automobile designers and companies. In July 1899, *Horseless Age* saw the future of the industry in this kind of vehicle rather than in the big "high-speed carriages and racing machines"; however, the trade journal admitted that the wretched American roads presented far more serious problems both to the manufacturers and to the drivers of vehicles of lightweight construction than was the case in France, with its excellent roads.[20]

In the United States the new light automobile, comparable to the Voiturette type in Europe, was most commonly designated as a runabout, the term for a particular body style that had been in use in the carriage industry since about 1880.

The term "runabout" was originally the trademark of the carriage company that had introduced the style, but it proved so popular that by the late nineties it was applied indiscriminately to "an almost endless variety of nondescripts." Nevertheless, the feature that distinguished a runabout from other carriages, according to *The Hub,* was its "long square body, suspended upon side bars and hung extra low." The typical runabout had one seat, holding two passengers, and had no top. Because of its lightness and ease of handling it had become "recognized as the only vehicle of the buggy class that can be used as a ladies' carriage."[21]

The adoption of the runabout by the auto industry in the late nineties again illustrates the extent to which the American automobile at that time was still essentially a horseless carriage in design, with a motor taking the place of the horse. It was convenient, of course, to make use of the manufacturing facilities of carriage companies in this manner, and there may also have been a belief that the public would more readily accept this new mode of transportation if it came in a familiar package. Furthermore, these carriages had proved to be well suited to American road conditions.

Many of the runabouts described and pictured in automotive publications in 1899 never got into production; but by the latter part of the year the Autocar Company of Ardmore, Pennsylvania was advertising for sale a two-cylinder gasoline runabout that was said to weigh only a little more than four hundred pounds and had been developed by the company's predecessor, the Pittsburg Motor Vehicle Company. The most widely advertised small car of the period was a two-passenger steamer developed by Francis E. and Freelan O. Stanley, which both the Mobile Company of America and the Locomobile Company were selling by the summer of 1899.[22]

In January 1900, a runabout was one of the models which the Detroit Automobile Company declared it would soon have on the market; and though a Ford-designed runabout failed to appear as scheduled, several were available from other companies by the summer of 1900. All of them had the same basic features: they were light in weight, they had a single seat that could hold two people, and they were usually powered by a one-cylinder engine housed beneath the vehicle. As he followed these developments and observed some of the lightweight models that were exhibited at the auto show in Chicago, Ransom Olds could scarcely have failed to see a popular trend emerging that favored a car incorporating the very benefits he had been hoping to achieve with his first gasoline vehicle of 1896—a small, uncomplicated mechanism with just enough power to meet the average motorist's everyday needs. Here, in the tradition of the little Olds steam and gasoline engines, was a car that would be easy to operate and inexpensive to produce. In an industry that has always been highly imitative, Olds jumped on the runabout bandwagon in the summer of 1900.[23]

For the most part, there was little to distinguish the Oldsmobile runabout from others on the market. It was not as light as the DeDion-Bouton Motorette or some of its other competitors, in the end weighing closer to 600 pounds than to the 500-pound figure Olds had hoped for. Subsequently, its weight would increase to 700 pounds and more. The one-cylinder gasoline engine was located under the vehicle; the driver sat on the right, controlling the engine with a lever located on his right and steering with his left hand by means of a tiller, still standard American automotive equipment. Very few American designers had as yet gone to the steering wheel, which one trade writer referred to as "that foreign freak," since the tiller or lever was regarded as a far superior steering device. Both the driver and his passenger sat completely exposed to the elements, although the purchaser was given the option of buying a cloth top, which when raised gave a certain amount of protection from the elements. At the side there were no doors—nothing but a low railing to keep riders from falling out. However, since twenty miles per hour was about as fast as it was practical to drive on the roads of that day, the likelihood of being thrown from the vehicle was not great.

All that was in front of the occupants of the car was the curved dashboard, which gave this Oldsmobile its nickname of the "curved-dash Olds" and was the one feature that most readily identified the car. Although the horsedrawn runabout traditionally had a straight dash, and most motorized runabouts retained this design feature, a runabout advertised in September 1900 by the People's Automobile Company of Cleveland had a slightly curved front. A steam runabout which the Kidder Motor Vehicle Company of New Haven, Connecticut unveiled early in 1901 bore an even closer resemblance in this one feature to the Detroit Olds car, whose appearance was just then beginning to be widely publicized in automotive circles. The Oldsmobile's dash, which curved out, up, and then in, was supposedly a functional part of the runabout's design, as well as one that might be pleasing to the eye. In his application for a patent on the car's cooling system, which was drawn up in September 1901, Olds claimed that when the runabout was moving forward, the curve of the dashboard helped to deflect the air currents down over the radiator, located in the footboard, "thereby greatly assisting in the dispersion of the heat." However, since the original curved-dash runabout had been built almost a year before Olds applied for a patent on the "cooler"—as he called it—it is possible that his inclusion of the curved dash as an integral part of the cooling system was an after-thought, intended to discourage competitors from copying the runabout's design.

Earlier, on May 1, 1901, Olds had also sought to protect his runabout by applying for a patent on the vehicle body. In his application he described the leading design feature of this body as "a concave-convex forwardly projecting portion . . . terminating in a scroll-like curve." He later amended this description by adding that the curved dash "rises to a slightly greater height than the rear portion of the body," in order to overcome the objection of the Patent Office examiner that the design as originally outlined was too close to that of a sleigh patented in 1895 and a carriage attachment patented in 1899. Olds' amended application satisfied the examiner and a patent on the runabout's body design was issued to him on July 23, 1901. A design patent was also awarded on the frame on September 10, 1901, and on the engine-cylinder head and chest on December 31, 1901. In the latter part of 1901, Oldsmobile ads were issuing warnings that "nearly every part" of the car was covered by patents and that "imitators and infringers will be prosecuted." But Ransom Olds had no better luck in enforcing his patent rights than did George Selden and his associates in the automotive field during this period—or John Harvey Kellogg in the breakfast food industry. Actually, there was no better testimony to the success of Olds' runabout by 1902 than the extent to which other manufacturers were trying to copy some or all of the curved dash's features, as observers at automobile shows often reported. But none of these imitations was to have quite the impact of the original.[24]

The price of the Oldsmobile runabout, initially set at $600 and then later raised to $650, where it remained for the life of the model, was no more innovative than was the overall style of the car. The curved-dash Olds was decidedly not—as has frequently been claimed—"the first cheap car on the market." At a very early stage the American automobile buyer began to develop a reputation as a consumer who was primarily interested in the price of the car. "English people look to the gearing, Germans to the engine," a French publication on "How to Sell Motor Cars" declared in 1906, but "Americans merely consider the price." Although the American whom this anonymous French writer had in mind was the rich man who regarded the automobile with the highest price tag a sure sign of greatest prestige, it was equally true that many Americans came to regard the automobile with the lowest price the best value. By 1900 the desirability of developing an inexpensive automobile was being discussed in print, and it remained a favorite topic among automotive writers for many years. Robert Bruce, writing in *Outing* magazine in September 1900, declared with great prescience that the major difference that would develop between the American and the foreign auto industry was in the price range of the cars on which they would concentrate their efforts. Bruce, apparently overlooking or ignoring the pioneering work of European manufacturers in the development of inexpensive voiturette models, contended that the foreign automakers catered to the aristocrats. "The American maker," on the other hand, "believes there are more people who have $300 to spend for a luxury than there are those who have $3,000 for the same purpose. This means that here we will see machines turned out by thousands, where abroad they have been slowly produced by scores."[25]

Although it would be a good many years before a person with $300 in his pocket had much of a chance to buy a new car, a considerable drop in the lowest figure at which one could purchase an automobile in the late nineties—around $1,000–$1,200—was evident by 1900. As early as June 1899, the Stanley-designed Locomobile steamer was being advertised for only $600, while the two-cylinder gasoline Autocar runabout advertised late in 1899 bore a price tag of $500. In 1900 the Thompson Automobile Company of Philadelphia introduced a lightweight, one-cylinder "gasoline rig" which likewise sold for $500; and in January 1901 the Crest Manufacturing Company of Cambridge, Massachusetts offered to supply the small carriage or bicycle manufacturers with all the parts they would need to produce a $400 motor vehicle. Although that Massachusetts firm's own Crestmobile, when it appeared later in 1901, sold for $550 instead of $400, this price, as well as that of several other runabouts produced at the time, was still less than the Oldsmobile runabout's, which also became generally available in 1901. By 1902 the unforgettably named Dingfelder runabout was being offered in Detroit for only $500, although few if any of those cars seem to have been produced; and by 1903 the Orient Buckboard of Waltham, Massachusetts was being touted as "The Cheapest Automobile in the World," with a price that was $275 under the Oldsmobile's $650. Even the Orient's price was beaten by those motorists who took advantage of the opportunity—apparently of limited duration—that was offered early in 1903 to buy a Canda Quadricycle, manufactured by George W. Condon of Newark, New Jersey, at the rock-bottom figure of just $195.

Meanwhile, the Oldsmobile, in addition to having to compete with other runabouts at equal or lower prices, also faced competition from numerous other lightweight models during the period between 1900 and 1903 which offered a more powerful engine or other attractive features. Although these models were priced at one hundred to two hundred dollars more than the Oldsmobile, the customer might feel that the added features more than offset the higher price. In this category, the Detroit-made Cadillac, Ford, and Northern runabouts, along with the Rambler from Kenosha, Wisconsin, were providing the Oldsmobile with its stiffest competition by 1903.[26]

All this adds to the significance of what Ransom Olds and his staff were able to achieve in pushing their runabout ahead of all others that were on the market. Lacking the elements of novelty and originality that might account for the appeal of a totally new product, and also lacking any advantage in terms of price over many of its rivals, the Olds runabout was a relative latecomer to the field and was probably no better than much of the competition. But it achieved its front-running position primarily because of the strength of the company Olds had built up over the preceding decade and a half, which now gave the Olds Motor Works both the time and the capability that were needed to plan, produce, and promote the car in a manner that others could not duplicate. Some of Olds' competitors lacked the financial resources that carried the Detroit firm through the many months that passed before its automobile production ceased to be a red-ink item on the pages of its account books. By the end of 1901, for example, both the People's Automobile Manufacturing Company of Cleveland and the DeDion-Bouton Motorette Company of Brooklyn were being driven out of business because of financial problems. The former produced a runabout quite similar to the curved-dash Olds in most respects, including price, and the latter offered a lighter— though more expensive—runabout which may have had some extra snob appeal through its connection with a well-known European automobile manufacturer. Other companies, such as Locomobile and Autocar, soon abandoned the low-priced field for the production of bigger, more expensive models.[27]

Eventually, therefore, as the little curved-dash Oldsmobile continued in production long after its early competitors had disappeared from the showrooms, there was a certain element of truth in the advertising claim that it was the first practical and successful runabout. And although many individuals contributed to this success, the claim seems equally well-founded that credited Ransom E. Olds with the distinction of being the designer of this popular car. As the individual who exercised undisputed control of the company's production during this period, he also deserves the major credit for seeing the car through to its ultimate great success, despite some serious and unexpected problems along the way.

*   *   *   *   *

By late November 1900 the Olds Motor Works was far enough along in its work on the new runabout model for sales promotion to begin. In response to an inquiry from a potential buyer in Palestine, Texas, Ransom Olds on November 28 pointed out that in addition to the $1,200 trap model about which the Texan had apparently asked, they were manufacturing "a light Gasoline Runabout" which "sells at $600.00." This was the price quoted in a brochure published by the Olds Motor Works sometime later that year; that price continued to be quoted until about the middle of the following year, when the price was raised to $650, although an undated company announcement issued that year said the new price would not become effective until January 1, 1902. In subsequent months and years rumors would periodically circulate through the industry that a further increase in the curved-dash runabout's price was about to be announced; but such an announcement was never forthcoming. Despite a substantial increase in the weight of the car, the price stayed at $650 for as long as the company continued to manufacture the model. Of course, this was the price of what a later generation of auto buyers would term a stripped-down model. In 1901, at least, the purchaser had to pay extra for such desirable features as a cloth top, curtains, rubber boot, and mud guards, which would add $85 to the base price. Nevertheless, this freezing of the base price at $650 helps to account for a good deal of the Oldsmobile's popularity, since continually rising prices were common among competing runabout models. The price of Autocar's run-

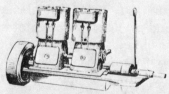
Courtesy of University of Michigan Graduate Library

One of the first ads for the Olds runabout, before the popularity of this vehicle caused the Olds Motor Works to abandon the electric car and also to shift its emphasis away from the manufacture of engines, the original basis of Olds' success.

about, which had started at $500 late in 1899, went up to $650 in February 1900, and by the end of the year had soared to $825, a figure that was further raised to $1,100 a year later. Locomobile prices, which started out in the $600 range in 1899, were boosted by $50 to $100 a year later. Improvements in the vehicles and the higher costs of materials and labor were reasons given for these increases. But Olds and his associates, though they could have used these same reasons to justify additional increases in the price of their runabout, did not do so.[28]

By January 1901, Olds was reportedly working on the production of one hundred runabouts. Other reports in February said that the car would be on the market in the spring; but a few were sold during the winter. An advertisement that appeared in February included a photograph of a curved-dash runabout that had been adapted for use as a commercial vehicle by a boot and shoe company, and *Horseless Age* reported at that time that a number of the runabouts were "already on the streets."[29]

A full-scale publicity campaign got underway in February 1901, with the publication of a special catalogue describing the new car. The campaign was a decided success. The trade journals paid far more attention to the curved-dash Oldsmobile than they had to any automobile or automotive development of Michigan origin up to that time. *Horseless Age* commented favorably on the catalogue, whose numerous illustrations in particular were "calculated to elicit praise for [the Oldsmobile's] running and handling qualities and appearance." *Motor World* reprinted three pictures of what it called "the younger and more drylandish brother of the famous Olds marine motor." Emphasizing the latter product and the reputation it had established for the company, and apparently attaching no importance to the automobile models that Olds had earlier developed, the magazine stated that the Olds Motor Works had "now turned a part of their attention to land vehicles, with the very pleasing results here shown, which will at once impress even the ordinary observer with their simplicity of construction, lightness and economy of operation."

To impress observers even more, Olds and his men staged a series of tests in and around the Detroit factory. These were pictured and described in the catalogue and early advertisements, and they were later to be repeated publicly with variations. In one economy test, two gallons of gasoline were placed in an empty tank and after the runabout had been driven fifty miles, three quarts of gasoline still remained in the tank. This was apparently the basis for the early advertising claim that the car got forty miles to the gallon. The lightness of the Oldsmobile—whose weight had slowly climbed to 580 pounds from the first reported 525 pounds—was demonstrated with a photograph of two husky men holding one of the runabouts several inches off the ground. At the same time assurances that the Oldsmobile, despite its lightness, was sturdily built were provided by a photograph of twelve men, with a combined weight nearly four times that of the car, standing on the runabout, causing no damage, it was said, to the vehicle. Other tests were designed to demonstrate the little car's braking power and its ability to handle grades of at least twenty-five per cent.[30]

In addition to issuing a catalogue, Olds had begun placing advertisements for the runabout by February, and the frequency of his advertising from that point on could be matched by few other auto manufacturers of the period. "The Oldsmobile is a MARVEL to most people," the copy for such an early ad began. "It is a simple fact, however, of what it is possible to accomplish. Runs forty miles on one gallon of gasoline; a child can play with it without danger; starts at will from seat; fully guaranteed." ("Safe for child to operate," another ad declared, seeking to drive home Olds' favorite advertising theme of the ease with which his machine could be operated.)[31]

Olds had dropped all mention of his steam engine from his national advertisements when he had introduced his gasoline engine; and he soon stopped mentioning his earlier automobile models when he introduced the runabout. His February 1901 catalogue, it is true, though it was devoted mainly to the runabout, did pay some attention to Olds' electrics, which were "built in several styles . . . specially adapted for city use, well made and run smoothly." But the advertisements, aimed at a wider audience, were devoted solely to boosting the runabout, and with good reason. The interest that had been created in the runabout by early March 1901 had already resulted in the receipt of over three hundred orders. Ransom Olds had obviously gauged correctly the trend in public opinion toward this type of automobile. There was no need to waste much further effort on promoting the other models which had never created a similar stir. The curved-dash runabout was clearly the winning entry Olds had been seeking in order to compete successfully for automobile sales. Confident in the wisdom of the decision that he had made, Olds established a production goal sometime that winter—possibly as early as December 1900—of one thousand runabouts for 1901, quite an ambitious figure for an automaker who had thus far made scarcely any autos. In fact, some no doubt felt that Olds could not meet such a production schedule. The first tire salesman with whom Olds discussed his needs, according to Charles S. Mott, "intimated that Olds could not get away with such a large order." Olds, Mott said, "was so indignant that he chased him out of the office and placed his order with another concern."[32]

* * * * *

Late in January, the slowest time of the year for the new auto industry, whose efforts were geared for a flurry of activity in the spring and summer when the public's fancy turned to thoughts of buying a car, Ransom and Metta Olds and their two daughters took off for a five-week trip to California, an annual vacation that had started when Olds' parents had moved to San Diego. The transcontinental journey was not, as the daughters recall, without its drawbacks. It was a tiring trip, since it took about a week to go from Michigan to the Pacific Coast, and although the passengers had the comforts of a sleeping car, there was no diner on the train out of Chicago, thus compelling them to leave the train several times each day at various stops in order to get something to eat.

Late in the day of Saturday, March 9, 1901, the Olds family was completing the long trip back to Detroit and had boarded a streetcar to take them from the train station to the stop nearest their home. Chancing to glance at the headlines of a Detroit paper that another passenger was reading, Olds was horrified to read that the Olds Motor Works factory in Detroit had been destroyed by fire earlier that afternoon. It was a strange and coincidental way for the general manager of the Olds Motor Works to learn of one of the most famous events in his company's and in the entire auto industry's history.[33]

At about 1:30 that afternoon an explosion of somewhat disputed origin—which Olds later said was traced to a natural gas leak—started a fire in the rear of the main building of the Olds plant. Two other explosions followed, and in moments someone shouted: "Rush for your lives, the building is all on fire!" What followed was described by one observer as "a scene of the wildest excitement. Men dashed for every exit." Fortunately, there were only about two dozen employees working that Saturday afternoon, but four men were injured as they were among several who were forced to jump from second and third floor windows as the flames spread with incredible rapidity through the plant, which had been completed scarcely a year earlier. Behind its imposing brick facade, the Olds factory, like most such buildings of that day, was built principally of wood, whose naturally combustible character was heightened by the oil and other inflammable substances with which many areas of the floor had become saturated in the course of manufacturing operations.

The first alarm was sounded at 1:37, and within a short time the fire department had eight engines and three trucks at the scene, plus the fireboat *James Battle* on the river side of the factory. However, the efforts of the fire fighters were to no avail. In what one reporter described as "a spectacle of rare magnificence," the flames spread through the plant "as though burning a house of cards." The conductor on a Jefferson Avenue streetcar passed the site just as the fire was breaking out, and by the time he made his return run past the same site sixteen minutes later "the walls had crumbled." Veteran firemen could recall few factory fires that had

The smoldering remains of the Olds Jefferson Avenue plant a short time after fire had broken out on the afternoon of March 9, 1901

spread so quickly. Their efforts were soon devoted to confining the conflagration to the Olds property; in this they were largely successful, although the adjacent Detroit Stove Works suffered some damage.[34]

Fred Smith was on the scene shortly after the fire started, and in the evening Ransom Olds arrived. The two officials were greeted by a dismaying sight. With the exception of the foundry, which escaped relatively undamaged, the factory buildings and most of the contents were a total loss, only a portion of which was covered by insurance. Olds readily admitted to reporters, as he poked about the charred rubble that weekend, that this was a great setback for his company. "While the material loss is great, we do not care half so much about that as we do for the setback it has given our business." Olds said that they had enough orders "to keep us working full-time for over a year, and a more inopportune time for such a calamity could not be. The automobile season is just coming up, and we expected to put machines on the market in a few days."

However, Olds refused to be defeated by this disaster. He

was confident, he said, that "in two or three weeks time we shall be running as though nothing had happened." Olds' optimism might have seemed exaggerated to some, but within a week of the fire plans were reported to have been completed by Edwin A. Bowd, the Lansing architect, for the rebuilding of the plant at a cost of $40,000. By the beginning of April, Olds was reporting that his men would be turning out ten automobiles a day by the middle of that month in the temporary facilities they were then occupying. Exactly when Olds actually succeeded in getting his runabout into production is uncertain and is a hotly debated topic among Oldsmobile collectors. Bob Huxtable of Lansing, owner of a runabout bearing the serial number twenty, which he believes is the oldest known production model curved-dash Olds, asserts that the vehicle was produced in April 1901. However, Charles E. Hulse of Flint, Michigan does not believe that any of the runabouts were turned out before June 1901, and he dates his own runabout number thirty at about July 1 of that year. The limited amount of available information would seem to bear out Hulse's point of view. Furthermore, even if Olds' men were indeed able to produce as many as ten cars a day, it does not appear that this goal was reached on a very regular basis, since by the end of 1901 only about 425 Oldsmobiles had been produced. This was far from the goal of 1,000 units which Olds had originally set for the year; nevertheless, it was an auspicious beginning toward the record production years immediately ahead.[35]

Viewed in this light, the ability of the Olds Motor Works to bounce back so quickly from the effects of the March 9 fire is a dramatic story in itself. The Cadillac Automobile Company, in its second year of production in 1904, would face and survive a very similar crisis in an equally remarkable manner. However, one can point to other automobile concerns that went out of business after fires had damaged or destroyed their production facilities, and this simply underscores the ability of Olds' company to recover in 1901 as another proof of Ransom Olds' capable leadership and Samuel Smith's solid financial support, which together enabled the company to survive this setback. These assets were present—though not always so dramatically visible—throughout these formative years and account for the spectacular success of the Olds Motor Works.

However, it was not this convincing demonstration of the strengths of the Olds organization that has caused automotive annals to record this disaster as a turning point of almost unparalleled significance in the development of the industry. These annals depict the fire as an accident that assured Detroit's emergence as the motor capital of the world.

This came about first of all, we are told, because the fire destroyed all of the work of Olds and his men except for one curved-dash Oldsmobile, which James J. Brady, a timekeeper who sounded the alarm when the fire was discovered, managed to get out of the blazing plant. In order to get something into production in the short time remaining before the peak period for auto sales arrived, Olds had to turn to the only model that had survived. The plans and patterns for all the models had been burned up, but by taking this one runabout apart they could reconstruct plans and patterns for that model, while that could not be done with any of the other eleven models. Fortunately for Olds, the runabout proved to be a hit with the car-buying public, and the success of the Olds Motor Works was thereby assured. But there is more to the story. Because the company's production facilities were knocked out, Olds was forced to turn to other Detroit firms that could manufacture the parts for the runabout, which the Olds employees could then assemble in their makeshift quarters. Thus, it is claimed, the Olds fire started the practice among automobile companies of contracting with outside suppliers for many of their parts. More important, that particular result of the fire led several of Olds' parts suppliers in Detroit, witnessing the success of the Oldsmobile, to turn to production of their own cars, several of which enjoyed lasting success and fixed in the public's mind the image of Detroit as the leader in producing the most popular cars.

All of this because of a fire that probably resulted from a workman's carelessness! The Motor Vehicle Manufacturers Association (formerly the Automobile Manufacturers Association) officially sanctioned the view that the fire was of overwhelming significance in shaping the future course of automobile developments in the United States. In its publication *Automobiles of America: Milestones, Pioneers, Roll Call, Highlights,* it links the Detroit fire of March 9, 1901 with the great Spindletop oil gusher in Texas two months earlier as the two events "that destined the gasoline engine to win over steam and electric." Noting that all that was saved from the Olds plant "was an experimental curved-dash roadster [*sic*]," the trade association summarizes what then supposedly happened: "In order to get back into business after the disaster, the firm had no choice but to use that one car as a model and to sub-contract orders for parts and sub-assemblies to small shops in the Detroit area. Most of the operators of these shops thus became automobile manufacturers, and, in consequence, Detroit became the Motor City."[36]

Accidental, unplanned occurrences, of course, do at times have momentous consequences and may, in fact, alter the course of history. But the Olds fire of March 9, 1901 was not one of those occasions. A reading of the contemporary news accounts of the fire reveals at once that a major assumption in the above familiar tale is totally without foundation in fact. The plans and drawings of the models, which Ransom Olds had been working on since 1899, were not destroyed. These records—as Olds announced and the press reported the weekend of the fire—had been recovered "uninjured in the vault in the building where they were kept." Furthermore, according to a notice sent out a short time later by the Olds Motor Works, the automobile patterns had also survived the fire. Thus, the action of James Brady—courageous as it undoubtedly was—of managing to rescue one curved-dash runabout from the roaring inferno ceases to be the event of pivotal importance which it has always been depicted in later accounts of this incident. If the patterns and drawings for this and other models were still available after March 9, Olds did not need the one rescued car from which to reconstruct the plans and patterns for the runabout.[37]

The fire, therefore, was not the reason Olds decided to concentrate solely on the runabout once he got production underway again. Had he wished to continue with any of the other models, the necessary information and materials were at hand; but he did not do so for the simple reason that he had decided weeks, if not months, before the fire that the runabout had the best chance to make it in the marketplace. The fire may have persuaded Olds to abandon the other models somewhat sooner than he might otherwise have done. Willis Grant Murray, factory superintendent of the company's automotive department, declared after the fire that several electric vehicles in various stages of production were among the vehicles destroyed, including one electric stanhope which crashed through the upper floor and landed on the safe in Fred Smith's office. Murray expressed his disappointment at this unhappy climax to what he claimed had been some two years of experimentation with electrics by the Olds staff. With the plans for the electrics still available, however, all that would have been required to resume the production of these vehicles was presumably a fresh stock of the necessary parts. But the 334 advance orders for the runabout that were reportedly received by the first week of March made it clear that this model had an appeal that none of the other models—electric or gasoline—had demonstrated. The demise of these models appears to have been inevitable whether there had been a fire or not. Keeping up with the orders for the runabout would have left the Olds automotive employees little if any time to work on any other models, even if there had been much sentiment in favor of any of them.

In short, even though Ransom Olds himself later liked to emphasize the dramatic impact the fire had had on the course of his career, the implication that the decision to concentrate on the runabout was forced on Olds by circumstances over which he had had no control cannot be accepted. Olds deserves the credit for having determined upon this course of action by the latter part of 1900, at least three months before the fire. The advertising and promotional campaign which his company had launched in the early weeks of 1901 clearly spelled out the nature of that decision. It was not a desperation move but one based on a correct assessment of the public's indications by 1900 of the kind of car it wanted to buy. Olds had simply exercised the same good judgment that he had shown earlier when in the mid-eighties he satisfied himself concerning the commercial prospects of the small Olds steam engine and again, a decade later, when he decided to come out with a gasoline engine.[38]

Upon close inspection, other parts of the story that has grown around the effects of the Olds fire are shown to be of approximately the same mythological character. The fire did not cause Olds to farm out the manufacturing of the run-about's parts because—as it has been claimed—he was left without the capability of producing these parts in his now gutted factory. As was noted above, Olds had never felt that he had this capability in the early stage of the development of his automotive interests; thus, as soon as he began to work with horseless vehicles he began the practice of contracting with outside firms for many of his parts. Even his first steam-powered vehicle in 1887 had gears that he had purchased from a company in Rhode Island, while such other parts as the wheels and body came from a local manufacturer. Any pioneering Olds may have done in developing this practice, which was common throughout the auto industry by 1901, was pioneering that had taken place in the 1880s, not in 1901. The practice by then had become widely accepted as the only course most automobile manufacturers could follow, in view of their limited factory facilities, personnel, and capital resources. In addition, it was argued, there was no need for manufacturers to try to make their own parts when the services of competent, well-established firms that could produce the engines, bodies, wheels, and any other parts needed to make a car were readily available.

Just a year before the Olds fire, *Motor Age* had counseled the auto companies to take advantage of these services and thus free themselves to devote their time to assembling the parts, "which is a sufficiently difficult task," and selling the cars. "This course requires the least investment, involves the least risk, gives the most rapid turn-over of what money is involved, and finally leads to success by the straightest and easiest road." The degree to which automobile companies in this period depended on parts suppliers varied considerably: after the Packard Motor Car Company became established in Detroit in 1903, it claimed to make all or nearly all of its parts; at the other extreme, some firms, such as the Ford Motor Company, initially did nothing but assemble parts which outsiders had contracted to make for them. The term "assembled car" would later be used in a derogatory sense; but this was not so in these earlier years, when companies even boasted that this was the kind of car they were selling. "All the car parts are made by contract with specialists," the Wayne company of Detroit told a trade reporter in 1904. "This gives the Wayne Company the advantage of the very best facilities of the best American constructors, far better than any one factory could hope to maintain, and reduces the flat cost to the lowest terms."[39]

When Ransom Olds first attempted to produce motor vehicles in 1896, he sought to place his activities somewhere between the extremes that would later be represented by Packard and Ford. He announced at that time that he would depend on other companies to supply him with such parts as bodies and wheels, while his own men confined their work to turning out the engine and related mechanical parts, plus handling the final assembling of all the parts. By 1900, as his auto manufacturing was beginning to become a reality, he was having auto bodies built by the C. R. Wilson Body Company, a Detroit firm that had formerly built carriages before beginning to supply bodies to the new auto industry late in the nineties. At the time of the Olds fire, the Wilson company, which had some of its materials stored in the Jefferson Avenue plant, was said to have "done considerable business with the Olds company."

When plans for the large-scale manufacture of the curved-dash Oldsmobile had been formulated in 1900, an order for five hundred sets of wire wheels was placed with the Weston-Mott Company of Utica, New York, which had begun to seek customers within the auto industry in the late nineties and by September 1900 was doing over half its business within this sector of the economy. Whether Olds was also buying wheels at this time from the Prudden Company of Lansing—as he seems to have done earlier—is not known; but by 1902–03, as Oldsmobile production boomed, Prudden became a major supplier to the Olds Motor Works. As noted above, by the summer of 1900 Olds had also contracted with a Cleveland company to supply batteries; and according to the later recollections of Alfred P. Sloan, Jr., it was at this time as well that Olds placed a preliminary order with Sloan's Hyatt Roller Bearing Company of Newark, New Jersey. The Hyatt company benefitted greatly from the large orders it received as the demand for the Oldsmobile increased. At its exhibit in the New York auto show of January 1903, Hyatt featured an Oldsmobile rear axle in which the firm's roller bearings were used.[40]

There are indications that by 1900 Olds was also beginning to go outside for the mechanical parts of his cars, which he had earlier expected to produce in his own factory. He was no doubt faced with the same dilemma that had earlier frustrated his efforts to produce motor vehicles in the engine plant in Lansing. In 1900 the Olds gasoline engines were still getting top billing in company advertisements for the very good reason that they still accounted for most of the company's sales. The latter, which had totalled about $72,000 in 1898, had risen to $120,000 in 1899 and would top $186,000 in 1900, following the move to Detroit. With the demand for engines showing this steady increase, the management doubtless felt that it would be unwise to divert much of the Olds work force from the production of engines for the general market to the production of engines for the company's own use in a product whose sales appeal had yet to be determined. (Nor were engines the only product other than automobiles that the Olds Motor Works was interested in. In 1901, Samuel Smith expressed much interest in the market possibilities of a pump which the Olds staff had developed, probably the same pump or an improvement of the one for which P. F. Olds & Son had announced production plans in March 1897.) The risks inherent in the introduction of automobiles on a large scale could be minimized if most of the company's employees and facilities would continue to be devoted to turning out the successful Olds engines while the manufacture of automobile engines and related parts would be turned over to outside firms. The final assembly operation would then require the services of only a handful of Olds employees. The entire work force of the Ford Motor Company in the spring of 1904, when its assembled car was one of the hottest items on the market, consisted of only thirty men and one woman, the woman apparently being employed in a clerical position. Most of the two dozen Olds workers who were in the factory on the afternoon of the fire seem to have been engaged in work on the twenty or so automobiles that were in various stages of assemblage. This would have been a sufficient force to handle the company's limited automobile output at that time if the job was primarily one of assembling—not manufacturing—parts.[41]

Although the evidence is not specific, it appears that by early 1901 the Detroit machine shop that had recently been opened by the two Dodge brothers, John and Horace, had contracted to produce engines for the Olds runabout. Around the same time Olds and his staff sought the assistance of the older, more established Detroit shop of Leland and Faulconer, asking Henry M. Leland, one of Detroit's most respected authorities on machines of all types, if he and his men could correct a noise problem in the runabout's transmission which Olds had been unable to eliminate. Leland took care of the problem and also contracted to build the transmissions for Olds.[42]

It is quite clear, then, that the fire of March 1901 was not the cause of Olds' decision to turn to outsiders for the parts that he needed; he had already made and implemented that decision long before the fire. However, this is not to say that the fire was of negligible importance in the development of the Olds business. The loss of the Detroit factory forced Olds to make some immediate decisions concerning what he should concentrate on with the limited facilities and equipment that remained available to him in Detroit. The sale later that spring to the Michigan Yacht and Power Company of Olds' marine engine division, which Charles King had been running since early in 1900, was the first step away from the emphasis on engine manufacturing to a new emphasis on the manufacture of automobiles. This move would be completed in the summer of 1903 with the sale of the Olds Gasoline Engine division to the Seager family. Thus the fire may have been a decisive factor in forcing Olds and his associates to make a choice between being an engine company or an automobile company. But it had no more effect on the decision about how the automobiles would be produced than it had on what automobiles would be produced.[43]

* * * * *

In 1901 and 1902, as the demand for the runabout grew, Olds expanded his network of suppliers. Byron F. Everitt, another Detroit carriage-maker turned automobile parts manufacturer, and H. Jay Hayes of Cleveland joined C. R. Wilson as suppliers of Oldsmobile bodies. Leland and Faulconer, as well as the Dodge brothers, began supplying engines, contracting for two thousand engines in June 1901, a huge order for that period. Later in 1901 a company as far away as Brooklyn, New York was supplying Olds with drop forgings. By early 1902 the Briscoe Manufacturing Company of Detroit was producing sheet metal parts, including fenders, gas tanks, and the radiators. Benjamin Briscoe later recalled that he thought a radiator was some sort of strange musical instrument when Olds first appeared with one in his office.[44]

As Briscoe would point out, the parts orders that Olds placed with Detroit companies during this period provided the most important initial stimulus to the growth of that city's auto industry. Not only did it lead to a concentration on the manufacture of automobile parts, which has been a major contributor to Detroit's economy ever since; but as Oldsmobile sales rose tenfold between 1901 and 1903, others were encouraged to follow Olds into producing not merely parts but the entire car. By late 1902, Henry Leland was involved in the production of the Cadillac, which simply started out as a slightly more sophisticated version of the Oldsmobile runabout. Earlier in 1902 another runabout, the Northern, was being produced in a factory a few blocks from the Olds plant. The Northern company was founded by Will

Barbour, who, though he did not supply parts for the Oldsmobile, had become interested in Olds' work while he was
heading the Detroit Stove Works, next-door neighbor to the
Olds factory. Barbour became acquainted with Jonathan
Maxwell, who took the stove manufacturer on test runs in
the runabout while expounding on his own ideas for a better
car. The result was Barbour's decision to back Maxwell in
the new venture. Later Charles King, another ex-Olds staff-
er who shortly joined Maxwell in the new company, claimed
that the Northern runabout did not operate satisfactorily
until King had corrected some of Maxwell's mistakes. In
1903, Maxwell left Northern to join Benjamin Briscoe, who
had decided that there was more money to be made in producing another new car that Maxwell had designed than
there was in making radiators. The Maxwell automobile,
originally produced in the former Mobile factory in Tarrytown, New York, would later be manufactured in Detroit
and would form the base from which Walter P. Chrysler was
to build his automobile empire two decades later.

Benjamin Briscoe's brother Frank struck out on his own in
1907 with still another runabout, which was designed by
Alanson P. Brush, who as an employee of Henry Leland had
earlier had a major role in the production of Oldsmobile engines. Meanwhile, the Dodge brothers had switched from
producing these same engines to making parts for a runabout the Ford Motor Company started putting out in 1903. It
was not until 1914 that the Dodges began producing their
own car. Still another Olds supplier, Byron Everitt, was one
of the three founders in 1908 of E-M-F, a Detroit auto firm
that resulted from the merger of the Northern and Wayne
companies. E-M-F was later taken over by the Studebaker
Company, which manufactured cars in Detroit until moving
these operations to South Bend, Indiana in 1925. In 1909
several former Olds executives, headed by Roy D. Chapin
and Howard Coffin, founded the Hudson Motor Car Company, a successful independent Detroit automobile producer
which became one of the two firms that merged in 1954 to
form the present American Motors Corporation.[45]

Thus, Ransom Olds and his little curved-dash Oldsmobile

Whenever one of the approximately five hundred lovingly preserved curved-dash Oldsmobiles appears at an auto show, it is the center of attention. Here at the 1976 Old Car Festival in Greenfield Village, Michigan, young Tim Stinedurf gingerly grips the strange steering mechanism of Charles Hulse's 1902 Oldsmobile. Hulse, left, is the proud owner of two runabouts.

served as an inspiration for some of the most successful manufacturers in the history of the automobile industry, including—in varying degrees—all four of the major surviving American automakers of the present day. From the perspective of history, this constitutes Olds' greatest industrial contribution, in a very real sense entitling him to the designation as father of the Michigan automobile industry. It is a title he earned through decisions that he had made by 1901 on the basis of his experiences with horseless carriages dating back to the 1880s. It was not the accidental intervention of a fire, as so many history books would have us believe, but those years of experience and experimentation that lay behind the phenomenal success of Ransom Olds and his runabout and the subsequent blossoming of Detroit as the center of the auto industry.

CHAPTER SIX

Producing the Curved-dash Olds

AFTER RANSOM OLDS moved his residence to Detroit in November 1899, he and his family did not remain strangers in the community for long. A combination of Olds' friendly nature, his desire to promote his business, and the influential character of his Detroit business associates enabled him to gain admittance to some of the circles usually frequented only by the more established leaders of the city. Information concerning Olds' social life in these years is sketchy, but it is known, for example, that he was a member of the Fellowcraft Club, which described itself as "the active commercial, professional and newspaper men's club of Detroit." In 1901, furthermore, when Detroit celebrated its bicentennial, Ransom and Metta Olds, newcomers though they were, were actively involved in the proceedings. Metta, who usually shunned the limelight, was one of the "Patronesses and Vice-Presidents" of the Woman's Bi-Centenary Committee, and her fellow committee members included some of Detroit society's most prominent names. Ransom Olds drove an Oldsmobile in the floral parade, a highlight of the three-day celebration in July. His business colleague Fred Smith and two officers of Mrs. Olds' committee rode in the vehicle as passengers.[1]

However, opportunities to indulge his love of social activities must have been limited during Olds' Detroit years, certainly one of the busiest periods in his entire life. To make matters worse, during the spring and summer of 1901, probably the busiest months of his three-year Detroit stay, Olds was hampered by some apparently serious and persistent health problems. The exact nature of his illness is not recorded, but it is clear that he was confined to a hospital sometime around April. It was from a window in his hospital sick-room that he is reported to have seen the first curved-dash runabout which his men assembled after the fire and which some of them drove over to show the boss. Even after being released from the hospital Olds apparently was not fully recovered, for that summer Samuel Smith was expressing concern about Olds' health and urging him to take some time off from work for rest and relaxation. Later in the year the state of Olds' health was still such a matter of concern that one of his associates, Reuben Shettler, quite bluntly urged him to buy some life insurance in order to provide his family, in the event of his death, with a more assured financial cushion than might be provided by Olds' stock holdings, whose future value no one could predict.[2]

In Detroit's Bicentennial Floral Parade in July 1901, the city's only active automobile manufacturing firm, the Olds Motor Works, entered this vehicle, elaborately decorated with four distinct shades of purple chrysanthemums, one of the several models which preceded the successful runabout. Ransom Olds (dark suit) is the driver, accompanied by Fred Smith and two officers of the Woman's Bi-Centenary Committee.

Courtesy of University of Michigan Graduate Library

It was precisely the pressure of the extra work load Olds had had to assume that spring which may have helped to bring on this unknown illness and also delayed the progress of his recuperation. A period that would have been very active under normal circumstances, as the wheels of production were greased to get cars to the market for the upcoming season, was made even more frantic by the need to provide temporary quarters to replace those that had burned to the ground in March.

In one sense at least, the fire proved to be of some benefit to the Olds company: a good deal of public attention was focused on its activities after the fire. For weeks the trade publications devoted far more space than normal to chronicle Olds' efforts to get back into production. The public's curiosity was aroused as it followed these reports and became increasingly interested in seeing just what kind of car the burned-out manufacturer would come up with. By early summer, when production models of the runabout first went on general display at scattered showrooms around the country, crowds of automobile enthusiasts flocked to examine the car. At the Chicago showrooms of Ralph Temple, the Oldsmobile distributor in that city, *Motor Age* reported, "without the slightest fear of successful contradiction," that the arrival of an Oldsmobile runabout on June 6, 1901 "attracted more comment and more visitors, in a short time, than any other vehicle that ever came into the city of Chicago. The store was the objective point, apparently, of every automobilist in the city, for it was well filled all day with men who know a good vehicle when they see one." One of Temple's brothers spent most of the day demonstrating the vehicle by driving it around on the showroom floor. Comments were almost uniformly favorable. Observers declared that Olds had come as close as was then possible to eliminate the vexing problems of noise and vibration. The appearance of the vehicle was also commended as a strong point, even though the finish of the display model "showed signs of haste in preparing it for shipment." Particular attention was paid to the fact that the operating mechanism was almost entirely hidden in metal cases, painted dull aluminum, "thus avoiding the formidable display of parts which so often bewilders and sometimes frightens prospective purchasers." Ralph Temple expressed his confidence that his ability to sell Oldsmobiles that summer would "be limited only by the ability of the factory to make deliveries."[3]

A month and a half later the editor of the same trade journal, in response to an inquiry from a resident of Kenwood, New York, reiterated his belief that the few curved-dash runabouts that had thus far reached Chicago had proved to be, from the editor's own personal experience and "the opinions expressed by other users . . . quite satisfactory. They are free from noise and vibration to a remarkable degree." Later in the year a former resident of Lansing who was then living in Brooklyn, New York congratulated Olds on having developed "the finest gasoline motor driven carriage in the world." Comparing the Oldsmobile runabout, which he had recently seen in New York, with Olds' "steam-engine driven 'wagon'" of twelve or fifteen years earlier, or even with Olds' first "neat Trap" of a later date, he declared that he "could not help but marvel" at the great progress evidenced in Olds' work.[4]

But Ransom Olds and his associates, though they had claimed early in 1901 that the Oldsmobile was such an excellent car that it sold itself—making it unnecessary for the company to "ask new customers to pay for $150 worth of advertising on each machine"—did not rely solely on word-of-mouth advertising and the comments of trade writers to publicize the runabout. In 1901 the advertising campaign of the Olds Motor Works, which had been promoting the company's automobiles on a modest scale while concentrating on beating the drums for the Olds gasoline engines, shifted to an emphasis on the runabout. And by the fall of 1901 all further mention of Olds engines was dropped from the advertisements for the automobile. Although separate small ads for the engines continued to appear from time to time in selected publications, the number and size of the ads for the Oldsmobile soon became—along with advertisements for the Winton and two or three other makes—among the most familiar sights on the advertising pages of the country. One unsupported report places the Olds expenditures for advertising at that time at $100,000 a year. This seems unlikely in 1901, when the firm's total sales of cars and engines amounted to less than half a million dollars; but such a figure may have been accurate by 1902 and 1903, when sales topped the one-and-a-half million and two-million-dollar levels. The Wayne Automobile Company of Detroit, whose sales came nowhere near those of the Olds Motor Works, claimed to have "spent upwards of $50,000 in judiciously advertising our cars" during 1904; and the records of Chalmers-Detroit, which was not among the leaders in auto sales at the time, show that its advertising-related expenditures for the year ending June 30, 1909 totaled $129,122.65. Thus, by 1903–04 at least, $100,000 was probably a conservative estimate of Olds' annual advertising budget.[5]

In the nineties the bicycle industry had blazed the trail for the auto industry: through its advertising it proved that a relative luxury, selling for as much as a hundred dollars, could be sold to the masses. Bicycle advertisements appeared on a scale never seen before, particularly in magazines. In their use of the art poster designed by topflight artists, as well as in their ad copy, which dwelt on technical features of the product and thus encouraged word-of-mouth advertising by the discussions it aroused among bicycle fans, the bicycle manufacturers foreshadowed some of the techniques employed in the later automobile advertising. However, despite the importance of these bicycle advertising campaigns, it was the automobile industry—advertising historian Frank Presbrey declares—that revolutionized advertising. Presbrey felt that the student of the subject in 1978, a half century after his history came out, "doubtless will regard as unimportant all progress made up to the time advertising was given the automobile to employ itself upon." The success that automobile advertising achieved put an end to any further questions concerning the desire and the ability of Americans to buy luxury items and opened the door in the twentieth century to the advertising and sale of many more luxuries that were thought beyond the reach of the mass market in previous generations. "The auto-

One of the earliest advertisements for the Olds horseless carriages in a national publication, this ad appeared in the May 1899 issue of *The Hub* at a time when the Olds engines were clearly regarded as that business's premier product.

mobile," Presbrey wrote, "provided the big opportunity which led to the conclusive revealment of advertising as a force of the first magnitude, a force comparable to steam, electricity and—the automobile."[6]

At the outset the auto industry concentrated on advertising in the trade journals. An ad for the Duryea Motor Wagon in the first issue of *Horseless Age* in 1895 is usually cited as the first such advertisement. And as late as 1909 it was estimated that more than half of the money spent by the industry on magazine advertising was still being spent in trade publications. The first such automobile advertising by Olds seems to have been in the spring of 1899 in *The Hub,* not strictly speaking a magazine for the automobile trade but one which nonetheless had by this time been forced to pay more attention to the new industry that was so closely related to the carriage trade. By early 1901, Oldsmobile ads were appearing with increasing frequency in the more orthodox trade publications, such as *Motor Age, Motor World,* and *Automobile Review,* although, strangely enough, not for some time in one of the best known, *Horseless Age.*[7]

It is a mistake to assume, as Frank Presbrey does, that this advertising was aimed at the dealers and not the consumers, since nearly all these magazines sought to direct their appeal to the motoring enthusiasts, not simply to dealers and other members of the trade. Nevertheless, the necessity of reaching a larger audience soon caused some companies to move into the general magazine field. They began to agree with what Henry Joy voiced in 1903, when he began to exercise the dominant authority in the Packard Motor Car Company: he said that the Packard staff's ad in the trade publication *The Automobile* was good, "but you ought to have such a thing as that in Leslies' or Colliers' or Harpers' Weeklies." Joy went on to declare that a recent full-page advertisement he had seen, "in Colliers' Weekly I think it was, put in by the Olds people, was the best add [*sic*] I have ever seen. You can't sell these goods without advertising or any goods without advertising." (Warming up to the subject and riding roughshod over any concepts he may have held regarding truth-in-advertising, Joy exhorted the Packard staff to "tell the biggest story about your racing machine that you can possibly invent, even if you never build it.")[8]

Ransom Olds was certainly not the first automobile executive to advertise his cars in the national, general circulation magazines, despite the claims of some curved-dash Oldsmobile enthusiasts that an ad for the "pioneer gasoline runabout" in the February 15, 1902 issue of *Saturday Evening Post* was a first for the mass-circulation periodicals. The Oldsmobile was not even the first automobile to be advertised in the pages of the *Post;* ads for three steam cars—the Skene, the Toledo, and the Stearns—appeared during the year preceding this first curved-dash runabout notice. Actually, Alexander Winton claimed that a one-inch ad he placed in *Scientific American* in 1898 was the first consumer advertisement for an American car. Whether he was correct or not, numerous other horseless carriages were being advertised in general circulation magazines from that time until the first Oldsmobile advertisements began to appear in 1901 in such magazines as *Review of Reviews, Scientific American* (Olds' long-time favorite), and *Harper's,* which had earlier carried ads for the Olds Gasoline Engines. In the following years few important magazines escaped what was obviously a well-coordinated effort to make the Oldsmobile the best-selling car by making it the most widely advertised car of its day.[9]

If the ads in the trade journals were designed to line up dealers for the cars, the ads in the general circulation magazines were also, in a sense, aimed at the dealer: they were intended to promote local sales by keeping the company's name in the public limelight. By 1905, however, *Horseless Age* stated that many manufacturers were beginning to question the value of much of their advertising in the popular magazines. They were increasingly shifting their attention to the local newspapers, which had previously been almost completely ignored. More and more companies, the trade magazine reported, were reimbursing the dealers, who knew the relative merits of the local papers, for the cost of such local advertising, which was felt to be a far more effective means of reaching the buying public. Olds may have been something of a pioneer in this trend, for as early as the summer of 1902 the Lockwood Brothers, Oldsmobile agents in Jackson, Michigan, began to run ads in the Jackson *Daily Citizen,* which before that time had carried virtually no automobile advertising. By the following winter the Lockwoods' ads, presumably paid for in part at least by the Olds Motor Works, were appearing with greater frequency—about once a week. Other examples that showed the Olds staff's increased attention to the newspaper medium could certainly be found; but *Horseless Age*'s prediction in 1905 that this form of advertising would soon "largely supersede advertising in the popular magazine" was never borne out. By about 1910 the industry was seeking to achieve a more balanced practice in the placement of ads, using newspapers, farm journals, and country weeklies, as well as magazines.[10]

The Oldsmobile company did not neglect other methods of promoting its cars. It claimed in later years that it was the first to publish a house organ, to issue a newsletter to its dealers, to put out sales manuals for its dealers, and to issue "comprehensive" instruction booklets for the Oldsmobile user. With a display of humor that was rare in auto promotions of that early period, the company also organized the Oldsmobile Club of America in 1901. Thousands were applying for membership, a company announcement claimed, and all that was required of the applicant was "a good character and an Oldsmobile." "The former," the announcement admitted, "we cannot always furnish, the latter is delivered on payment of the initiation fee, which, beginning January 1, 1902, will be $650 at the factory." Another, more traditional, advertising device consisted of sets of postcards using the Oldsmobile as the central illustrative material; these cards have become highly prized collectors' items in recent years. Outdoor advertising, which came into its own as a major advertising medium and frequent blight on the landscape with the advent of the automobile-travelling public, was used extensively by Olds. In fact, when W. C. Durant was negotiating General Motors' acquisition of the Olds Motor Works in 1908, which had by then greatly declined in importance, he declared that he was paying a million dollars for a lot of road signs and—he implied—not much else. At the same time, however, he recognized that those signs and billboards had helped to keep the Oldsmobile name before the public, easing considerably the task he faced in refurbishing the reputation and the sales of the product that name represented.[11]

A few minutes spent within the pages of the 1902–03 *Ladies' Home Journals* suffice to disprove another long-accepted Olds claim—that an ad for the Oldsmobile in the April 1903 issue was "the first automobile copy" to appear in the magazine with the largest circulation of any magazine published in the United States. More than a year before the Oldsmobile ad, an ad for the Waverly electric appeared in the February 1902 *Journal,* picturing a buxom woman, appropriately garbed, about to go motoring in "The Ideal Automobile for women." Another Olds first is lost; but here again the real story may have more significance than the claim that turns out to have been fiction. The Oldsmobile does appear to have been the only automobile other than the Waverly to be advertised in the columns of the *Journal* during those years; thus it was the only gasoline-powered vehicle to be represented there. In its April 1903 advertisement, as well as two new ones that followed in the May and June issues, the Olds Motor Works sought to counter the electric auto's principal appeal to women drivers by emphasizing the great ease with which "this mechanical marvel" could be started and operated. The first of the one-third-column ads showed an elegantly dressed woman leaving a millinery shop to get into her curved-dash runabout: "The Best Thing on Wheels—The ideal vehicle for shopping and calling—equally suitable for a pleasant afternoon drive or an extended tour." This last suitability, which was scarcely possible with the limited driving range of the electric, was stressed in the two following Olds ads in the series, one showing two stylishly attired women driving their runabout over a country bridge ("The pleasure of automobiling is enhanced by the delightful days of spring"), and the other depicting a woman in an equally rural setting driving her little Oldsmobile with one hand and with the other waving her

The
*best thing
on wheels*

The Oldsmobile

Physicians use the Oldsmobile in preference to any other because it saves time—and a Doctor's time is money. The Oldsmobile has proved itself by long, hard service to be the ideal Motor Vehicle for Physicians. It outwears a dozen horses, is always harnessed, always fed—is built to run and does it. All months are good months for the Oldsmobile, but the autumn months are best of all. If you want prompt delivery, order promptly.

Price $650.00 f. o. b. Detroit

Write for book 21, which tells all about it.

SELLING AGENTS

Oldsmobile Co., 138 W. 38th St., New York
Oldsmobile Co., 1124 Connecticut Ave., Washington, D. C.
Quaker City Auto. Co., 138 No. Broad St., Philadelphia
H. B. Shattuck & Son, 239 Columbus Ave., Boston
Banker Bros. Co., East End, Pittsburgh
Oldsmobile Co., 411 Euclid Ave., Cleveland, Ohio
William E. Metzger, 254 Jefferson Ave., Detroit
Ralph Temple & Austrian Co., 293 Wabash Ave., Chicago
Fisher Automobile Co., Indianapolis
Olds Gasoline Engine Works, Omaha
W. C. Jaynes Auto. Co., 873 Main St., Buffalo, N. Y.
Day Automobile Co., St. Louis and Kansas City, Mo.
George Hannan, 1455 California St., Denver
Clark & Hawkins, 903 Texas Ave., Houston, Tex.
The Manufacturers Co., 26 Fremont St., San Francisco
A. F. Chase & Co., 215 So. Third St., Minneapolis
Oldsmobile Co., 728 National Ave., Milwaukee, Wis.
Abbott Cycle Co., 411 Baronne St., New Orleans, La.
Autovehicle Co., 79 Orange St., Newark, N. J.
Hyslop Bros., Toronto, Canada
Rochester Automobile Co., 170 South Ave., Rochester, N. Y.
Mason's Carriage Works, Davenport, Ia.
C. H. Johnson, 55 So. Forsyth St., Atlanta, Ga.
Sutcliffe & Co., 411 Main St., Louisville, Ky.
Texas Implement and Machine Co., Dallas, Tex.
Jas. B. Seager, Tuscan, Ariz.

Olds Motor Works
Detroit, Mich., U. S. A.

Courtesy of Eastern Michigan University Library

Since members of the medical profession were often the first in a community to purchase a car, this August 1902 ad is aimed at attracting a larger share of that rapidly expanding market. As always, Olds' ad writers did not miss the opportunity to take a swipe at the horse.

handkerchief at a horse, an action in keeping with the heading which read: "Good Bye, Horse."[12]

After June 1903, Olds abandoned the pages of the *Ladies Home Journal,* at least for the rest of that year. Perhaps the high cost of advertising a product that still appealed primarily to a male clientele in a woman's magazine resulted in the decision to leave this field to the Waverly, whose ads claimed that it was driven by more women than "all other types of vehicles combined." However, these three ads for the Oldsmobile help to support the suspicion that no matter who was in immediate charge of the company's advertising—the name of the ad agency or the officials on Olds' staff who were involved is not known—Ransom Olds kept a close watch on what was published. The language of the advertising copy, with its constant emphasis on the practical nature of the runabout and the simplicity of its operation, is clearly reminiscent of Olds' advertisements in earlier years for his engines, and also of the points he had always stressed in discussing his motor vehicles. The continually changing content of the ads also recalls the frequent changes in ad copy for the Olds engines in a time when other engine manufacturers had tended to keep the same ad running for long periods of time. Tailoring the ads for a particular audience or time of year was reflected not only in the *Journal* ads but in others: Olds aimed one advertisement at medical doctors, one of the first groups to adopt the automobile in sizable numbers; others were intended to fit the needs of a particular season, such as those attempting to convince the potential buyer that this lightweight vehicle was suited for the rigors of winter traveling. Finally, Ransom Olds' influence on the advertising can be seen in the continual repetition of that favorite theme of his—the superiority of the runabout to the horse. One advertisement claimed that the Oldsmobile would "do the work of six horses at an average cost [for gasoline] of $35.00 a year (10,000 miles). Board alone for one horse costs $180.00 a year, so the economy is very evident." (Olds and his ad writer conveniently forgot to mention that any Oldsmobile owner who drove his car for anything like ten thousand miles in a single year would almost certainly have been saddled with a huge bill for the repair and general maintenance of such a well-used vehicle.)[13]

In conjunction with the advertising campaign, interest in the Oldsmobile was constantly promoted by public demonstrations of the practical, sturdy nature of the runabout, again reflecting Ransom Olds' interest in this kind of activity, in which he had been engaging at least since he demonstrated his steam carriage for *Scientific American* in 1892. Despite the great increase in the size of his staff since the early nineties, Olds still did a good deal of the demonstrating himself. Photographs accompanying early ads for his automobiles usually showed him in the driver's seat of the vehicle depicted, although without identifying him (Olds apparently realizing that at this point his name did not yet have commercial value).

As he had done in the earlier days of his engine business, Olds liked to personally install and demonstrate his new cars. For example, when Henry M. Leland ordered a curved-dash runabout in 1901—the first car this future automobile magnate ever owned—it was Ransom Olds, not one of his salesmen or mechanics, who drove the car up to the Leland residence in Detroit and showed Leland how to operate the machine. Teaching someone to drive an automobile in these early days was generally handled in a rather casual manner. For example, some years later, when Olds had a summer home on Grosse Ile, he drove his car into nearby Trenton to catch a train for Lansing, taking along with him the groundskeeper of his island residence. On the way to the train station Olds made some brief comments about how the car worked. The groundskeeper, who had never driven a car, learned to his astonishment when they reached Trenton that the comments were intended to enable him to drive Olds' car back to the island. Fortunately, the instructions were clear enough and the traffic light enough for the workman—despite understandable nervousness—to make it back· in safety. On other occasions, Olds sought to impress potential customers by putting the runabout through its paces, sometimes backing it up a hill, clearly demonstrating the surprising power of this little one-cylinder car. What Olds did not

Courtesy of Michigan Historical Collections

Olds used this unusual testing device to demonstrate the runabout's high degree of control in braking and forward-reverse movement and, incidentally, the car's light weight. The driver of the center runabout may be R. E. Olds.

tell the onlookers was that the car could not always be trusted to make it up the hill going forward—ordinarily considered the normal direction.

Olds also continued to drive an Oldsmobile before large audiences, as he had done earlier at county fairs and in Detroit's bicentennial floral parade in July 1901. Although he did not follow the example of some of the other automobile company executives—such as Henry Ford and Alexander Winton—of taking to the race track to demonstrate the speeds his vehicle could attain, he did claim to be the first one to recognize the value of the packed sand surface in the Ormond-Daytona Beach area of Florida for speed trials. In April 1902, Ransom Olds, driving the specially built racing vehicle known as the "Pirate," and Alexander Winton, driving his more powerful "Bullet," engaged in an informal contest under the auspices of the proprietors of the Ormond Beach Hotel. However, when official speed runs were held beginning in 1903, Olds turned the driving over to others.[15]

Olds occasionally pressed his older daughter Gladys into

service to demonstrate the truth of his claim that the runabout was simple enough for a child to handle. Once, when Gladys could not have been more than ten years old, she was driving an Oldsmobile around a track in Lansing when an on-looker was heard to question Olds' sanity, suggesting that he ought to be "sent away to Kalamazoo" (site of a state mental institution) for exposing his daughter to such dangers. However, reports of other children as young or younger than Gladys Olds driving automobiles were fairly common at a time when few states or communities had adopted driver licensing regulations. Through the establishment of minimum age requirements, children were eventually prohibited from driving Oldsmobiles or any other automobiles on public thoroughfares.[16]

Olds also continued the practice of demonstrating various features and qualities of the Oldsmobile by means of circuslike stunts. The physical demonstrations used during the winter of 1900–01 at the Detroit plant were now repeated at county fairs and elsewhere. On these occasions it was customary to have two men, carefully selected for their physical prowess, lift a runabout off the ground, to demonstrate its lightness; the ability of the runabout to be driven after as many as seventeen adults had been loaded on the car demonstrated the sturdiness of the vehicle; and the ability of a tight-rope walker to maintain his balance on a high wire attached to and suspended above a moving Oldsmobile dramatically affirmed the machine's steady, vibration-free operating qualities. Among other stunts, Olds had a runabout driven up the steps of a public building on one or more occasions, a stunt apparently introduced in Detroit in March 1901, when a Mobile steamer was driven down the Wayne County Courthouse steps. This publicity device was carried to its logical extension in 1904, when a Cadillac was driven up the capitol steps in Washington.[17]

As the curved-dash Oldsmobile went into full-scale production, "demonstrators" or test drivers were hired to put each newly assembled car through a series of road tests. Until the Olds Motor Works and other Detroit auto companies developed their own proving grounds, the drivers used the city streets for testing purposes, as well as nearby Belle Isle, linked with the mainland by a bridge that was only a short distance out Jefferson Avenue from the Olds plant. On the island there were mounds of dirt that had been excavated during the digging of canals for pleasure craft, and these provided a sterner test for a car's hill-climbing ability than could be conducted in the city proper. The Olds company claimed that each car had to be driven up a grade of thirty per cent as one of the tests it had to pass before being shipped out. Detroit's generally flat terrain was a significant asset in that city's early development as an automobile center, however, since a hillier surface would have been a constant source of embarrassment to salesmen trying to impress customers with the superior merits of cars that usually had trouble negotiating any but the gentlest grade.

Horace Loomis and Jonathan Maxwell, in addition to their work as engineers and designers, did some testing for Olds in 1901–02, before Maxwell moved on to become one of the designers of the Northern and later of the Maxwell. Two other Olds testers were Miner E. Haywood and Theodore E. Barthel, brother of the auto pioneer Oliver Barthel. The latter recalled the difficulties he had during the summer of 1901 persuading the captain of the Detroit-to-Windsor ferry to transport Barthel's curved-dash Oldsmobile over to Canada so that he could drive it there and thus enable the Olds company to advertise its runabouts as internationally tested. However, the most famous and apparently the chief Olds test driver by the fall of 1901 was Roy D. Chapin, whose family had been acquainted with the Olds family in Lansing, where Chapin was born in 1880.[18]

In 1899, the year in which the Olds family moved to Detroit, young Chapin went to Ann Arbor to enroll in the University of Michigan. He never completed his studies there (though in later years he was a loyal and generous supporter of the university), dropping out of school in the spring of 1901 to take a job with the Olds Motor Works in Detroit. Olds' acquaintance with Chapin may have had something to do with Chapin's being hired: as Olds' need for more workers rose quickly, he became something of a soft touch for any

Courtesy of Michigan Historical Collections

A test driver, apparently the intrepid Roy Chapin, puts the frail-looking Oldsmobile through a rugged hill-climbing exercise.

relative or acquaintance who approached him about a job. But Horace Loomis, another acquaintance of Chapin from Lansing, seems to have been the one who was responsible for interesting Chapin in coming into the company. Loomis took Chapin for a test run in one of the first runabouts produced after the disastrous fire, and as they drove down Detroit's Grand Boulevard, Loomis said to his companion, "I'll open her up, and you'll see how fast she can go." After experiencing the resulting speed, as high as eighteen miles an hour, Chapin was ecstatic: "Wonderful," he exclaimed, "this is the stuff for me. I'm going to quit school and join up."[19]

Chapin was initially a jack-of-all-trades for Olds. He saw considerable service as a photographer, employing a skill that he already had to prepare illustrations for a new company catalogue. In May 1901, during a machinists' strike, he received a crash course of instruction in a variety of jobs when Olds kept the plant operating with his non-striking staff. But later in 1901 Chapin's principal responsibility came to be vehicle testing, a job he enjoyed and would come back to from time to time in later years, even when he was the head of the Hudson Motor Car Company.

In October, Chapin and Jonathan Maxwell were the drivers in what was apparently Olds' first attempt to go beyond test runs or demonstrations as a means of publicizing the runabouts—running them in races. The first automobile races in the Detroit area—and probably anywhere in Michigan—were held on October 10, 1901 at a dirt track in Grosse Pointe. The races were billed by their promoter, William E. Metzger, Detroit's pioneer auto dealer, as the World Championships of auto racing, and Olds gave all the employees of his Detroit plant the afternoon off—a Thursday afternoon at that—to go to the track. There they and the rest of the large crowd that assembled as the afternoon wore on saw more curved-dash Oldsmobiles on display than any other make of car, which is perhaps not surprising since it was still the only car in commercial production in the city. On the track's infield some of the Oldsmobiles were put through some of their familiar stunts designed to demonstrate some of the positive features of the vehicle. On the track itself Chapin and Maxwell drove two runabouts in a ten-mile race for cars weighing under a thousand pounds. They came in second and third respectively to a White steamer from Cleveland. However, the unfavorable publicity that might have resulted from this defeat was largely forgotten in the excitement generated by the unexpected result of the final race of the day: Henry Ford was launched on the road to national fame with his victory over Alexander Winton, who at the time was probably the best-known auto racing figure in America.[20]

Other drivers would win races and set speed records with Olds-built cars in the following years, but Roy Chapin's greatest achievement came not on the track but in the endurance run. In mid-afternoon on October 29, 1901, Chapin set out alone in a standard curved-dash Oldsmobile which he and Maxwell had selected from those coming out of the factory; he was on his way from Detroit to New York as another means of publicizing the superior qualities of the car.[21]

Alexander Winton had very successfully promoted his early motor vehicles by driving one of them from Cleveland to New York in 1897 and then repeating the feat in 1899, thereby pioneering in the use of a publicity device that would remain a favorite in the industry from that time on. Of course, the average motorist in those years was, as a practical matter, forced to confine his driving to short trips in and around town because of the formidable combination of the generally poor road conditions and the imperfect nature of the automobiles. Cross-country trips such as Winton's were stunts, therefore, designed to create an image of a car's

Young Roy D. Chapin, impeccably attired, appears ready to test a new curved-dash Oldsmobile in this photograph, probably taken in the summer of 1901.

Courtesy of Michigan Historical Collections

durability; few drivers were willing to endure the physical hardships and the expensive repair bills that were almost an inevitable result of any effort on their part to duplicate such long-distance runs.

In a letter to Alvan Macauley of the Packard Motor Car Company in 1941, Ransom Olds claimed that it was his idea to have a runabout driven to New York and that he gave the assignment to Chapin, his chief test driver. Whether Olds would have been as ready to be associated with the trip had it been less successful is open to question; and there are some who believe that Chapin himself made the original suggestion, since he later provided ample evidence that he had a feeling for publicity that was at least equal to Olds'. In any event, the result was one of the most famous incidents in automotive history.[22]

The timing of Chapin's departure—and the real reason behind the trip—revolved around the annual auto show to be held in New York City's Madison Square Garden, November 2-9, 1901. The idea was to have Chapin arrive in New York in time to have the event help promote interest in the Oldsmobile. Although this was only the second such show to be staged, it was already recognized as *the* show of the year for all those interested in the latest developments in motor vehicles. Olds, who had exhibited at an early show in Chicago during the summer of 1900, had not exhibited at the first New York show in November of that year. The company had been scheduled for a show in Chicago in March 1901, but the fire at the Detroit plant had forced the cancellation of that appearance. The decision to exhibit an Oldsmobile at the New York show the following November was apparently made at the last minute, since advance reports on the upcoming show in late October did not include Olds' name among the exhibitors who had been scheduled up to that time. This may indicate the hesitance of Olds and his staff until late October about the length of the odds Chapin would face in making it through to New York safely.[23]

When young Chapin finally drove up on November 5 in front of New York's Waldorf-Astoria Hotel, he is said to have been refused admittance. The doorman looked askance at

Chapin's mud-spattered appearance and his battered little runabout and ordered him to go around to the servants' entrance in order to find Olds, who was registered there after wisely taking the train to New York, and tell him of his safe arrival. The left rear wheel of the runabout had been damaged that morning as he swerved to avoid hitting a pedestrian on Fifth Avenue; earlier on the seven-and-a-half day trip he had had major repair problems with the transmission, the steering, the main side spring, and the axles; and there were constant minor difficulties with the tires and the cylinder gaskets, which frequently blew out on hills. Nevertheless, as Chapin reported in a telegram to the main office back in Detroit, the car had arrived "in good order," having consumed thirty gallons of gasoline and an amazing eighty gallons of water on the 820-mile trip, and having achieved an average speed on the road of fourteen miles per hour.[24]

Chapin set no long-distance records on this trip, despite what Chris Sinsabaugh, among others, would later assert. There are on record a number of longer automobile trips in the United States prior to the time of Chapin's journey, including at least one from New York City to Detroit in 1899, the reverse of Chapin's trip two years later. Nor did the trip cause a sensation in the press, as others have declared. Not a word about Chapin's achievement can be found in the columns of the hometown *Detroit Free Press* or *Detroit News* of that time, and little or no attention was paid to the event in other newspapers and periodicals, even in New York. During the early days of the show the arrival of various motorists from some distance, including a steam car from Toledo, Ohio, took the edge off what impact the curved-dash Oldsmobile's arrival from Detroit might otherwise have had.[25]

Roy Chapin went on to become one of the founders and the head of the Hudson Motor Car Company, secretary of commerce under Herbert Hoover, and until his death in 1936 a leader in national automobile and good-roads organizations; but this 1901 motor trip remains the most frequently mentioned event in his eventful life. Aside from the boost this trip gave Chapin's career, however, the real importance of the cross-country adventure for the company lies in the effective way Olds and his associates used it to promote the runabout. The little car was cleaned and polished and proudly exhibited by Olds during the remaining days of the Madison Square Garden show, adding a distinctive and show-stopping element to the Olds exhibit which helped to single it out from among the fifteen other runabouts other companies had on display. Full-page, illustrated advertisements, detailing none too accurately the eventful trip (the copy writer referred to Roy Chapin as "O. H. Chapin" and declared that during the trip the driver had experienced no car trouble), appeared in automotive trade publications within a matter of days.[26]

Although the Oldsmobile's price of $650 was something of an attention-getter in a show that featured many cars far more expensive—including an imported French model sold to a buyer at the show for $17,000—the Detroit runabout's performance record was more important in distinguishing it from its competitors, at least one of which was being offered for a hundred dollars under the price of the Detroit car. Roy Chapin's arrival in New York, therefore, helped to improve the reputation of the Oldsmobile at a critical moment and in a location that was vital to the future success of the car. By the fall of 1901, Olds had lined up dealers at a number of points in the Middle West and at certain other spots in the country, but he still lacked a strong connection with the all-important New York City market. In May, Olds had received a letter from an acquaintance who had recently moved from Detroit to Morristown, New Jersey, a short distance west of New York: "I should think there might be quite a sale for your machines here now," the friend informed him, going on to express his surprise at the number of automobiles he saw in the East, where three years earlier such vehicles were still "a rare sight." At about that time there were some discussions under way between the Olds Motor Works and the New York department store magnate John Wanamaker, who, because his competitors in the Macy Company had begun importing automobiles from Europe in the mid-nineties, was interested in adding automobiles to his line of merchandise. Although Wanamaker would play a major part two years later in the early distribution of Ford automobiles in the East, for some reason he did not reach an agreement with Olds in 1901 to become the New York distributor of the Oldsmobile.

Sometime later in 1901 such an agreement was made with the New York firm of Spalding & Bidwell, which was connected with the sporting goods firm of A. G. Spalding and Company. In fact, Spalding & Bidwell were in charge of the Oldsmobile exhibit at the New York show in November. While the show was in progress, however, the company had second thoughts about the contract it had signed with Olds, which called for them to sell one hundred Oldsmobiles in New York during the following year. The directors of the company decided they could not possibly meet that figure, though the Winton company is reported to have sold more than one hundred cars during the seven days of the show alone. Before he left New York, however, Olds had made a far more favorable arrangement with Ray M. Owen than the one from which Spalding & Bidwell had backed away.[27]

Owen, who during the next decade became the best-known seller of Olds-manufactured cars, was an automobile pioneer in his own right. In 1896 or 1897 he and his brother Ralph had purchased a gasoline-powered car built by Dr. Carlos C. Booth of Youngstown, Ohio. They converted it into a delivery vehicle for their carpet-cleaning business in Cleveland. In the late nineties Ray Owen claimed that he built three more vehicles on his own before selling the carpet-cleaning business and, with the financial backing of Roy and William Rainey, opening up "an automobile emporium" on Euclid Avenue. It is said to have been the first auto dealership in Cleveland and possibly in all of Ohio.[28]

In November 1901, Owen attended the New York auto show and, when he heard that Spalding & Bidwell did not intend to go ahead with their contract with Olds, began negotiating with Olds. As a result of these talks, Owen, who had been selling Oldsmobiles in Cleveland, became the Oldsmobile distributor for New York and New Jersey as well as Ohio, again with the Raineys' support. At first the plans called for Owen to agree to sell five hundred runabouts the first year, five times the number the Spalding organization had shied away from and more than all the runabouts that Olds had produced in 1901. However, as the contract was being drawn up, Olds is reported to have urged Owen and the Raineys to increase their order to achieve the maximum publicity impact. "I would like to see you make this order for a thousand cars," Olds said. "Then the public would drop its jaw and take notice." (By way of contrast, a little over a year later one of Olds' major competitors, the Thomas B. Jeffery Company of Kenosha, Wisconsin, closed a deal with John Wanamaker to sell 150 of its popular Rambler runabouts.) Owen and his backers agreed to the change, although the cagy Roy Rainey apparently insisted on a guarantee that the Olds Motor Works would be able to produce enough cars to meet the quota for which Owen was being held responsible.

By January 1902, Owen's New York agency was reporting sales at the rate of twenty runabouts a week, while in Cleveland he published the names of thirty-nine companies and individuals to whom he had made "recent sales," including the prominent Ohio politician Myron T. Herrick. As it turned out, Owen is said to have sold "only" 750 Oldsmobiles in New York in 1902; but despite his failure to reach the agreed quota, his success in selling even that many cars— almost certainly the largest number any dealer had ever sold in a single year—was the major factor in making the Olds curved-dash runabout the volume leader in sales in the country.[29]

By the summer of 1902 the Olds company had selling agents throughout the East and Middle West, plus a few in the South, the West, and in Canada. The Olds dealer in Denver reported that he had sold fifteen cars in the first weeks of the year, including six to doctors. One of these was Dr. J. B. Clymer, a general practitioner, whose son Floyd (later a noted collector and publisher of automobile lore and memorabilia) reported that the Oldsmobile his father purchased was the first car sold in Colorado north of Denver, and it "created a sensation" when Dr. Clymer drove it home. In June, James B. Seager, a member of the family that had a major stock interest in the Olds company, became copartner in a firm that acquired the Oldsmobile distribution rights for Arizona, New Mexico, and Mexico. By the following year the Oldsmobile was reported to be the "most extensively used" of the light runabouts that had become the most popular type of automobile in Mexico City.[30]

Invaluable publicity for the Oldsmobile came from the sight of such a prominent public figure as Chauncey Depew, an automobile enthusiast—though he is reported to have cautioned a relative at this time against investing in automobile stock—driving an Oldsmobile on the streets of New York. Mark Twain and the actress Maude Adams were other American celebrities who were among the announced purchasers of curved-dash runabouts. Outside the United States the little Oldsmobile was attracting attention as early as July 3, 1901, when one of the runabouts (the thirtieth of Olds' production after the fire the preceding March) arrived at the depot in Oil Springs, Ontario. It had been purchased that spring by Richard Whittaker, a wealthy citizen of the town who had ordered his car after going to Detroit for a personal inspection of the Olds plant. (Unfortunately, although the car subsequently performed quite well, the engine quit on Whittaker after he had driven about a mile from the station and he had to hire a team of horses to haul the car back into town to have the problem corrected.) By the end of 1902, Oldsmobiles were said to be "rapidly becoming one of the favorite cars" in Europe, and a photograph showing Sir Thomas Lipton seated in his curved-dash runabout was used to drive home this point. On the continent, Queen Helena of Italy and other members of her royal family became Oldsmobile owners; in Germany an Oldsmobile which the Krupp family purchased was still seeing active service three decades later, causing the family to turn down requests to allow the ancient runabout to go on exhibition in Europe. The extent of the Oldsmobile export business in Europe was dramatically illustrated in 1905 when a company-sponsored gathering of dealers in Paris attracted Olds agents from not only the French capital and London, but also Berlin, Naples, Florence, St. Petersburg, Copenhagen, Munich, Milan,

Amsterdam, Christiana, Odessa, Moscow, Bucharest, Lisbon, and Hamburg, as well as Algeria. Sales of Oldsmobiles in other parts of the world included two that were ordered by the colorful Julio A. Roca, president of Argentina, who presumably wanted two runabouts, the trade journals mused, "so that if he has a puncture and a rebellion at the same time he can use the second machine to seek calmer pastures."[31]

Sales figures as reliable as those published today are not available for the early years of the auto industry. It is usually believed that the Olds Motor Works produced or sold (the terms are used almost interchangeably) 425 runabouts in 1901; in 1902, when the company had predicted a production of 5,000 cars, sales rose to 2,500 (if we accept the most conservative estimate). Other sources, however, state that the number "built and sold" that year was 3,229, while others mention a figure of 3,700, apparently the highest total for 1902 that has appeared in print. By the winter of 1902–03, Oldsmobile ads were referring to "5000 satisfied" users of Oldsmobiles; if the statement meant that there were 5,000 Oldsmobile runabouts in use by that time, this number is far in excess of the most optimistic figures available for total sales through the end of 1902. By the time of the Detroit Auto Show in February 1903, however, new claims were being made that there were by then 8,000 curved-dash runabouts in use all over the world; and by the end of 1903 the Olds Motor Works was claiming a total of "20,000 Oldsmobiles in use in every part of the world," an unbelievable increase of from 12,000 to 15,000 cars over the figures quoted less than a year before. That total was even far in excess of the company's typically exaggerated prediction early in 1903 that it expected to produce 10,000 runabouts that year. The most commonly cited figure for the number of Oldsmobiles produced in 1903 is only 4,000 vehicles. Thus the total number of runabouts produced by the end of 1903, if one accepts the highest estimates available, would be only slightly more than 8,000, about forty per cent of the sales figures cited in ads for the end of that period.[32]

From figures jotted down by Ransom Olds—apparently for his own private information and not for publication—we can form more precise judgments with regard to the dollar amounts of his company's sales. These figures were spectacular enough in themselves, revealing a growth in 1902 and 1903 that far exceeded any that the Olds business had enjoyed in the past. Sales totaling $410,401 in 1901 jumped to $1,626,475 in 1902 and $2,325,580 in 1903, with automobiles accounting for virtually all of this income by 1903.[33]

In marketing his car Ransom Olds has been credited with initiating the policy of insisting on cash on delivery of the runabout to the distributor or to customers who bought directly from the factory. This claim stems largely from statements contained in one of several frequently quoted articles on the early history of the industry by John K. Barnes, published in 1921. Barnes said that Olds' insistence on cash on delivery constituted one of the most "important contributions" in placing the young industry on a sound footing. At a time when few automotive companies had very large cash reserves, the burden of providing the funds needed to pay the automaker's employees and his suppliers was passed on to the dealers. Roy Chapin, recalling these early days, said: "Dealers' deposits often paid half the sum necessary to bring out a full year's production; and if the assembling were efficiently directed, drafts against the finished cars could be cashed as rapidly as the bills from the parts-makers came in." The dealers in turn, in order to replenish their depleted financial reserves after paying the sight drafts that accompanied their shipments of cars from the Olds plant, were virtually compelled to insist that their customers pay cash also. According to Barnes, Olds told his dealers that it was to their own advantage not to sell on credit, because by demanding that the customer pay the full price at the time of the purchase of the car they were also transferring outright ownership of the vehicle to the purchaser. The latter was then likely to operate the car with greater care than he would if he were paying for it in installments, in which case if something went wrong with the vehicle, which was more than likely to happen, he might return the car to the dealer and refuse to make any more payments.[34]

Until we know more about the marketing practices of other early automobile companies, it is not possible to say whether Barnes was overstating the precedent-setting character of Olds' practices in this regard. Allowing a customer to buy a product on time was by no means unknown in the business world of Olds' day, and Olds was undoubtedly aware of such practices. In Lansing during the nineties, bicycle dealers sometimes agreed to sell a bicycle on the installment plan, "a small amount down being demanded and weekly or monthly payments for the balance," according to a Lansing newspaper report of that period. However, the average cost of these bikes was only fifty to fifty-five dollars, a far different figure than what automobiles began selling for during these same years. Even then, the bicycle dealers gave credit only in the exceptional case. In the early days of the automobile industry, when the cheapest cars available were ten times as expensive as the average bicycle, neither the manufacturer nor the dealer could have considered any credit plan as a normal merchandising technique until banks or other financial agencies became willing to assume the economic burdens that went with such credit arrangements. Since it was not until well into the second decade of the twentieth century that bankers began to become aware of the profits that could be realized from auto loans, it seems safe to assume that at the beginning of the century all manufacturers, not simply Olds, had adhered to the cash-on-delivery plan—or as Henry B. Joy of Packard more picturesquely phrased it: "When the money's in my pants, the automobile is yours." However, Olds remained convinced of the wisdom of this policy long after many other manufacturers had seized the new opportunities to sell their cars on the installment plan. "I believe that plan is dangerous and a menace to the business," Olds declared in 1923, and he added that the widespread adoption of such credit techniques by the industry would eventually "prove to be bad for this country," thus pinpointing what would eventually be regarded as one of the major causes of the Depression of the thirties.[35]

* * * * *

In order to achieve the production and sales records which he set by 1902 and 1903, Ransom Olds had had to improve very substantially the methods he initially employed in assembling his cars. A case can be—and has been—made for viewing Olds as the pioneer in impressing the American auto industry with the commercial possibilities of the light-weight, practical, inexpensive car, more than a half-decade before Henry Ford made the same point with his Model T. But Olds was also the pioneer, again in advance of Ford, in developing the techniques needed to mass-produce the vehicles. Even before it had begun to produce cars in any quantity, the Olds Motor Works was saying that one reason it was able to offer its new runabout at a price of only $600 was because all the car's parts were "built to a standard, and these parts being produced in great numbers at one time are made at low cost, and at the same time a better class of work is secured." This was certainly one of the earliest statements of what would shortly become perhaps the most frequently voiced argument set forth to defend the mass-produced car. Of course, Olds' annual production figures of 2,500 or 4,000 would not be considered in the category of mass production today, nor would they have impressed anyone only a few years after 1902 and 1903; but in 1902 the situation was quite different. Total production in the American automobile industry that year was probably no more than 9,000 cars. Thus, depending on which production figures one accepts, Olds was producing anywhere from twenty-eight to forty per cent of all American-made automobiles in 1902, and the 4,000 cars he produced the following year would have constituted about thirty-six per cent of the car production for 1903.[36]

To gain the proper perspective on what Olds was doing during these years, however, one must realize that he was not alone in having to alter earlier manufacturing techniques to keep up with the demand. It is true that Autocar, whose runabout—from the attention it received in the press and advertisements—one would have thought to be a runaway best-seller in 1899–1900, is reported to have produced only twenty-seven automobiles in all of 1900. But other companies were turning out vehicles at rates that were much closer to those Olds was reaching by 1902. French automobile manufacturers, whose work has been generally ignored by American automobile historians, were reaching substantial production levels by 1901: Alexandre Darracq produced 1,200 cars that year, and DeDion, Bouton, et Cie achieved a monthly production of 200 of its Voiturettes by December 1901—about half as many cars as Olds produced during that entire year. In the United States, the Electric Vehicle Company is reported to have produced 2,000 electric taxicabs at its Hartford, Connecticut plant in 1899, while from four to six thousand of the lightweight Locomobile steam cars are variously reported to have been produced from 1899 to 1901, which was probably more than the total of all Oldsmobiles produced until 1903. Furthermore, between 1899 and 1903 "about 6000" Mobile steam cars are said to have been assembled in the company's Tarrytown, New York factory. In the Midwest the Thomas B. Jeffery Company turned out nearly three thousand of its Rambler runabouts during its first two years of production in 1902 and 1903, nearly equaling the production record of Olds during the first two years of the curved-dash runabout's production. Finally, by 1903 two Detroit-made cars, the Cadillac and the Ford, had begun to appear in numbers which were soon to surpass the Oldsmobile's records.[37]

Thus Ransom Olds, in seeking ways to make his production more efficient, was dealing with problems that others in the United States and Europe were also confronting, in some cases prior to the time he would have begun tackling them. Nevertheless, Oldsmobile figures by 1903 had clearly surpassed anything that any other company, American or European, had yet been able to achieve. In the summer of that year *Horseless Age,* though not identifying the companies by name, reported that the leading American automobile manufacturer—and the reference to the Olds Motor Works was clear—was turning out over one hundred cars a week, about twice as many as any other American companies were known to be producing. At the end of the year that same well-informed trade journal estimated that of the total estimated American production of over 25,000 automobiles for the upcoming year, Olds would "undoubtedly" have "the largest" share, with a production conservatively pegged at from 6,000 to 7,000 vehicles. This was compared with the estimates for the other leading firms: Cadillac with an estimated production of 4,000, Ford and Thomas B. Jeffery with 3,000 each, and Winton with 2,000. It is no wonder, then, that *Scientific American* in January 1904 singled out the Olds Motor Works as an operation that exemplified the new trend in automobile manufacturing. Some manufacturers had workers scurrying about the factory getting parts from hither and yon, and slowly piecing together one car at a time. For example, the head of the Dowagiac Automobile Company in southwestern Michigan in 1908 reported that it took two weeks for two of his workers to put together one car. To avoid such inefficiency Ransom Olds no doubt drew in part on the experience of such manufacturers as Detroit's railroad car companies in assembling their rolling stock, methods with which some of Olds' associates, such as Henry Russel, would have been quite familiar. At any rate, Olds began to organize the assembly work in a manner that suggested the later, more sophisticated automobile production lines. The work of putting the car together proceeded from station to station in the plant, with the vehicles being moved along on wooden platforms equipped with casters. The workmen were assigned specific tasks at each point in the assembly operation, and the parts they needed were close at hand in large bins. It was scarcely mass production in the sense in which the term would be used after Ford and his staff introduced the moving assembly line in 1913–14 at their Highland Park plant; but what Olds did over a decade earlier was a notable advance for its day. And it was one more of Olds' activities that served to fix in the public's mind the image of Detroit as a manufacturing center of automobiles produced in a particular fashion.[38]

Ironically, however, by 1902 an increasing number of Oldsmobiles were being assembled not in Detroit but in Lansing. This change had originated with the fire of March 1901, which had presented Olds with the problem of providing for the company's long-range needs, which would require replacements for the temporary quarters that were initially used in place of the burned-out Jefferson Avenue factory.

Immediately after the fire Olds had announced his intention to rebuild the Detroit plant as soon as possible, and within a few days architectural plans were said to have been completed for the project, which would cost an estimated $40,000. But before the end of March rumors were circulating that Olds officials were not committed to rebuilding in Detroit "if the right kind of inducements" were to make it worthwhile for the company to relocate elsewhere. It seems quite likely that the rumors were planted by Olds and his colleagues who were hoping to start an active competition among communities that might want to become the new home of this up-and-coming young company. If Detroit wanted to retain the Olds factory, it would have to outbid these other communities. It was a tactic similar to the one Olds had employed in 1897 to secure financial support from his hometown of Lansing, and which he appears to have used again in 1898 to get these same supporters to come up with more money. The device was a familiar one in the early history of the auto industry, when chambers of commerce and other promotional groups made offers of land and financial aid in order to persuade companies to move to a particular community or to keep them where they were then situated, while the companies exerted all the pressure they could muster to obtain such inducements. W. C. Durant became a master of the game through his success in wringing additional concessions and assistance from his hometown of Flint by threatening to move his operations elsewhere if his demands were not met.[39]

Before the end of March a committee had been formed in Pontiac to try to convince the Olds company to move to that city, the site of a flourishing carriage industry—perhaps the second largest center of this activity in the state. Such a location would be an important advantage for a company making horseless carriages. However, the Olds company announced its intention at that time to maintain and enlarge its engine-manufacturing plant in Lansing so that that factory could handle the production of engines previously made in the Detroit plant, in addition to those already being produced in Lansing. This may have been a signal to Lansing business leaders that this was an appropriate time to make Olds an offer that would induce the company to transfer the rest of its operations back to the birthplace of the Olds enterprises.[40]

In Lansing, the Lansing Business Men's Association had been organized the preceding January. A promotional group similar to the old Lansing Improvement Association, they met sometime that spring and decided that one of their initial moves would be to extend an invitation to Lansing's prodigal son R. E. Olds to come home. According to C. W. Otto, who served for many years as the manager of this association's successor, the Lansing Chamber of Commerce, Harris E. Thomas, then president of the association, was appointed to go into Detroit to see what it would take to get his old friend Olds to accept such an invitation. Thomas carried out the assignment and secured Olds' acceptance of the offer by promising to give the Olds Motor Works a fifty-two-acre site on the southwestern outskirts of Lansing. The agreement was no doubt subject to the condition that Olds' fellow directors would have to agree also before the commitment became binding. The site Thomas referred to had once been the fairgrounds of the Central Michigan Fair Association. In 1889 the latter group was deeply in debt and had been bailed out of its financial difficulties by the Michigan State Fair organization, which had agreed to locate its annual fair on these grounds provided the site was free of debt. The Lansing Improvement Association spearheaded a successful drive to get the voters of Lansing to authorize the sale of $12,000 in bonds to clear the debt of the Central Michigan Fair Association in order to bring the State Fair to town. However, the State Fair did not prove to be profitable in its new home; after a few years it was pulled out of Lansing, and the fairgrounds reverted to the Central Michigan Fair Association. By the summer of 1898 this group, finding it impossible to pay off the mortgage the State Fair management had given local banks on the fairgrounds, plus the $12,000 bonded indebtedness, had declared bankruptcy. This left concerned citizens of Lansing—particularly its bankers—with a financial mess to clear up and a valuable piece of property to dispose of. It was this problem that Harris Thomas, three years later, proposed to solve by turning the property into a revenue-producing industrial site.

The other members of the Lansing Business Men's Association were said to have been taken aback when Thomas returned to Lansing and told them of the promise he had made to Ransom Olds on their behalf. By this time the amount of money that was required to wipe off the debt on the fairgrounds had been knocked down to the rock-bottom figure of $5,200, one hundred dollars an acre. When the association tried to raise this money through voluntary contributions so that it could present the deed to the property to the Olds Motor Works, it was able to get only $1,800, indicating the limits to which the Lansing business community was willing to extend itself to add an auto plant to the city's industrial economy at this time. The remaining $3,400 had to be borrowed from two individuals, Fred Thoman, an Olds stockholder, and Charles P. Downey, influential proprietor of Lansing's best-known hotel. Others involved in the land deal were individuals who had ties with Lansing banks, including J. Edward Roe, an officer with the American State Savings Bank who would have close business links with Ransom Olds in the future, and whose son Clarence would later marry Olds' daughter Bernice.[41]

By the last week of June, Olds and some of his staff and associates, including Fred and Samuel Smith, had inspected the Lansing site. On June 30, Olds and the Smiths met with Henry Russel in the latter's home and voted to accept the Lansing offer, which the board minutes indicate Thomas had presented to the company on June 10. On July 19 the elder Smith, vacationing at Harbor Springs in northern Michigan, wrote to Olds and expressed his wish to see "this matter closed at Lansing as soon as possible or before the offer lapses & gets away from us." Smith and Henry Russel both wanted construction of the first building at the new site to get started in time to have it completed by December, with a second building to be completed shortly thereafter, in order to have the new factory ready to meet the anticipated demand for the Oldsmobile that was to be developed by the spring of 1902. Money was no problem, Smith assured Olds. They already had invested so much in the company, and the prospects for financial gain now appeared so promising, that Smith was ready to advance whatever additional funds were needed to insure the speedy completion of the contemplated new facility.[42]

One major hurdle remained to be cleared, however, before the Lansing deal was closed, and it is at this point that Reuben Shettler enters the picture, a man who would continue to appear during the next decade, exerting a major influence on Ransom Olds' business activities. Details of Shettler's life are known only to a very sketchy degree. Sources indicate that he was a native of Lansing and probably somewhat older than Ransom Olds, though the date of his birth is not known. In 1891 it was reported in a local paper that he had acquired space in Lansing from which to carry on his business as the state agent for the Huber Manufacturing Company of Marion, Ohio, makers of agricultural machinery. Shettler prospered, and he and his wife were accepted members of the best Lansing society. Early in the summer of 1897, for example, Mrs. Harris Thomas and Mrs. Hugh Lyons, wife of one of the city's leading industrialists, were among the guests whom Mrs. Shettler entertained at a "charming thimble party"; and later that summer Mrs. Lyons was again among the guests whom the Shettlers had aboard their launch, the *Jessie S.*

Toward the end of 1898 the Shettlers left Lansing to reside in southern California, partly because of Mrs. Shettler's ill health. Shettler exchanged some of his Michigan business interests for a cattle ranch, although he and his wife made their permanent residence in Los Angeles. However, this apparently did not mean that they were cutting their ties with Michigan. They returned to Lansing in May 1899 for a stay of several months, during which Shettler looked after some of his remaining Michigan investments. These would bring him back on frequent occasions in subsequent years. The Olds automotive activities soon became the principal attraction drawing him back to the Wolverine State.[43]

Whether Shettler came to know Ransom Olds within a

social context or—as seems more likely—their acquaintance grew out of their closely related business activities, Shettler had in 1898 invested in the Olds Gasoline Engine Works when the capital stock of that company was increased. One of the reasons for this business connection was that the Olds engines were adaptable to some of the agricultural operations for which Shettler's machinery was designed. Shettler would later claim that he had only loaned Olds $5,000 at this time, but the company's annual report shows Shettler as a stockholder in the firm. The following year, when the engine company became part of the Olds Motor Works, Shettler received $5,000 plus an equal amount of stock as his share in the distribution that was made to the stockholders in the two concerns that were merged to form the new Detroit-based company. The organization of the Olds Motor Works in the spring of 1899 may, in fact, have been the immediate cause of Shettler's return to Lansing at that time.[44]

In a statement he prepared in 1936, and which he said the Lansing *State Journal* refused to publish, Shettler—who had long since broken with Olds—said that he had been approached by the Lansing Business Men's Association in 1901 and had been asked to act as that group's intermediary in its negotiations with the Olds Motor Works because of his known friendship with R. E. Olds. Whatever the *State Journal*'s reasons were for refusing to accept Shettler's five-page statement either as a news item or as a paid advertisement, the general accuracy of much of what he wrote would not have been subject to debate. Certainly Shettler's associations with Olds prior to 1901 had been well publicized. He was credited in 1898 news stories with being one of the Lansing businessmen principally responsible for the increased investments that temporarily succeeded in keeping the Olds business enterprises in that city. And in June 1899, the Lansing *State Republican* noted that Shettler had accompanied Olds on a trip in the Olds motor vehicle to Pine Lake.

However, Shettler was not being entirely candid in 1936 when he stated that he had agreed to accept the assignment of the businessmen's group as a community service to Lansing, which, he declared, had been badly in need of the kind of boost that a promising new industrial enterprise such as the Olds Motor Works could give to its lagging economy. Actually, of course, Shettler, like Fred Thoman, was a major stockholder in the Olds Motor Works and had a personal interest in arranging matters in a way that would be most beneficial to the company. Contemporaneous letters tend to confirm Shettler's claim that he was a major force in the final decisions that brought about the location of the Olds operations on the site where Oldsmobile manufacturing has been centered to the present day. But they also show that Shettler was acting in the negotiations as an agent for the Olds Motor Works and not simply out of a public-spirited desire to help the community.[45]

It is not clear whether Shettler rather than Harris Thomas, as other sources would indicate, first approached the Olds directors about the land offer. It is clear that it was Shettler who, at the request of these Olds officials, took on the job of securing from the Grand Trunk Western Railway, the only railroad serving the area of the proposed new plant, a number of concessions that the Olds board desired before it would give final approval to the deal. Shettler conferred with Grand Trunk officials at meetings in Lansing and at the office of this Canadian railroad's president in Montreal. The railroad agreed to bear the entire expense of running a spur line into the new factory, to haul materials needed to build and equip the new plant at nominal rates, part of which would be rebated to the Olds Motor Works, and to provide regular twice-daily freight service from the factory to the main freight terminal in Lansing. In reporting the terms of the agreement to the Olds directors, Shettler emphasized the railroad's concern that the arrangements be kept strictly confidential—and with good reasons, since some of the provisions, especially those relating to rebates, would probably have been regarded as illegal had they been publicized.[46]

With this obstacle to final agreement out of the way, an official announcement was issued on August 12 stating that the Olds Motor Works had accepted the land in southwestern Lansing as the site on which it would begin immediate construction of permanent facilities to replace those destroyed in Detroit the previous winter. The formal transfer of title to the land from the businessmen's association to the company took place in September. The devotion to the economic welfare of Lansing which had motivated these few local businessmen to put up the money for the property did not extend to any willingness to write off this money as a gift. The Olds' directors were under the impression that only if they were to fail to build a factory on the fairground site would they be required to refund to the businessmen's association the amount that group had spent to secure the property. However, in August 1902, months after the promised factory had been completed and put into operation, the Olds board, under some considerable pressure from the Lansing association, voted to reimburse the association for the cost of the land. But it was not until July 1903, at the urging of R. E. Olds, that the money was finally paid.

Meanwhile, Reuben Shettler claimed to be $800 out of pocket, that being the amount of his expenses during his prolonged negotiations with the Grand Trunk. Although Fred Smith claimed that when he raised the issue with Shettler, the latter had said he did not want to be reimbursed for these expenses, the seeds of the subsequent blowup between Olds and Shettler in 1910 can perhaps be found in Shettler's lingering bitterness at what he regarded as the failure of Olds' company to compensate him for the time and money he had contributed to smoothing the way for the company's move to Lansing.[47]

Exactly why the Olds directors, who had shifted the company's operations away from Lansing to Detroit just two years before, should now have decided to move them back to the state capital is not quite clear. One of the stated reasons was the "labor troubles" that had beset the company in Detroit. It is true that in May 1901 the company had become embroiled in a machinists' strike that threatened at one point to erupt into violence. This could well have predisposed company officials to flee the city; but second thoughts on the matter would quickly have recalled the labor dispute at the Olds engine plant in Lansing in 1898, which made it evident that they could not escape from such problems simply by moving out of Detroit. The second reason given to explain the move was the shortage of skilled labor that existed in Detroit. But it was scarcely reasonable to believe that the supply of such labor would be greater in a city as small as Lansing, particularly when one of the reasons they gave for leaving Lansing in 1899 had been the insufficient number of skilled workers found there. The truth of the matter is that the supply of skilled workers needed in the auto industry was limited no matter where they might have gone in Michigan. As a company like the Olds Motor Works developed, it soon outgrew the local supply of such workers and had to import them from other parts of the country or from Canada.[48]

State labor statistics do reveal a development in 1901 that may well have been an important—if unstated—cause of the company's decision. The average wage of the workers at the Detroit Olds plant showed a very sharp increase over the same average for the previous year, perhaps a result of the labor troubles in May. During that same period, wages at the Lansing plant remained relatively unchanged; thus, whereas there had been little difference between the rates paid at the two Olds plants in 1900, the prevailing rate in Lansing in 1901 was a third less than that paid in Detroit. Such a marked wage differential would seem to have been an important economic consideration in switching the company's operations entirely to Lansing.[49]

No doubt the major reason the Lansing offer was viewed with favor by the Olds directors, however, was the amount of land and the cost involved, when compared with the Jefferson Avenue site. Olds and his associates apparently first thought that they were getting the fairgrounds free; but even when the company paid the Lansing Business Men's Association for the property, the price of the entire fifty-two acres was nearly $35,000 less than the reported cost of the five acres the Olds Motor Works had purchased in Detroit in 1899. At the new Lansing site sufficient space was now available for plant expansion, whereas the expense of obtaining additional land for a comparable expansion at the Jefferson Avenue site would have been almost surely prohibitive.

In addition, one suspects that besides the concessions the Olds company received from the Grand Trunk, other inducements were forthcoming from Lansing businessmen who stood to gain from an affirmative decision by the Olds directors. For example, William K. Prudden, one of those whose name was attached to the land offer, would benefit enormously as a manufacturer of wheels from the orders he would soon receive from the Oldsmobile company. He could supply wheels to the Lansing plant without any of the transportation costs that were tacked on to the purchase price of those Olds was getting from Weston-Mott in New York. Harris Thomas and Lawrence Price, another Lansing businessman who had helped to secure the old fairgrounds, took the lead in the summer of 1901 in organizing a new Lansing firm, the Auto Body Company. Although it was denied that this concern had been formed solely as a supplier to the Olds Motor Works, it seems doubtful that Thomas and Price would have gone ahead with their plans without some assurances that they would obtain much of the Oldsmobile business formerly given to Detroit body manufacturers. By the same token, the willingness of the two men to organize this company assured Olds that he would have a supplier of bodies for his runabouts close at hand to the new Lansing plant.[50]

As it turned out, however, none of the above factors, which seemed to favor complete relocation in Lansing, caused the Olds company to abandon Detroit altogether in 1901. Announcement of Olds' plans to move to Lansing had inspired the Merchants and Manufacturers Exchange, an organization that had helped bring Olds to Detroit in 1899, to attempt to keep the company in that city. These efforts may have influenced a new decision by the Olds Motor Works, announced in November 1901, that in addition to building the new plant in Lansing they would also rebuild the Detroit plant. The announced reason for this partial reversal of the decision of the previous August was that sufficient housing was simply not available in Lansing to house the Olds work force if all operations were moved to that city. Already in the

Courtesy of Michigan History Division

These thirteen curved-dash runabouts, with the new Olds Motor Works factory in the background, signaled the return of Olds' manufacturing activities to Lansing.

fall of 1901 the company had been forced to use some of the old fair buildings in Lansing as temporary housing for the relatively small number of Olds workers who had by then been transferred to Lansing; this might indicate that the housing situation was a major factor in the decision to remain in Detroit. However, given the relatively small size of the auto industry at that time, the decision to maintain two widely separated factories may have been regarded as merely a temporary measure. In August 1902 the directors did, in fact, discuss the advisability of concentrating all production work in the Lansing plant. Although they decided against such a step at that time, the size of the Lansing site and its far greater expansion opportunity over the Detroit site made it almost inevitable that a decision in favor of just such a concentration would ultimately be approved—as it was in 1905.[51]

Beginning in 1902, Oldsmobiles would be produced both in Lansing and in Detroit for a period of three and a half years. Initially, Ransom Olds, in addition to serving as general manager of all the Olds manufacturing activities, had immediate responsibility for the Lansing plant; Fred Smith, in addition to continuing to serve as company secretary-treasurer, took over the supervision of the day-to-day operations at the Detroit plant. However, by the time Oldsmobile manufacturing was shifted entirely to Lansing, Fred Smith had been in complete managerial control of the company for over a year, replacing Ransom Olds, who had ceased to have any connection with the firm to which he and his father had given their family name.

CHAPTER SEVEN

R. E. Olds Leaves
the Olds Motor Works

ALTHOUGH RANSOM OLDS, beginning in the summer of 1901, spent much time in Lansing overseeing construction of the new plant and then getting its production underway, he apparently did not move his family back to Lansing until the summer of 1902; as late as June 12, 1902, when he applied for a patent on a carburetor, the Olds residence was still listed as Edmund Place in Detroit. Upon their return to Lansing that summer, the Olds family lived on South Capital Avenue, within hailing distance of the State Capitol. This was to be only a temporary arrangement, however, until a new residence could be completed, which was to remain the home of Ransom and Metta throughout the remainder of their lives.

The site of the new house was located at the corner of South Washington Avenue and Main Street, a convenient location since it was only a few blocks east of the new factory and also a short distance southwest of the older River Street engine plant. At the same time the site was near the homes of other prominent Lansing citizens, including Eugene Cooley's and the fabulously ornate residence Orlando M. Barnes had built a few years earlier. The site Olds chose had originally been occupied by the Benton House, one of Lansing's oldest buildings and its first brick structure, a hotel erected when Lansing was founded in the late 1840s. In later years the hotel was renamed the Everett House, but for a time in the 1860s it had housed a private school operated by the Rev. Carmi C. Olds, father of Schuyler S. Olds. Under subsequent owners the building had deteriorated until it became "an eyesore in the neighborhood"; it was torn down around 1900 by Judge Edward Cahill, from whom Ransom Olds purchased the property a short time later.[1]

The Olds home was designed by the architect D. B. Moon, who had designed the new Oldsmobile plant in Lansing and who had earlier designed several other Lansing residences. The house, which was completed by 1904, was a two-and-a-half-story, L-shaped structure that fronted on Washington Avenue but had the longer extension of the "L" facing Main Street. Both in its exterior and interior appearance it was quite typical of the homes of the well-to-do being constructed during the later years of the Victorian Era. The exterior walls were of buff-colored brick, trimmed with red sandstone. The hip roof was covered with green slate, and in the corners were towers; these were removed in 1952, when a deep veranda extending along almost the entire front of the house was also removed.

The interior was impressive, with its paneled walls, its paneled or decorated ceilings, and its marquetry floors with three- and four-tone borders. Passing through a vestibule into the reception hall, one entered the parlor to the left, beyond which was the dining room and the kitchen, with an attached pantry and separate dining room for the servants. On the right side of the first floor was a music hall and library, and off that a separate study.

On the second floor was a large music room with paneled walls and a double-coved ceiling on which were painted musical emblems and other decorative features, including a partially draped woman swinging on a garland of flowers. The architectural historian Harley J. McKee, who was impressed by the high level of workmanship in the construction of the house, described this room as "an example of creative adaptation; not a 'period' design in any sense, it achieved much of the delicacy and light gaiety that we associate with Louis XV interiors." A large pipe organ at one end dominated this room and reflected the love Olds quite obviously had for music. It was the love of an untrained amateur, one who was unable to play a musical instrument. Years later, Olds encouraged his young grandson, R. E. Olds Anderson, to keep up his piano lessons, telling the boy that "he would give all the money he ever made if he could play the piano himself." Rather than taking lessons himself, however, Olds fulfilled his desire to participate in the performance of the music he loved in a manner quite consistent with his skills and training as a mechanic: he had the organ in the music room adapted so that it could be played manually or mechanically with the use of perforated paper rolls.[2]

The purchase of this organ should not be interpreted as the act of a businessman who, having acquired material wealth, suddenly felt the need to add a little culture to his life. Olds' musical interests had been manifested at least as early as 1891, when he and his wife had sponsored a musical entertainment for the Baptist young people in their home. In April 1901, despite the business pressures he was then experiencing and the poor state of his health, Olds had taken the time to purchase a new Mozart Grand Piano from a Detroit music store; the fact that he used his old piano as a trade-in indicates that there had been a piano in the Olds household for some time prior to this date. During his later years Olds would purchase numerous pianos, both grands and uprights, which, like his organ, he was able to operate mechanically. Especially on Sunday mornings before church and in the afternoon, when other forms of entertainment were forbidden in this Baptist household, Olds would sit and play roll after roll, with members of the family and any visitors joining him in songfests that might last for hours. Hymns were naturally among his favorites on these occasions, but his interest in the classics was also evident at these song sessions. Titles of roll and sheet music that he copied into his diaries in the 1920s show that his tastes also encompassed the popular songs of the day, such as "Moonlight and Roses," "You Can't Stop Me From Dreaming of You," "Velvet Lady," "The Dream of Love," "Somewhere My Love Lies Dreaming," "Hawaiian Butterfly," "Look for the Silver Lining," "A Little Home With You," and numerous other tunes of a similarly sentimental character.

A tune that became a long-time favorite with Olds, for

obvious reasons, was "In My Merry Oldsmobile," even though this song—the only one of many that have been written about a particular make of car that achieved lasting popularity—was composed after Olds had ceased to be associated with the production of the Oldsmobile. In December 1945, he had an electronically controlled carillon built into the Olds Tower in downtown Lansing, and one of the tunes it could peel out for all the citizens of the town to hear was the familiar strains of this Gus Edwards melody, although for-

The music room in the Oldses' Lansing home, dominated by the pipe organ, around which the family and friends joined in so many songfests over nearly half a century

Courtesy of Gladys Olds Anderson

tunately for the sanity of the townsfolk the song was never played with the frequency that Olds had originally envisioned.[3]

The entire top floor of the Olds home was devoted to still another love of Olds—dancing. Here in the ballroom dancing parties were frequently held. On one such occasion in 1911, the Roes, Pruddens, Edmondses, Davises, and two other Lansing couples were in attendance for what Olds described in his diary as a "Big party." Unlike Henry Ford, who preferred the old-fashioned folk dances and helped to spark a revival of interest in them, Olds preferred such traditional dances as the waltz and the two-step.[4]

However, as interesting as the music room and the ballroom may have been in providing insights into lesser-known aspects of Olds' personality, those features in his new home that were more in keeping with his public image were the ones that attracted the most attention at the time. The *Detroit Free Press*, describing Olds' "handsome residence," paid particular attention to the "automobile room" at the right rear of the first floor. The trade journal *Automobile* showed a similar interest, describing the Olds residence as "one of the first of a type of house which bid fair to become almost a necessity with the growing popularity of the automobile. In designing this house the owner and architect had in mind the housing of several automobiles in the most accessible and convenient way for the owner." Accessibility and convenience in this case meant an area for which the term "automobile room" was much more appropriate than "garage," as that term came to describe residential adjuncts in later years. With over a thousand feet of floor space, the room was completely finished off and heated; it was furnished with a washstand, sink, work bench, "and such tools as are usually found in a private automobile stable," and a turntable— perhaps added later—so that Olds would not have to bother backing his car out. Years later, Olds' young grandson and a friend were amusing themselves one Saturday by spinning the turntable with their feet. The motion caused a trailer to go crashing off into a nearby Pierce-Arrow. (Olds, like many automobile magnates, did not confine his personal car purchases to those his company produced.) The horror-stricken youths hastened to tell the grandfather of what had happened, but Olds, a typical indulgent grandparent, laughed it off, declaring that if that was the worst thing that ever happened to the boys they would not have much to worry about.

Entrance to the automobile room from the house was through a door from the kitchen and another that led from the library. From the study that adjoined the library two windows overlooked the automobile room, so that Olds, when working at home, could keep an eye on his cars, "a consistent detail," *Automobile* felt, "for an owner as interested in the self-propelled vehicle as is Mr. Olds." The same publication noted that one drawback resulting from the inclusion of such a garage area as part of the house plan was a "considerable" increase in fire insurance rates; "but to the majority of owners of expensive automobiles and fine stone residences, this is almost a negligible factor in view of the great comfort of having the cars under the same roof as the living apartments, particularly in rainy and extremely cold weather."[5]

Although the Olds home would often be referred to as a mansion, it was scarcely in the same class with some of the palatial homes other Michigan automobile magnates would build in later years; nor was it even the grandest residence in Lansing. The total reported cost of the house was $25,000, certainly a bargain compared to what it would cost to construct such a house in later years; but this figure was only a tenth of what Henry Ford would spend four years later on a home in Detroit. And it was only a small fraction of the cost of Ford's subsequent Fair Lane mansion in Dearborn or the equally expensive residences built in Grosse Pointe, Birmingham, and Bloomfield Hills by other automotive multimillionaires. But Olds, though he would later build some elaborate summer homes elsewhere in Michigan and a winter residence in Florida, remained content with his comparatively modest Victorian home in Lansing. In this apparent willingness to live with less than he could have had, however, one sees more than anything else the essentially conservative side of Olds' personality that helps to explain much of what happened to him in the last half of his long business career.[6]

* * * * *

By the time he returned to live in Lansing in 1902, R. E. Olds had achieved a degree of national recognition for his work with automobiles that far overshadowed the recognition he had earlier received for his engines. As the Oldsmobile became the best-selling automobile of the day and probably the most widely advertised, each of these cars and ads helped to publicize the man whose name supplied the first four letters of this increasingly familiar marque. Within the auto industry itself, some indication of Olds' high standing with his peers was demonstrated in 1902, when he was placed on the executive committee of the National Association of Automobile Manufacturers, the only Michiganian on this group's governing board. By 1903, Olds was also serving on the Road Improvement Committee of the American Motor League, the oldest automotive organization in the country. It seems unlikely, however, that Olds exerted himself much to obtain either of these posts: the former organization was one primarily concerned with the management of the annual automobile shows, and the latter was a group that, despite its age, had never succeeded in winning great acceptance as a major spokesman for the industry. Had he desired to occupy positions of power in the industry, there would have been within his grasp more influential offices, which less important but more aggressive men seized at this time.[7]

Great as Olds' prestige in the outside business world undoubtedly was by 1902, the degree of control he exerted within his own company had been eroding steadily since the time he first accepted outside capital in 1897. By 1901, when he was on the threshold of his greatest success, his authority was being increasingly restricted. In January the directors voted to make Samuel Smith the president once again, as he had been in 1899, and returned Olds to the position of vice president, which he had held prior to his election as president at the board meeting of January 1900. Press reports

concerning the Olds factory fire two months later referred to
Olds as the president of the firm, suggesting that Olds gave
the reporters the impression that he still held that office; if
that is true, it would indicate that he was not happy with his
fellow directors' decision to shift him out of the position.
However, since Olds retained the title of general manager
and thus presumably continued to be in charge of the manufacturing side of the business, he may have viewed the action in January as relieving him of administrative responsibilities which had made it difficult for him to devote his full
attention to the aspect of the business that interested him
most. But in the months following the January administrative shuffle it became increasingly clear that Samuel
Smith—and especially his son Fred—intended to exercise a
degree of control over company policy and its execution that
was bound to place them on a collision course with Ransom
Olds and his conception of his responsibilities as general
manager.

In July 1901, Samuel Smith's letter to Olds, in which he
expressed his wish to see the final details of the Lansing land
deal speedily wrapped up, was couched in the man's typically
courteous style; yet its overall tone can most appropriately
be described as that of a directive from a chief executive to
one of his administrative aides, not as the exchange of views
between the company's two ranking officers and largest
stockholders. Another hint of the reduced status of Olds' position appears to have come in August, when Reuben Shettler reported on the details of the freight arrangement he
had worked out with the Grand Trunk Railway. It turns out
that he had taken the action not in accordance with instructions from Olds, but "in accordance with agreement and
understanding with Mr. F. L. Smith." It is true that Shettler
at the same time expressed the hope "that Mr. Olds will
speedily recover," thus suggesting that a recurrence of Olds'
ill health of the previous spring may have compelled the
younger Smith to take on some of the responsibilities which
Olds, as vice president and general manager, would otherwise have been expected to handle. After Olds was fully
recovered, however, Fred Smith continued to insert himself

into areas that would not usually be considered the domain of a secretary-treasurer. The continuation of these presumptions by Smith made almost inevitable the clash between the two which ultimately led to Olds' being forced out of the company in 1904.[8]

So long as the direction of the Olds Motor Works had remained centered in Detroit, Olds and the Smiths seem to have worked well together. They were in constant contact, and it would have been natural for Samuel Smith and his sons Fred and Angus (the latter, though coming to hold a substantial amount of stock, apparently never played a major policy-making role in the company) to have deferred to the judgment of the more experienced Ransom Olds on questions about the manufacturing side of the business. With the division of the Oldsmobile operations between Detroit and Lansing, and the splitting up of the responsibility for running the two plants between Fred Smith and Olds—even though Olds retained the title of general manager over the entire company—Smith began to feel confident about his own managerial talents and to feel less of a need to follow Olds' lead in such matters. At least as early as the spring of 1902, Smith was trying to influence company managerial policies in a way that could scarcely have been regarded by Olds as anything but an infringement of his rights and authority.

The issue that is usually cited as having precipitated Olds' departure from the Olds Motor Works is the Smiths' alleged desire to replace the inexpensive runabout with a bigger, heavier, more expensive model and Olds' opposition to such a change. Although Ransom Olds himself came to be the leading advocate of this theory, a careful study shows that, although the issue of car size, weight, and price may have helped create a break between Olds and the Smiths, it was only one element in a situation that was far more complex in its development. By the time the final break between these business associates took place in the latter part of 1903, any arguments regarding models seem to have been settled.[9]

At least as early as the spring of 1902, work was underway at the Lansing plant on the development of a two-cylinder

Oldsmobile touring car. Fred Smith was obviously enthusiastic about the project, but he cautioned Olds to "keep this thing under cover—as far as opening it up to visitors." Nevertheless, rumors of what was going on in Lansing did leak out, and *Horseless Age* in the summer reported "on good authority" that the Olds Motor Works was developing a two-cylinder model for 1903 that would sell for $800. This report was denied by the Olds company in September and again in November, when Fred Smith was quoted as saying that there would be "no important change" in the Oldsmobile during the following year. At the end of that same month, however, Smith was writing to Olds, urging him—if he was satisfied with the touring car—to complete two of these models for display at the upcoming auto show in New York.[10]

Olds, Fred Smith, Roy Chapin, and W. G. Morley of the Olds staff attended the third annual New York show, which was held from January 17 to 24, 1903 in Madison Square Garden. The Oldsmobile exhibit contained some distinct surprises which more than confirmed the accuracy of the rumors going the rounds the previous summer. In addition to a standard curved-dash runabout, which had become the most popular car on the market since its initial appearance at the second annual show fourteen months earlier, Olds exhibited a runabout cut in half, giving the observer an unusual insight into the working mechanism of the vehicle. A new model, featuring a closed coupé body with glass front, fitted on a runabout chassis, was especially designed for doctors and was said by one reporter to have been "the sensation of the exhibit" because it had not been expected. But the most attention was paid to the two-cylinder, ten-horsepower, 1350-pound tonneau model. Olds and his crew in Lansing had produced a touring car that was in appearance and mechanical features simply a big brother of the runabout. The curved dash was retained but with a French-style "bonnet" in front containing the tubes of the cooling system. The engine was beneath the body, in the same location as the runabout's less powerful motor. The entrance to the rear seat, which doubled the seating capacity of this model over the normal capacity of the runabout, was a door on the side, something of an innovation at a time when other tonneau models generally featured a rear entrance. "The whole appearance" of the Oldsmobile tonneau, the *Cycle and Automobile Trade Journal* commented, "suggests gracefulness and practicability.... It is the evident intention of the Olds people to meet all demands for a touring car, having the same practical features which have made the Oldsmobile so popular, and judging from the construction and appearance of the new car it, like its popular companion, is built to run and does it."[11]

At this stage in the auto industry's development, however, the mere display of a model at an auto show was no guarantee of its immediate availability to the public. Companies frequently sought to attract attention by displaying superbly finished mock-ups that were not actual working vehicles; some of them did not even contain an engine under the hood—or seat, as was more probable in this era. The Oldsmobile tonneau displayed in January, 1903 was apparently not one of these fakes, but at the same time it was not yet ready to go into production, in spite of the company's indication that it would soon be in the dealers' showrooms.

On April 22, three months after the debut of this car at the Madison Square Garden show, Fred Smith expressed to Olds his great distress that they had not yet begun to produce the touring car. Oldsmobile agents, Smith reported, were angry at the company for not delivering the car, and he said that they should never have promised such deliveries if they knew they could not fulfill them. He felt that the Olds Motor Works could not continue to operate during the coming year with only the runabout model to offer the public. The dealers, Smith said, were unanimous in demanding cars with "more power, stiffer construction, and a more conventional dash—say french 'bonnet.'" Evidence that Smith was accurately reflecting the feelings of dealers came late in 1903, when Reuben Shettler, who had acquired the Oldsmobile distributorship in southern California, wrote to Ransom Olds, warning him that if the rumors to the effect that the Olds Motor Works was dropping its plans to put out a bigger car were true, then "we are up against it good and hard." Without "a big machine," Shettler declared, they could not keep pace with the competition.[12]

Early in February 1903, an article by Ransom Olds was published in the *Detroit News*. It appeared in a special section on automobiles that came out just prior to the opening of the second annual Detroit auto show. This was a strange event in which the automobile exhibits—including a repeat of the Oldsmobile exhibit from the New York show—had to compete for attention with exhibits of boats, pianos, and dogs, which were all present under one roof as part of a week-long show. Olds declared that the automobile by 1903 was ceasing to be regarded as a mere "fad" and was commencing to be granted its "rightful place in the world of business and pleasure." Assessing the developments up to that date, Olds repeated many of the same points he had included in his remarks before the Michigan Engineering Society in 1897. Comparing the horsedrawn vehicle with the automobile, he again expressed no doubt that because of its greater convenience and economy the motor vehicle would continue to replace the older form of transportation with increasing rapidity. Among the three types of automotive propulsion, Olds was still confident that the gasoline-propelled automobile would be favored by an ever greater margin, though he indicated somewhat greater respect for the electrics than he had shown in 1897. He decried the efforts of some American manufacturers to follow the lead of French and German companies in trying to make "the automobile the child of luxury, instead of the child of necessity." However, Olds felt that the "freaks and exaggerated monstrosities" of the early period of automotive development were now giving way to cars that were built for "every-day use." Vehicles of from twenty to one hundred horsepower would continue to be built for racing purposes, but, he predicted, "the lighter and lesser horse-power vehicle will certainly be the future automobile." Through much of the article, Olds emphasized his preference for the runabout, which was reflected in his concluding prediction "that within the next 10 years the automobile most generally used will be one of 700 to 800 pounds in weight, small, compact, and always under instant control."[13]

The general tenor of Olds' remarks, particularly his emphasis on the lightweight runabout and his criticism of a trend toward larger, more luxurious, and expensive cars could be interpreted as an implied criticism of his own company's decision to develop a touring car, a photograph of which was printed adjacent to a portion of Olds' article with the caption "A New Departure." If this was the impression Olds wished to leave with his readers, it would confirm the notion that it was his continued commitment to the production of a small, cheap car that caused the break with the Smiths and ultimately his departure from the company. It may well be, as Fred Smith and Henry Russel appear to have believed in the spring of 1903, that Olds, because of his preference for the runabout, had been dragging his feet on the touring-car project and was thus principally to blame for the company's failure to put the new car into production on schedule. But even if this was true, by the fall of the year—according to a statement he made in 1904—Olds had come to accept the idea of a touring car as a necessary and desirable vehicle for its day. After all, the touring car model which the Olds staff had been working on, despite being heavier by more than 500 pounds than the ideal weight mentioned by Olds in his article in February 1903, and twice as costly as the runabout, was scarcely the very costly, prestigious type car for the wealthy that he had been decrying. The Oldsmobile touring car had been modeled after the runabout, but because of its greater roominess, power, and durability, it came closer to achieving Olds' goal of a practical car for everyday use than did the runabout, certainly for those who wanted to travel any distance. That Olds had begun to recognize the greater possibilities of this kind of touring car was shown in 1904 when, in his new automobile company, it was the Reo touring car, not the Reo runabout, that was featured in the advertisements appearing by the end of that year.[14]

Just as these actions demonstrated that Olds' attitude toward a bigger car was not as inflexible as some have depicted it, there is also evidence to indicate that Fred Smith, though he may have initially been more enthusiastic about the touring car than was Olds, was at the same time much less opposed to the continued production of the runabout than has generally been assumed. In fact, in the same letter of April 1903 in which he was critical of Olds for the lack of progress in producing the tonneau model, Smith stated that the top priority of Olds and his staff should be the runabout. "As I have always claimed," Smith said, "the big work is still ahead in planning a campaign to lead the trade with something new, practical & cheap." These were almost exactly the sentiments that Olds had expressed in February and were scarcely what one would expect from the man who has been portrayed as having driven Olds out of the company because of his desire to shift the emphasis away from the cheap runabout to more expensive vehicles.

Similarly, in September 1903, Smith, rather than insisting on immediate action in the production of the touring car, was telling Olds that it would be "unwise to push out any great number of Touring Cars this year in their present shape and there is no question but that we will be gainers in the long run by making haste slowly." Thus, although bigger Oldsmobile models would ultimately come to represent Smith's major manufacturing interest, they do not seem to have been his over-riding interest in 1903. And in 1904 and 1905, when Olds was no longer around, and Fred Smith had undisputed control over management policy decisions, the little curved-dash runabout continued to provide the bulk of company sales; in fact, the car continued in production until 1907, by which time most of the companies that had earlier competed with the Olds Motor Works in the low-priced runabout market had abandoned these models for bigger, more advanced vehicles.[15]

It is clear, then, that what was at stake in the conflict that developed between Ransom Olds and Fred Smith in 1902 and 1903 was something much more basic than what kind of car they should produce; on that issue they should have been able to resolve their differences by at least the latter part of 1903. By that time, however, their relationship had greatly worsened: the issue that divided them was simply the question of who should run the company. Since the time Samuel Smith's money had made possible the establishment of the Olds Motor Works, Ransom Olds had not been assured the kind of control he had held earlier in the family-owned engine company, or even in the Olds Motor Vehicle Company, where he had controlled an amount of stock equal to that of all other stockholdings. But as long as the Smiths and the other officers and stockholders in the Olds Motor Works depended on the judgment of Olds in matters of policy affecting the company's product, Olds could justifiably continue to feel that he was still in charge of the operations.

As the automotive division grew into a healthy and prosperous organization, two developments may have served to decrease the degree to which Olds' associates would feel the need to defer to him on manufacturing policy matters. With the growth of the company, additional help was required, and among those who were hired were some obviously talented individuals—like Charles King and Jonathan Maxwell—whose experience and knowledge in the area of engines rivaled Olds'. King, of course, was a Detroiter whose employment early in 1900 coincided with the Olds company's acquisition of his struggling little marine engine business. Many others who applied or were recruited came from Detroit or Lansing, the latter in particular often recalling to Olds some past contact they may have had with him. The hiring of Maxwell in 1900, however, was an early indication of how the automobile industry would ultimately act as an insatiable magnet, drawing and absorbing workers from outside the immediate locality. Maxwell, although originally from Indiana, came to the Olds company from a job he had held in Montreal; and Canada would continue to prove a fruitful source of labor for the Michigan auto industry. Olds had already hired the Canadian Richard Scott in 1898, and Milton Beck, who came to the company in 1899, was reportedly from Toronto. The hiring of these outsiders may have been relatively unplanned, but in the spring of 1901, as Olds began to swing into full-scale car production, advertisements for workers were placed in out-of-state papers, with the response coming from applicants scattered throughout the Midwest. Again, many of them seemed to be individuals with extensive experience with machines, carriages, or automobiles. Others who may have lacked such work experience were obviously talented individuals: for example, Robert Hupp, who within a few years would strike out on his own with the Hupmobile; or Roy Chapin and several of his fellow students from the University of Michigan—particularly the brilliant engineer Howard Coffin—who within less than a decade after they went to work for Olds were recognized leaders in the industry as the heads of their own companies. In short, within two years after the Olds Motor Works had been formed, the Smiths could, if they desired, get advice from numerous staff members whose credentials made their views appear every bit as trustworthy as those of Ransom Olds.[16]

The second development that served to diminish the importance attached to Olds' methods and opinions resulted from Fred Smith's becoming the official in charge of the Detroit plant in 1902. To carry out his new responsibilities, Smith had to develop a staff that could advise him on problems that could not wait for a decision from General Manager Olds now that the latter was located in Lansing, ninety or so miles away. As he gained experience in this job, Smith began to go beyond merely supervising the day-to-day operations in Detroit and began to seek to institute changes in overall company policy, sometimes in opposition to ideas and practices favored by Olds.

One area in which Smith became very active was sales. It appears that Smith took Roy Chapin under his wing and gave the young test driver increasing responsibilities in the sales end of the business, ultimately promoting Chapin to the post of sales manager by 1904. By the summer of 1902, Chapin had instituted policies governing the distribution of automobiles that characterized the kinds of arrangements that would become universal in the industry but were not in keeping with Olds' rather more informal practices. An example of the latter was recalled by Donald Wilhelm, who said that in the early days of Oldsmobile he had written to

Olds personally, asking that he be made the Oldsmobile agent in Wilhelm's home town of Defiance, Ohio. Olds replied at once, giving Wilhelm the desired appointment, apparently without bothering to inquire into the applicant's qualifications. Had he done so, he would have discovered that Wilhelm was only a high school freshman. When he was unable to answer questions about automobiles posed by his first prospect, the family doctor, he decided on the spot to abandon the life of an automobile salesman for a career in writing.

A more qualified Binghamton, New York firm, which had been selling Olds' engines for years, wrote to Olds in the summer of 1902 objecting strenuously to the way it was being treated by "this Kid C"—apparently referring to Chapin—who had informed the New Yorkers that if they wanted to sell Oldsmobiles they would have to deal with the agent who had been awarded the franchise for that area of New York state. The easterners, accustomed to dealing directly with Ransom Olds, complained that Chapin's policies "will not win many friends for the Oldsmobile." Olds apparently agreed with their view and wrote to Fred Smith to voice his own criticisms of Chapin's work. Smith, who told Chapin's mother that same summer of his "great confidence" in her son's "good sense and sound judgment," responded that he felt Olds was being unfair to Chapin. Smith stated: "Chapin does *good* work in the office. You don't perhaps realize it, but he is posted thoroughly on the business being done in the various agencies. I don't think you do the boy Justice, quite." Nor did Smith agree with Olds' contention that a sales manager of a firm such as theirs had to have a deep knowledge of machines above all. It was more important, Smith felt, for the man to be a good judge of human beings. "The very best tobacco salesman in Detroit doesn't nor ever did smoke or chew and doesn't really know what he's talking about," Smith told Olds, "but he's the best judge of human nature I ever ran across."[17]

Smith seems to have emerged the victor in this argument. And just as he was taking hold of the sales end of the business by the summer of 1902, he was also grabbing the reins of command in another area that was of importance not only to his company but to the future of the auto industry. As early as the spring of 1902, Smith had become involved in a movement trying to block the efforts of the Electric Vehicle Company to force producers of gasoline automobiles to pay royalties to them. The Electric Vehicle Company argued that the Selden Patent, which it controlled, applied to all such vehicles. A suit had been brought by the patentholders against the Winton Company of Cleveland, the outcome of which was still in doubt by 1902; but if the patent's validity would be upheld by the courts in Winton's case, manufacturers such as the Olds Motor Works would be faced with the unwelcome prospect of paying a royalty on all the cars they had sold in the past as well as on current and future sales. In May 1902, therefore, Smith initiated talks with George H. Day, president of the Electric Vehicle Company. These negotiations ultimately led to the formation in March 1903 of the Association of Licensed Automobile Manufacturers, a group of companies which agreed to pay the patentholders a royalty in order to avoid the expense of a court fight. Part of the royalty was to be returned to the ALAM to enable it to operate as a trade association that would—according to the organization's supporters—police the industry and assure the public that the cars from their licensed companies would have to measure up to high standards of workmanship and performance.

Fred Smith, who was elected the first president of the new association (a far more influential office than any Olds had held or ever would hold in the industry), acted as spokesman for the Olds Motor Works throughout the long, drawn-out negotiations. Actually, on June 27, 1902 the directors named Olds, Smith, and Henry Russel as a special committee charged with handling this patent issue; however, though Smith kept Olds informed of what was going on, there is little evidence to indicate that he sought the advice of the general manager or that he tried to bring him into the talks. Instead, when the discussions with the Electric Vehicle Company were reaching a critical stage during the fall of 1902, Smith brought his own father and Henry Russel into

Courtesy of University of Michigan Transportation Library

Motor Way's artist in 1905 succeeded in depicting Fred Smith as the stubborn, tough-minded executive whose opposition Olds was unable to overcome

the negotiations—not Olds. The latter, like most of the automotive pioneers, later claimed that he questioned the validity of the Selden Patent insofar as it applied to the kind of vehicles he was manufacturing and thus opposed a compromise with the patentholders, believing correctly that their claim would not stand up in court.

There is no indication from Smith's letters to Olds, whose replies in this instance have not been found, that Olds pressed his views very vigorously or that he attempted to insert himself into the negotiation proceedings. Olds declared in 1904 that when the question whether the Olds Motor Works should enter the Association of Licensed Automobile Manufacturers came up at a board meeting in the

spring of 1903, he had voted against joining, only to be out-
voted by the majority of directors who sided with Fred Smith.
However, the board minutes for March 2, 1903 show that it
was Olds himself who moved that they ratify the arrangements Smith had made on behalf of the company in these
patent negotiations, which included membership in the
licensed manufacturers group. The following month Olds
seconded a motion by Eugene Cooley to approve the license
agreement that had been drawn up between the Olds Motor
Works and the holders of the Selden Patent. It may well be
that Olds expressed his opposition in the discussions that
preceded these motions but that he voted the way he did
simply to keep out of the official company records any impression of internal dissension. In any event, it is clear that
Fred Smith had the votes to sustain his viewpoint and Olds
did not. No longer was Olds' reputation alone sufficient to
swing his fellow directors around to his point of view, as it
had been at that memorable first meeting of the board of the
Olds Motor Vehicle Company in 1897, when Olds had been
able to convince the other directors that it was not possible to
do what Edward Sparrow was asking.[18]

Although Olds may not have been happy with Smith's actions in the area of sales and in dealings with other companies
in the industry, he was probably willing to tolerate Smith's
assumption of control over such matters so long as the
wealthy Detroiter did not attempt to throw his weight around
in the manufacturing of the automobile. But by 1902, Smith
was doing just that. In the spring and summer of that year he
was not only pressing a somewhat reluctant Olds to proceed
with the development of the touring car, but he was even
more insistent that Olds take steps to correct some defects in
the existing runabout model. Complaints about the car were
coming in at what Fred and Samuel Smith considered an
alarming rate. The younger Smith informed Olds that something had to be done: "The repair items are a fright and the
black eye our runabout will get from breakage complaints
will grow worse the deeper we get in." Early in August,
Samuel Smith instructed Olds to spare no efforts to correct
the Oldsmobile's defects: "Don't rest a day or [sic] put away

work on anything new until you have planned & *perfected* part of this machine as far as practicable." At the end of August, however, Fred Smith could see no signs that Olds had initiated the steps needed to improve the car, although some of the defects had been awaiting action for two months. Firmly, Smith asked—"demanded" is perhaps the proper term—that Olds sit down and study the list of defects carefully so that on Smith's next trip to Lansing the two men could come to definite decisions on what would be done to correct these problems.[19]

Other officials and stockholders in the company shared some of the Smiths' concerns regarding the quality of the runabout. James B. Seager, when he became the Oldsmobile distributor for Mexico and the American Southwest, sent in a thirteen-page letter reciting all the changes required to make the runabout an acceptable vehicle for use in that rugged country. Earlier, in 1901, Reuben Shettler had written to Olds with a report of some annoying problems that had developed with two of the runabouts that were shipped to California. In August 1902 the directors of the company were given a report on the improvements that had been made on the runabout; but they were not satisfied, and in January 1903, Cooley moved—with Angus Smith's support—that the officers "be instructed" to bring the runabout "up to date as fast as possible" in terms of the strength and general quality of the vehicle. Several months later, President Henry Russel was reporting that unfavorable opinions regarding the little car were becoming fairly widespread among knowledgeable people. Talking with a group of Detroit's "important and intelligent business men," Russel discovered, as he told Olds, that these men had a rather low opinion of the Olds Motor Works, declaring that it was *"not a good permanent* business. They said it was banking on a temporary popularity & selling a cheap made machine."[20]

Plenty of evidence can be found that would support the view of these company officials that the Oldsmobile runabout was beginning to be regarded as an inferior product. As early as April 1902, a member of the prominent Westinghouse family wrote to a business acquaintance that he had heard so many complaints about the Oldsmobile that he had decided to delay until the next year any automobile purchases in the hopes that by 1903 a greatly improved vehicle would be available. But in the fall of that year there was an embarrassing public demonstration of the inadequacies of the Oldsmobile's brakes: during the New York to Pittsburgh Endurance Run, an Oldsmobile that had stopped on a hill began rolling back downhill despite the application of the brakes. "Several men held it until the engine was speeded up and the clutch thrown in, pulling the car up the grade all right." Ransom Olds' daughters recall, in fact, that their mother's job when she was riding in the car was to be ready, if their father stopped or stalled on a hill, to jump out and place blocks of wood under the rear wheels, a responsibility also assigned to Metta Olds with her husband's earlier steam vehicle, before the girls were born.

Cracks were made about the Oldsmobile that may or may not have been intended as good-natured ribbing. One suggested that a question mark would be appropriate at the end of one advertising slogan which said of the Oldsmobile: "Built to Run, and Does It." Another familiar advertising slogan was: "The Oldsmobile—Nothing to Watch but the Road," to which a frequent rejoinder was said to have been: "Yes, but you get damned tired watching the same piece of road all the time." Another remark of a condescending character was attributed to other automobile dealers who reportedly told their customers that the Oldsmobile "is a good little machine to buy for practice and experience," but then they should "throw it away and buy a high power machine."[21]

In defense of the small Oldsmobile and the reputation of its designer, it should be pointed out that no automobile produced in this early era measured up to the standards of performance that came to be expected of automobiles by later generations of car buyers. According to the standards of its own day, the curved-dash Oldsmobile seems to have been a reasonably good product. The rapid rise in sales between 1901 and 1904 is a clear indication that whatever the public's awareness may have been of the vehicle's defects, it did not stop them from buying the car. This point was made in 1902 by the New England Oldsmobile agent who admitted that there were those who criticized the Oldsmobile, "but let me tell you that there is no vehicle that is giving less trouble or more satisfaction," a statement that he felt was supported by the fact that he had sold some two hundred Oldsmobiles, far more than any of the other cars he handled.[22]

Beginning with Roy Chapin's cross-country trip in 1901, the relative durability and reliability of the Oldsmobile was repeatedly demonstrated and publicized during the next four years. Motorists a few years later would never have tolerated the problems Chapin had to contend with, but the important point in 1901 was that he and his runabout made it through to New York. The following April, Oldsmobiles performed creditably in a one-hundred-mile endurance run on Long Island, with one driven by Ray Owen finishing in six hours and fifty-eight seconds and earning a first-class certificate. Later, on August 2, 1902, Roy Chapin, Milford M. Weigle, Miner Haywood, and E. A. Brown were the drivers of four Oldsmobiles that were among twenty-nine cars entered in a one-hundred-mile endurance run at Chicago. Chapin, using three and seven-eighths gallons of gasoline, an outstanding showing in terms of fuel economy in this event, finished in five hours, eleven minutes, and thirty-nine seconds, fifty-one minutes behind a Winton, which had the best overall time in the contest. Weigle finished the course twenty-two minutes behind Chapin, while both Haywood and Brown took more than six hours to finish. In October, Ray Owen, driving an 800-pound Oldsmobile, was the only driver of a vehicle in the class of one thousand pounds and under to complete the five-hundred-mile New York to Boston Reliability Run without any penalized stop.[23]

The evidence from these events of 1902 that the Oldsmobile runabout must be ranked at or near the top among the runabouts of that day was further confirmed by the results in 1903. In March the flamboyant Oldsmobile dealer in Indianapolis, Carl Fisher, who would later develop the most famous of all the annual American racing events in that city, accepted a local newspaper's challenge of $1000 to the winner of a one-hundred-mile endurance race between an Oldsmobile and a competing Detroit runabout, apparently the heavier, somewhat more expensive Cadillac, though the trade journal report of the event did not specify the name of Fisher's opposing driver and car. Although he had no Oldsmobile runabout in stock, Fisher borrowed one from a customer and drove it to victory, over terribly muddy roads, in a little over five hours. The other runabout broke a connecting rod halfway through the race. Fisher returned the Oldsmobile to its owner and promptly wired the Olds Motor Works to ship him ten carloads of new cars immediately.[24]

In October of that year Ransom Olds himself took part in the New York-to-Pittsburgh Endurance Run, in which three of his Oldsmobiles were entered. Olds, however, was not entered in the event as a driver of one of his cars but as an observer in a Columbia car, which had to be abandoned on the second day of the run. Olds was forced to go by horse-drawn stage to the nearby railroad station, where he proceeded on by train. He was reported to be "very much incensed" at the choice of such a difficult route for this endurance test. He expressed the fear that by the time the press learned of the problems the automobiles were having—making it necessary in some instances for automobile manufacturers to revert to horse-drawn conveyances to go on their way—the impression the general public received would be similar to that expressed in the Binghamton *Republican,* which reported the early events of the run under the headline: "The Horse Still Stands Near the Head in Endurance Contest." Olds announced that he intended to withdraw his Oldsmobiles from the run at Binghamton if he reached that city in time. However, when he arrived there he was greeted by more encouraging news. One of the Oldsmobiles had been the first gasoline car to arrive at that stopping place, even though it had been forced to make an unscheduled detour off the road and over a hill on the way into town in order to bypass a Stearns automobile that was stuck and was blocking the road. Eventually, two of the Oldsmobiles made it through to Pittsburgh, the least expensive of any of the cars that accomplished the feat. One trade writer observed that "it certainly looks as though a purchaser gets his money's worth" with an Oldsmobile.[25]

The most demanding test an Oldsmobile had yet passed came in the summer of 1903, when a runabout was driven by Lester L. Whitman and Eugene I. Hammond from San Francisco to New York in seventy-seven days, only the third automobile to have made a transcontinental crossing. A few weeks earlier that summer, a Winton had been the first to accomplish this feat, and a Packard had made it a little later. Two years later two other runabouts, "Old Scout" and "Old Steady," crossed the continent in the other direction; assisted by Milford Weigle, Dwight B. Huss drove "Old Scout" across the country in forty-four days.[26]

Abroad, an Oldsmobile was the only American-made gasoline-powered car entered in the 1902 reliability trials sponsored by the Automobile Club of Great Britain and Ireland, and the following year two Oldsmobiles received the top awards in their class in the same event. On the continent the durability of the curved-dash runabout—as well as the superior character of European roads—was demonstrated in spectacular fashion when Maurice Fournier (brother of the great French racing car driver Henri Fournier) drove an Oldsmobile on a 3,125-mile tour of Europe in December 1904, taking only twenty days and winning a $20,000 bet his brother had made with a French sportsman who had not believed such a trip could be made in that short a time.[27]

Although the Oldsmobile runabout had perhaps its greatest success in long-distance endurance events, additional fame was brought to the Oldsmobile name by performances in shorter races and speed trials, which improved considerably on the second- and third-place showing of Chapin and Maxwell at the Grosse Pointe races in 1901. Between 1902 and 1904, Milford Weigle picked up three gold medals and twelve silver cups while driving an Oldsmobile in various dirt track events. In the spring of 1903 the young Oldsmobile engineer Horace T. Thomas drove the Oldsmobile *Pirate,* a specially built lightweight racing machine—not a standard runabout—to a new American mile record for cars under one thousand pounds; later that summer Dan Wurgis enjoyed considerable success driving the *Pirate* in races for cars in its weight class, although when he attempted to race bigger cars he found that the little Oldsmobile racer could not keep up the pace.[28]

The Oldsmobile's record in these and other tests of its durability and speed, together with its leadership in sales, was unquestionably a source of great satisfaction to Ransom Olds. It is little wonder, then, that the developer of this car found it hard to listen with any degree of patience to the critical comments of his fellow directors and stockholders. Talking with Henry Russel in 1903, Olds argued against any tinkering with a car that had proven to be a veritable gold mine, but Russel replied that "while as you say, there is no harm against making as much money as we can, we must sustain the reputation of the concern as well as make profits."[29]

It was this seeming lack of interest on Olds' part in adopting vigorous measures that would protect the reputation of the company and its product that finally led to an open breach between Olds and Fred Smith. According to Roy Chapin, Olds' attitude was "that it was time to correct a fault when the fault made itself evident on the road." This rather casual attitude toward the concept of quality control comes through in Duane Yarnell's 1949 biography as well: discussing the handful of cars that were produced before the appearance of the runabout, Yarnell says that when customers complained about their vehicle, "R. E. would gather his crew together and they would make a combined attack upon the defect until it was completely obliterated." Olds told Yarnell that he knew these early cars were defective when they were sold and that it was only the eagerness of his backers to have something to sell that made him decide to put these models into production. Olds admitted that he was concerned about the effect this might have on his reputation, but he had felt that he could protect himself by his readiness to deal with the owners' complaints when the defects showed up on the road.

He adopted the same wait-and-see attitude, however, toward the curved-dash Oldsmobile, whose production—by his own accounting—was due to his own initiative and not to any pressure from his backers. When a customer came in with a complaint about the runabout, which Olds freely admitted was a frequent occurrence, Olds was always available, he said, to discuss the problem and replace a defective part at no cost to the customer. The other stockholders, he recalled, complained that he "was giving too much away." He said that his response was: "Each satisfied customer is an advertisement for more business." On the other hand, when Eugene Hammond told Olds of some of the mechanical problems he had had with the Oldsmobile on his cross-country trip in 1903, Olds replied: "Well, we have to sell parts too."[30]

The Olds Motor Works acknowledged that problems sometimes did develop with its cars. Late in 1902, in response to a query from a reader of *Horseless Age,* the company stated that all Oldsmobiles would perform as well as those that had been so successful in endurance runs if the cars were kept in proper order. "The great trouble is that repair men throughout the country do not understand them as well as they might," a spokesman explained. "We expect to do something along this line in the near future to educate them more thoroughly as to the requirements of a gasoline motor." This may have been the origin of the Oldsmobile publication that set down a series of "don'ts," although these were directed more to the driver than the garage mechanic. "Don't imagine that your motor runs well on equal parts of water and gasoline. It's a mistake." "Don't do anything to your motor without a good reason or without knowing just what you are doing." These and the other elementary admonitions on the lengthy list suggest that ignorant drivers as well as inexperienced repairmen were regarded as the cause of a good many of the complaints received by Olds and his associates. Nevertheless, Arthur L. Eddy, an experienced motorist, wrote in 1902 that ninety per cent of the problems that developed with an automobile—and there was not an automobile made, he claimed, that was not without its problems—were the result of defective construction in the factory.[31]

It was precisely at this point that Fred Smith and Ransom

Olds differed the most. While he was willing to concede that they should continue to provide service to customers after the car was sold, Smith felt that Olds should put forth more effort to eliminate defects in the cars before they left the factory. Olds contended—and it was undoubtedly true—that the state of technological knowledge at that time made it inevitable that some parts that would have to be used in producing automobiles were not going to withstand wear as well as other parts of the vehicle. But Olds also failed to take advantage of some of the knowledge that was then available toward improving the quality of the car. Although he took preliminary steps in the direction of mass production of the automobile, it does not appear that Olds saw the need to insist on the kind of standardized, uniform, and precision-made parts that were later required to increase the speed and efficiency of the assembly operations and the quality of the assembled vehicle. Instead, considerable time in the Olds plant was taken during the assembly of each car to file and grind and otherwise adjust the various parts so that they would fit together, with the result that no two Oldsmobiles were exactly alike. Olds recognized this. When he delivered Henry Leland's runabout, for example, he had difficulty getting the engine started when he tried to show Leland how to operate the car. Olds casually passed off the problem by remarking that each Oldsmobile was an individual. Leland, on the other hand, was an extremely meticulous man who insisted on precision work of the highest quality. He had purchased the runabout in order to get a better idea of the engine which he had contracted to produce for Olds. After he and his staff had torn down the Oldsmobile's engine and studied it, they proceeded to eliminate the individuality of these engines by machining the engine parts they manufactured to such a degree of uniformity that when the engines were assembled they all performed in a similar fashion. Because of the interchangeable character of these parts, furthermore, Leland's workers were able to turn out the engines so rapidly that Ransom Olds remarked, with some astonishment, that Leland "must have a motor incubator" in his shop.[32]

By the summer of 1902, Fred Smith was expressing his

dissatisfaction with Olds' manufacturing methods. He kept urging the general manager to establish an experimental shop where changes and improvements in the automobile could be planned and carried out. Rather than waiting for public complaints to force the company to change, as they had been doing up to that time, Smith declared that Olds should show some initiative and keep ahead of the public by constantly seeking new ways to improve the runabout.

When Olds showed no great inclination to adopt Smith's suggestions, Smith threatened to set up an experimental shop under his own supervision in the Detroit plant. Even the work that Olds was doing in Lansing on the runabout, which included bringing in Wallace Olds to tinker with the engine, did not satisfy Smith, who felt that radical changes were needed. "The old model is too weak and flimsy and none of our agents want it," he fumed. "I can't see any point in puddling away with that old batch of stuff—and I tell you quite frankly, that you are laying yourself open to future criticism in having your brother waste time and money on what you know is an insufficient engine." If Olds would not go ahead on the development of an improved engine, Smith said, he would take on the job himself. "I haven't any great doubt of being able to push it through and get something the trade really wants." Ransom Olds could hardly have taken these immodest, untactful remarks as anything other than direct criticism of the way in which he was managing the company, which is no doubt what Smith intended them to be. And it must have been difficult for Olds not to take offense at such comments from a man six years younger than he and with only four years' experience with the problems of building and manufacturing automobiles, in contrast with Olds' nearly two decades of work in the field.[33]

Finally, at the end of April 1903, Smith did in fact establish an experimental engineering operation in the Detroit plant under his own direction—without consulting Olds. Three months later Smith filed an application for a patent on what was presumably one of the first fruits of the experimental work he had undertaken. The patent, which was issued to Smith in November 1903, was on an improved vehicle spring designed for use in heavier cars, another indication of Smith's growing interest in this kind of automobile. Earlier springs, such as those Olds had patented and used in the runabout, were satisfactory, Smith said, only "for a certain class of motor-vehicles in which the weight is not excessive."[34]

When Ransom Olds learned—"by a round about way"—of Smith's action in establishing an experimental shop without his authorization, his reaction was prompt and explosive. "Now if this is your policy to do business underhanded and unbeknown to me, as you have several other things," he informed Smith, "I do not care to be associated with you. I am Vice-President and Manager of this company and such things should not be taken up without my consent or the consent of the board. I have had all I want of this treatment." The remarks in this letter reveal a rare expression of anger from the usually mild-mannered Olds. Olds was no milquetoast: although he is remembered by those who knew him outside the business world as a kindly, good-natured man who never cursed, those who had business dealings with Olds recall that he could be tough when he wanted to be. After years of association with mechanics he had learned all the salty expressions in the workingman's vocabulary, and he did not hesitate to use them if the occasion warranted. One suspects that Olds regarded Fred Smith's actions in the spring of 1903 as such an occasion and that he spoke out more forcefully and colorfully in discussing the subject with his aides in Lansing and in face-to-face confrontations with Smith than in the more carefully chosen language of his letter to his fellow officer.[35]

After this letter of May 1, 1903, the relationship between Olds and Fred Smith—though undoubtedly strained—was of a correct, courteous nature for the remainder of the year; but Olds' days with the company were now numbered. At a board meeting on December 7, 1903, a motion by Olds was approved to turn over to Charles B. Wilson the general supervision of production in the Lansing and Detroit plants, while Olds was reassigned to work "exclusively" with the engineering and experimental divisions. However, this was but the prelude to the final dramatic move at the board meeting late on the afternoon of January 11, 1904: a motion introduced by James H. Seager and seconded by Eugene Cooley to name Fred Smith to the positions of vice president and general manager previously held by Olds was unanimously approved. The action followed the annual stockholders meeting, at which Olds had been re-elected to the board of directors, along with Samuel, Fred, and Angus Smith, James H. Seager, Henry Russel, and Eugene Cooley. After the board meeting Olds was still a director, but he held no other office in the company. In a letter to Fred Smith at the end of January, Olds referred to an agreement the two had made earlier whereby Olds would step down as general manager while Smith in turn would help Olds sell some of his stock. However, in a September 1904 letter to a former stockholder, Olds indicated that he had fought to retain his managerial position; but when the selection of officers came up at the January board meeting, "I was voted down," and Smith "was elected in my place."[36]

"It was a hard thing for me," Olds remarked, "when I had been manager since 1885 ... working day and night to develop the business to a wonderful success." It appears that he saw the move coming, however, and made some preparations to soften the blow. In October 1902, Samuel Smith had stepped down as president of the Olds Motor Works, to be succeeded by Henry Russel. Russel's choice was perhaps the first sign that Olds was on his way out, since the latter had served as president earlier, and with the reduction in Samuel Smith's earlier large stockholdings he had come to own more stock in the company than anyone else. However, during 1902, Olds had sold off one thousand shares, bringing his total down to 6,500 by the end of the year. In January 1903 he was seeking to sell some more of his stock to the New York Oldsmobile distributor Ray Owen. Later in the year he was successful in disposing of a considerable amount of stock to Henry Russel. By the time he was removed from his executive positions in January 1904, Olds claimed to have sold over 3,000 shares of stock at $30 a share during the preceding two years.[37]

Perhaps Olds had to sell some of this stock to raise money for his new home and to finance other personal projects; but such actions, which further weakened his ability to influence decisions on which the stockholders were consulted, would hardly seem consistent with the ambitions of a man who had any thought of staying with the company in a position of major importance. It seems likely, therefore, that long before his defeat in the board meeting of January 1904, Olds, finding it impossible to work with Fred Smith, was beginning to ease himself out of the firm.

In June and July of 1903, Olds took part in a series of meetings whose object was to separate the Olds Gasoline Engine Works from the Olds Motor Works. An arrangement was agreed upon whereby the independent engine works would refrain from manufacturing automobiles, while the Olds Motor Works in turn would not manufacture engines, other than those required to power its vehicles. Olds, Eugene Cooley, and Frank Robson had been serving as the directors of the engine works, whose corporate existence had been officially retained since 1899, even though it was entirely controlled by the parent Olds Motor Works. Now the board of the engine works was expanded to include Samuel and Fred Smith, Henry Russel, and James B. Seager, who—along with other members of his family—now became the major stockholder in the company. Once the separation had been accomplished, on July 1, Olds resigned from the board and from the position of president that he had held since his father had stepped down from that office. Henry Russel replaced Olds as president, Angus Smith took his place as director, and Fred Smith replaced Frank Robson, who had been serving as secretary-treasurer and who also resigned at this time.

On July 14, Olds was present at the meeting of the board of the Olds Motor Works which revised the company's articles of association to bring them into line with the action involving the engine works and also to increase the number of shares of stock in circulation from fifty thousand to two hundred thousand. However, the document that incorprated these changes and was filed with the secretary of state on August 7, bore only the signatures of Henry Russel, James

H. Seager, and Samuel Smith and his two sons; the signature
of the company's general manager was conspicuously absent.
As the document noted, the five signatories together controlled over two-thirds of the capital stock. Their concerted
action at this time made it evident that Ransom Olds' presence was no longer regarded as necessary in the determina-
tion of company policy.[38]

A further indication of the changing relationship between
Olds and his associates in the company may perhaps be seen
in the fact that the patent which Olds had applied for in 1901
on the runabout's cooling system was issued by the patent
office on December 1, 1903 not to Olds but to the Olds Motor
Works. All previous patents that Olds had applied for had
been issued to him, as the inventor, even though all of
them—with the possible exception of the elevator gate, of
which Olds and George E. DeVore were co-inventors—were
for inventions that were used on products that Olds' company manufactured. The patent application files do not indicate at what time the patent office was directed to assign the
cooler patent to the Olds Motor Works instead of Ransom
Olds; but the action was obviously taken some time before
December 1903, when Olds was still vice president and general manager. It may be that the other officers, suspecting
that Olds might not want to stay with the company much
longer, had insisted that the ownership rights to the cooler
patent and to four other patents that Olds had applied for in
1901 and 1902—and on which final action was also still
pending—be assigned to the company. This would prevent
Olds, if he did leave the company, from using these devices
on any other automobiles that he might build in the future.[39]

Following the fateful board meeting of January 1904, it
was almost inevitable that Olds would dispose of the remainder of his stock, since, as he later declared, for him to
have retained a financial interest in the company would
amount to an admission that he felt the firm would prosper
under its new management. By the summer of 1904, when
Olds resigned from the board of directors, thereby cutting all
remaining ties with the company, he had sold the remainder
of the stock he still held at the beginning of the year. He was

forced to take far less than the thirty dollars a share he allegedly received for the stock he sold in 1902 and 1903. Apparently the best he was able to get in 1904 was ten dollars a share. Olds blamed Fred Smith for this, because the latter had promised to assist him in disposing of his stock at a good price. Smith had failed to live up to that promise, Olds charged, and indeed Smith may have driven the price down by advising brokers that he considered ten dollars—par value—a reasonable sum to pay for the stock. However, Olds failed to recognize that he himself was partially responsible for depressing the price of the stock by dumping all of his shares, a huge block of the existing shares in the company, on the market at one time. More important, he seems to have totally ignored the fact that the four-for-one split in the number of shares that had been voted in 1903 was bound to reduce the market value of the new shares, even with the remarkable upward surge in company earnings. Thus, ten dollars was indeed, as Fred Smith claimed, a reasonable price to get in 1904, representing as it did a rate of return equal to forty dollars on the stock held before the split in July 1903. Later, in 1907, Eugene Cooley could find no takers when he tried to sell his stock for five dollars a share, half of what Olds received in 1904.[40]

* * * * *

Alongside his development of the curved-dash Oldsmobile, Ransom Olds' departure from the Olds Motor Works has been the most frequently mentioned incident in his life and the one which many have felt provides the key to an understanding of his personality. At the time of Olds' death in 1950, a *Detroit Free Press* editorial expressed what had long since come to be—and has remained—the standard interpretation of Olds. The Motor City editor wrote that Ransom Olds was "a kindly Christian man" who would not fight his stockholders when they opposed his low-priced car. In contrast—and the contrast has been drawn on numerous occasions—Henry Ford, when faced with a similar problem in 1905–06, stood up to his dissident stockholders and beat them, thereby gaining the complete control of the company that bore his name. Therefore, it is reasoned, Ransom Olds, who let the control of his company slip through his hands, was a weaker man than Ford, which is why Ford ended up as the most famous automaker in history and Olds ended up among the also-rans.[41]

Aside from the fact that the reasons behind the conflict between Olds and the Smiths were much more complex than those set forth by the *Free Press,* as well as others who have advanced the same interpretation, this entire argument is essentially faulty. Since 1899 the Smiths had had the power to take over complete control of the Olds Motor Works at any time they chose to use it. From the standpoint of any effort he might have made to resist such a move, Olds' position was untenable. He could not have won a stockholders' fight even if he had sought to arrange some kind of compromise on the issues over which he and Fred Smith disagreed; it appears that by at least 1903 Fred Smith was determined to take over the management of the company, and with the number of shares of stock that Smith and his supporters controlled, there was nothing that Olds could have done to prevent Smith from getting his way. The best Olds could have hoped for under the circumstances would have been to stay on as a figurehead director, a kind of living symbol of the Oldsmobile—with no real power. Henry Ford, on the other hand, had substantial support from other stockholders in the Ford Motor Company. That enabled him to defeat his opposition in 1905–06, which was centered around Alexander Malcomson, who lacked the widespread support Fred Smith had been able to call upon to defeat Olds. Furthermore, Ford had gone down to defeat—and in a rather meek fashion at that—in the earlier Detroit Automobile and Henry Ford companies, before finally gaining complete managerial control on his third try with the Ford Motor Company. It took Ransom Olds only one such experience for him to come back with a new company, with which he quickly demonstrated his true mettle to Fred Smith and to the world.

The split between Ransom Olds and the Smiths was a permanent one. Within the space of only five years of close association, they had enjoyed a measure of success beyond that of anyone else in the new auto industry; but in 1904 they went their separate ways. Under Fred Smith's management the Olds Motor Works enjoyed two more outstanding years of sales, and a *Detroit Free Press* story in the spring of 1905 hailed Smith as one of Detroit's "Captains of Industry," crediting him specifically with having "introduced a number of time- and labor-saving devices in the [Olds] plants which are administered in a thoroughly modern and up-to-date manner." But Smith's shift from the production of low-priced, low-powered vehicles to high-priced, high-powered ones apparently came too fast for the public to adjust to Oldsmobile's new image, and a sharp decline in sales left the company a mere shadow of its former self. By late 1908 the Smiths gladly agreed to William C. Durant's offer that brought the firm into the General Motors organization. By the fall of 1909 the Smiths ceased to have any connection with the management of the Olds company, and their further involvement with the auto industry, the prospects of which had seemed so bright only a half-decade earlier, was for all practical purposes at an end.[42]

Ransom Olds continued in the auto industry in a direct management capacity for a quarter of a century after the departure of Fred Smith from the Olds Motor Works. One can only wonder whether his career, as well as Fred Smith's, would not have been better served if the two had found ways of continuing to work together in the same organization. But it was not to be. Instead, bitter feelings remained that time did not wipe away. In 1928, Fred Smith wrote his memoirs, *Motoring Down a Quarter of a Century,* which originally appeared in the magazine *Detroit Saturday Night* and were then published in booklet form with funds supplied by Smith's former protégé Roy Chapin. In this recollection, devoted almost entirely to his experiences with the Olds Motor Works, Smith does not mention the name of R. E. Olds once.[43] And Olds clearly did not like to make any reference to Fred Smith in later years either, although his feelings toward Samuel Smith seem to have been of a friendlier nature. But eventually Olds could see no point in keeping alive an ancient grudge. Thus, when he received a communication from Fred Smith sometime during this later period—apparently a rather virulent attack by Smith on his one-time business associate, though the Olds family does not seem to wish to discuss its contents—Olds laid it aside and refused to make any response. For him, the years with the Olds Motor Works were a part of his past. He could look back with great pride on what he had accomplished, but it was the past.[44]

CHAPTER EIGHT

Olds Re-enters the Auto Industry

AT THE TIME of Ransom Olds' death in 1950, Dr. Julius Fischbach, pastor of Olds' church in Lansing, described the late businessman as one "who forever faced forward."[1] It was, on the whole, an apt characterization, as Olds had repeatedly demonstrated: he had moved steadily ahead from steam engines to gasoline engines to lightweight automobiles, in each case enthusiastically embracing the new course of his career with few backward glances at what he was leaving behind. This was also the case when he left the Olds Motor Works in 1904. Of course, he continued to express some lingering bitterness at what had happened; that was only to be expected under the circumstances. But the plans he was developing for the future seemed of greater moment to him than his regrets about the past.

With the funds he had obtained through the sale of his Olds Motor Works stock and the generous dividends that stock had earned during the four or five years he had held it, Olds was able to devote his time in the winter of 1904 to the fulfillment of his desires to diversify his business interests. He had hinted at these desires a decade earlier with his co-invention of an elevator gate and his later efforts to manufacture pumps. Already by the spring of 1904 he was going far afield from his earlier engine and automotive interests. He acquired the Bancroft Peat Fuel & Cement Company; as it turned out, this was one of his few ventures that was not successful, and he eventually abandoned it in 1910. Through the trade of some of his stock he gained the controlling interest in a gold mine, which likewise seems to have been of only

241

passing significance in terms of the long-range development of his business holdings. Of greater importance in this latter regard was his increasing emphasis on the acquisition of real estate and its management and development; this would ultimately come to absorb most of Olds' investment capital. This particular interest had been revealed at least as early as 1899, when Olds, burdened as he must have been with the task of managing the shift of many of his manufacturing operations from Lansing to Detroit, still found time to go forward with the entirely unrelated job of constructing a two-story brick building on a lot he owned in downtown Lansing. It may have been in 1904 that Olds also acquired an apartment building in Chicago that would later be important in the development of his real estate holdings, since it was at the time of Olds' break with Oldsmobile that a Chicago broker offered to arrange an exchange of real estate for some of his automobile stock. In any event, it was in 1904 that Olds became the owner of Lansing's Hollister Building. From his office in this downtown structure, still one of the city's most familiar though no longer one of its more prestigious business addresses, Olds began to busy himself with the details of his new interests, even going so far as to decide on the kind of toilet paper that might be most suitable for the tenants of his office building. Soon, however, he gladly turned over to his older brother Emory, who now began to serve as Ransom's personal and confidential secretary, the task of looking after these property management details so that he might devote himself to his revived automobile interests.[2]

Following the directors' meeting on January 11, which had stripped Olds of his managerial offices in the Olds Motor Works, public announcements by both the company and its former general manager depicted the change as one that he had desired in order to allow himself more time to devote to other activities and to travel. The events of the next few days and weeks seemed to confirm the report published by *Horseless Age* on January 13 that the automotive pioneer was retiring completely from the industry of which he had been a principal founder. At the New York auto show some ten days later, Olds was not present; thus he attended neither the banquet hosted by the Olds Motor Works for its dealers, an event that was described as "a big family reunion, and a most enjoyable evening," nor the meeting of the executive committee of the National Association of Automobile Manufacturers, where he was the only committee member to be absent. Olds was reportedly elected third vice president of the association at this time; but not only was this report quickly revealed as erroneous, but by March, Olds had been replaced on the NAAM's executive committee by Roy Chapin. All of this was consistent with Olds' own efforts during this period to create the impression that he had no further intention of getting back into the automobile industry; but to a few close associates his real intentions were soon to be revealed.

Olds' experiences in the auto industry, far from souring him on it, had convinced him more than ever of the spectacular prospects for growth the industry offered. In answer to a question concerning the future of the industry, Olds informed one of his brokers in January 1904: "There is no end of it." Characteristically, Olds equated the future success of the automobile with the declining use of the horse. He predicted that within at most a decade "the horse will not be allowed on the streets in the larger cities. Did you ever stop to think what that means?" Olds asked. To him it meant that automobiles would have to take the place of horsedrawn vehicles; and he estimated that Michigan carriage and wagon manufacturers alone produced over 200,000 such vehicles a year. Actually, the figure was considerably higher, since the production of the state's largest firms had totaled 371,769 horsedrawn vehicles in 1898, and all indications show that production rose in the early years of the twentieth century. Thus, at the beginning of 1904, when annual United States automobile production was only about twenty thousand cars, Olds was boldly projecting production figures over ten times as great within the space of ten years in order to replace the market for horsedrawn conveyances.* "I have made a careful

---

*Olds' assumption—a common one among his contemporaries—that users of horsedrawn vehicles would be the major purchasers of automobiles was not entirely correct. For one thing, the horse was not banned from city streets, as Olds had predicted, and it proved much harder to displace than he had anticipated. Many

study of the business for a great many years," Olds went on, "and predict that the automobile business will be one of the greatest industries that the country has ever seen. Every successful Company will see its business multiplied many times in order to keep up with the demand."

It is true that this optimistic appraisal in January 1904 partly reflected Olds' desire to convince his broker that his Olds Motor Works stock was a bargain at the price Olds was asking for it. Six months later, however, he expressed the same confidence in the future of the industry to a newspaper acquaintance in New York. "If I was anxious to pick up a few barrels of money I do not know of anything I would attack quicker than the automobile business," Olds declared. Although in that particular letter Olds disclaimed any personal interest in getting back into this business, his plans for such a re-entry were actually almost complete at the time he was writing the letter.[3]

It would have been difficult for Olds not to want to get back to manufacturing motor vehicles at this time: the pioneer car maker could not help but witness the boom in the industry from his unaccustomed position on the sidelines. In Lansing alone, not only was the Olds Motor Works forging ahead to new production records, but others with whom Olds had also been associated in the past were entering the field with their own companies. In 1903, Frank G. Clark, Olds' partner in the construction of his original gasoline vehicle in 1896, joined with Arthur C. Stebbins, at one time secretary of the Olds Motor Vehicle Company, and Harris E. Thomas, Olds' frequent legal advisor, to form a company that would produce a one-cylinder runabout. Clark had developed the vehicle, and it would be called, of course, the Clarkmobile. That same year, Stebbins' brother Bliss joined

---

persons who were using horses continued to prefer them to the horseless vehicle well into the second and even third decades of the century. Far more customers for the automobile seem to have come from among the much larger group who had never owned a horse but who now saw in the motor vehicle a more convenient, practical, carefree, and perhaps less expensive form of transportation than the horse and buggy. Eventually, auto manufacturers recognized this and rather than harping on the automobile's superiority to the horse simply concentrated on selling the automobile on its own merits.

with J. Edward Roe, the banker, James P. Edmonds, one-time secretary of the Olds Gasoline Engine Works, Fred M. Seibly, a former stockholder in the Olds Motor Vehicle Company, and Madison F. Bates, former Olds employee and co-inventor of the Olds gasoline engine, to form the Bates Automobile Company. Departing from the trend that Olds had helped to start with his inexpensive Oldsmobile, it would produce the Bates touring car, bearing a price tag of $2,000. Neither the Clarkmobile nor the Bates—nor several other attempts during the same period to establish new Lansing automobile plants—proved successful. But Ransom Olds could not be sure of that in 1904. Instead, he could only see his long years of experience being wasted while others, with less experience, were seeking to cash in on the rapidly rising tide of the public's demand for automobiles.[4]

It was only natural, moreover, that others, seeing the same trend in automobile sales, would seek to enlist the services of a man of Olds' reputation to head up a new automobile company. Olds told Duane Yarnell that he was approached by a Detroit firm, Holmes and Brother, with their offer to back him in forming a company that could get into production quickly: they would be able to take over Detroit's Diamond Match factory and use it as their manufacturing facility. Olds (who may have been confusing this offer with the one made to him in 1898 by Detroiters John Holmes and John Nicol) said he turned down the proposal in part because it would be financed by a public sale of bonds, a method he objected to because of the large number of investors it would bring in, each one of whom would be a potential critic of his manufacturing policies. In addition, he said he rejected the offer because Holmes and Brother would retain a controlling share of the common stock, and Olds was not about to make the same mistake that he had made in 1899, when he gave up stock control of the Olds Motor Works in order to obtain Samuel Smith's financial backing.[5]

On August 4, 1904, Olds reported to Ray Owen that he had also received a proposal from individuals representing a New York syndicate. According to his later recollections, this group claimed to have behind it some very substantial finan-

cial resources, including those of "friends in the Equitable
Life Insurance Company." Olds no doubt was referring to the
Equitable Life *Assurance* Society, one of the "Big Three"
insurance firms of that day. Officials of the Equitable were
concerned about the decline in the firm's position around
1903–04, which some of them felt would be strengthened if
more attention were given to investments in stocks. Railroad
stocks appear to have been what they mainly had in mind,
but taking a flier on an automobile company might well have
appealed to these New York financiers. This may have been
especially tempting since some of J. P. Morgan's partners,
whose interests were closely allied to those of the Equitable
officials, had just helped to finance a new automobile company organized by Olds' former associates Jonathan Maxwell and Benjamin Briscoe. However, Olds rejected the New
Yorkers' bid for his support, citing his desire to remain retired from the auto industry. The real reason may have been
his reluctance to become involved with an eastern group
after the unhappy results of his earlier involvement with
another eastern group in 1898–99. The New Yorkers in 1904
offered Olds, he informed Ray Owen, about double what he
would receive in the way of initial financial rewards from the
Lansing-based group with which he did become associated.
However, he felt that he would profit more from the latter
association in the long run because, it seems clear, he knew
these people and was confident he could maintain control of a
company with this kind of backing; the easterners were unknown to him and represented financial interests he might
not have been able to control.

Thus, for the second time a New York group lost a chance
to establish an Olds automobile company in that area. By
1904, with the success of a powerful line-up of Michigan-
made cars, such as Oldsmobile, Cadillac, Ford, Packard,
Northern, plus a number of promising new entries like
Buick, it was probably too late to reverse the trend that had
already made Michigan the leading center of automotive
production. Even so, the news that the best-known Michigan
automotive figure had been persuaded to move East could
not but have had a salutary effect on the morale and prestige

of the eastern segment of the auto industry as it fought to survive against the competition of the Michigan firms.[6]

In addition to the offers Olds received to head up new companies, there were reports in 1904 that he also received "several good offers from big concerns," apparently automobile companies that were already in operation. In later years, when the position of a few large manufacturers had become so strong that it was increasingly difficult for a new company to gain a foothold in the automotive marketplace, the only avenue open to an automotive executive who wanted to continue in the industry once he had left one automotive company was to try to obtain a position with another of the established firms. William S. Knudsen did this in the twenties when he moved from the Ford Motor Company to General Motors, and his son, Semon E. Knudsen, did it a half century later when he moved in quick succession from top positions in General Motors to Ford to White Motors. In 1904, however, although someone with Ransom Olds' reputation and experience would have been viewed by the backers of a number of struggling automobile companies as just the man they needed to transform their firm into a profit-making venture, the opportunities that were still present to make it big with a new company of one's own creation seemed far more attractive to a man like Olds. And this was the direction in which he chose to go when he returned to the industry.[7]

The plans for what would become the Reo Motor Car Company had begun to take shape early in February 1904, when Olds and his family made their annual trip to southern California to visit Pliny and Sarah Olds. When he left Lansing late in January, Olds provided his brokers with his itinerary so that they might reach him if they found any buyers for his Olds Motor Works stock. On February 6 and 7, Olds said, he could be reached at Reuben Shettler's office in Los Angeles. It was undoubtedly at that time that Olds and Shettler worked out the preliminary details of what Shettler later recalled was "an understanding" between the two men "that as soon as Olds could dispose of his Olds Motor Stock, we would organize a new Automobile Company in the Spring, providing I would undertake the responsibility of financing it." Aside from Olds, himself, and his "confidential clerk," Shettler declared, no one else knew of this proposition.

Despite the incompleteness of available records, the evidence there is confirms the essential accuracy of Shettler's 1936 recollections of what took place in 1904. That Shettler was the central figure in the discussions and negotiations that led to the organization of Reo was known and reported at the time. What is not clear, however, is who originated the idea to establish the new company. Whether it was Ransom Olds who thought of this as a way of getting back into the auto industry and then sought Shettler's help in carrying out the details; whether the suggestion first came from Shettler; or whether the concept was developed jointly by the two men in the course of their discussions is not known. What is certain, however, is that Olds was in on the planning from the outset and that his later protestations to the contrary were only his attempt to make it appear that he was coming back into the industry only at the insistence of friends and acquaintances, who—unknown to him—had gone ahead and organized a company and, in order to secure his consent to head the firm, had made him an offer he could not afford to turn down.[8]

By March, after Olds had returned from California, the plans for the new business were sufficiently well advanced for Olds to be able to outline them in a letter to Horace Thomas, the former engineer with the Olds Motor Works who had left that company some months earlier to take a position with the Electric Vehicle Company in Hartford, Connecticut. Olds had a high regard for Thomas' abilities and wanted to line him up for a top job in his new company. Since that company did not yet exist and might not for several months, Olds asked Thomas in May if he would be interested in a temporary job as superintendent of Olds' peat company. Thomas, who was not happy with his $100-a-month job with the eastern firm and correctly foresaw that its prospects were not promising, accepted Olds' offer, appar-

Courtesy of University of Michigan Libraries

An alert Reuben Shettler pictured at the time of Reo's organization in 1904

ently with the understanding that he would receive the position of chief engineer in Olds' automotive organization when it took shape later that year.[9]

Meanwhile, Reuben Shettler had been helping Olds dispose of his Olds Motor Works stock. It was Shettler who arranged the exchange of some of this stock for a controlling interest in a gold mine. By June the end of this phase of the operation was in sight; Olds wished to have this completed before he moved ahead with the new company. At the same time, Shettler had been clearing his own desk in preparation for the new venture. In the spring he sold his California Oldsmobile agency.

In June, Reuben Shettler came east to arrange the financial backing for Olds' second automobile manufacturing effort. After conferring with Olds, Shettler contacted Edward

F. Peer, a young Lansing businessman who had started out in the early 1890s first as a clerk and then a bookkeeper for Shettler. Later he had gone on to become the local manager of the Huber Manufacturing Company, which Shettler had represented, a position Peer still held in 1904. He now became the third member, with Olds and Shettler, of the new organization's hierarchy, and would become secretary-treasurer when the company was formed.[10]

From Shettler's discussions with Peer came a definite proposition to be presented to Olds for his consideration early in July. The plan, which Shettler subsequently explained to prospective investors, must have been eminently satisfactory to Olds. As Benjamin F. Davis, chief executive officer of Lansing's City National Bank, outlined the matter in a note to Eugene Cooley on August 5, shortly after Shettler had left Davis' office, the company would be capitalized at a million dollars, divided equally into preferred and common shares. Of the $500,000 in common stock, Olds would receive $260,000 or 52 per cent of the voting stock in the company. In return for this stock Olds was to pay no money. Instead, the company would get Olds' "genius," that is, the use of his name, reputation, and years of experience as a developer and manufacturer of automobiles. It would also get the rights to Olds' patents and some of his Lansing real estate to be used as a site for the company's factory. In the incorporation papers that were filed on August 16, a valuation of $100,000 was placed on two engine patents that Olds held, $5,000 on two of his automobile designs, and $25,000 on his real estate, for a total of $130,000, half the par value of the stock that he received in return. It is not clear which of Olds' patents this document refers to, or whether Olds actually retained any rights to the patents issued him during the years he was with the Olds Motor Works. Since he applied for patents on new mechanical improvements shortly after the new company was formed, it is possible that the incorporation papers referred in part at least to ideas that Olds had and regarded as patentable, and not to patents already issued to him.

After Olds' share of the common stock, the remaining

$240,000 worth was to be sold—again at half its par value—thus raising a nucleus of $120,000 in cash with which to launch the venture. The half million in preferred stock, Shettler informed Davis, was to be held off the market until after the organization of the company, when it would be sold to raise additional funds as they were required.[11]

Thus, while he would get the money he needed to resume the manufacturing of automobiles, Olds was making sure that he did not repeat his mistake of 1899, when he had traded away control of the Olds Motor Works in order to secure the necessary funding for that company. That Olds was consciously taking this lesson to heart is made clear in the letter that he wrote to Ray Owen on August 4, in which he invited the New York Oldsmobile dealer to buy some of the new stock. Olds emphasized that the plan was "to give me controlling interest in the Company...had I never allowed the controlling interest of the Olds Motor Works to get away from me, I know that the Company's matters would be going up the ladder instead of tumbling down the other side." This remark, incidentally, was premature in its gloomy prognosis of how Olds' former company was faring without his steady hand at the tiller.[12]

By the second week in August, Shettler had completed his work; Olds was called back from northern Michigan, where he had been vacationing, to receive the final terms of the agreement, as set forth in a document dated August 9. "As I stepped off the train [in Lansing] I was met by an old friend who handed me a very interesting looking paper," Olds told the business writer O. D. Foster some twenty years later. "Reading it I found that a group of my friends had organized a half-million dollar company of which I was to be the head, and within three hours had raised the money to finance it. Of this I was to have a controlling interest, or $260,000. To say that I was astounded would be putting it mildly." Two decades later the story was slightly altered in the version that Olds narrated to Duane Yarnell. Two friends, probably Shettler and Peer—not just one friend, as in the earlier account—met him at the station, and it was not until the three were "comfortably seated" at Olds' home that the pro-

posal was presented to Olds, informing him that the eleven
men whose signatures accompanied the document were offering him the controlling interest in the company, "provided
he accepts and takes over the management of the company."
Olds admitted to Yarnell that he had known before he went
north that an effort was being made to form the company but
that it was only upon his return that he became aware of all
the details. Yarnell wrote: "Never in his wildest imagination
had he dreamed that he would receive such backing as this."
Olds' response was to accept the offer, for he realized, as he
told Yarnell, that he had been deluding himself in believing
that he was ready for retirement: he was only forty years old.
As he had told Foster, "I was still young enough to enjoy the
harness."[13]

Perhaps Olds eventually persuaded himself and others
that this is how he came to be involved with Reo. However,
like the story of how he learned by chance of a more efficient
way to start his gasoline engine through an unsolicited letter
from the electrician at Sing Sing prison, or how the disastrous fire of March 1901 miraculously directed Olds on the
path to automotive success, this version of the Reo Motor Car
Company's birth portrays Olds as an individual who owed
his rise in the business world to a very great extent to for-
tuitous circumstances. Dramatic as these stories are, and
flattering as it may have been to Olds' ego to appear so
highly esteemed by the public that investors came pleading
with him to head up their company, the real facts are certainly not undramatic or unflattering to Olds. Whether it
was originally due to his modesty or a certain lack of self-
respect reinforced by the forgetfulness of old age, Olds
seemed strangely willing to deny himself the credit for having exercised good judgment and for having taken the initiative in making the right decisions; these qualities advanced
his career earlier, and they moved him back into a major
position in the industry in 1904, only months after he had
been dumped from his earlier top executive post. It is true
that news accounts published at the time of Reo's formation
presented much the same story of Olds' having to be persuaded to join the new firm. But Olds' correspondence at that

time indicates beyond a doubt that whatever his reaction may have been when he came back from northern Michigan, surprise could hardly have described his feelings about a proposal which he had helped formulate months before and whose subsequent development he had followed with close attention. Interestingly enough, a biographical sketch of Olds that appeared in the mid-twenties, which he certainly approved before publication, simply states that Olds "organized the Reo Motor Car Company."[14]

* * * * *

The new company was incorporated on August 16, 1904, and as news of the venture first became generally known, it was obvious to all that the incorporators were banking on Ransom Olds and his "genius" to establish the company's credentials as a major new entry into the fierce competition for automobile sales. The name of the new firm was the R. E. Olds Company. And at their meeting on August 16, the stockholders chose R. E. Olds to be president and general manager, a choice that was to be expected since Olds cast fifty-two per cent of the votes. Little wonder, therefore, that the press reports tended to be variations on the theme expressed in *Automobile*'s headline: "R. E. Olds Starts Again." *Horseless Age* reported that Olds, "of Oldsmobile fame," had formed the R. E. Olds Company, and that a factory, "capable of accommodating 900 to 1,000 men," would be built, with cars "of Mr. Olds' latest design" to be ready by the early part of 1905. "Lucky Lansing," the *Detroit Free Press* exclaimed, for having as one of its residents a man so well known in the automobile industry that his "connection with the new enterprise will give it immense prestige."[15]

Olds' name stood out all the more prominently in the new company because the other stockholders were relatively unknown in the automobile industry. Reuben Shettler, who owned the largest amount of stock after Olds and was elected vice president of the firm, had been associated with the Olds Motor Works, of course, both as a stockholder and as an agent for the Oldsmobile. Lawrence Price and Edgar S. Porter, who each held five hundred shares in the R. E. Olds Company, had been among the group of Lansing businessmen who formed the Auto Body Company three years earlier. But it would have taken a close observer of the auto industry to recognize the connection Shettler, Price, and Porter had had with that industry. Although the list did not include the socially prominent and influential names that were among the investors in the Olds Motor Works, the stockholders in the R. E. Olds Company were all men of importance in Lansing, where—with the exception of Shettler—they all resided.

Shettler, in particular, had been successful in providing the new company with solid financial backing by securing investments from men who were connected with Lansing's banks. Benjamin F. Davis of the City National Bank had been persuaded by Shettler's sales talk of August 5 to take two thousand shares of common stock; J. Edward Roe, who had been cashier of the American State Savings Bank since its founding in 1892, and William H. Porter, brother of Edgar Porter and an officer in the People's State Savings Bank, each took a thousand shares. Originally a lumberman, Porter had established the Lansing Spoke Company; because of Porter's new connection with the auto industry, this company began to produce wheels for automobiles. The mayor of Lansing, Hugh Lyons, was another businessman whose career took a new turn as a result of his acquisition of five hundred shares in the new Olds company during the summer of 1904. Hugh Lyons & Company, which had been making showcases, soon began manufacturing bodies for Olds' new car. Elgin Mifflin, another officer in the Lyons firm, also became a charter stockholder in the R. E. Olds Company. Still another major investor was the Lansing hotel proprietor Charles P. Downey, with three thousand shares; Edgar Porter, Lawrence Price, J. Edward Roe, and he had helped make possible the land offer that brought Ransom Olds back to Lansing in 1901.[16]

The expectation of these Lansing businessmen that Olds would enjoy the same success with this new automobile company that he had with the Olds Motor Works, thereby further strengthening the economy of their community, caused them to invest in the R. E. Olds Company. In remarks to reporters Olds himself also emphasized the hometown ties, declaring that he hoped this new enterprise would make Lansing even more important in the auto industry than it had already become through the efforts of the existing companies. There was still room, he said, for more automobile manufacturers; the more there were the better it would be for the continued growth and development of the young industry. Olds also sought to divorce himself from his previous association with the Oldsmobile, declaring that he would be producing cars of a new design, not related to those with which his name had been previously attached. His new venture, he maintained, was in no way the result of any feeling of hostility toward the Olds Motor Works; but at the same time he served notice of his intention to "use all his energies in devotion to what he says shall be the largest automobile factory in the world."[17]

News of the formation of the R. E. Olds Company was not welcomed by the Olds Motor Works, whose officials had been aware for some time of their former vice president's plans to re-enter the auto business. On August 18, the day after the company's organization was reported in the papers, a coldly impersonal letter signed simply "Olds Motor Works," probably written by Fred Smith, informed Olds that although the Oldsmobile manufacturers were not surprised to learn that Olds had decided to return to the production of automobiles, "we are surprised that you should take the name which so clearly and unmistakably will conflict with the name of the company which you assisted in organizing and in which you were a large stockholder." Perhaps, the letter continued, Olds had acted out of ignorance in taking "a name which would conflict with that of the Olds Motor Works"; nonetheless, it went on:

> ... we take this opportunity of calling your attention to the fact that in our opinion and in that of our attorneys, the use of the name 'Olds' by you in an automobile company, or in the automobile business, is clearly an infringement of our rights. We are sending you this notice at an early date so that you

> may know our position in the matter and so that if your dispo-
> sition is to avoid litigation and conflict between the two com-
> panies because of the similarity of names, you can without
> any loss to yourself in prestige and advertising make a
> change which will eliminate the name Olds and save the
> trouble and annoyance and expense of litigation that neces-
> sarily must follow in case you do not change.[18]

Olds, who until that time had continued to hold his seat on
the board of directors of the Olds Motor Works, now resigned
from that position, and his place was taken by Edward W.
Sparrow. Explaining his association with the new automobile company in a way that was consistent with the
view he generally expressed from this time forward, Olds
informed the Olds Motor Works on August 19 that thirty
days before he had had no intention of entering the automobile business again: "I have only done so because the
trade in general requested me to do so; numerous friends of
mine throughout the U. S. have urged this upon me, while
the people in my own town organized and had the stock all
signed up before they submitted the proposition to me." He
could not see, however, how the association of his name with
the new firm should be any concern of his old company. The
name that had been chosen did not "in any way appear like
the Olds Motor Works," and the name that would be used on
the automobiles the company would produce "certainly will
not be a name that will in any way sound like Olds
Mobile."[19]

However, in a letter as early as August 14 to Reuben Shettler, and to others on August 18—possibly to all of Olds'
fellow stockholders in the R. E. Olds Company—the Olds
Motor Works not only threatened to take legal action if the
name Olds was not stricken from the title of the new company but also claimed that "any use by [the new] Company of
the name Olds in its corporate name or as applied to automobiles is clearly an infringement of the rights sold by Mr.
Olds to the Olds Motor Works and the Olds Gasoline Engine
Works." When that sale had taken place was not stated, but
when Olds was informed of this claim he denied that he had
ever sold the rights to the use of his name. He even told

Henry Russel that he might seek a court order to prevent the
Olds Motor Works from using his name any longer on what
Olds now contended was an inferior product, since the defec-
tiveness of the current Oldsmobiles "had a tendency to injure
my reputation as a manufacturer." However, this was pure
bluster on Olds' part. Advised by legal counsel that the Olds
Motor Works stood a good chance of winning any suit it
might bring over the use of the Olds name, Olds and his
fellow stockholders voted on September 27, 1904 to change
the name of the company from the R. E. Olds Company to the
Reo Car Company, amended later still to Reo Motor Car
Company.[20]

It is not known who had the inspiration to make an acronym of Olds' initials; nor is it known whether or not that
person was aware that "reo" is the Greek verb meaning "to
run." It appears, however, that from the outset the intent
was to apply this name to the automobiles the R. E. Olds
Company would manufacture: within two weeks after the
formation of the company, *Horseless Age* reported that it
understood that the new cars would be called Reos. Using
initials as a designation for a company's automobile was not
new. Several years earlier the French firm of Charron,
Girardot, and Voigt had begun producing a car which was
called simply the CGV; in 1903 the United States saw the
first imports of the Italian Fiat, whose famous name is an
acronym of its manufacturer's name, Fabbrica Italiana Au-
tomobili Torino. In the United States a few instances of the
use of initials in car names can be found that predate the
Reo, for example, the ABC steamer of 1900, whose initials
stand for the American Bicycle Company. But the Reo certainly must rank as the most successful example of this type
in American automotive history, surviving long after the
E-M-F, the KRIT, the RCH, the IHC, and many other makes
had long since vanished. It may or may not be true, as has
been alleged, that Ransom Olds boasted when the decision
was made to change his company's name that he was now so
well known that his initials alone were sufficient to enable
the public to identify him with the company and its automobile; but it is certainly true that Olds and his associates

lost little or nothing in a publicity sense by agreeing to remove the Olds name from their corporate title.[21]

In addition to threatening legal action over the use of the
Olds name, the Olds Motor Works—led by Fred Smith, Olds
was convinced—harassed its former vice president and his
new company in other ways in the early weeks of Reo's existence. Lansing's banks received letters which were, Olds
concluded, intended to discourage these institutions from extending credit to Olds and his associates; but, he said, Smith
"might as well talk to a stone," for all the effect his actions
would have. Then, in what can only be regarded as a display
of petty spitefulness, Smith took legal action to force Olds to
pay for three Oldsmobiles that were in his possession at the
time he resigned as a director of the Olds Motor Works and
which Smith claimed were company property. Olds contended that all three vehicles were more or less experimental
in character, that he had been using them for a long time,
and that he had assumed he had more than paid for them
during his years with the company. When Smith remained
adamant in his demand that Olds surrender the vehicles,
Olds retained the services of Harris Thomas' law firm to
represent him in the matter. After several weeks of negotiation, the dispute was settled with Olds' payment of $1,800.[22]

In addition to these external pressures, the Reo company
was beset by some problems of internal origin, according to
Reuben Shettler. The latter, who later claimed to have assumed most of the burden not only of organizing the company but of providing the cash raised by the sale of common
stock—since he had not only paid for his own stock but had
loaned Edward Peer and others the money they needed to
pay for their stock—contended that Olds reneged on two
promises he had made to Shettler. For one, Shettler stated,
Olds had promised to turn over to him two thousand shares
of the common stock that Olds received if Shettler succeeded
in securing the financing the company needed. Shettler
claimed that he could never get Olds to honor this promise,
although he admitted that Olds did give him $5,000 in cash,
which Olds may well have felt was ample compensation for
the time and effort Shettler had put into organizing the com-

pany. However, Shettler also claimed that when the company was organized, Olds had agreed to buy five thousand shares of preferred stock but had subsequently refused to do so. Shettler had arranged for "several hundred thousand dollars'" worth of credit with the Old Detroit National Bank, which was to be made available when all the stock in the company had been subscribed. Olds' refusal to purchase his share of preferred stock threatened to invalidate these credit arrangements, according to Shettler.[23]

Although they were a foretaste of more serious internal difficulties that would erupt in 1910, these problems seem to have been successfully surmounted at this time, for the new company progressed with its plans to get into operation at an amazing pace in the weeks following its organization. At the beginning of August, Olds told Ray Owen: "If I decide to move in this matter, I shall move quick and be ready for next year's business." He was true to his word. By August 19, three days after the organizational meeting of the company's stockholders, draftsmen were reportedly working on drawings for the patterns that would be used for the new car, and temporary work quarters were being readied in a section of the Lansing Pure Food Company's factory. Olds joked that "it was probably the only time in the history of the automobile industry that food could be purchased from one section of a building, and automobiles from another." Machinery for the plant was being purchased and shipped in from Detroit and Chicago by the following week. By the end of August more than a score of men had begun work in the temporary plant, and by the first of September, Olds declared that orders for the car were coming in at such a rate that their entire first year's output could be spoken for within a month.[24]

On September 5 construction of a permanent factory was begun at a site that had remained a secret up to that time so as not to endanger the closing of several deals that were underway to secure various tracts of land. These were in a ten-block area bounded on the west by South Washington Avenue and on the north by the Grand Trunk tracks and depot. The two-story brick buildings of the Reo industrial complex, which were completed by early 1905, thus became more visible to Lansing visitors traveling on the Grand Trunk as a sign of the city's automobile manufacturing development than was the Oldsmobile plant some blocks to the west of the railroad station.

Unlike its cross-town rival, Reo had direct access to a second railroad, the Lake Shore and Michigan Southern. The latter ran a spur line into the factory from its main tracks on the east side of the Reo property, and the decision to locate the factory at this site was partly dictated by just such an advantageous arrangement for the shipment of freight in and out of the factory over two major railroads. Another reason, however, was that the property Olds had assigned to the company in return for a portion of his stock was part of this site. Other parcels of land that comprised the total site included a farm that Benjamin Davis' father had purchased a half-century earlier, perhaps another reason—in addition to Davis' banking connections—why Shettler had been anxious to draw him into the circle of Reo investors.[25]

Directing the work on the automobiles Reo would produce was Horace Thomas, who, as Olds had promised, was moved from the peat company into the position of chief engineer for Reo, an office that he would continue to hold for thirty years. Olds brought in another former aide, Richard Scott, to be factory superintendent. Scott had continued on in the supervisory position he had held with the Olds Gasoline Engine Works since 1898 and had not been directly involved with the production of Oldsmobiles. And, although Olds claimed that he made no direct effort to lure staff members away from his earlier manufacturing firms, it was only natural that many others who had worked for him before now followed the example of Thomas and Scott and took advantage of the opportunity to work for Olds again. The result was that the staff of the Reo company was soon loaded with men who had previously worked for the Olds Motor Works or the Olds Gasoline Engine Works, or who had had some other direct business connection with Ransom Olds. Cities like Lansing, where successful automobile manufacturing operations had already developed, now possessed a nucleus of skilled workmen experienced in automotive work, and this was one of the major reasons new automobile companies chose to locate in such cities rather than in localities where the experienced staff would have to be made up of individuals brought in from other areas.[26]

By October of 1904, the first Reo model, based on designs Olds and Thomas had been working on before the company was organized, was completed and ready for testing; on the afternoon of October 14 it was given its first test drive of some seventy miles in and around Lansing. The car was markedly different from the vehicle with which the Olds name had been associated earlier. This was no doubt partly a results of Olds' desire to assure the public that he was making a fresh start in the industry and that he had no intention of simply imitating his past successes. More importantly, however, Olds was obviously trying to keep pace with the times by incorporating features in his 1904 model that had gained favor with other automotive designers since the day when he drafted plans for the curved-dash runabout. The car he and Thomas came up with was, in fact, the kind of car Fred Smith—and perhaps more significantly, Reuben Shettler—had been urging Olds to build the previous year.

In appearance the Reo was recognizably an automobile, not a horseless carriage. In front of the driver, where there had been nothing but the curved dash in the Oldsmobile runabout, there was a hooded area that was referred to at this time as a "French bonnet," after the French designers who had introduced this feature in the early 1890s as a convenient location for the car's engine. While copying this body detail, as he had done in the Oldsmobile tonneau model the previous year, Olds did not immediately make the mechanical adjustments that would have been required to move the car's engine from its position beneath the vehicle, where he, like most American designers, had always placed it. In this sense the Reo's bonnet was what has been termed a "dummy hood," housing not the engine but merely the gas tank, radiator, and batteries. Nevertheless, no one could mistake this vehicle for a carriage minus its horse.

Olds made two other notable changes from the design of the earlier horseless carriage. Stepping into the Reo was facilitated by a running board along each side, a sturdier feature than the carriage step which Olds had used previously and which he recalled had collapsed on one occasion under the weight of a particularly hefty individual who was inspecting a curved-dash runabout at an auto show. The tiller steering bar Olds had previously used was replaced by the steering wheel, now no longer viewed as a "foreign freak" but an acceptable feature of the American car. Olds claimed later that this was another change made partly because of the difficulties the tiller supposedly created for big drivers with large, protruding stomachs.

Most importantly, Olds' first Reo marked a departure from the kind of car he had talked about in 1896 and which he had become famous for with the introduction of his runabout in 1900, in that the new car was a touring car with room for five passengers—as opposed to the two persons the standard runabout could carry. At 1,500 pounds it was twice as heavy as the curved-dash runabout, it had more than twice the power with its two-cylinder, sixteen-horsepower engine, and at $1,250 its price was almost twice that of the runabout. It is true that in the fall of 1904 Olds and Thomas also brought out a competitively priced two-passenger Reo runabout model at $650, although it too had the advanced automotive design features they had incorporated in the touring car, including the dummy hood and steering wheel. But it was the more expensive touring car that received the bulk of the advertising attention when the campaign for the Reo cars was launched at the end of the year.[27]

The name of Ransom Olds had been generally associated with low-priced cars up to that time; but now and throughout the remainder of his career in automobile manufacturing, a period of more than thirty years, Olds would be linked with automobiles in the medium price range. The first hint of this change had been the appearance of the Oldsmobile tonneau model in 1903, which was not yet in production when Olds left the Olds Motor Works. The new direction was now made official with the introduction of the Reo touring car late in 1904, and it was this crucial turn of events that determined the position that Olds and his company could hope to achieve in the industry. As Ford, and later General Motors and

Chrysler, were to demonstrate—and as Olds had learned earlier with the Olds Motor Works—the production of a popular car in the low-priced field was essential to any company that expected to maintain a front-running position in the auto industry. Reo never really had such an entry in its early days, and twenty years later, when Richard Scott tried to develop a wider range of models, it was too late to alter the patterns that had been set at the time of the company's formation.

The Reo, however, does not represent as great a shift in R. E. Olds' basic thinking regarding automobiles as it might first appear. Olds did not abandon his belief in the desirability and importance of producing practical, inexpensive cars suitable to the everyday needs of the common man. Toward the end of his life, when he had long since left the business of manufacturing cars, Olds repeatedly criticized the automobile of that later day as over-priced. In 1949 he told a Lansing reporter that the auto industry could, if it wanted to, produce a car that would sell for no more than a thousand dollars; and a year later—a few weeks before his death—he told the same writer that he was confident that he could, if he were a younger man, put out a small car that would sell for only $500. If he could have done that, the reporter said, he would have given the big companies "a battle for the market." As the unhappy experience of independent auto manufacturers who tried to develop a market for small cars in this postwar period would indicate, it was probably just as well for Olds that he did not have the opportunity to put his words into action. But later, when the public's interest began to shift away from the over-built automobiles of the fifties to the compacts and subcompacts of the sixties and seventies, Olds might have been able to put up a better fight.[28]

Why then did Ransom Olds, if he continued to believe in the kind of motor vehicle that he had first set out to build in 1896, raise his sights in 1904 from the runabout to the more expensive touring car? The answer is found in the biography Olds published in 1949: that first Reo automobile, Olds told Duane Yarnell, "was as lightly constructed as R. E. could make it, while still retaining the necessary strength to take

From the Four Winds

Courtesy of University of Michigan Transportation Library

Ransom Olds, always eager to demonstrate the ease with which his machines could be operated, towers over the "Baby Reo," a two-horsepower, exact working model of the standard-size Reo. The tiny car was the delight of children visiting the auto shows in 1906 and was later featured in the Barnum and Bailey Circus.

the buffetings of country roads." As the creator of the curved-dash runabout, Olds had fiercely defended that vehicle while he was still with the Olds Motor Works; but in his new situation he felt freer to agree with the critics in their analysis of that model's defects. If the automobile's full potential was to be realized, he thought, it had to be capable of being used for intercity, cross-country travel as well as for the convenient short trips around town. The runabout satisfied the latter need, but it was too fragile to be a practical vehicle for long-distance traveling. In order to provide the strength that was needed "to take the buffetings of country roads," the only solution, Olds and most of his contemporaries felt, was to give up the lightweight qualities of the runabout for the heavier, more durable qualities of the touring car. Because of the increase in weight, materials, and labor costs that went into such models, of course, the low price of the runabout also had to be sacrificed.[29]

Almost a half-century later, when Olds criticized the automobiles of that day for being too expensive, he said that the industry should be able to produce a low-priced car, "considering the vast strides in metal developments and the scientific machines made for mass production." However, those advances were still in the future in 1904, and thus Olds, the early leader in the production of low-priced automobiles, felt compelled by the available technology to raise the price of his product in order to provide the improved quality that was demanded. Advertisements for the Reo, however, continued to emphasize that, with the exception of the touring car's price, it still had the other features for which earlier Olds' products had been famous—simplicity of operation and a practical, common-sense approach to its construction.[30]

During this same period Henry Ford strove to achieve the same results that Olds was after with his Reo touring car. But Ford attempted to do this without an increase in price by improving the existing technology. By doing so, Ford ultimately succeeded and far surpassed Olds as the leader in production of cars for the masses. By the time Ford and his staff had developed the techniques that could have enabled Olds to make a determined bid for a share of the cheap car market, he had lost the urge to do so. As a result, he was apparently satisfied to speak of his later cars as "popularly-priced," which had some validity if one were comparing a Reo with a Cadillac or Pierce-Arrow, but not if one were using the Ford or Chevrolet as a yardstick.

Of course, the full ramifications of Olds' decision in the fall of 1904 were not evident at the time. So far as he was concerned, he was exercising his customary sound business judgment in following a trend in the industry away from the lightweight, buggy-type runabouts to the more durable touring cars. That this movement was underway had been evident to those who attended the auto shows earlier in 1904; and by 1905, when the Reo touring car was exhibited, it was obvious that the trend to the bigger car had won industry-wide acceptance.

Olds himself did much of the testing of the prototype of his Reo touring car. He claimed that he drove it some two thousand miles over some of the worst roads he could find in the Lansing area and during the rainy fall season, which was, other than spring, the time of year when the dirt roads were at their very worst. Nevertheless, Olds said that he failed to uncover a single major defect in the vehicle. Within sixty days after the small crew of Reo employees had begun work, Olds was ready with the car that would bring him back into the automobile marketplace.[31]

Just as in the production of the car, Olds once again called on the services of an associate from his Oldsmobile days to sell the Reo, in this case Ray Owen. When Olds had written to Owen on August 4, asking him if he wished to invest in the new company, Owen had replied that he and his backers, the Rainey brothers, were interested; but by the time his letter arrived in Lansing all the Reo stock had been subscribed. Olds assured Owen that he could persuade some of the stockholders to part with enough of their holdings so that Owen could still be one of the major investors. But on August 30 the correspondence took an entirely new turn: "How would you like to have us take the exclusive selling agency for your car," Owen inquired, "on some satisfactory basis for all concerned?" By exclusive Owen did not mean that he would control the rights to sell the car in one area, as he had with the Oldsmobile in New York City since 1901; he meant that he would contract to sell the entire Reo output. In a sense, he would be acting as sales manager for the Reo company. He would not be drawing a salary from Reo; instead, he would be operating independently of the Reo organization as the head of his own distribution company. The advantages of this arrangement for Owen were that the financial rewards would be greater than if he were simply a member of the Reo staff.

For Olds and his Reo organization the advantages of accepting Owen's proposal were that it would free them from the immediate need to concern themselves with anything beyond the actual production of automobiles by shifting to Owen's shoulders the burden of lining up dealers and arranging the details of distributing and marketing the car. It was an unusual arrangement but one that was not unknown in the industry during these early years. For example, four years later Studebaker, the South Bend carriage manufacturer, made its first big move in the automotive field by contracting to sell the entire output of the Detroit auto company E.M.F. In 1904, therefore, a contract was drawn up and approved that made the Reo Motor Car Company of New York—later reorganized as R. M. Owen & Company—the exclusive sales agents for the Reo, an arrangement that lasted until 1914.[32]

Ray Owen apparently made his original proposition to Olds without any clear conception of what kind of car Olds had in mind to produce. Two days later, realizing that he ought to know what it was he was proposing to sell, Owen wrote to Olds suggesting that they get together and go over the plans Olds and his staff were developing. Owen was apparently satisfied with what he was shown. But in the following weeks, as he went around the country lining up dealers, he became increasingly convinced that the new car, in order to be successful, had to represent a complete break with the kind of car Olds had been associated with earlier. One trade journal declared that the past successes of Owen and the Raineys in selling cars had "caused a general lining up of agents who are anxious to get territory for the Reo car." It is undoubtedly true that with a salesman of Owen's established reputation in charge of the distribution of the Reo, the task of lining up the experienced local dealers to make the new car a success was greatly helped. But Ransom Olds' connection with this car may not have been initially an asset to Owen in carrying out his job. Although Olds later claimed that Oldsmobile dealers fell over each other in their eagerness to secure Reo agencies, Owen said that he encountered great reluctance and resistance among these and other dealers in his efforts to persuade them to sell the Reo.

Part of Owen's difficulty when he first approached dealers in September, and for some weeks thereafter, was that he had nothing to show them in the way of a completed automobile. In addition, however, he discovered that Olds' reputation as a designer and builder of cars was not a strong selling point, at least among allegedly knowledgeable automobile people. There was, he informed Olds, "the general impression . . . that you are very much inclined to cut the material down on your cars. . . . You will, therefore, have this prejudice to overcome, and I would not hesitate, if I were in your place, to put in the best material obtainable in these cars, even at a slight additional cost." Furthermore, as Owen learned of the plans other auto manufacturers were then working on, he advised Olds to increase the size of his touring car to make it competitive with similar models that others would shortly have on the market. Thus Owen served as another of the influences that convinced Olds to abandon his earlier commitment to smaller, less expensive automobiles.[33]

In spite of what Ray Owen encountered in securing dealers for Reo, these and other difficulties were overcome as the new Lansing company proceeded with rapid and remarkably smooth progress toward achieving its goal of introducing its models at the start of 1905. Upon his return from his latest trip through the country in December, Owen reported that he had signed up dealers in Chicago, St. Louis, Cleveland, and Buffalo, and no matter what he may have been telling Olds in private, he now announced for public consumption that the interest in the Reo shown by prospective dealers was "something out of the ordinary."[34]

By this time the first advertisements for the Reo were appearing, one full-page ad having already appeared in the November issue of *Motor* magazine. This would indicate that the advertising campaign was getting underway with extraordinary speed, since it had only been on November 9 that Olds received a letter from the Philadelphia advertising firm of Powers & Armstrong expressing their pleasure at being named the Reo agent. J. O. Powers informed Olds that he would be coming to Lansing in the middle of the month to get the information he would need to prepare the ad copy; in the meantime he asked to have some clear sideview photographs of the models sent to him as soon as possible. But the first Reo advertisements dispensed with any attempt to show a likeness of the car. Instead, the public's curiosity was aroused by art work that showed nothing but the outlines of a vehicle covered by a curtain. If the details of this new vehicle were a mystery at that time—possibly even to the copywriter—there was no attempt to hide the identity of the car's designer. And when the curtain was finally raised on the Reo touring car in the January 1905 issue of *Motor*, showing a frontal view of the "Great Reo Car," seated at the wheel was "Mr. R. E. Olds, inventer and builder of the first practical gasoline runabout, and recognized everywhere as foremost among the world's motor engineers and builders."[35]

From the outset, in fact, the advertisements had emphasized not the car but its designer. "Curtain Still Down," a December advertisement declared, "but we'll tell you what's behind it—The Man R. E. Olds, with his world-wide reputation as a skilled and scientific inventor and builder of motor-cars, who made the first practical gasoline Runabout and who, on January 1st, 1904, withdrew from the concern with whom he and his father had been identified for many years." Thus, without mentioning the Olds Motor Works by name, and by referring to Olds' father (one of the rare occasions, incidentally, in which any attempt was made to link Pliny Olds with his son's work), Powers & Armstrong sought to establish an image of Olds with a reputation not simply based on the curved-dash Oldsmobile. That automobile, after all, had been on the market for only four years in December 1904. Instead, the ad suggested that Olds had acquired his skills long before the Oldsmobile, during the course of his earlier business career and through his association with his father.

What did this mean to the consumer? Powers & Armstrong spelled it all out in still another early Reo ad: "You need no longer pay fabulous prices for intricate mistakes and doubtful experiments," the buyer was assured, because R. E. Olds, with his "twenty years of practical experience, his inventive

The Man   R. E. Olds

You know him, the foremost designer of gasoline motor cars in the United States. He has built motors for twenty years and built them right. Any car that he makes is sure to be successful with the greatest possible use of every bit of power the gasoline can give.

He is not satisfied with simply an "idea." Every detail is worked out to the fullest possible perfection. He doesn't spend your money in learning how. He knows what he is going to do before he does it.

Above all, he knows what kind of a car to build for American Roads; and he knows what the American people want. His first car was a success. His latest car,

the REO, is a Wonder.

Everybody who has seen the Reo says it is a beauty, stylish and luxurious. The picture (from an amateur photograph) gives a fair idea of how it looks from the side, but you must look it all over and all through to realize the perfection of detail which makes its wonderful effectiveness. You should see.

Its **powerful engine**, simple and compact. Giving 16 horse-power for the 1450 pounds weight of the entire car—The greatest power for its weight of any motor car made and with the least possible loss.

Freeze-proof and jar-proof radiator made of removable sections for making repairs without laying up the car.

Its **convenient gasoline and water tanks and batteries** under the hood.

Its **entire self-enclosed mechanism.**

Its **one-piece cylinder** without jackets.

Its **valve mechanism** at the top of the motor, with every valve mechanically operated.

Its **original and effective carbureter** insuring a perfect mixture under all conditions.

Its **sensitive spark and throttle control.**

Direct transmission with ample clutch surface.

Practical steering gear and brakes.

Full elliptical springs in rear.

The body, seats, guards, steps, every detail of design, construction and finish, are a splendid example of convenient and luxurious carriage-making.

The Reo Touring Car is the car people want at the price they are willing to pay.

It is handsome, roomy, powerful, simple and easy to control. No amount of money could make the working parts of the car better in any essential detail

$1250 f. o. b. Factory.

The REO Runabout

is a single cylinder 8 H. P. car and weighs 850 pounds. The same attention has been paid to every detail as has made the Reo Touring Car a success.

$650 f. o. b. Factory

REO Motor Car Co.

R. M. Owen, Sales Manager.

AGENCIES THROUGHOUT THE UNITED STATES

Factory:
Lansing, Mich.

Sales Offices:
138 West 38th St., New York

The   Car

Courtesy of University of Michigan Transportation Library

The connection between Reo and the name of R. E. Olds could scarcely have been made more explicit than in this early Reo advertisement.

genius, mechanical skill and thorough knowledge of American requirements [has designed] the best 16-horse power Touring Car that human brain and skill can conceive and put together." By February 1905 a full-page advertisement, featuring a photograph of Olds at the top, was calling his latest car "a Wonder." Any automobile that Olds made was "sure to be successful. . . . He is not satisfied with simply an 'idea.' Every detail is worked out to the fullest possible perfection. He doesn't spend your money in learning how. He knows what he is going to do before he does it."

Indicative of the conscious effort to alter the public's image of the typical Olds-designed car was the secondary place given in most of these ads to the Reo runabout, any mention of which seemed to come almost as an afterthought. On the other hand, there was no desire to throw away the sales advantage that might come with the public's association of Olds with an inexpensive car; as a result, the agency's copy emphasized that with all of the Reo touring car's advanced features it was still priced at only $1,250, unquestionably a reasonable price for this kind of automobile, though not quite as unusual as the ads implied.[36]

CHAPTER NINE
The Reo

THE PUBLIC got its first look at the Reos when they were exhibited at the auto shows early in 1905, beginning with the Madison Square Garden show in New York during the third week of January, and followed by appearances at Chicago and several other cities (although a snow storm prevented the company from getting its demonstrators from Chicago to Detroit in time for the opening of that city's auto show the following week). Ransom Olds, as had now become his custom, attended the New York show, and it was perhaps indicative of his position both in his new company and in the industry that while Ray Owen was busy at the show promoting the Reo, Olds, the pioneer auto industrialist, was looked upon as a kind of elder statesman who stood somewhat above such crass and mundane matters as the promotion and sale of a product. Olds was asked his opinion of the future of the industry, and as always he was bullish: "The great majority of American manufacturers have worked hard and faithfully to design simple and practical machines, and to build them honestly," he told *Horseless Age*. "They have won the approval of the public by that effort, and by the real merit of their cars, and now they are to reap the benefits." The closest he came on this occasion to talking about his own car was when he indicated that he was especially optimistic about the future of popularly priced high-powered vehicles, the category in which he would have placed his Reo touring car.[1]

While Olds himself had little to say about his new car, Ray Owen was very enthusiastic about the Reo, being quoted in

Horseless Age as saying that demand for the car "exceeds our fondest expectations." A writer in *Automobile Review* became almost ecstatic, describing the Reo as "a new star in the auto firmament which promises to glow with increasing brightness." *Scientific American*, which had been keeping track of the progressive products of Ransom Olds' genius since 1892, made the Reo the only Michigan-produced car that it included in an article entitled "Some Leading Automobiles of the Present Year." Despite the newness of the Reo, the magazine felt that "there is every reason to believe that it will prove itself to be one of the finest light-weight touring cars for 1905." However, aside from the radiator displayed at the Reo exhibit, which was of a new design that claimed to be "freeze-proof and jar-proof," the Reo did not seem to live up to advance reports that Olds was incorporating in the vehicle "some entirely new ideas."[2]

In addition to a large-scale advertising campaign and appearances at the major auto shows, the Reo company kept interest in the new car alive through an extensive use of various methods that had been devised by 1905 to demonstrate the superior qualities of an automobile. In November 1904, Ray Owen, no doubt recalling Roy Chapin's success in piloting an early Oldsmobile runabout from Detroit to New York, announced that he planned to have a Reo driven from the factory in Lansing to New York, "a distance of about 1,000 miles ... if the weather remains good." Since there is no further mention of this proposed test drive, it may be assumed that the weather or some other considerations forced its cancellation.[3]

Nine months later, however, a Reo touring car, specially equipped with a hand windlass, tire chains, camping gear, searchlight, and other paraphernalia, was launched on the most ambitious and arduous road test thus far attempted in the United States. The Reo Mountaineer, as the car was dubbed, was to be driven by Percy Megargel, of the Buffalo Automobile Club, and David F. Fassett, a mechanic from the Reo factory, from New York to the Pacific and back. If successfully carried through, the feat would mark the first round-trip automobile journey across the continent. The trip was officially sponsored by the touring committee of the American Motor League, but the Reo company would naturally benefit from the publicity surrounding the trip, just as the Olds Motor Works had from the transcontinental trip of Whitman and Hammond in 1903 and the New York-to-Portland contest between "Old Scout" and "Old Steady" in the summer of 1905.

By November 1905, after three months on the road, Megargel sent the Reo company a telegram from Portland signaling the successful completion of the first half of the trip. The two intrepid tourists then headed down the coast to California so that they could head back east via the southerly route. Their original intention had been to arrive back in New York in time for the auto show in January 1906, publicizing the durable qualities of the Reo in the same way Chapin and Olds had promoted the Oldsmobile in New York in 1901. But the length of time they had taken to reach the West Coast had ruled out any possibility of their returning to New York in time for the annual auto show; and bad weather, bad roads, and the rugged western terrain they encountered on their way back east forced a drastic revision of the tour's time schedule. By the end of February 1906, Megargel and Fassett had only reached Gallup, New Mexico, and it was not until June 9 that the Reo Mountaineer, still performing amazingly well, arrived back in New York City after a trip of 11,742 miles, reportedly the "longest continuous automobile tour on record."[4]

Other events in which Reos participated in 1905 were of greater value in promoting sales among the great majority of car buyers, most of whom had no thought of attempting transcontinental trips in their vehicles. As early as April, Reos were taking part in hill-climbing contests, and a standard Reo touring car, "fresh off the train," was successful in winning three cups at the Paddock Hill contests in Cincinnati on May 17. This success was especially played up by Reo officials, who no doubt wished to dispel any doubts concerning the hill-climbing capabilities of an Olds vehicle that might linger from the public's recollections of the Oldsmobile runabout's somewhat spotty record in this regard.[5]

In addition to entering their cars in hill-climbing events, Olds and his associates made a determined effort to publicize the Reo through victories on the racing circuit, where they were considerably more successful than Olds had been in his Oldsmobile days. A special thirty-two-horsepower racing vehicle, the "Reo Bird," was built in the spring of 1905 and, with Daniel J. Wurges as the driver, was one of the most successful entries in that season's races. On Memorial Day, Wurges won two of the three races he entered at the Empire City track in Yonkers, New York. Ten days later, at the so-called National Championships at Morris Park, New Jersey, Wurges did not fare so well, losing to the legendary Louis Chevrolet. The latter, however, was driving a Fiat that was three times as powerful as the "Reo Bird."

In August, at the Grosse Pointe track, which had earlier launched Henry Ford and Barney Oldfield on their racing careers, Wurges won the first two races in his car's class. Following those he was entered in the big event of the day, to compete against Webb Jay in his "Whistling Billy" steamer, Oldfield in his "Green Dragon," and other famous cars of that period. On the second turn of the first mile Wurges was blinded by dust, and by the time it had cleared one of his wheels had struck Oldfield's right rear wheel. The "Green Dragon" tore through a hundred feet of fence and was wrecked, pinning Oldfield under the machine, injured but alive. The "Reo Bird" spun completely around, went across the track, through the fence, down an embankment, through brush to the track's outer barrier, where it came to a halt. Miraculously, both the car and driver escaped unharmed. Undaunted, they went on their way to Syracuse in September and set what was said to be a new mile record for middle-weight cars.[6]

R. E. Olds does not seem to have been directly involved to any great extent in these various Reo promotions; but he was an active participant in what would have to be regarded—in the perspective of a later period—as the most famous of all motoring events that year. It was the first of the tours conceived by Charles J. Glidden, the retired telephone executive and motoring enthusiast, as a spectaculr method of promoting automobiles and their manufacturers. The initial Glidden Tour began on July 11, 1905 at the headquarters of the Automobile Club of America on Fifty-Eighth Street and Fifth Avenue in New York, proceeded up through New England to Bretton Woods, New Hampshire, and came back to the starting point in New York on July 22, having covered a distance of 870 miles. Of the thirty-two cars that began the tour on July 11, only four were Michigan-made cars: two were Cadillacs, and the other two were Reo touring cars. (Benjamin Briscoe also took part in this tour, but, though Briscoe was from Detroit, his car—the Maxwell—was produced in New York.) Ray Owen was in car No. 31, along with a chauffeur and three other passengers. C. C. Singer was the chauffeur of car No. 30, the other Reo, and his passengers included Duncan Curry, a New York newspaperman, Alfred Reeves, a pioneer newspaper automotive editor from New York, and Mr. and Mrs. Olds.

The tour produced some excitement. On the first evening Mrs. Olds, together with the other women on the tour, including Mrs. Ray Owen, Mrs. Percy Pierce, wife of one of the producers of the Pierce-Arrow, and Mrs. John Newton Cuneo of Long Island, a socialite and the only woman driver on the tour, were entertained at a private dinner in Hartford, Connecticut. In New Hampshire the tourists had breakfast at five a.m. on top of Mount Washington, the site of an extraordinary hill climb, "Climb to the Clouds," in which one of the Reos won first prize for cars priced under $2,000. On the return trip, the Olds party received something of a scare during a cloudburst, when lightning struck and splintered a tree only twenty feet from their car.

But the most celebrated feature of the first Glidden Tour began to unfold on the morning of July 12 as the touring cars entered the Massachusetts town of Leicester. There Channing Smith, the chairman of the board of selectmen, had been upset earlier that morning at what he considered the recklessness of a passing motorist, who apparently was not connected with the Glidden group. Smith directed the local constable, a man named Quinn, to set a trap for any other speeders that day. Quinn, who was described as having "a hatred of motorists," responded to this order "with alacrity." At the foot of a steep hill he measured off 308 feet at a point where, as the journal *Motor Way* related the story, "every motorist who is blessed with ordinary common or garden-horse sense would make a rush to get up another little grade, and there he stationed his men with stop watches and flags and waited." As the Glidden tour group came through, some were going too fast for Quinn to catch their numbers. He was reported to have added the times of these faster cars to those of the cars that were going slow enough to be identified, with the result that he came up with seventeen tour cars that were exceeding the speed limit. Subsequently, it was decided to press charges against only eight individuals, among whom were Benjamin Briscoe, Mrs. Cuneo, and R. E. Olds. All of the alleged speeders, *Motor Way* maintained, "have the reputation of having been careful in all towns, and it is probable that not one of them reached the speed with which they were credited."

The Gliddenites who had been charged with speeding were to appear in court in the nearby city of Worcester on the return leg of the tour. The anticipation of "the coming seance with the Worcester authorities over the Leicester affair" added an extra touch of excitement as the tourists left New Hampshire for New York on July 19. The next day they arrived in Worcester, where they had an overnight stop. As a result of conferences between the Leicester officials, representatives of the tour, and the Worcester Automobile Club, Constable Quinn was to serve Olds and the other alleged speeders with warrants at a "soiree d'arrest" to be held in the rooms of the Worcester Club in the Bay State hotel at six that evening. But en route to this function Quinn was accosted by one of the tourists, who informed the former of how the participants in the tour felt about him in such blunt terms that the constable decided he did not want to proceed with his part in the affair. The warrants were finally served by the clerk of the Worcester court and were accepted "gracefully" by Olds and all the others, except two of the charged who were not present. After further conferences, the offenders decided to plead guilty when they appeared in court the next morning. Although they could have put up a good defense, they decided they did not want to hold up the further progress of the tour.

The following morning the arrested tourists, plus most of the remaining tour participants, appeared in the court of Judge Utley, whom *Motor Way* described as representing "as fine a speciman of the genus motorphobus as ever happened." Utley quickly disposed of the cases of several drunks in order to get to the cases of the six Gliddenites. The attorney for the Worcester Automobile Club pleaded for clemency, stating that the reputations of those who were charged had been falsely maligned and that they should be treated as guests. Utley brushed aside the attorney's pleas, declaring that the Gliddenites "were no guests of his and that he deplored the fact that the law no longer gave him the power to send them to jail." After condemning the Glidden Six as outlaws in the same class with murderers, the judge fined them each fifteen dollars, apparently the maximum penalty the law allowed. The fines were paid, and the Glidden party returned to the Bay State House to resume their trip back to New York.

But the Leicester affair was not over. When the Glidden cars left Worcester they were draped in crepe, while drivers and passengers sported crepe rosettes in protest to what they felt was the unfair way some of them had been treated in this incident. The cars maintained a safe speed of fifteen miles per hour on the road to Leicester, but when they reached the outskirts of the newly notorious town, the drivers slowed the pace down to one or two miles an hour. Preceded by the town band, which apparently sympathized with the tourists and marched solemnly along playing a funeral march, the cars took an hour to crawl through the village, with much honking of horns and assorted remarks by the tourists expressing their opinion of the village and its infamous speed trap. The entire party halted in front of the shop where the hapless Constable Quinn was employed, but the latter did not respond to the Gliddenites' more or less good-humored request that he come out and greet them. "The population of the town, great and small, cheered and danced with delight," *Motor Way* reported. "Leicester was infamous as the most inhospitable and the most unreasonable town on the motorists' black-list. But it had got on the map." When the cars finally had passed through town, the crepe was ripped off, the band dismissed, and the tourists sped off to luncheon in Springfield and the conclusion of the tour in New York City the following afternoon.

Although Ray Owen continued to publicize the Reo through active participation in subsequent Glidden Tours, Ransom Olds seems to have had little or nothing to do with the tours after the first one in 1905, although this most famous of all the early American automobile promotions was held until 1913. The Leicester affair may have cooled Olds' enthusiasm for this kind of publicity, or perhaps he—like a good many other participants—was dissatisfied with the method by which awards were made to the contestants at the end of the tour. Olds and Owen both received certificates stating that their cars were among twenty-two vehicles that had been driven "for the required distance, registering according to conditions at all controls." Seven contestants were said to have had "clean records," but their names were not disclosed. Olds' car would not have been in this latter category in any event, because of the speeding violation in Leicester. Each contestant voted for his or her top three choices of the car with the best record, which would be awarded the Charles J. Glidden Trophy. Percy Pierce and his entry won the award with a total of fifteen votes. Olds and Owen each received two votes, each presumably voting for the other and himself. At least they fared better than Benjamin Briscoe, who received only one vote.[7]

No matter how unhappy Olds may have been with the results, however, within a week after the Glidden awards were announced, Reo ads were playing up the fact that two of the Reo touring cars had received "First-Class Certificates of Honor" in the "famous Glidden Tour," and that the car which had won the top award had twice the horsepower of the Reo and cost three times as much. The tour demonstrated that the Reo did everything the $3,000 car could do, "except burn your money." Summarizing the results of the contests of all sorts in which the Reo had participated that summer, an advertisement in September declared that they had proven that "from their very beginning Reo cars were right."[8]

* * * * *

There is no way of determining how effective the Reo's performances in hill-climbing, racing, and endurance events were in stimulating sales of the car in 1905; but the sales record alone was an impressive one for a new firm just starting out. Although first year sales came nowhere near Ray Owen's typically optimistic forecast of 3,000 in December 1904, or the more restrained prediction of 2,000 that was being heard the following month, the actual production of 864 cars from March 1905, when the first of the new factory buildings was completed and the first car shipments were made, through August 31, the end of the company's fiscal year, was an auspicious beginning. Net sales of $955,905 for this six-month period were translated into a profit of $323,457, about two-and-a-half times the amount of money that was to have been raised through the sale of common stock at the company's organization in August 1904. Production rose in 1906 to 2,458 cars, continued up in 1907 to 3,967, and reached 4,105 for the fiscal year ending August 31, 1908. The lower growth rate of the last year was attributable to the fact that this fiscal year began at a time when auto sales in general were sharply depressed by the Panic of 1907. Sales of 6,592 cars for the year ending August 31, 1909 reflected both the strong rebound in industry sales following the panic and also Reo's continuing strong position in the industry, which since 1906 had ranked it among the top half-dozen largest manufacturers in America in terms of sales. Reo's dividend record was also outstanding and was cited by the pioneer automobile historian James R. Doolittle as evidence of the spectacular growth record the successful firms enjoyed during these years. From a ten-cent dividend in 1905, the company went to a fifty per cent stock dividend plus a thirty-five cent cash dividend in 1906. Dividends continued to rise in the following years, with a hundred per cent stock dividend being declared in 1909, plus a cash dividend of sixty cents a share.[9]

Clearly, Ransom Olds could point with justifiable pride to what he had been able to accomplish on his second try at manufacturing automobiles. And not only did he have undisputed control of one of the foremost automobile companies in the industry; he had expanded his business interests into related areas. Faced with the problem of being dependent on outside suppliers for his parts, which sometimes led to production delays when they failed to deliver certain parts on schedule, Olds made decisions in 1906 that led rapidly to the organization in Lansing of the National Coil Company, Michigan Screw Company, and Atlas Drop Forge Company. These companies would assure the Reo plant of a steady flow of certain parts, although they did not do business solely with Reo. Familiar figures who had been associated with Olds in earlier days or were with him at Reo—like Eugene Cooley, Edward Sparrow, E. F. Peer, Richard Scott, and Horace Thomas—were among the investors and officers in these parts companies; but in each case the company president was R. E. Olds. Olds also broadened his interests into the field of banking, helping to organize the Capital National Bank in Lansing in 1906. When this institution opened its doors, Olds' name once again appeared in the familiar position of president.[10]

On January 1, 1907, Olds jotted down in his little pocket diary the names of the several firms which he then headed. He must have been reflecting on how far he had come in the three years since he had been removed from his position as vice president and general manager of the Olds Motor Works. And while his fortunes in the auto industry were in the ascendancy, he was no doubt well aware—with what must have been some satisfaction—that the fortunes of his former company, under the management of Fred Smith, had by 1907 taken a sharp downward turn.

That year marked the passing of the curved-dash runabout from the scene. Little attention was paid to this development, which was indicated by the little car's absence in the

This 1908 Oldsmobile "Toy Tonneau," a luxury touring car, was as representative of Olds Motor Works autos by that time as the cheap little runabout had been of the company's products five years earlier.

Oldsmobile company's exhibit at the Madison Square Garden show in January. *Horseless Age* wrote the vehicle's obituary in February, observing that it was "extremely doubtful whether any other make of car has been so widely advertised as this one, been made in as great numbers and found its way into so many parts of the world." It was this car "that sounded the death knell of the steam runabout, and now the curved dash car in turn is passing away before the onward march of the multicylinder principle." While Olds continued to recognize this trend by introducing a four-cylinder Reo in 1906, along with a variety of other models, he also continued to emphasize the less expensive two-cylinder touring car. Fred Smith, on the other hand, seems to have allowed his obvious enthusiasm for the bigger cars to cloud his judgment of what the public wanted or was prepared to buy. In 1906, Oldsmobile introduced what was reportedly the first medium-priced four-cylinder car on the market; and the first six-cylinder Oldsmobile was brought out in 1907. These were the automobiles Smith now emphasized, in a company that but a short time before had been the leading manufacturer of low-powered, low-priced cars.[11]

In Lansing, where Oldsmobile production had been entirely concentrated since the final abandonment of the Detroit plant in 1905, Smith's and Olds' companies maintained a fierce competition that left few in the community untouched. *Motor Age* reported:

> Everybody works either for one or the other of the two big motor car factories, has a friend who does or knows a friend's friend who expects soon to be employed. So strong is the rivalry between the two factories, however, that the man who leaves skimmed milk at the door of the Olds employe knows better than to solicit trade from the family whose breadwinner dallies with an envelope from the Reo paymaster.

In the spring of 1907, when it was announced that President Theodore Roosevelt would be coming to town on May 31 to deliver an address at the semicentennial celebration of the opening of Michigan Agricultural College, the Olds Motor Works and Reo vied for the honor of having one of their automobiles used in transporting Roosevelt out to the college campus east of the capital. For many, the President's awaited decision on that matter came to overshadow the main purpose of his visit. In the end, Teddy availed himself of the services of both companies. With Ransom Olds at the wheel, the president was driven out to the college in a Reo. Upon entering the car, Roosevelt reportedly asked Olds whether this was one of the cars of the Association of Licensed Automobile Manufacturers or an independent. Olds assured him that his company was one of the independent auto manufacturers. However, if the reply pleased the famous Trust Buster, it did not prevent him from riding back to Lansing in an Oldsmobile, a product of the group that supported the Selden Patent and was denounced by the independent producers as "The Trust." "At nightfall," *Motor Age*

Courtesy of Michigan History Division

With his hands on the Reo's controls, Ransom Olds drives President Theodore Roosevelt and his fellow top-hatted passengers out to Michigan Agricultural College on May 31, 1907. Jonathan L. Snyder, the college president, is seated beside Roosevelt, and William Loeb, Roosevelt's secretary, occupies the front seat with Olds.

reported, "when the nation's first citizen was well on his way eastward, the battle lines were withdrawn, and good judges and critics regarded the day's motoring engagement as a drawn battle."[12]

On the battleground where it really counted, however, in the dealers' showrooms, the competition between Reo and Oldsmobile was strictly no contest by 1907, when Reo's sales placed it far ahead of its rival. By 1908, Oldsmobile had dropped to sales of barely a thousand cars, and Samuel Smith had been forced to pump over a million dollars into the firm to keep it going. It is no wonder that the Smiths and their fellow stockholders welcomed the opportunity offered by William C. Durant in November 1908 to transfer control of the Olds Motor Works to the new General Motors combine. But any sense of triumph Ransom Olds may have felt at how things came out was to be relatively short-lived. Within a few years, under new management Oldsmobile regained the ascendancy in Lansing, while under old management the business empire Olds had created gradually shrank in importance.

CHAPTER TEN

"My Farewell Car"

IN 1911, CLAUDE C. HOPKINS, one of the acknowledged advertising geniuses of all time, who represented the equally famed advertising agency of Lord and Thomas, was called in to plan the advertising campaign for the 1912 Reos. Hopkins' forte was planning and carrying out campaigns that succeeded in creating consumer interest in relatively new products or restoring it in those that were not doing well. He loved emergencies and by the same token disliked what he regarded as the monotonous task of directing an advertising campaign once a successful approach had been developed. He preferred instead to move on to another problem product that would again challenge his ability to make people want to buy the product. Bissell Carpet Sweepers, Van Camp's beans, Palmolive soap, and—among automobiles—the Overland and the Hudson represented some of what he considered his greatest triumphs in applying his techniques to product advertising.[1]

The arrival of Claude Hopkins on any scene, therefore, could well be a sign that a company was in trouble. And Reo's troubles in 1911 were rather obvious. The sales of its cars had crested at 6,592 in 1909, which had placed the Lansing firm in sixth place in passenger-car production, behind Ford, Buick, Maxwell, E-M-F, and Cadillac. However, even in 1909, Reo's growth had not kept pace with the growth of the industry as a whole. Reos produced that year constituted only a little over five per cent of the country's passenger-car production, down from more than nine per cent of the market in 1907, when Reo had ranked third behind Ford and Buick, and down from six-and-a-half per cent in 1908, when it had dropped to fifth place in output. Production figures for 1910 show 6,588 Reos manufactured, only four cars less than the 1909 totals; but that figure now represented less than four per cent of the national total. A sharp decline to 5,278 cars in 1911 dropped the company down to tenth place in passenger-car production, selling less than three per cent of all the cars produced that year. Even more serious, the company whose dividend record in its early years had been outstanding omitted paying a dividend in 1911 for the first time in its history.[2]

The reasons for the decline are not difficult to spot. Reo had simply not kept pace with the rest of the industry with regard to model design and mechanical improvements. The 1911 models were still basically the same ones Olds and his staff had developed in 1904. In the meantime the competition had come out with new models that had drawn the attention away from the Reo. The company now sought to reverse this trend by coming up with a new model of its own and by getting Claude Hopkins to apply his talents to boost the Reo's sagging sales appeal.

Hopkins came to Lansing, studied the problem, and then went off to meditate on what course of action to pursue. He returned shortly and told Ransom Olds that he would take the assignment on several conditions. The first was that the new model was to be called "Reo the Fifth." The term was, as Hopkins knew, without any real meaning; but it would dramatically and succinctly serve to set the car apart as a new model, the latest in a succession of models. This would help dispel the public's image of the Reo company as a stodgy firm that had stood still while others had pushed ahead.

The second condition Hopkins insisted on was that Ransom Olds be featured in the ads for the car. "People like to deal with men whose names are connected with certain accomplishments," he said. "They would rather do that, I have found, than deal with soulless corporations. Naming an expert in the advertising campaign indicates a man of unique ability and prominence ... people accord him respect." In the advertising copy that he had earlier written for the

Chalmers-Detroit and the Hudson, Hopkins had featured Howard E. Coffin, the former Oldsmobile engineer who was in charge of designing these cars. Although earlier ads for the Reo had singled out Ransom Olds as the designer of that car, Hopkins now went a step further. His ads for "Reo the Fifth" were to be signed by Olds, thus giving the impression that Olds had authored them. The idea was to capitalize on the greatest potential of Olds' reputation. "I told him," Hopkins declared, "I would write ads. he would be proud to sign, and he agreed."

What Hopkins proposed to do was not new. Full-page advertisements for the 1906 Thomas had featured a "personal statement" from E. R. Thomas, head of the Buffalo company that produced these cars, in which he sought to assure the public that a man with his long experience in the industry would naturally want to protect his reputation by employing

The Reo — about 1910 — a large, commodious automobile which this Ypsilanti owner and his three passengers seem to find most satisfactory

the very best workmen and by using the best equipment and materials in order to produce the best car on the market. Hopkins adopted the same approach for what turned out to be one of the most famous campaigns in advertising history.[3]

By January 1912, Hopkins' advertisements for the new Reo, which have come to be regarded as among the classics of the copywriter's art, had appeared in publications with a combined circulation of thirty million, making this, according to R. M. Owen & Company, the most massive advertising drive in automotive history up to that time. The appearance of Ransom Olds as the author of these advertisements has deceived some writers, including his biographer Glenn Niemeyer, into believing that the ad texts literally reflected Olds' thinking. Thus the great emphasis that is found in the ads on the most minute details of the manufacturing of the cars—"I *analyze all my steel*.... My carburetor is *doubly heated*.... I carry tests and inspections, throughout the construction, to what men call extremes"—these are cited by Niemeyer as examples of Olds' "obsession for quality and detailed inspection."[4]

While it may be true that Olds had become conscious of the need to pay greater attention to such matters than he seems to have shown in his earlier days with the Olds Motor Works, these statements in 1912 only represent Claude Hopkins' use of one of his favorite techniques in distinguishing a product that was otherwise indistinguishable from other similar products. Thus, in launching an ad campaign for Schlitz beer, for example, he had gone to great pains in his copy to describe how the company made its beer. Schlitz executives protested that "the processes we use are just the same as others use. No one can make good beer without them." Never mind that, Hopkins had replied, "others have never told this story. It amazes everyone who goes through your brewery. It will startle everyone in print." At a time when every brewery was advertising its beer as "Pure," a claim that made no impression on the consuming public, Hopkins, through his approach, "gave purity a meaning." "Washed in Live Steam!" was the heading of one Hopkins ad in which he described how Schlitz cleaned its bottles, a standard method

My Farewell Car

By R. E. Olds, Designer

Reo the Fifth—the car I now bring out—is regarded by me as pretty close to finality. Embodied here are the final results of my 25 years of experience. I do not believe that a car materially better will ever be built. In any event, this car marks my limit. So I've called it My Farewell Car.

My 24th Model

This is the twenty-fourth model which I have created in the past 25 years.

They have run from one to six cylinders—from 6 to 60 horsepower.

From the primitive cars of the early days to the most luxurious modern machines.

I have run the whole gamut of automobile experience. I have learned the right and the wrong from tens of thousands of users.

In this Farewell Car, I adopt the size which has come to be standard—the 30 to 35 horsepower, four-cylinder car.

Where It Excels

The chiefest point where this car excels is in excess of care and caution.

The best I have learned in 25 years is the folly of taking chances.

In every steel part the alloy that I use is the best that has been discovered. And all my steel is analyzed to know that it meets my formula.

I test my gears with a crushing machine—not a hammer. I know to exactness what each gear will stand.

I put the magneto to a radical test. The carburetor is doubly heated, for low-grade gasoline.

I use nickel steel axles with Timken roller bearings.

So in every part. The best that any man knows for every part has been adopted here. The margin of safety is always extreme.

I regard it impossible, at any price, to build a car any better.

Center Control, Finish, etc.

Reo the Fifth has a center, cane-handle control. It is our invention, our exclusive feature.

Gear shifting is done by a very slight motion, in one of four directions.

There are no levers, either side or center. Both of the brakes operate by foot pedals. So the driver climbs out on either side as easily as you climb from the tonneau.

The body finish consists of 17 coats. The upholstering is deep, and of hair-filled genuine leather. The lamps are enameled, as per the latest vogue. Even the engine is nickel trimmed.

I have learned by experience that people like stunning appearance.

The wheel base is long—the tonneau is roomy—the wheels are large—the car is over-tired. Every part of the car—of the chassis and the body—is better than you will think necessary. No price could buy anything better.

Price, $1,055

This car—my finest creation—has been priced for the present at $1,055.

This final and radical paring of cost is considered by most men as my greatest achievement.

It has required years of preparation. It has compelled the invention of much automatic machinery.

It necessitates making every part in our factory, so no profits go to parts makers.

It requires enormous production, small overhead expense, small selling expense, small profit. It means a standardized car for years to come, with no changes in tools and machinery.

In addition to that, by making only one chassis we are cutting off nearly $200 per car.

Thus Reo the Fifth gives far more for the money than any other car in existence. It gives twice as much as some.

But this price is not fixed. We shall keep it this low just as long as we can. If materials advance even slightly the price must also advance. No price can be fixed for six months ahead without leaving big margin, and we haven't done that. The cost has been pared to the limit.

Catalog Ready

Our new catalog shows the various styles of body. It tells all the materials, gives all secifications. With these facts before you, you can easily compare any other car with this Reo the Fifth.

If you want a new car you should do that. Judge the facts for yourself. Don't pay more than our price for less value. After 25 years spent in this business, here is the best car I can build. And the price is $1,055. Don't you think you should know that car?

Write now for this catalog. When we send it we will tell you where to see the car. Address—

R. M. Owen & Co. General Sales Agents for Reo Motor Car Co., Lansing, Mich.

Canadian Factory, St. Catharines, Ontario

Center Control

Brake and Clutch Pedals

Reo the Fifth
$1,055

30-35 Horsepower Wheel Base

112 Inches

Wheels— 34 Inches

Demountable Rims

Speed— 45 Miles per Hour

Made with 2, 4 and 5 Passenger Bodies

One Front Door Open to Show Center Control

Top and windshield not included in price. We equip this car with mohair top, side curtains and slip-cover, windshield, gas tank and speedometer all for $100 extra. Self-starter, if wanted, $25.00 extra.

(25)

Courtesy of Motor Vehicle Manufacturers Association

Claude Hopkins' famous Reo the Fifth ad, featuring a message from R. E. Olds himself

used throughout the industry. Hopkins, explaining his frequent use of this tactic, said: "Again and again I have told simple facts, common to all makers in the line—too common to be told. But they have given the article first allied with them an exclusive and lasting prestige." The statements that Hopkins now put into Olds' mouth, which had him boasting of doing what most other automobile manufacturers were also doing, thus marked the continuation of a practice that Hopkins had used many times in the past.[5]

The most famous element in Hopkins' Reo advertisements, however, resulted from one of the conditions he had insisted on. Combining the appeal of Olds' reputation as a builder of automobiles and the painstaking exposition of the processes used in building his latest car, Hopkins had Olds declare that the Reo the Fifth represented the culmination of his many years of experience. It was the best car that he was capable of designing. By cutting corners, of course, he could have put out a car that would have sold for less; but, he said, he refused to cheapen his product in that way. Someone else could possibly design a better car, but for Olds the Reo the Fifth "marks my limit"; it was "My Farewell Car." Thus, Hopkins said, he shaped his text "to typify the man, the man of rugged honesty, of vast experience. The man who knew. The man who scorned to do anything but the best that was possible, regardless of its cost. The man who put his reputation far ahead of profits."

When Hopkins went over the advertising copy and layout with Olds, the forty-seven-year-old automaker immediately objected to the theme that the Reo the Fifth was his "farewell car": "I don't intend to retire," he informed Hopkins. The latter quickly set Olds' mind at rest, assuring him that he need have no fears that the statements in the ads were going to force him to get out of the automobile business. After all, Hopkins reminded him, "Sarah Bernhardt made seven farewell tours"; Olds was entitled to at least "two or three. Every farewell is subject to reconsideration." In the meantime, Hopkins was banking on the hope that some buyers, thinking they might never have another chance to purchase a new car designed by this master craftsman, would be all the more anxious to obtain one of these automobiles while the supply lasted.[6]

In actuality, however, Hopkins was striking closer to the truth than he may have realized. For several years Ransom Olds had been looking for the right kind of opportunity that would have enabled him to retire from the Reo Motor Car Company. Had any one of several deals worked out, the Reo the Fifth or one of the earlier Reo models would have in truth been Olds' "farewell car."

* * * * *

As far as R. E. Olds was concerned, it seems clear that the high point in his business career came in the years from 1896 to 1906, when he was pioneering in the development and production of practical gasoline-powered automobiles. As he looked back on this period, he told Duane Yarnell that these were "the greatest, most exciting" years of his entire life. During his years with the Olds Motor Works he had succeeded in demonstrating that these goals could be achieved with a high rate of profit to the manufacturer. If there was any doubt that he could succeed without the support of Samuel Smith and his sons and friends, he had then repeated the demonstration a second time with the Reo Motor Car Company. By 1906, Reo was clearly established, under Olds' guidance, as one of the leading automobile manufacturers in the country.

By 1906, then, Olds' position in the industry had ceased to be that of a pioneer, one of those who were seeking to prove that they could survive in this new industry. Having twice proved just that, Olds was now an established leader who was faced with the far different task of maintaining and adding to the lead that Reo had acquired over most of the competition. The job of running a business under those circumstances came more and more to follow certain set patterns, and Olds was not endowed with the kind of personality suited to that kind of routine, particularly in as fiercely competitive an industry as the auto industry was turning out to be. He found it perhaps boring, certainly less challenging than the conditions he had faced when he was trying to prove himself. For many businessmen who have found themselves in a similar position, a desire to attain increased power and wealth has been sufficient incentive for them to be willing to apply themselves as diligently to their jobs under these more settled circumstances as they had when they were first starting out. But neither power nor greater wealth seem to have held that great an attraction for Olds. He said as much in 1949 through the medium of his official biographer, and although the sentiments that he expressed then could be taken as an old man's excuses for his failure to capitalize fully on the opportunities he had had during his lifetime, his actions in the preceding decades seem to have borne him out.

As a result, although it appears that Olds was essentially satisfied with the way things had gone for him personally in the years after 1906, his neglect of the affairs of his automobile company was perhaps the major cause of Reo's declining importance during these years. The magic touch of Claude Hopkins may account for Reo's rebound in sales in 1912 from the decline of the previous two years. However, though the increase pushed Reo back up to seventh place in the country, it did not halt the subsequent drop in the percentage of national car production that Reo's totals represented. Continued improvements in sales over the next several years only succeeded in stabilizing the company's output for a time at about one-and-a-half per cent of the national total. Never again would Reo regain the position it had held in the industry during its first three or four years.[7]

By 1907, the evidence from Olds' diaries makes it clear that he was giving little attention to the day-to-day activities of his company. He spent far too much time traveling and vacationing to have been able to maintain close contact with company operations. The mails and telegraph did not give the service later provided by the long-distance telephone, still in a somewhat primitive stage of development, which would enable the vacationing or traveling executive to maintain continuous contact with developments in the home office.

Olds' yearly routine had started becoming well established

shortly after he became active in the auto industry. The early part of January invariably saw him off to New York for the annual auto show. Upon his return home he might take in the shows at Chicago or Detroit, which were held shortly after the close of the national show in New York; but normally the Olds family was headed for Florida by the end of January, since Ransom's parents had moved from San Diego to what is now Daytona Beach in 1905. The family stayed in the South until late winter. After returning to Lansing in late March or early April, they would stay in their home for several weeks, although Olds might well make business trips to Detroit or New York during this period. Summers they were off for northern Michigan or other places in Michigan where Olds could indulge his love for yachting. Olds would be back in Lansing during the fall more than at other times of the year, although he might go down to Florida for a time before Christmas to make preparations for the family's return to the South a month or so later.

This, however, was only the regular schedule of trips. A year rarely passed without special trips that took Olds and his family off in other directions. In 1907 they went to Europe, the first of a number of trips abroad that the family would take. Although many American automobile manufacturers were going to Europe during those years to pick up pointers from European engineers and designers, it seems likely that Olds' trip in 1907 was more for pleasure and much less for business than he later claimed it had been. The family returned to Europe in 1910, sailing for Hamburg on June 25 and not returning to Lansing until September 3. From what is recorded of this tour of the continent and the British Isles, there is no indication from Olds' diary notations, aside from a visit that he paid to a Swiss watch factory in Geneva, that he was doing much business. Rather, this wealthy American tourist was deriving pleasure from doing what he never could have done on the income he earned only a few short years before. In 1911 he was off to the Pacific Northwest, Alaska, and back home through western Canada. The next year he toured eastern Canada; a few months later, in January 1913, he traveled to the Caribbean, concluding this particular trip with a three-week stay

Courtesy of University of Michigan Transportation Library

Motor Way's whimsical sketch of the 1906 Chicago Auto Show depicts a shoeless Ransom Olds (bottom right) next to Henry Ford, who is wearing a derby several sizes too small and an overcoat not long enough to hide his lack of trousers. Harvey Firestone, appropriately enough, sports a tire around his waist. Between Elmer Apperson (no. 8) and E. R. Thomas (no. 10) is a glum-looking Fred Smith.

in Bermuda. Interestingly, the auto magnate rarely traveled long distances by car, preferring—as did most sensible travelers on land during these years—to use the railroads. One exception, however, came in the summer of 1908 when Olds, his wife, their two daughters, and a guest took a leisurely month-long motoring trip through the Northeast, though even then both ways of the Detroit-Buffalo part of the trip were by lake steamer.

Even when Olds was in Lansing, his diary rarely indicates that he spent the day "in the office." Generally the entries for days—or even weeks—at a time read simply: "at home." From there it was possible, of course, for him to be reached by his staff at the Reo plant, a few blocks away, enabling him to keep abreast of business developments. But in a more formal sense, his contacts during the year with the activities of his company and of the auto industry were few in number. He attended the annual Reo stockholders' meetings and usually attended the meetings of the board of directors; and since the New York auto show was the major social as well as business function of the year for the industry, he was invariably present at it. For the rest, however, he was content to allow his staff to run Reo.

As Olds recalled in later years, he had recognized that production goals that may have seemed enormous when he first started out—the one thousand runabouts he had aimed for in 1901, for example—were soon over-shadowed by the actual production figures a few years hence as the demand for automobiles blossomed. Keeping up with this demand required changes in management. It was no longer possible for one man to keep tabs on every detail of the operation himself. Therefore, Olds said, he had learned to delegate more and more responsibility to experienced staff members.

No doubt this picture of what happened contains a good deal of rationalizing on Olds' part to conceal the fact that he was probably not that interested in continuing to play an active role in the management of Reo. If this was the case, Olds was indeed fortunate to have a staff, headed by Richard Scott, that seems to have been an unusually devoted and loyal force, in an industry notorious for its high rate of employee turnover. On one occasion, Yarnell relates, a Reo executive in the $25,000-a-year bracket was offered a job with a competing firm at a beginning salary of $100,000. Olds told the man that he could not match such an offer, but the executive turned it down anyway, telling Olds: "I'd rather work for Reo at what I'm getting than to take the other position at four times the salary." Unlikely as it may seem, Yarnell claimed that this example "was a typical employee reaction."[8]

The one area in which Olds continued to maintain an interest and exert his authority appears to have been the design and mechanical features of the cars. However, even here there is evidence, at least from the patent records, of a very decided slowdown in the productive nature of Olds' work from his earlier years. Shortly after the organization of Reo, Olds applied for a patent on the Reo's running gear in October 1904. Over a year later, he applied for a patent on a "Convertible Automobile Body," designating a body that could be quickly and easily converted from a one-seat to a two-seat vehicle. In July 1907, Olds, together with Horace Thomas, applied for a patent on a gas engine that operated on a six-cycle principle. No further applications—at least no successful applications—were forthcoming from Olds until one on a tire patent made in 1910 and issued to him the following year. Only eight other patents would be issued to Olds during the rest of his life, almost none of them directly related to automobiles. The four auto-related patents he did receive during the first seven years of his association with Reo were decidedly different from the eighteen he had successfully applied for in the years 1894 to 1902. During the time that the volume of his innovative work dropped, Olds' diaries also seem to indicate that he was spending more time on the details of the yachts he was building for his leisure enjoyment than he was on the design of the automobiles that had provided him with the wealth to enjoy himself in that luxurious fashion.[9]

* * * * *

Even before Olds had relinquished much of his authority over the operations of his Reo company, he was showing an unwillingness to use his power and prestige as the head of a major automobile company as a means of influencing issues, even when he recognized their importance to the development of the industry. The best example of this was his vacillating stand regarding the Selden Patent. At the time Olds was involved with the organization of Reo during the summer of 1904, almost a year had passed since the Association of Licensed Automobile Manufacturers, headed by Fred Smith, had brought suit against the Ford Motor Company for its continued production of gasoline automobiles without a license from the holders of the Selden Patent, which they claimed covered this kind of car. The suit had proceeded along its involved and tedious course and was still years away from final settlement. Ransom Olds, like most of his fellow automobile pioneers, agreed with Ford's position that the Selden Patent did not apply to his automobiles or to those of most other American manufacturers of gasoline-powered cars. Olds would be among those who testified as an expert witness for the defense in the suit against Ford. His views had not been generally known earlier because of his position with the Olds Motor Works, one of the charter members of the ALAM. Shortly after Reo's formation was announced, however, Olds was forced to declare himself openly when he received a letter on August 29, 1904 from the attorneys for the Selden forces, warning him that if he proceeded with his plans to produce a gasoline automobile without the permission of the patentholders, "you will render yourself liable to a suit for an injunction and accounting for your infringement of the said Selden Patent."[10]

On a trip to New York at this time, Olds discussed with Ray Owen and Roy Rainey whether or not he should apply for a license, and the three men decided that it would be safe for Olds to proceed without one, even though Olds suspected that Fred Smith might attempt to get the ALAM to institute action against Reo as another one of his harassing tactics of his former colleague. The very fact that Smith was a leader of the licensed automobile manufacturers' group may also have convinced Olds that he stood little chance of getting a license even if he applied for one. By mid-September, however, after talking with George H. Day, general manager of the ALAM, Roy Rainey had changed his mind about the wisdom of going ahead without a license. Impressed with what seemed to be the great power the ALAM represented, Rainey now joined with Ray Owen during the next months in urging Olds to seek membership in the licensed organization.[11]

The fact that Owen and Rainey were the distributors in New York City of the Franklin, a licensed car produced in Syracuse, placed them in an embarrassing position if the Reos, which they had also contracted to handle, continued to be produced in defiance of the expressed opposition of the Selden interests. It was more than embarrassing: the ALAM declared that part of the licensing arrangement was an understanding that the licensed manufacturers and their agents would "not sell, keep on hand or in any manner dispose of or deal in directly or indirectly any unlicensed new or second-hand gasoline vehicle infringing said Selden patent." Earlier in 1904, Cadillac, a member of the ALAM, had taken its Philadelphia agency away from John Wanamaker when the latter acquired the Ford agency in New York. Officials of Cadillac explained at the time that they did not want to run "any risk with the Selden Patent by Wanamaker selling a licensed machine in one shop and an unlicensed one in the other."[12]

Ray Owen, who may have feared that the Franklin company would now threaten to follow Cadillac's example if he did not give up his Reo distributorship, was reassured by H. H. Franklin, head of the New York firm, who promised Owen that he would use his influence to get the ALAM to approve an application from Reo. Owen told Franklin that he thought Olds would submit such an application if he were given some assurances that it would be acted upon favorably. This would suggest that Olds' fears of being turned down by the association and the damage this would do his reputation caused him to oppose entry into the organization and to speak out against the ALAM, rather than the force of his opinions regarding the validity of the Selden Patent and the methods the group was using to enforce it.[13]

However, for whatever reason, Ransom Olds refused to

heed the advice of Owen and Rainey on the Selden issue during the autumn of 1904, despite the importance he must have attached to the need to remain on good terms with the men who would be responsible for selling his cars. For a time Olds even seemed about to take the leadership of the anti-ALAM forces in the industry. In his testimony in the patent suit proceedings he declared that he would go back to making steam cars before he would agree to the terms demanded by the patentholders. Early in September, Olds informed Henry Ford of his support of the fight Ford was waging against the ALAM, and by the end of October he was suggesting to Ford that they take the lead in forming a rival association of unlicensed manufacturers. Ford liked the idea, but the two apparently decided that it would be best to have the new organization headed by a manufacturer who was less controversial and not so clearly identified with the opposition to the patent and to the ALAM. Their choice for the job was a relatively obscure Peoria manufacturer, J. B. Bartholomew, who had produced a gasoline-powered car called the Bartholomew from 1901 to 1903 (when the name was changed to the Glide). Reuben Shettler set up a meeting in Chicago between Olds and Bartholomew early in November. Shettler explained to the Illinois automaker that Olds was so involved with getting Reo on its feet that he could not assume the leadership of the new association; but Bartholomew, if he agreed to take on this job, could rest assured that Olds and Reo would do everything they could to make the association a success. Olds was, after all, Shettler declared, "the best advertised automobile manufacturer in the world." The mere fact that he was a member of the association would add enormously to its prestige.[14]

Later in November, however, Olds began to back away from the aggressive position he had thus far assumed toward the ALAM. It would appear that this was partly because of some consideration that came up in his meeting with Bartholomew. But it is also true that these were crucial weeks in the development of Reo: not only did the work in Lansing demand Olds' full attention, but he also probably came to believe that he might be subjecting his company needlessly to the danger of attack from Smith and the licensed automobile forces if he became too openly identified with the operation. To be sure, he continued to resist the pressures from Ray Owen, who hammered away at the theme that admission to the ALAM was the safest course for Olds to take. And in mid-January 1905, Olds was still expressing his support—at least to Owen—of an association of independents in opposition to the ALAM. Yet when such an association, the American Motor Car Manufacturers' Association, was formed on February 24, 1905, Reo was not among the score of companies that became charter members of the group. Furthermore, Henry Ford had changed his mind about keeping his company in the background of the organization; the first president, or chairman, of the AMCMA was not J. B. Bartholomew but James Couzens, business manager of the Ford Motor Company. Bartholomew was elected treasurer, while officers of the National Motor Vehicle Company of Indianapolis and the Mitchell Motor Car Company of Racine, Wisconsin, were elected vice chairman and secretary respectively. Thus Ford, who had already reaped invaluable publicity for himself and his company as the defendants in the Selden Patent suit, capitalized still further from his company's leading position in the fight against what Ford had effectively branded the monopolistic forces which the ALAM represented.[15]

Reo subsequently did join the AMCMA, but without the fanfare that would have resulted had this action taken place when the organization was formed and when Ransom Olds could have been identified as one of its founding fathers. Likewise, Reo eventually was included among the group of unlicensed manufacturers who were being sued by the Selden forces, but again Olds' company was cast in a secondary role to that played by the Ford Motor Company, which the public correctly viewed as the firm that had borne the brunt of the ALAM's attack since the suit was initiated in 1903.[16]

When a federal district court ruled in September 1909 in favor of the Selden Patent, Reo continued in the AMCMA for several months. In fact, in January 1910, Olds served as chairman in charge of the association's annual show in

Grand Central Palace, New York, an event which the
AMCMA had staged since 1906, when the older Madison
Square Garden auto show had begun to be limited to members of the ALAM. Olds' report at the conclusion of the show
said that it had been a financial success and that attendance
had been greater than at any of the previous exhibitions the
group had held in the Palace. Members of the association
voted to present "a suitable token" to Olds in appreciation of
his work. But the action came at a time when the unlicensed
manufacturers association was rapidly disintegrating and
members—in the face of the federal court decision—were
scurrying to join the ALAM, on whatever terms the trium-
phant rival association was demanding of the holdouts. Reo
was one of the joiners; in fact, the day after Olds had accepted the plaudits of the AMCMA members, he attended a
meeting of the ALAM's board of managers that was being
held in conjunction with the Selden forces' rival auto show in
Madison Square Garden.[17]

Later that spring Olds, together with fellow Michigan auto
executives Henry Joy and Benjamin Briscoe, served on a
five-member committee that arranged a banquet of the
ALAM, billed as the first annual affair of this nature, which
was held at New York's Hotel Astor on April 7. And the
presence of Michigan's Governor Fred M. Warner as the
principal speaker on that occasion no doubt partly reflected
the influence of Ransom Olds, who was active in Warner's
Republican party. Olds himself, of course, was among the
distinguished group of automobile men who attended the
formal affair, along with Ray Owen, who had urged Olds to
join this group five and a half years earlier. Ironically, Fred
Smith, one of the founders of the organization, was absent,
probably because he had left the Olds Motor Works the preceding September and was no longer very active in the industry.[18]

Another prominent absentee was Henry Ford, who had
stubbornly refused to bow to the Selden forces. Instead, he
had appealed the district court's decision regarding the validity of the patent as it pertained to his car. Early in 1911 a
federal court of appeals reversed the lower court's judgment

and ruled that the Selden Patent did not apply to the automobiles that Ford and nearly all other American companies, including Reo, were producing. This was what Ransom Olds had contended all along; but it was Henry Ford alone who would forever have the distinction of fighting for this viewpoint through to final victory in the courts and compelling the surrender and ultimate dissolution of the licensed automobile manufacturers association. Olds could have gained a share of those honors had he not wavered from his initial inclination in the autumn of 1904 to take a strong stand against the ALAM.

It turned out that Olds' advisors Ray Owen and Roy Rainey had grossly misjudged the impact the ALAM's opposition could have upon Reo sales. That the association was really something of a paper tiger was proved by Ford: instead of seeing his company wither in the face of the vaunted power of the Selden combine, he saw it prosper to the point that by 1911 sales were up to nearly 40,000 cars a year, almost eight times the sales of Olds' licensed company, and far beyond those of any other automobile manufacturer.[19]

CHAPTER ELEVEN
Merger Talks

RANSOM OLDS failed to use his power and influence to the best advantage not only in the case of the Selden Patent but also in the case of another trend that was developing during that same period. This was the consolidation of automobile manufacturers and parts companies into larger combinations that could compete more effectively for a larger share of the market. In August 1907, *Horseless Age* predicted that a period of reorganization was imminent in the industry. For the first time in the history of the industry a number of agents had failed to sell all of their cars, and within the month previous to the article's publication at least a dozen automobile companies were reportedly encountering severe financial problems. The multitude of small concerns that had sprung up would, the trade journal declared, find it increasingly difficult to survive. Already, the advantages which manufacturers like Olds had earlier demonstrated of "producing on a large scale" had "practically forced the small companies from the low priced runabout field." In the future, small firms would be able to survive "only if they offer a vehicle of decided merit, and run both their manufacturing and business departments in a businesslike manner in accordance with the most up to date methods." For the rest, however, *Horseless Age* stated: "The same economic laws which have brought other industries under the control of a relatively small number of large firms will assert themselves in the automobile industry."[1]

Just as in the Selden dispute, there is evidence that Olds' basic judgments on the need for consolidation were sound.

Duane Yarnell quotes one of Olds' statements during this period: "I believe that the next big development in the motor car industry will be the merger of a number of independents into one gigantic corporation. Just what companies will be taken into this merger I cannot say, but competitive conditions are forcing the development." The date and the occasion for this pronouncement are not given, but Olds would seem to have been moving in that direction himself in 1906, when he added to his control of a single automobile company the control of three suppliers of essential automotive parts. "By following the ruthless policy of monopolizing sources of supply, by taking over control of parts companies, by operating solely upon public funds [that is, through the sale of large amounts of stock]," Olds, Yarnell speculates, "might easily have built up the greatest monopolistic empire in the history of American industry."[2]

Yarnell would seem to have been naive in the extreme if he assumed that anyone could have created such an empire with ease; but he was even more naive if he actually thought that R. E. Olds could have attempted such an undertaking. Not only would no one be likely to have described Olds as "ruthless," but Olds was lacking in the promotional talents that were needed to pull off a large-scale merger and to arrange for its financing through huge public stock offerings, a method he never favored anyway. Olds was not an entrepreneur; he was a master mechanic who was interested in engines and their uses. He was satisfied with what are now seen as quite modest goals but which were at the same time, so far as Olds was concerned, far beyond anything he had dreamed of attaining when he and his father started out in the mid-1880s to make a success of their little machine-shop business. The empire-building that took place in the industry from 1907 onwards was not the work of the mechanics among the auto pioneers—the Duryeas, Charles King, Jonathan Maxwell, Henry Ford (whose manufacturing operation grew to enormous size through means other than consolidation), and Olds—but of relative latecomers to the industry. The consolidators Benjamin Briscoe and William

C. Durant lacked the mechanical interests and abilities of Olds and Ford, but they possessed the vision, the incentive, and the special skills needed to create a General Motors.

It was Briscoe, the one-time manufacturer of sheet-metal parts for Olds' runabout, who first proposed to Durant sometime in 1907 that they merge their Buick and Maxwell-Briscoe companies along with any other manufacturers they could persuade to come in. Briscoe was probably prompted to take this step by the great Wall Street investment house of J. P. Morgan and Company, which had a large financial interest in Briscoe's automobile company and then saw an opportunity to pull off in the automobile industry the same kind of coup Morgan had carried off a few years earlier in the steel industry with the formation of United States Steel and in the farm equipment field with the creation of International Harvester.[3]

Although the idea of the merger was not initially his own, it immediately attracted Durant's enthusiastic support. It was in keeping with ideas he had earlier sought to advance in the carriage industry with his Durant-Dort Carriage Company, before he took over control of Buick late in 1904 and began a whole new career in the auto industry. Briscoe, according to Durant's recollections, had no very well-conceived ideas about where to go after the Buick and Maxwell operations were brought within one corporate structure. In his conference with Durant he named a group of automobile manufacturers Durant felt would be inappropriate for them to approach since they had little in common with each other or with the kind of cars that Buick and Maxwell-Briscoe were producing. Therefore, Durant suggested that Briscoe concentrate his efforts on the four largest auto manufacturers, which included—in addition to Buick and Maxwell—Ford and Reo. Although there were some considerable differences between the four companies, they were all concentrating their efforts on automobiles in the lower price ranges which they were producing in large quantities. Thus the four were distinct both in the cars they produced and the manufacturing techniques they employed, from firms that were concentrating on high-powered, high-priced, and low-volume automobile production.[4]

The chronology of the early talks concerning these merger plans cannot be precisely reconstructed, but there is evidence to support the assumption that Briscoe had contacted both Ford and Olds before the end of 1907 about a possible consolidation of their companies with his and Durant's and had clearly found both men interested in the idea. Subsequent developments indicate, however, that there were some basic differences in the views of Olds and Ford on the one hand, and of Briscoe on the other, about the method by which this consolidation was to be carried out, differences which were either not made entirely clear to Briscoe during the course of his talks with the two men or which he chose to overlook.

The best clues to the progress of the negotiations from that point on are to be found in Olds' diary for 1908. There he noted that on January 17 he boarded the Grand Trunk train long before dawn to go into Detroit for a meeting with Briscoe, Durant, and Ford later that morning. The meeting was held first in the Penobscot Building, and then when that location seemed too public a place for the kind of discussions they were engaged in, they adjourned to Durant's suite in the Pontchartrain Hotel, the favorite gathering place in Detroit for automobile tycoons during those years (not to be confused with Detroit's present hotel of the same name). James Couzens, a tough bargainer, accompanied Ford to some of the negotiating sessions and may have been present at this first meeting of the representatives of the four interested companies; but there is no evidence that Olds brought along any of his associates to this or any of the later meetings.[5]

At the January 17 meeting Briscoe proposed that the four top executives present agree upon a plan of consolidation that they could present to the Morgan company, which would handle the necessary financial arrangements for the new corporation. Durant is said to have suggested placing a value of $10 million on the Ford Company, and on the basis of that figure he thought that $6 million would be a fair value to set on Reo's worth and $5 million on Maxwell-Briscoe. He set no figure on Buick's value, saying that he would leave that open to negotiations, the result to be based on the reports of the appraisers and auditors. However, the accuracy of these figures, which Durant included in a memoir he prepared many years later, is questionable. James Couzens, in notes that appear in a memorandum book he kept in 1907, reported— probably as a result of the discussion he and Ford had with Briscoe at that time—that the merged firm was to be capitalized at about $35 million, of which Ford, Reo, and Buick would each represent $7,125,000, and Maxwell-Briscoe $6,125,000, with the remainder of the stock to be sold or distributed as bonuses to the participants in the merger. These figures closely parallel the totals that Olds scribbled (his handwriting is not entirely legible) in his diary opposite the page containing entries for the week of May 31 to June 6, 1908. Thus it would appear that Olds and Couzens, at least, had the same understanding of what proportion of the worth of the new firm their own companies would represent. This same entry in Olds' diary, incidentally, is the only source indicating that the Brush Runabout, produced by Briscoe's brother Frank, was also part of the merger discussions at this time.

The four major participants in the January 17 consolidation meeting apparently did not come to a final agreement on the kind of corporate organization the merger would take. Briscoe favored a real consolidation of the companies, with one central committee deciding the operating policies, and with the purchasing, engineering, advertising, and sales activities of the individual firms combined into single departments serving all the manufacturing units that made up the merger. Durant, on the other hand, wanted simply a holding company that would control the stock of the several companies but would leave the existing management of the separate companies free to continue operating with only a minimum of direction from the management of the holding company. If Olds or Ford expressed any opinions on this subject, there is no record of their remarks. From accounts that Durant and Briscoe wrote of this first meeting of the four men, it would appear that Ford and Olds did little talking and that at this stage in the negotiations they were maintaining a wait-and-see attitude.[6]

Olds returned to Lansing by train late that evening, but a week later, on January 24, he was in New York, where the merger talks were resumed in the law offices of J. P. Morgan's son-in-law, Herbert L. Satterlee, who represented the Morgan interests in the merger discussions during the next several months. The meeting, according to Olds' diary, lasted all that day and was continued from ten o'clock the next morning until three in the afternoon, when Olds left. No doubt correspondence was exchanged between the several interested parties during the following weeks, although none to or from Olds has yet turned up. The next occasion in which face-to-face bargaining took place, according to Olds' diary, was on May 11, again in Satterlee's office; and another session may have taken place on June 8 and 9, when Olds was again in New York. However, by that time the talks had taken an unexpected and, for Durant and Briscoe, disappointing turn.

At one of the meetings in Satterlee's office, probably that of May 11, the question of the value to be placed on the four companies came up once again. Benjamin Briscoe expressed his dissatisfaction with what he regarded as the undervaluation of his company by the other participants in the negotiations. It was an important issue, of course, because Briscoe and Durant were agreed that control of the several companies was to be obtained through an exchange of the stock of Buick, Maxwell-Briscoe, Reo, and Ford for a proportion of the stock of the new corporation; the proportion was to be based on the agreed-upon valuation of each of the four companies. Thus the higher a company's appraised value, the greater the amount of stock it would receive. Durant's and Briscoe's plans called for little or no cash to be paid to any of the companies. At this stage in the industry's development it was difficult to obtain money from financial institutions, since the latter generally took the view that the automobile's future was too uncertain for them to consider loans to such enterprises safe investments. However, in the view of Durant and Briscoe the stock they would receive in the new corporation would be a far more valuable consideration than cash, because past experience showed that the whole would become greater than the sum of its parts: that is, the market value of the stock of corporations such as they were now proposing soon far exceeded the combined value of the stock in the firms that had been merged. However, Ford and Olds took quite a different view of the matter. These two mechanics were practical men who were more interested in cash in hand than they were in what they might get in the future from the sale of any stock. They had kept their views to themselves at the earlier sessions in January; but in May they brought them out into the open, throwing the discussions into complete disarray.

According to Olds, he and Ford had talked the matter over together and had agreed that they would both hold out for a large cash settlement before they would agree to bring their companies into the merger. Thus, when Briscoe reopened the subject of the financial details of the merger by questioning the value to be placed on his company, James Couzens announced that if the Ford Motor Company was to be part of the merger, the company would have to receive $3 million in cash—according to Briscoe's recollections of the figure— before agreeing to accept stock for the remainder of its appraised value. This was the cue for Ransom Olds to speak up and announce that Reo would also have to receive a $3 million cash payment before it would join the new corporation. Actually, Olds' recollection was that he and Ford had asked for $4 million each, not the $3 million Briscoe recalled; in any event, whether the total sum was $6 million or $8 million, it was completely beyond any amount that Durant and Briscoe had contemplated or that J. P. Morgan and Company was prepared to furnish.[7]

But the problems did not end with the demand for cash which Ford and Olds had suddenly injected into the talks. The Morgan company, Satterlee later said, had been expecting the participants in the merger to make large subscriptions for the stock of the corporation, thereby helping to underwrite the venture. But when Satterlee asked Ford how much stock he planned to purchase, Ford replied, according to Durant's account, that he had no intentions of buying any stock at all. Whether the same question was put to Olds, Durant does not say; but it is likely that Olds' reply would have been the same as Ford's, because both men had agreed with each other that they wanted no connection with the corporation once it had been formed. "I don't like the idea of mixing up with these New York bankers," Ford reportedly had said to Olds. "I say we should make a clean break if we're going to get out at all. If you'll agree to sell your company, I'll agree to sell mine. We can turn the whole thing over to them and retire."[8]

It was Satterlee's recollection in later years that it had been understood all along that Ford and Olds planned to retire and that this was why they were interested in giving up their companies. However, Olds had quite a different recollection. He claimed that it was not so much the cash he and Ford demanded that upset the Morgan representatives as it was their announcement that they would not continue to manage their companies once they became part of the merger. Olds even claimed that the elder J. P. Morgan himself "threw up his hands" and said that without Ford's and Olds' continued direction of the Ford and Reo operations the merger "would be no go." Even though Olds was almost certainly mistaken about J. P. Morgan's presence at the meeting,* it seems logical that there would have been some individuals at the meeting in Satterlee's office who would have considered the Ford and Reo companies less valuable properties in the future without the direction of the two men who had enjoyed such success in running the firms since their organization. In fact, Olds stated on another occasion that when the bankers (he did not mention Morgan this time)

---

*Although Morgan was in New York at the time of the meetings in Satterlee's office on January 24 and 25, there is no evidence that he was present at those sessions; and at the time of the May meeting, when the exchange Olds mentions more likely occurred, Morgan was in Europe. Furthermore, it would have been highly unusual for the senior member of this great Wall Street firm to be present for any of these talks, in view of the fact that at this late stage in his life Morgan was leaving the details of his business affairs for his associates and staff to handle, and particularly since the Morgan company seems to have regarded the proposed automobile merger as one of the less important deals in which it was then involved.

learned that he and Ford intended to retire, they declared that the "deal is off." If Olds and Ford "didn't have faith enough in the industry to stay with it," Olds recalled the Wall Street financiers' reasoning, "they didn't want any part of it either."

On the other hand, continuing with their companies after a merger understandably held no appeal for either Ford or Olds. Each man was at the moment the president and majority stockholder of his company. Each would lose that status in a merger and would have to go back to a situation very much like the one he had found so annoying earlier in his business career: to the Olds Motors Works for Olds, and to the Detroit Automobile Company and the Henry Ford Company for Ford. There they had been minority stockholders, forced to work with—if not for—those who had actual control of the company. Olds felt no special obligation to his fellow Reo stockholders: they had already received more money than they had invested in 1904 through the dividends their stock had earned. They could decide for themselves what to do if Reo became part of the merger. As for himself, Olds undoubtedly saw the straight cash deal as an opportunity to make a very profitable exit from an industry that had lost much of its attraction for him.[9]

But Olds was not to have that opportunity in 1908. Herbert Satterlee, greatly distressed at the statements of the Ford and Reo representatives, called Durant and Briscoe aside into an adjoining office, where he angrily demanded an explanation for the sudden and unexpected direction the talks had taken. Durant replied that he was as surprised as Satterlee by the statements of Couzens and Olds. Briscoe, however, was forced to confess that Henry Ford had given him some indication earlier that he was interested in cash, not stock, for agreeing to his company's becoming part of the consolidation. Briscoe said he had assumed that Ford had changed his mind in view of his apparent acquiescence in the general tenor of the progressing discussions. Satterlee obviously felt that Briscoe should have briefed him on the earlier conversations with Ford so that he could have been better prepared to counter Ford's demand for cash. As it was, Satterlee thought the matter over for a few minutes and then returned to the meeting, where he informed Ford and Olds that there had been an unfortunate misunderstanding. The financial arrangements, he explained, were entirely up to the bankers to determine, not the automobile executives. Therefore, Satterlee declared the meeting adjourned until such time as the bankers had had an opportunity to complete their plans.[10] This seems to have effectively ended the discussions.*

It is of course, easy enough today to see that each side showed poor judgment in not accepting the other's terms in that fateful meeting in Herbert Satterlee's Wall Street office. The Ford and Reo motor companies were well worth the money Couzens and Olds were asking, as an examination of their earnings would have seemed to indicate, even without any attempt to project future earnings. Reo's net profits for the year ending August 31, 1907 had topped $800,000, while Ford enjoyed its first million-dollar-plus profits in 1907. By the spring of 1908, with sales recovering from the depressed levels of the previous months' recession, it should have been evident to any well-informed industry observer that the prospects for both Reo and Ford were for continued improvements in their earnings record. If the Morgan officials failed to assess correctly the profitable character of the companies they were turning their backs on, however, Ford and Olds were equally guilty of failing to see how enormously valuable the stock they had refused to accept would become in a few years. How could investors refrain from frantically

---

*When the first rumors of these previously secret talks began to appear in print later in May, Reo was reportedly still one of the companies that was involved, and Olds' diary contains notes relating to the merger on a memorandum page accompanying entries for the end of May and the first part of June. It also indicates that he was in New York on June 8 and 9, but without specifying the nature of the business that brought him there. Although it is possible that the climactic turning point in the merger discussions took place at this later time rather than at the May 11 meeting, evidence against this appears in a story in *Horseless Age* during the first week of June: it states that talk had by then narrowed down to a merger of only Buick and Maxwell-Briscoe, indicating that Ford and Reo had been dropped from consideration. Later, in July, Edward Peer, secretary of Reo, admitted to a reporter that the company had earlier been approached about a merger; but, he said, Reo had never "seriously considered the proposition."[11]

scrambling to obtain stock in a company that would have started out producing the Buick, Ford, Reo, and Maxwell, the four best-selling cars in the industry—in the world, for that matter! Charles S. Mott, who soon took advantage of the kind of deal Olds and Ford turned down, saw the General Motors stock that he was given for control of his Weston-Mott Company—proportionately far less than what Ford and Olds would have received for their companies—spiral into a personal fortune that was at one time estimated at $800 million.[12]

It is impossible to say what would have happened, of course, if the merger talks in the spring of 1908 had ended in agreement. The objections that the Morgan interests raised, according to Olds, to acquiring the Ford and Reo companies without also getting the services of Henry Ford and Ransom Olds had considerable merit. In later years W. C. Durant said that there was no doubt in his mind that without Henry Ford, the Ford Motor Company would not have reached the important position in the industry as a division of a consoli-dated firm that it did as an independent manufacturer under Ford's continued direction. On the other hand, Reo might have fared better under the consolidation. With the medium-priced Reo in his stable, Durant would probably not have had as much interest in acquiring the financially trou-bled Olds Motor Works; thus the successful effort of Durant and General Motors to restore Oldsmobile to a strong posi-tion in the industry might have been applied to Reo. The acquisition of Oldsmobile was something of a stopgap action that was forced on Durant if he was to have any merger at all; had Ransom Olds not joined Henry Ford in balking at the J. P. Morgan Company's merger proposal, the public might still be buying Reo passenger cars today.[13]

However, the discussions that were terminated in the spring of 1908 were not the last chance Ransom Olds had to be part of a merger. The words "General Motors" followed by several figures appear on the memorandum page of Olds' diary oppo-site the entries for October 19, 1908. After the collapse of the merger negotiations in the spring, Durant and Briscoe, continuing to work with Satterlee and the Morgan interests, tried to work out a merger simply of their two companies. But by the beginning of August these efforts had also failed. It was then that Durant went ahead on his own and organized the General Motors Company, a holding company whose articles of incorporation were filed in New Jersey on September 16, 1908. Within two weeks Durant had completed arrangements for the new company to acquire control of Buick, through an exchange of stock, and after that he worked at bringing in additional companies.

The first of these was the Olds Motor Works. The previous summer, Durant had been searching for an ace in the hole in case other merger plans collapsed and had found the Smiths receptive to the possibility of merger. As noted above, their decision in 1906 to shift their emphasis from the production of the inexpensive runabout to much more powerful and expensive cars had had a disastrous effect on Oldsmobile sales. Serious discussions regarding a merger were underway by October. Fred Smith, however, balked at the terms of Durant's first offer on October 10. Olds' diary entry would indicate that following this initial rebuff from Fred Smith, Durant had communicated with Olds to inquire again about the availability of Reo. It was absolutely essential at this time for Durant to get control of some other automobile company besides Buick—which he had already controlled anyway—if General Motors stock was going to be attractive to potential investors. Olds would have almost certainly told Durant in October what he had told the gathering in Satterlee's office in May: a large cash settlement was still the prerequisite if Durant wanted Reo to be included in his latest merger scheme; Durant would still have been unenthusiastic about such a response from Olds. And shortly afterward his need for Reo became less urgent when the Smiths' objections to his first offer were resolved and the Olds Motor Works was acquired on November 12, 1908 on the basis of an exchange of stock, with little money changing hands.[14]

On a trip to New York the following year, Olds noted in his diary on September 28: "Saw Durant." No mention is made of the nature of the conversation; but since Olds was not

given to trivial diary entries—or comprehensive accounts of
what he did during a particular day, for that matter—it can
be reasonably assumed that the meeting dealt with matters
of some importance. In view of Durant's amazing success
since the previous fall in adding a host of additional automobile and parts manufacturers to those already controlled by General Motors, it would have been surprising
indeed if Durant had not broached the subject of Reo's acquisition again. However, Durant's acquisition of the Oak-
land company (GM's future Pontiac Motor Car Division), together with his ownership of Oldsmobile, further lessened
any real necessity to acquire yet another medium-priced car.
The discussions would certainly have ended quickly if Olds
had brought up the subject of money, since only a few weeks
before that Durant had been forced to come up with about
$4.5 million to gain control of Cadillac. The effort had largely
exhausted his credit at the banks, although shortly after his
September 28 meeting with Olds he would go out on a limb
by securing an option to purchase the Ford Motor Company
for eight million dollars. The deal did not go through, however, because the banks turned down Durant's bid for a loan
of $2 million to make the first payment to Ford.[15]

In addition to seeing Durant, Olds had talks the day before
with Benjamin Briscoe and Alfred Reeves, Olds' companion
on the 1905 Glidden Tour. The latter was now working with
Briscoe on merger plans of their own. After the efforts to
merge Buick and Maxwell-Briscoe had ended in failure during the summer of 1908, Briscoe, like Durant, had tried to go
it alone. In November 1908 he had reportedly had an option
to buy controlling interest in Cadillac, but he had been unable to raise the money demanded by Henry Leland, head of
Cadillac. Then in 1909, Durant and Briscoe tried again to
unite their interests. A deal had been arranged in July
whereby General Motors would acquire control of the
Maxwell-Briscoe Company, plus the Briscoe sheet metal
company in Detroit and Frank Briscoe's Brush Runabout
firm, for $5 million in stock. Ironically, however, the
Morgan interests, which had to approve the merger because
of their large holdings in Briscoe's enterprises, refused to

accept a stock-only offer, insisting instead that General
Motors pay $2 million in cash, the same kind of deal Ford
and Olds had demanded the year before and the Morgan
company had refused to accept. Now Morgan's insistence
that Durant come up with a large amount of cash ended
hopes for the merger of the Briscoe interests with General
Motors.[16]

In the next few months Benjamin Briscoe again set out to
create a rival combination with his Maxwell-Briscoe company as the nucleus, just as Durant's Buick had been the
nucleus around which he had organized General Motors. In
January 1910, Briscoe succeeded in forming the United
States Motor Company, with Maxwell-Briscoe as its first acquisition. Briscoe's major financial backing came from the
prominent Wall Street investor Anthony Brady, who had
large holdings in the Columbia Motor Car Company in
Hartford, Connecticut, and who now brought this company
into the U. S. Motor organization; he also arranged to provide the new company with one million dollars in new funds.
During the following months Briscoe acquired a number of
other auto manufacturers, including his brother's Brush
Runabout. But his inability to persuade his supporters to
come up with the cash he needed, when stocks alone were not
enough to swing a deal, prevented him from getting the big
name cars that were required for the lasting success of his
combine.[17]

Briscoe later claimed that he, like Durant, had had the
opportunity to gain control of the Ford Motor Company in
the fall of 1909, but the $8 million in cash Henry Ford was ask-
ing was just as impossible for Briscoe to raise as it had been for
Durant. At the same time Briscoe also sought to acquire Reo,
even though this too would require a substantial amount of
cash if the effort were to succeed. Briscoe and his aide Reeves
perhaps made the preliminary overtures to Ransom Olds at
their meeting on September 27, 1909. After U. S. Motor was
organized in early 1910, rumors persistently linked Reo with
Briscoe's company; some reports by that spring even asserted
that the Lansing firm had already been taken over by U. S.
Motor.

These rumors gained some substance by the acknowledgment that some Reo stock had passed into the hands of U. S. Motor backers. However, when he was questioned by a Lansing newspaper early in May, Ransom Olds denied that any Reo stock had been acquired by U. S. Motor or any other company. On the other hand, he would not deny that discussions had been held between Reo representatives and officials of other companies and that a possibility existed that Reo would be sold. Declaring with some pardonable exaggeration that Reo was "the greatest money maker in the automobile world," Olds said that it was not surprising that others were interested in getting their hands on such a profitable business. They could do so, Olds announced, if they came up with $7 million in cash "for our holdings." He apparently meant that that was the asking price for his own majority stockholdings in the Reo company, since he indicated at the same time that he would not sell his stock unless all other Reo stockholders were included in the deal on a similar cash basis. Thus the cost of purchasing all outstanding Reo stock could have greatly exceeded Henry Ford's eight-million-dollar price tag, which Briscoe and Durant had both found beyond their reach when they had wanted to acquire the Ford Motor Company the previous fall.[18]

By the beginning of 1911, Olds was indicating to insiders that he would be willing to sell his stock, regardless of what the other stockholders might do. Throughout that year and on into 1912, despite public statements to the contrary, he was actively seeking to find a buyer or buyers for his holdings. At the end of September 1911, he went to Chicago to confer with one of W. C. Durant's former aides, Arnold H. Goss, who was at that time apparently involved with the promotional plans of John North Willys (though it is possible Goss was still doing leg work for Durant, who was involved in a host of new automobile schemes since he had been forced to give up managerial control of General Motors in 1910).[19]

Willys had entered the auto industry a decade or so earlier as an automobile salesman; in 1906 he had contracted to sell the entire output of the Overland company of Indianapolis, just as Ray Owen was doing with the Reo Company. Late in

1907, when the management of Overland had failed to deliver the cars Willys had contracted for, and the company was, in fact, on the verge of bankruptcy, Willys gave a virtuoso display of his promotional talents by raising the money needed to save the company. He then proceeded to take it over. He renamed the firm the Willys-Overland Company and moved the operations to Toledo, beginning a successful automotive manufacturing development in that Ohio city that survives today as the Jeep manufacturing division of American Motors. By 1909, Willys-Overland, which had been a negligible concern in the industry earlier, had advanced under Willys' direction to seventh place in automobile production, ranking right behind Reo. By 1910, when Reo's production began its downward slide, Willys-Overland's output increased threefold, shooting the company up into third place; after 1911 it was second only to Ford for the next six years.[20]

But John Willys, like Durant and Briscoe, was never content with the success of one company; he was constantly on the lookout for opportunities to expand his interests. It appears that 1911–12 was a period of intensified development of Willys' expansion plans, and his activity culminated in 1912 in the acquisition of two motor-truck manufacturing firms. Since Ransom Olds had by this time become involved in the manufacture of trucks, as we shall see below, it may have been this interest that first brought Olds and Willys together; but it seems likely that Olds would soon have sought to expand the talks to a more general consideration of Olds' entire automotive holdings.

Whatever the purpose or the outcome of Olds' discussions with Arnold Goss in September 1911, something was definitely in the wind by the first of the next year. On January 3, 1912, Olds noted in his diary that on his way to New York, he had conferred with Willys in Toledo. Four days later, in New York, he "went over to see Willys" at the latter's hotel. On the ninth Olds left by train for Detroit, where he spent the entire following day in conference with Goss, although his diary indicates that he had also expected to see Willys at the same time. And a week later Olds was in Chicago, where he again spent nearly the entire day in further discussions with Arnold Goss.[21]

Nothing appears to have come of these talks, and assuming that Olds was trying to sell his Reo holdings to Willys, this was typical of all of Olds' efforts along these lines. Despite the fact that he was now willing to accept an offer whereby payment for his stock could be spread over several years, there were no buyers. As Olds confessed to an associate in May 1912, it seemed that "no one could raise the money for so large a proposition." Those who might have raised the money were probably unwilling to meet Olds' price because of doubts about the value of the company they were being asked to buy. With the leveling off of Reo sales by 1910 and the sharp decline that began in 1911, Olds' asking price of $7 million would have seemed more and more out of the question to Benjamin Briscoe, John Willys, and any other interested individuals. In Briscoe's case, however, his failure to acquire control of Reo may have contributed to the demise of his U. S. Motor combine. With only its Maxwell car continuing to be a strong contender for automobile sales, the company was forced into bankruptcy in 1912. It might have been able to survive had Olds been less insistent on cash as the only basis for the transfer of the control of his company at the time Briscoe was putting his merger together in 1909–10.[22]

CHAPTER TWELVE

The Reorganization of Reo

DURING THE SAME PERIOD in which Olds was carrying on his fruitless merger talks with Durant, Briscoe, and Willys, major changes were taking place within the Reo organization that were of crucial importance both to the future of that company and to Olds' position within it. In 1908, Reo became one of the first American companies to establish a branch in Canada as a means of getting around the high tariff rate imposed on American-made cars imported into that country. The Reo Automobile Company, Limited (renamed the Reo Motor Car Company of Canada shortly thereafter) was initially located at Windsor, and later moved to St. Catherines, Ontario. The parent company held all the stock in the Canadian firm except for single shares held by Olds, Richard Scott, Edward Peer, Donald E. Bates, and W. G. Morley, the former Olds Motor Works official who now became manager of the Canadian operations.[1]

Far more significant, however, were developments in 1910. In May of that year Ransom Olds purchased the plant of E. Bement & Sons Company, the long-time Lansing stove and farm equipment manufacturer, which had fallen on bad times and had gone bankrupt some time earlier. Within a few days newspaper stories revealed the motive behind Olds' move: the Bement factory was to be converted into a temporary facility in which Reo would soon begin to produce trucks. Olds had had some experience with commercial vehicles: he had reportedly intended to produce them when he first attempted to manufacture motorized conveyances in the late nineties; in fact, he did produce some commercial vehicles in limited quantities while he was still in charge of Oldsmobile operations. Shortly after Reo automobiles were first produced, Olds' new company was said to be readying "a commercial car that will be so low in first cost that the horse cannot compete with it." Plans for and a sketch of a Reo delivery wagon were published early in 1906. However, this work remained largely experimental until 1910, when the decision was reached to produce two such vehicles: one was to be a light delivery wagon that would sell for $600, and the other a heavier fifteen-hundred-pound truck that would be priced at $750. Production was scheduled to begin in 1911. In October 1910 a separate firm, the Reo Motor Truck Company, was organized to manufacture Olds' commercial vehicles. The company was capitalized at one million dollars, and it paid the Reo Motor Car Company a hundred thousand dollars for the Bement property, including the machinery and other contents of the buildings.

In 1911, nearly a thousand Reo commercial vehicles were produced under what soon became the familiar "Speed Wagon" trade name. From the outset Reo's decision to produce trucks proved to be one of the best that Olds and his associates ever made. Ultimately, Reo trucks would continue to be produced for nearly forty years after the last Reo passenger car had come out of the Lansing factory. Although the commercial possibilities of motor vehicles had been widely discussed since the very first horseless carriages were produced, the pace at which such vehicles were adopted lagged far behind that of passenger automobiles. Thus, despite what might seem a late start by Olds in entering this field, he was still in plenty of time to benefit from the full development of interest in this type of motor vehicle manifested by the third decade of the twentieth century.[2]

As was to be expected, Reo ads gave the familiar depiction of this latest vehicle as yet another result of the experience and ingenuity of the company's founder. "Reo trucks... Built by R. E. Olds ... The Famous Designer." "It goes without saying that R. E. Olds knows how to build a truck," one early ad declared. "The dean of designers with 25 years of experience. The builder of myriads of pleasure cars. The

creator of Reo the Fifth. Mr. Olds should be—and he doubtless is—the best qualified man in the business." Efficiency,
durability, simplicity of operation, and low price, the
hallmarks of nearly all of Olds' products since his small
steam engines of the mid-eighties, were now said to be also
embodied in his trucks. "This truck is built so a twelve year
old boy can drive it.... It is immensely economical." The
price? "Only $750.... Most trucks which do what this truck
does, cost from $1,200 up." Finally, there was the oldest of
the familiar refrains from so many of Olds' promotions of
past vehicles—its advantages over comparable horsedrawn
forms of transportation. The fifteen-hundred-pound truck
"does five times the work of a one-horse truck, and it does it
three times as quick. It is always ready—never gets tired."[3]

The continued use of Ransom Olds' name in promotions, to
the exclusion of all other officials in the company, created
the impression that Olds was still in complete control of his
firm's affairs. However, the deterioration of Olds' actual control was accelerating from 1910 on, and it became more and
more clear to insiders, at least, that Richard H. Scott was the
man who was really in charge. According to Reuben Shettler, opposition to Scott's growing power in the company sur-
faced early in 1910. Shettler said that he and others objected
to what they regarded as the unwarranted and unauthorized
manner in which Scott had taken over many of the "official
rights and activities for the company," which had been dele-
gated to Olds. At the same time, however, Shettler complained, the growing involvement of Scott, an ardent prohibitionist, with the activities of the Anti-Saloon League was
causing him to neglect his assigned responsibilities as factory superintendent. Shettler's views on this subject were
echoed by others, who for many years would feel that Scott's
outside interests not only led to his neglect of company responsibilities but also had a detrimental effect on Reo sales
and profits. Herman Staebler, a pioneer auto dealer in Ann
Arbor who was for a time the Reo sales representative in the
Midwest, told of one occasion when he had negotiated a sizable sale of Reo vehicles to the Anheuser-Busch brewery in St.
Louis, only to have the deal called off at the last moment

when August Busch, Sr. realized that Richard Scott was a top executive in the firm Staebler represented. "Do you think I am going to buy from someone who's trying to put me out of business?" the incensed beermaker asked Staebler. The latter could only sit there without a response and watch a good sale yanked out of his grasp. Years later, after the end of national prohibition in 1933, it was Scott's refusal to approve large truck orders from the revived liquor industry that was thought to be a major contributor to the company's financial distress at that time.[4]

Ransom Olds was also a well-known supporter of prohibition, and it was his refusal to allow liquor to be dispensed in the Olds Hotel in Lansing that helped keep that city dry until after his death.* However, where his business interests were involved, and at locations other than Lansing, Olds was considerably more tolerant than Scott, not allowing his personal views to interfere with opportunities to make money. The point was, however, that Scott, not Olds, was making more and more of the decisions regarding Reo by 1910.[5]

According to Shettler, therefore, he sought to arrange matters in the early months of 1910 so that Ray Owen, whom Shettler referred to as "a thorough business man," would assume control of Reo's management. Shettler gave Owen an option on a portion of his own stock in the company, and then he sent off a letter to Olds, who was in Florida, "asking him to give Mr. Owen an option on enough of his stock, so that Mr. Owen, Mr. Peer, and myself would hold controlling interest." If Olds refused to agree to this request, Shettler threatened to take the train from Los Angeles back to Lansing, where he would "take away Scott's authority in the factory and disposses [sic] Mr. Olds of the gift of Common Stock he had received, and divide it among the stockholders, setting up the fact that he was not carrying out his agreements." Shettler would step down from the position of vice president that he had held since the formation of the company in 1904, and the job would be given to Owen, who

---

*It also contributed to some serious and ultimately unhappy conflicts within the family, since Olds' son-in-law, who managed the hotel, felt that a liquor license was essential to the continued success of this business.

would also take over Olds' position of general manager. Olds was apparently to be permitted to stay on as president, but without any real power, while Richard Scott would presumably be relieved of any further managerial responsibilities.

At first, Shettler later recalled, his plan seemed about to go through. Olds telegraphed Shettler and Owen that he was willing to go along with the idea, and Owen went to Florida where he obtained from Olds the requested option to purchase the stock necessary to carry out the scheme. But then, Shettler said, something happened, and "for some unaccountable reason, best known to Messers. Olds and Scott, Mr. Owen allowed this option to lapse, after I resigned in his favor. This created a situation where there was nothing E. F. Peer . . . and I could do but sell our stock and retire from the Company."[6]

Entries in Olds' diary for the period from February through April 1910 confirm some of the details of the account Shettler wrote in 1936; they also provide some evidence that there may have been more involved in these intrigues and negotiations than Shettler cared to reveal or perhaps knew. Olds did give Owen an option on a substantial block of Reo stock, but the purpose behind this move does not seem entirely consistent with what Shettler claims to have had in mind. Notations on the memorandum page of Olds' diary opposite the week of February 27 to March 5, at least, indicate that major changes in the Reo hierarchy were being contemplated at that time. Shettler would be out as vice president, to be replaced by Owen; but Shettler's partner Peer would also be ousted, his dual job as secretary and treasurer to be divided between J. Edward Roe and Donald Bates respectively. Shettler and Peer may have been willing to agree to complete exclusion from their former managerial positions, as well as to Olds' continuing on as president. But for Richard Scott to remain factory manager—as Olds also indicates was the intention of these negotiations—while Olds also held onto the title of General Manager, would seem to have been entirely contrary to the main intent of the Shettler-Peer plan.

Later, during the third week of March, Olds jotted down

notes for a letter to Owen, which indicated that by that time negotiations were underway for Owen to purchase all of Olds' stock. Olds said that he had been "thinking the stock matter over" and had decided that he "would not care to take less than $32—per s[hare] for 80000 s[hares] not under option." The other stockholders were to be given the same offer, Olds said, "but whether they sell or not would depend on how it was handled." In any event, Olds thought it was a good bargain that Owen should take advantage of. Between April 17 and 20, Olds was busy getting options on the stock of some or all of the other stockholders, and he was conferring with bankers in Detroit and with Owen in Detroit and Lansing about the progress of these stock negotiations.

No further mention of Olds' activities in this regard appear in his diary after April 20 (though he rarely wrote very detailed entries and frequently made no entries at all for days and even weeks at a time). From the information Olds does provide, it would appear that there was considerably more in the wind during the late winter and early spring of 1910 than Shettler relates in his account. If Shettler and Peer were originally teamed up with Owen in an effort to gain control of Reo, Owen eventually seems to have become a part of a larger plan that contemplated the acquisition of all the outstanding shares of stock in the company. With the numerous New York contacts he had acquired since becoming the Oldsmobile distributor there in 1901, Owen was quite possibly acting as the front man for U. S. Motor Company in that combine's widely rumored attempts to acquire Reo in the spring of 1910. Even though these larger schemes failed to be carried out, the plans that Olds had noted earlier in the winter for a change in Reo's managerial hierarchy were put into effect. Olds' April 5 diary notation, "Made RMO v. pres.," seems to indicate that Olds was thoroughly in favor of the change and, in fact, personally responsible for it. The announcement of the Reo directors' move appeared in the trade journals with the explanation that Owen had been elected to this position after "having purchased the interest of R. Shettler, retiring vice president." Two and a half months later, the other managerial change foretold by Olds' diary entry of the previous winter took place when J. Edward Roe was elected to the post of secretary, succeeding Edward Peer, who likewise was reported to have "resigned."[7]

Thus the result of those events in early 1910 was exactly as Reuben Shettler later related. He and Edward Peer had been out-maneuvered and forced to retire from the company. Instead of combining forces with Ray Owen to gain control of Reo, and forcing Richard Scott out—while placing Olds in a position of little influence—Shettler and Peer were out; and although Owen was in, Scott's position in the company remained unaffected by the changes, as had Olds'. It is quite possible that Scott was, as Shettler certainly believed, responsible for persuading Owen not to play the role assigned to him by Shettler in his plot to unseat Scott. Part of the explanation for Owen's willingness to heed Scott's advice—if that is what happened—may have appeared in October 1910: an agreement was announced whereby the Reo Motor Truck Company, through an exchange of stock, took over Ralph Owen's financially hard-pressed Owen Motor Car Company, thus relieving Ray Owen's brother of a potentially embarrassing business interest. This arrangement also had some advantages for the Reo organization, giving it control of a patented gear shift which it could use in the Reo cars, although it soon dropped any idea of keeping Owen's expensive RO car in production.* The possibility that such a deal could be worked out may have helped to change Ray Owen's mind earlier in the year about exercising the options that were part of Shettler's plans. Ray Owen's being awarded the contract to sell the new Reo trucks may also have been part of the arrangements that won him over to Scott's side.[8]

What Ransom Olds' role was in all these complicated maneuverings is difficult to say, aside from the obvious fact that he concurred in the decisions that were ultimately made. Given what was clearly his desire to retire from the business, Olds no doubt supported any developments in the winter and spring of 1910 that would have resulted in the sale of his

---

*Interestingly, Reo's action also helped to bail out Olds' former colleagues and rivals, Fred and Angus Smith, who were among the largest stockholders in the Owen company.

stock at the price he was asking for it. Once the prospect of such a development became unlikely, and it became rather clear that he would be forced to retain his stock, it is probable that he would have favored keeping Reo under the management of Scott. Although he rubbed many people the wrong way, Scott was an experienced factory manager with whose methods Olds was thoroughly familiar; the latter would not have been in favor of shifting over to a management team headed by Ray Owen, whose experience was not in the area of production. Thus, to protect his investment, Olds supported Scott in the final showdown over who was going to run the company.

For Edward Peer, who had been a resident of Lansing for over twenty years and had established a position of some importance in the business community there (with interests other than those he held in Reo), the forced resignation from his Reo position led shortly to his leaving Lansing and disappearing from the Olds story entirely. As for Reuben Shettler, Olds visited him in Los Angeles on at least one trip to California, taking a "long drive" with his former colleague on March 31, 1915, and two days later going to Shettler's home for dinner. Olds did not confide to his diary the nature of his conversations with Shettler, but whatever they may have been, the visit did not mark a lasting reconciliation between the two former partners and friends. Twenty-one years later, Shettler's typewritten recollections of his business associations with Olds showed so much hostility toward Olds and Scott that the Lansing *State Journal,* according to Shettler, refused to print the document, either as a news story or in the form of an advertisement paid for by Shettler.[9]

Despite the executive position Ray Owen gained as a result of the shuffling in 1910, his future with Reo was actually less secure as a result of Richard Scott's increased strength; this led to the termination of Ray Owen's sales contract with Reo three years later. There had been dissatisfaction within the company for some time with the arrangement that gave Owen the exclusive distribution rights to Reo vehicles. In fact, as early as the spring of 1906, Olds had jotted down in his diary what were apparently notes for a letter he planned to write to Owen, in which he would ask Owen if it would "not be better for both of us [for Olds' company] to take over sales ... and give you personally N. Y. & vicinity." He declared that Owen himself would probably not lose financially by such a change. But a more important consideration, Olds argued, was the probability that if Owen agreed to such a reduction in his sales responsibilities, it would avoid the danger of "R" taking some action about which Olds was apparently apprehensive. Although "R" could have referred to Reuben Shettler, the high regard Shettler later professed for Owen's ability and his support of the Owen contract suggests that Olds' 1906 reference was to Richard Scott, and that Scott at that early date was already raising objections to Owen's handling of Reo sales. If so, Scott finally got the support he needed in 1913, when the minutes of the Reo board of directors' meetings show Scott taking the lead in expressing the board's dissatisfaction with Owen's record in selling Reo automobiles. The day after Christmas, the board voted unanimously to terminate the contract with R. M. Owen's ability and his support of the Owen contract suggests apparently paid Owen's company over a quarter of a million dollars, while Owen's personal holdings of stock in both the Reo Motor Car and Reo Motor Truck companies were purchased by Richard Scott, adding very substantially to the latter's holdings.[10]

The actual state of affairs at Reo was finally recognized in December 1915, when Olds formally relinquished his title of general manager to Scott, who had been acting in that capacity in all but name for nearly a decade. Olds retained the title of president until December 20, 1923, when he also relinquished it to Scott and accepted instead the post of chairman of the board. The admittedly honorary nature of this position in the Reo organization was completely in harmony with Olds' desires to rid himself of all but the flimsiest of ties with an industry of which he had been one of the principal founders, but in whose subsequent development he had formed little interest in remaining involved.[11]

CHAPTER THIRTEEN

Olds' Later Business Career

LATE IN 1921, L. Gaylord Hulbert went to work for the Detroit patent law firm of Whittemore, Hulbert & Whittemore.
Like so many Detroiters of his generation, Hulbert had returned from service in World War I to seek his fortune in the
automobile industry; but after a couple of years he had found
himself unemployed when the postwar depression had a
severe—if brief—impact on the sale of cars. Gaylord's father,
Prescott M. Hulbert, persuaded his son to come to work in his
law office, where Gaylord's engineering training at the University of Michigan would be useful in evaluating many of
the patent applications the firm handled.

Over a half-century later, Gaylord Hulbert, who had originally accepted his father's offer only as a measure to tide him
over until he found a permanent position elsewhere, but who
had stayed on to become the senior member of Whittemore,
Hulbert & Belknap (as this venerable firm is now known),
recalled that one of his early assignments took him to Lansing to consult with Horace Thomas, chief engineer of the Reo
company, about some patent work that Hulbert's office was
handling for Reo. It happened that Ransom Olds was in the
office that particular day and asked Hulbert to see him when
he had completed his business with Thomas. Olds was well
acquainted with the elder Hulbert from the days, twenty-five
years before, when his Detroit firm (then known as Thomas
Sprague & Son) had handled all of Olds' patents during that
most productive period in Olds' automotive career. In the
1920s, however, Prescott Hulbert's son was surprised to dis-
cover that, although the president of the Reo Motor Car

Company wanted to discuss with him a pending patent application, it was one that had nothing to do with automobiles or with the Reo company.[1]

This incident exemplifies what seems to have been characteristic of Olds' later business career. Although he retained a connection with the automobile industry during much of this time, as symbolized by his office at Reo, his interest—even on those rare occasions when he was in the office—was likely to be in activities other than those connected with the production of cars and trucks. At the time of Hulbert's visit in the early twenties, when Richard Scott was securely in control of the management of Reo, Olds had applied at the United States Patent Office during 1919–20 for patents on a detachable propulsion unit for railway vehicles, a root extractor, and an auxiliary tread for pneumatic tires, all of which were issued to him in 1923. He had already been awarded a tractor patent in 1921.

This spurt of energy on Olds' part during the postwar period seems to indicate that he was never entirely satisfied or comfortable with the life of leisure that his automobile wealth had made possible. Furthermore, it was only natural that his lifelong love of machines would be one way in which he would satisfy his need to keep busy. But the further fact that the intervals between patents were now longer, and the inventions themselves lacked the closely related character of most of Olds' earlier inventions, supports the observation that none of Olds' later business activities seems to have aroused in him the kind of sustained interest he had had in his automotive work. In the years just before World War I, it had been power lawnmowers and tractors, with the latter continuing on into the next period of inventive energy during the early twenties, only to be followed in the thirties by a return to Olds' earliest mechanical interest, the engine—particularly the diesel engine.[2]

Some of Olds' later inventions were translated into new manufacturing ventures. The gasoline-powered lawnmower, which he patented in 1915, one of the earliest of those devices that would become such a familiar sight and sound on the American suburban scene, was put into production by

A widely used, 1920s era portrait of Olds, complete with celluloid collar

the Ideal Engine Company, a small Lansing firm that Olds had acquired. Next to motor vehicles, the lawnmower was probably the most successful product with which Olds was associated, and the company was soon renamed the Ideal Power Lawn Mower Company.[3]

Olds' work on diesel engines in the thirties and forties was an outgrowth of his investment in the 1920s in the Bates and Edmonds Motor Company, which Olds' former associates Madison Bates and James Edmonds had organized in 1899. From gasoline engines, which this company had manufactured and sold through the Eastern Fairbanks Company, it had turned to diesel engines in the early twenties, when the Fairbanks company ceased to order any more engines. In 1924, Harry Hill, who had obtained the controlling interest in the Lansing company, appealed to Olds for financial help to save the faltering business. Olds proceeded to purchase James Edmonds' stock for about $420,000. The company was reorganized as the Hill Diesel Engine Company in 1929, and Olds increased his investments in the company to more than $700,000. During the following decade Olds tried to combine his new interest in diesel engines with his continuing interest in automobiles, but without much success.[4]

In his later years, like a number of other automotive pioneers—notably Henry Ford, Charles King, and William E. Metzger—Olds took a fling at manufacturing airborne vehicles, although in this case he was involved only as an investor. Hugo Lundberg, Sr., who had been brought to Lansing in 1906 to manage the Michigan Screw Company, persuaded Olds, Richard Scott, and several others to invest $10,000 each in Driggs Aircraft, a new Lansing business that he was starting up in the twenties. Olds also was involved, along with Charles S. Mott, Charles F. Kettering, and Roy Chapin, with the organization of the Detroit Aircraft Corporation. However, neither of the two firms proved to be successful; instead, they helped to demonstrate that Michigan's success in becoming the center of the auto industry did not necessarily project into other areas of transportation.[5]

In 1932, Olds learned of a new refrigeration idea for trucks that had been developed in Greenville, Michigan. He bought the rights to the idea and formed the Kold-Hold Manufacturing Company. The name derived from the process that enabled an insulated truck to be connected to a refrigeration system which brought the temperature inside the storage area of the truck down to the desired level and maintained that temperature for several days by means of the insulating materials. Olds had several Reo trucks converted to the system and sent them around the country to promote the process, which reportedly enabled an ice cream truck, for example, to be refrigerated for only ten cents a day.[6]

Machines and mechanical devices, however, did not represent Olds' principal nonautomotive business interests in his later years. Indeed, if any one interest deserves first place it would have to be real estate. In 1912, Olds formed the R. E. Olds Company, reviving the name that had briefly been employed with his second automobile manufacturing company; this time around it was applied to a firm that would—from that time to the present—manage the Olds family's investments, mainly those connected with land and property holdings, although Olds was also interested in investments on the stock market (information in his diaries indicates that he came to be especially interested in certain Canadian stocks). Olds' real estate holdings had grown steadily from the relatively modest acquisitions he had made in Lansing in earlier years. Particularly after the sale of his Olds Motor Works stock, he added to his holdings and went far beyond the confines of Lansing. The most ambitious and potentially most important of Olds' land development projects was one that he launched in 1916 on Florida's Gulf Coast. There he attempted to establish a new community: it was not to be a resort for the well-to-do such as his friend and one-time Oldsmobile dealer Carl G. Fisher was building in Miami Beach during this period; instead, it was to be a community that Olds, consistent with his own background, hoped to make attractive for persons of modest means through the jobs that he would offer them in the factories he planned to locate there or through the farming opportunities that would also be made available in the surrounding countryside.[7]

Olds' initial interest in Florida had been on the east coast, where he had been among the first to see in the hard-packed sands of Daytona Beach ideal conditions for automobile competitions, and where he had acquired property in 1905 that would be his winter residence for the remaining forty-five years of his life. His west coast Florida development a decade later grew out of the desire he had expressed at least as early as 1912 to invest in Florida land and also out of his efforts to rid himself of an unprofitable Chicago apartment building. He received an offer from Richard G. Peters, who was willing to accept the apartment building, which Olds valued at $125,000, as partial payment on 37,541 acres of undeveloped land Peters owned on the north side of Tampa Bay. Olds was immediately interested, and by the early part of 1916 arrangements were completed for the purchase of Peters' property. The total cost to Olds, according to a news story, was $500,000, a figure that made this the largest real estate transaction ever handled in Lansing up to that time (though Olds' business records would seem to indicate that the price he paid was actually somewhat less than this published figure).[8]

On March 27, 1916, Olds noted in his diary that he had spent the entire day in the woods looking over this Florida acreage. He was apparently satisfied that he had chosen wisely. The land included ten miles of waterfront on the bay, and although the land itself was undeveloped— consisting of little more than scrub pine—it was bisected by the Seaboard Air Line Railway and by a paved road that linked Tampa with the Gulf Coast. Developed property bordered Olds' property on all sides, and in addition to Tampa, the communities of Clearwater, St. Petersburg, and Tarpon Springs were close at hand. Shortly after his on-the-spot assessment of the site's possibilities, therefore, Olds organized the Reo Farms Company (later renamed the Reolds Farms Company), with a capitalization of $1 million, to handle the development of a community that was at first dubbed

Reolds-on-the-Bay, but was later changed to Oldsmar. Although Olds tried to persuade Herman Staebler, the Midwest Reo agent, to join him in this venture—and he may well have approached other automotive associates—the names of the individuals who did become associated with him in this land development seem to have been drawn from a different group of acquaintances, including Charles Ecker, his longtime aide in the R. E. Olds Company.[9]

Olds was seized with an enthusiasm for his new project that led him to devote more attention to it for a time than almost anything else he had become involved in after stepping down from an active managerial role in the automobile industry. His diary shows that he spent a great deal of time at Oldsmar in 1917, and especially in the early part of 1918, as well as a considerable number of days in the years immediately following. The laying out of the town proceeded with the same kind of speed that had characterized the construction of Olds' factories in earlier years. Oldsmar was to have many of the features common to Florida land developments of the twentieth century: the resort hotel, complete with private bathing beach, boating facilities along the waterfront, an area that would feature "choice bungalow sites" priced at from $1,000 to $1,500, an 800-foot canal to accommodate more pleasure boats, curving drives lined with palm trees and flowering oleanders, golf courses, and other tourist-oriented attractions. But the distinctive character of Olds' development was reflected in the space set aside in the town for industrial plants and for numerous small farm plots on the outskirts. These were intended to make it possible for the working man and his family, through employment he would be able to obtain in a factory or through citrus-growing, cattle- or poultry-raising, or other farming activities, to be able to "enjoy the subtropical tourist advantages with as much zest as any millionaire."

Oldsmar was vigorously promoted in ways that would be familiar to anyone who is acquainted with the later promotional campaigns of such Florida land developers as the Mackle Brothers and General Development Corporation. Newspaper ads extolled the site as a "veritable garden spot";

salesmen, each with his own assigned territory, opened their offices in the North (principally in Michigan), and chartered trains carried prospective land buyers from Detroit to Oldsmar. The entire operation was directed by the Reolds Farms Company, which would do everything—from the sale of the home to the clearing of the land and the construction of the residence or any other desired buildings. In the case of a farm site, they would prepare the land for cultivation, build fences, drill wells, provide the necessary machinery, and even supply farm animals from livestock Olds planned to raise on his farm on Grosse Ile, Michigan. Payments could be made on the installment plan (cash and carry may have been feasible when Olds was selling his cheap runabouts but not for what he was selling at Oldsmar, at least not for the working-class customers he hoped to attract). The terms were approximately one-fourth of the total amount paid at the closing of the deal, and annual payments thereafter of ten per cent of the remaining total, at six per cent interest.[10]

Reolds Farms officials were soon boasting that Oldsmar had made more progress in one year than some other projects had made in ten. It was referred to as the "Wonder Town" of the area, and by 1922 one writer was claiming that Florida and the entire South was "astonished" at the town's "rapid growth." This growth, of course, was predicated on Ransom Olds' success in attracting or developing the economic activities that would supply employment for the residents. The prospects for such success appeared good when, less than a year after Oldsmar had been launched, the Kardell brothers, Reo agents in St. Louis, approached Olds about taking on the presidency of a company that would manufacture a tractor they had developed. Olds indicated that he would do so on the condition that they located the factory in Oldsmar. He told them that they would be close to a source of iron in Alabama, the climate would enable them to test their tractors throughout the year, and, "most of all," Olds pointed out, "ordinary labor down there can be had for about $1.65 per day as against $3.00 per day in the North." The Kardells visited Oldsmar, were impressed with the site, and by the end of 1917 had completed arrangements to move the Kardell Tractor and Truck Company to Oldsmar, where the name was soon changed to the Oldsmar Tractor Company.

This was reported to be the only tractor plant in Florida at that time, and the development was hailed as the start of "a new era" for that state, offering the farmer a serviceable, moderately priced tractor, and helping to advance the cause of manufacturing in Florida. This was a period in which both Henry Ford and William Durant sought to move their automotive companies into the farm tractor business, and it was a move that Olds had apparently been contemplating even before he was approached by the Kardells, since he had received a patent on a tractor in 1914. It is not known whether this invention, or the other tractor patent Olds obtained in 1921, were to be manufactured by the Oldsmar Tractor Company; but it would seem logical to assume that Olds had this in mind when he responded as he did to the Kardells.[11]

Olds did announce that the root extractor which he patented during the postwar period would be manufactured at Oldsmar, and it was clear that the invention was developed as a direct result of the difficulties that were encountered in clearing the Oldsmar property. Olds also became involved with the production of an improved heater to be used in Florida citrus groves when frost threatened the crops. Two other Oldsmar firms developed in response to some of the locally available resources: the Turpentine Products Company and the Palmetto Brush and Fiber Company, which made scrub and hand brushes from the fibers of palmetto roots left over when the land was cleared. The Gulf Lumber and Power Company operated a saw mill, planing mill, and dry kiln, which Olds had originally contemplated would be a logical outgrowth of the local timber resources. In addition, the company supplied power to Oldsmar as well as the nearby community of Safety Harbor. As for the planned agricultural development, it too seemed to show promise of success, particularly when the Carmen Grape Company introduced varieties of grapes that were well adapted to Florida conditions and which, because they matured early, could reach the eastern markets a month ahead of California grapes.

By 1920, the Oldsmar State Bank had over a million dollars in deposits, the Wayside Inn was doing a healthy tourist business, and before long the number of cars on the streets of Oldsmar were leading some residents to worry about the problems of traffic congestion. Oldsmar was optimistically said to be well on its way to achieving the original goal of a population of 100,000. However, other reports indicate that by 1923 the town contained no more than 200 residents; and failure, not success, was at that moment just around the corner. Olds may well have seen his hopes for his development dimming several years earlier, during World War I. Although he probably had not foreseen the American involvement in the war when he went ahead with his plans for Oldsmar—over a year before the American declaration of war on Germany—Olds did seek to take advantage of the war, when it came, as a means of stimulating interest in Oldsmar and of boosting its economy. In 1918 he declared that he was proceeding as rapidly as possible with the clearing of his Florida property so that it might be farmed and thereby contribute to solving the critical food problems of the day. "I can see no reason why Florida should fail to be the garden spot of the future," Olds told a Tampa paper in March, 1918. "It has the climate to produce three or more crops a year on plenty of good land, and Florida should be able to yield food enough to supply many of the northern states, as well as some of the foreign countries, and thus help to win the war."[12]

Of more immediate bearing on the winning of the war and on Olds' desire to attract a major industry to Oldsmar was his effort in 1917 to interest the federal government in establishing a shipyard in the new town. In April, barely two weeks after war had been declared, Olds telegraphed President Woodrow Wilson, offering to donate the land for such a facility and the timber from ten thousand acres of his property if the government agreed to establish a navy yard in Oldsmar. The thought had occurred to him, he told the president, that the government might be interested in his offer since he had already been approached by a private shipbuilding firm that had shown some desire to locate on Olds' property; in addition, "parties claiming to be agents of a foreign government" had sought to purchase the rights to this timber. Olds received the president's thanks for his "generous and patriotic offer," which, Wilson's secretary informed Olds, was being referred to the Secretary of the Navy.

When he heard nothing from that quarter, Olds approached his one-time employee at the Olds Motor Works, Howard E. Coffin, who was with the Council of National Defense. Coffin passed the idea along to the United States Shipping Board, which informed Olds that the government was indeed pushing ahead on a massive campaign to build as many wooden cargo vessels as possible, just what Olds had in mind. However, the board intended to work through existing private shipyards and was not intending to put up any government shipyards. Olds then pressed for some assurance that government contracts would be forthcoming if he persuaded private shipbuilders to locate at Oldsmar. Important as it would have seemed to keep the interest and support of a person of Olds' manufacturing experience and reputation, neither the Navy nor the Shipping Board gave him any further encouragement. The Shipping Board even informed Olds that the plans for the wooden vessels were as yet incomplete and the board did not know when their completion could be expected. By May 1917, therefore, Olds had abandoned his hopes of developing a shipbuilding industry at Oldsmar and of the boost to the town's prospects that a large transfusion of government money and contracts could have provided.[13]

Without such outside aid, Olds was left to his own resources. By 1923, he had poured some $4.5 million of his own funds into Oldsmar, which appears to have been a very sizable investment in terms of Olds' net financial worth at that time. In his search for something that would attract residents and investments to Oldsmar, he had even sunk $100,000 into an unsuccessful oil-drilling project. As the twenties wore on, however, and he had little in the way of returns from his investment, Olds began to give up on Olds-mar. His judgment, as usual, had been basically sound; but in this case his timing was too far off for his expectations to be realized. Eventually, Florida land developments that were aimed not at the old and wealthy but at younger people of working age but modest financial resources, as was the case with Oldsmar, would enjoy spectacular success. Whether there were enough people in this category in 1916 who would have been willing to take a chance on a move to Florida is not certain; in any event, the unsettling effect of the war and the severe postwar depression of the early twenties killed the prospects for the kind of rapid growth that Olds had been anticipating. Whether or not Olds foresaw the 1926 crash that ended the great Florida land boom of the twenties, a boom that was associated with the more traditional Miami Beach-resort development and not the Oldsmar type, he had begun to unload his Oldsmar holdings several years earlier, thus avoiding even greater losses—than his estimated loss of $3 million—had he held on to Oldsmar longer. After 1926 land values throughout the state collapsed.

He first traded the Oldsmar race track for the Fort Harrison Hotel in Clearwater; neither property was complete, but the hotel was at least potentially of far greater value than the racetrack Olds gave up. In 1923 he acquired the Bellerive Hotel in Kansas City, built at a cost of $2.5 million in exchange for the remaining unsold sections of Oldsmar and a "large amount of cash." Finally, in 1926 he sold the tractor company for $100,000, his experience seeming to confirm Walter P. Chrysler's view that automobile manufacturers—among whom Henry Ford proved to be the exception—should leave tractors to the farm equipment companies. At least Olds' venture into this field cost him considerably less than did Billy Durant's decision to acquire a tractor company, which cost General Motors $30 million before it decided that Chrysler had been right when he advised Durant against this move.[14]

At least as late as 1932, Olds continued to retain a small financial interest in Oldsmar, but after 1926 others assumed the responsibility for keeping the Florida development alive. First Charles P. Bland of St. Louis, and later investors from New York, took a crack at it. The name of the town was changed briefly from Oldsmar to Tampa Shores, but the results remained disappointingly the same, until the Great Depression reduced the development to the point where, as one resident recalled, it "just stopped functioning." Actually, it did continue to function to some slight degree, and the growth in the town's population from 878 residents in 1960 to 1,538 in 1970 aroused new hopes that Oldsmar might yet fulfill the hopes of its founder.[15]

Despite the failure of his Florida land venture, however, Olds did not lose faith in real estate and various other kinds of property developments as suitable investments. Hotels became one of his continuing interests. He sold or traded the Bellerive Hotel in Kansas City in the 1930s, but he retained control of the Fort Harrison Hotel in Clearwater for the rest of his life. In addition, Olds headed up a group in the late 1920s which constructed the Hotel Olds in Lansing. Olds also continued to control this hotel until the time of his death in 1950, and the management was handled by his son-in-law, Bruce Anderson. The Hotel Olds became for Lansing of the twentieth century what Charles Downey's Downey House had been in an earlier day—the city's foremost hotel. Its location directly across Capital Avenue from the State Capitol building made it immediately the most convenient meeting place for state officials and all who had business with them. After Olds' death, the site he had chosen enabled the hotel, under different management—and for a time under a different name—to continue to thrive; but by the mid-seventies the problems affecting older hotels in downtown city locations were threatening to close the doors of Lansing's Olds Hotel as they had earlier that once proud hotel in Flint bearing the name of Olds' great contemporary, W. C. Durant.[16]

One of the last business ventures in which Olds became involved, this one of a nonprofit character, also involved a hotel, the Daytona Terrace Hotel in Daytona Beach. He purchased it for $60,000 in 1942, and renamed Olds Hall, the hotel was converted into a retirement home for ministers and missionaries who could rent one of the seventy-five apartments for a low rate. Olds paid frequent visits to this interdenominational facility, and he declared that nothing he had done had given him more satisfaction.[17]

In 1929–30, Olds erected a twenty-six-story office building at the corner of Capital and Allegan in Lansing, adjacent to the Hotel Olds. The circumstances by which he obtained the land for this building from the investors in the Blackstone Theatre, an unfinished structure on the site, are by no means clear. But LeRoy A. Brown, an officer in the theater company, bitterly contended in a number of highly inflammatory public statements in later years that he and his associates had been "sold down the river" by Olds. Brown declared that Olds had entered into an agreement with the Blackstone Theatre Company in 1924, which the investors in that company hoped would result in Olds' completing the theatre building, thereby preventing them from losing the money they had put into the unfinished venture. However, Brown said, Olds was not legally bound to take such action and in actuality he had never intended to do so. His intent all along was to get his hands on the property, tear down the unfinished theater, and put up his office building. Others in Lansing with some knowledge of the circumstances surrounding Olds' acquisition of the site say that there may be some truth to Brown's charges that Olds was guilty of sharp practices, although it may have been his associates in the deal who were primarily to blame and not Olds himself.[18]

When the Olds Tower, as the new office building was named, was opened, the R. E. Olds Company had offices on the tenth floor, where this family investment company has been housed ever since. The main reason for constructing the building, however, was to house the Capital National Bank, which Olds had founded in 1906 and served as president from then until 1932, when he became chairman of the board. According to Duane Yarnell, Olds never "took desk space" in the bank, his role being essentially one of encouraging his friends and business associates to deposit in a bank of which he was head. Inactive as he may have been in the day-to-day operations of the bank, his family believes

This photo of May 20, 1930 shows the steel superstructure of Olds' bank and office building, for many years the tallest building between Detroit and Chicago, looming up beside the Hotel Olds along Lansing's Capital Avenue.

that of all his nonautomotive business interests, Olds probably enjoyed his contacts with the banking world the most. Its fiscal and political conservatism suited his own personality and outlook, which became increasingly conservative as he grew older. At the same time, his position with this bank gave him an opportunity to be of assistance to fellow Lansing residents in the quiet, unpublicized manner he preferred.[19]

* * * * *

Capital National Bank's failure to reopen after the bank holiday President Roosevelt declared in March 1933 as a means of dealing with the emergency the Depression had created in the nation's financial institutions was one event—with the problems of the Depression in general—that helped bring Olds back into a more active role in the automotive industry. During the twenties Olds had maintained contact with the industry through the annual New York shows that he had enjoyed attending since the beginning of the century. On January 6, 1925, his pioneering efforts in the industry were recognized by the National Automobile Chamber of Commerce: at its Silver Anniversary Dinner it presented Olds, along with Charles King, Charles Duryea, Jonathan Maxwell, Edgar Apperson, Elwood Haynes, Alexander Winton, A. L. Riker, John S. Clarke, and Rollin H. White, huge silver medals designating them as the individuals who contributed the most to the mechanical development of the car.[20] It was an interesting and prestigious group with whom Olds was thereby associated.*

A little over a year before that dinner in New York, it had been announced at a special meeting of the Reo directors on December 20, 1923, that Olds was stepping down as president—a position he had held throughout the company's nineteen-year history—and that he was taking over the newly created position of chairman of the board. It was certainly assumed by Olds, the directors, and the industry that the essentially honorary nature of the new office accurately reflected the role he had actually been playing in Reo for over a decade. The advancement of Richard Scott to the presidency completed the task of making the titles of the chief officers correspond to their actual status in the company. The change also seemed related to Olds' desire to reduce his investments in some of his older manufacturing interests. After World War I, he had pulled out of the Michigan Screw Company, which he had headed since the founding of the company in 1906. On an original investment of only $10,000, Olds reportedly now received a million dollars for his stock

---

*The selection was marred by the exclusion of Henry Ford, whom one would assume to be a natural choice for such an honor. The exclusion was probably a result of Ford's refusal to join the industry's trade association, which was the successor to Ford's old and vanquished legal adversary, the Association of Licensed Automobile Manufacturers.

in that company. In 1922, when reports circulated on Wall Street that Olds also intended to dispose of his Reo stock, Olds called the rumors "bunk"; but in March, 1923, the other Reo directors accepted Olds' offer to sell back to the company 50,000 shares of Olds' Reo stock at $14 a share, less than the selling price on the open market. Subsequently, additional shares of the stock Olds and his family held were sold off, until by 1928 only a token amount remained in their hands.[21]

It seems unlikely that Olds, at a time when the prospects of the automobile industry had never seemed brighter, would sell his stock because he had any inkling of the rocky days that lay just over the horizon, following the stock market crash of 1929. It seems more probable that Olds, who was by nature cautious and from his childhood seems to have had a certain fear of being poor, sold his stock at the good prices available in the twenties in part to offset some of the losses he had suffered in his Florida land development, and in part to place a larger share of his financial resources in safer kinds of investments.

As it happened, of course, Olds was fortunate to have cashed in most of his Reo stock during the bull market of the twenties. The Depression of the following decade and the unprecedented collapse in the stock market would have enormously decreased the amount he could have received had he waited until then to sell the bulk of his stock. Even had economic conditions in general remained good, however, the value of Reo stocks would have dropped sharply because of changes in company policy that were instituted in the mid-twenties, which by the end of the decade had caused Olds to belatedly regret his decision to turn over the reins of the company to Richard Scott.

Until the mid-twenties Reo had consistently concentrated on producing a limited number of models in the medium-priced range of vehicles. This conservative policy had enabled some of Reo's more venturesome competitors to widen their lead in sales. However, Reo's declining share of the passenger-car market was offset by the success of its truck sales, which, from 1919 on, exceeded Reo car sales during all but one of the next ten years. Unspectacular as the Reo operations may have been compared with those of Ford and the several units of General Motors with which they had briefly vied for top ranking in the industry during the early days, the combination of car and truck sales had nevertheless resulted in a steady increase in the company's net worth and an unbroken record of profits. After considerable fluctuation in the early years, this progress had enabled dividends to be stabilized at an annual rate of seventy cents by 1917, and then to be increased to three times that amount by 1923, the highest cash dividend in company history.[22]

It was at this time that Richard Scott, feeling increasingly secure in his management of Reo, decided to break with the past and expand the ranges—both in style and price—of the vehicles the company produced. He planned to strengthen Reo's competitive position by following the marketing trends of the day. In retrospect, it is easy enough to criticize Scott for showing bad judgment in making this decision. It can be argued that Reo would have been far better off in the long run had Scott phased out car production entirely at this time and concentrated the company's efforts on strengthening its position in the commercial vehicle market. Its competitive position in that market, in terms of the share of the total sales that it held, was far better than what it had been able to hold among competitors in passenger-car production. But it is just as easy to understand how Scott felt that his decision was the correct one for Reo at this time.

The twenties witnessed an enormous increase in auto sales. This was the decade in which the motor car became the dominant means of transportation for most segments of American society. At the same time that the number of potential customers was greatly increased, however, many of them were also becoming more sophisticated in their view of the product. The lesson of the twenties seemed to be that the future lay with the companies who offered the public a wide variety of cars in all price ranges and in frequently changing styles. Ford, with its unchanging, unsophisticated Model T, which had given that company a commanding lead over all other companies in the previous decade, lost out in the twenties to General Motors, which emphasized diversity and constant change in its models. As the decade wore on, it became increasingly clear that the many smaller companies, such as Reo, which lacked the diversity of General Motors' cars, or the strong entry in the low-priced field which enabled Ford—despite its lack of diversity—to hold the number two spot in the industry, were going to find it more and more difficult to survive.

Richard Scott wanted to strengthen Reo's competitive position, but in a manner that was consistent with his own and his company's traditionally conservative approach. Rather than attempting to achieve diversity quickly by acquiring control of some other automobile manufacturing firms or by seeking outside financial help through large new stock issues and bank loans—as W. C. Durant and Walter Chrysler were doing during the twenties—Scott proposed to expand the range of Reo models and to finance this expansion out of Reo's earnings. By 1925 Reo's profits had reached a level at which Scott felt he might safely move ahead with plans to add new models at price levels both above and below those of the current Reos.

Scott began to make his move late in 1923: at a cost of $200,000, he had Reo acquire the vacant Duplex Truck factory, a few blocks from the Reo plant, thus providing some of the added space that increased production would require. In October 1925 he brought in an Italian-born designer, Fabio Sergardi, who had served as chief engineer at the Olds Motor Works in the past—only one of many additions to the Reo staff that Scott made during this period. In January 1927, the first of Sergardi's new models, the Reo Flying Cloud, was unveiled at the New York Auto Show, and it received rave notices in the trade press. Available in four body styles, it was somewhat more expensive than the 1926 Reos. The Flying Cloud was followed that spring by the Wolverine, a lower-priced model, although at $1,195 it was not competitive—nor did Scott intend it to be—with Ford or Chevrolet in the lowest-priced automobile range. It did, however, meet what the company declared was a need for a model "smaller and lower in price than the old traditional line of Reo products." Still later, in the summer of 1927, Reo announced a similar diversification of its Speed Wagon line of commercial vehicles, including Speed Wagon Junior, a low-priced, light delivery truck. Richard Scott was thus attempting to revise the public's prevailing image of Reo as the producer of only medium-priced vehicles.[23]

By the end of 1927, Scott's efforts seemed to be paying off: Reo production figures for the year topped 40,000 cars and trucks, 6,000 more than the figures for 1926, the best previous year in the company's history. Particularly gratifying was the fact that passenger-car production, which more than doubled the previous year's totals and surpassed the figures for truck production for the first time since 1918, accounted for Reo's improved position in the industry. The following year, therefore, Scott moved ahead with the Flying Cloud Mate, a new car whose price was between the Wolverine and the original Flying Cloud model, now referred to as the Flying Cloud Master. However, while the Flying Cloud had achieved considerable popularity with the public, the prospects for the overall success of Scott's ambitious plans for Reo's sales development were dimmed by the clear evidence that the Wolverine had not done well. It was said that many buyers failed to connect the car, because of its name, with the Reo company. Furthermore, it was well known that it was an assembled car, Scott having stretched Reo's manufacturing capabilities to their limits in putting out the Flying Cloud. And by the late twenties the term "assembled car" instantly lowered that vehicle's reputation with knowledgeable buyers. As a result, the Wolverine was soon quietly, and without fanfare, dropped. Meanwhile, two new Speed Wagon models were also introduced in 1928, a year that again saw total production for the year surpass the previous year's record, this time by nearly 7,000 vehicles. However, an ominous note was sounded that year by the decline in passenger-car production, with trucks once again accounting for a majority of the vehicles coming out of the Lansing factory. This was the first sign that Scott's hope that restyling and diversification would revitalize Reo's passenger-car sales was not being realized. The upturn in car sales in 1927, it now appeared, had not led to a permanent change in automobile buyers' attitudes toward Reo.[24]

The following year started on a brighter note. Sales for the first five months were the best for any comparable period in Reo's history. A deluxe Flying Cloud Master was introduced on a very limited basis to test the market for the high-priced, luxury Reo which was already on the designing boards. By June, however, the early prospects for a record year were dimming, and by the end of the summer, well before the stock market crash in October began depressing sales throughout the industry, it was clear that Reo was in trouble. At the end of 1929, a year that saw the combined industry totals for passenger-car and truck production soar far beyond any previous year's figures, Reo slipped backwards, reaching only about seventy-five per cent of the production of the preceding year. Net sales were off nearly twelve million dollars from the $59,800,000 total rung up in 1928. Net profits dropped to their lowest total since the depression year of 1921, and for the first time in Reo's history, its net worth, which had shown a steady growth each year, was less than it had been in 1928.[25] Auto sales for 1929 declined to the levels of 1925, and truck sales were lower than they had been at the start of the decade. The ratio of profits to sales was by far the lowest in Reo's quarter-century history, and, although the stockholders received a cash dividend for the year of $2.40 per share, this was a drop of sixty cents from the 1928 rate and eighty cents under the record dividend that had been paid in 1926, the year before Scott's new models had begun to appear in dealers' showrooms.[26]

Ransom Olds had apparently had doubts for some time about the wisdom of Scott's diversification program, and the events of 1929 only served to convince him that he had been right in feeling that Scott had over-extended the limited resources of the company on a program that had failed to achieve the anticipated amount of increased sales. Olds, backed by three other board members, Donald E. Bates, the secretary-treasurer, George H. Smith, the purchasing agent, and Carlton H. Higbie, a Detroit stockbroker, openly split with Scott, whose supporters on the seven-man board were Horace Thomas, the chief engineer, and Harry Teel, Scott's brother-in-law and successor as factory superintendent. Olds' dissatisfaction with Scott's management led to the latter's being replaced as general manager in February 1930 by William Robert Wilson, a veteran automotive executive with such well-known companies as Studebaker, Dodge, and Maxwell. Scott, however, who retained the post of president, got the Olds group to agree to the creation of a voting trust, under the direction of Scott, Wilson, and Bates, which was to run to the end of 1932 and was designed to maintain the control of the present management during that period.[27]

If Olds had had any idea that the new general manager would call a halt to further implementation of Scott's grandiose expansion program, he was soon to be disillusioned. Under Wilson's management, Reo continued to introduce new models in 1930, including two intermediate-weight Speed Wagon trucks, a restyling of the Flying Cloud lines, and on October 9, 1930 the long-awaited entry in the luxury-car bracket, the eight-cylinder Reo Royale. The decision to go ahead with the production of this last car a year after the stock market collapse had begun to send automobile sales into a tailspin seems, in retrospect, almost incredible. It is true that other companies also chose this time to introduce some of the most expensive and luxurious cars ever produced, including Cadillac, which came out with twelve- and sixteen-cylinder models. Despite the prestige that had long been associated with Cadillac and Packard, for example, their sales fell off almost as sharply in the early thirties as those of the less expensive cars. The new Reo Royale was without question a magnificent car, perhaps the most beautiful automobile in the United States. The automobile historian Beverly Rae Kimes states that several of her friends who owned Royales swear "that there was nothing on the road like it." But without the long-established status that was instantly conferred on the owner of a Packard, Cadillac, or Lincoln, Reo's new car faced an almost impossible task from the outset in grabbing any appreciable share of the rapidly shrinking market for such high-priced

The Five-Passenger Victoria

The Two-Passenger Coupe
with Rumble Seat

The Reo Royale, announced in the *Saturday Evening Post* (Oct. 11, 1930) in a suitably sumptuous, understated manner appropriate for the luxurious, limited-edition automobile

Courtesy of Eastern Michigan University Library

cars (though its original price of $2,485 made the 1930 Royale almost a bargain-basement luxury car). The Royale ultimately proved to be the single most costly mistake Olds was in any way involved with during his entire automotive career. Reo reportedly lost over six million dollars on the Royale.[28]

The new models introduced under Wilson's management did not appear until late in 1930, a year in which Reo sales suffered an even sharper drop than they had the previous year. The decline was not as sharp as that suffered during this first year of the Depression by some of Reo's competitors; but this was of no consolation when the year-end financial accounting showed Reo for the first time experiencing not a profit but a net loss of nearly $2 million. When 1931 brought more of the same bad news, with losses reaching more than $2.7 million and production of vehicles dropping to its lowest point since 1913, support for William Wilson evaporated. The three-year voting trust arrangement (which had not served the desired purpose anyway, since only a fourth of the stock had been converted into trust certificates) was terminated on June 30, 1931, a year and a half ahead of schedule. That September, Wilson and the directors agreed to terminate his contract as general manager, although his formal resignation did not come until March 5, 1932. The return of President Scott once again to the general manager's position that Wilson was vacating was a clear sign that he had come out on top in this phase of the struggle for control of the company.[29]

The events of the next four years are part of an ever-deepening tragedy, as one after the other, the members of Reo's old guard—Scott, Olds, Thomas, and Bates—struggled in vain to save Reo from the deadly blows the Depression was dealing an organization already gravely weakened by the costly expansion program. Cost-reduction measures that were now instituted by Scott were insufficient to prevent the continuation of annual losses that had begun two years before; in 1932, Reo failed to pay its stockholders a dividend for only the second time in its history and the first time since 1911. The decline in passenger-car sales reached the lowest levels since 1907, and truck sales dropped to their lowest

REO

Over a period of 26 years Reo has established its product on every continent; its record of service lies directly behind the world's confidence in Reo.

As an institution Reo is alone in having developed its business in almost equal volume from year to year in both the passenger and commercial car fields.

This widespread acceptance in both fields is a tribute to Reo's engineering forethought, its sound manufacturing and its stable business policy.

Today its great plant facilities, its world-wide dealer loyalty, its cash resources, clean financial structure and established executive cohesion are ready for another quarter-century of service in the world's greatest industry.

REO MOTOR CAR COMPANY
LANSING, MICHIGAN

Courtesy of Eastern Michigan University Library

One of a series of statements run by Reo in national publications at the end of 1930 in place of its regular car and truck ads, with a message designed in part to calm the general economic fears of the Depression era but more particularly to offset growing reports of Reo's financial instability

point since 1916. New models, both in the Flying Cloud and Speed Wagon lines, were introduced, with the attention directed at a drastically reduced price tag—not body or mechanical changes—in the hopes of catching the public's attention during those depressed times. Sales did in fact turn upward beginning in 1933, as the economy began its painfully slow recovery from the depths it had reached in 1932; but the recovery was not sufficient to offset the complex and widening financial problems that beset the Reo management.

Only three months after the directors and stockholders

had agreed to cut the par value of Reo common stock in half in December 1932—a desperate move to enable the company to write off some of its accumulated losses—additional losses were sustained when Olds' Capital National Bank, in which Reo had cash deposits of over a million dollars, failed to reopen for business in March 1933. Reo's loss in this case resulted from the conflicting banking interests of its two principal officers: late in 1931 the City National Bank, headed by Richard Scott, was also threatened with collapse. Olds' bank agreed to save Scott's bank by assuming City National's deposit liabilities, on the condition—among others—that Reo, which was one of the larger depositors in its president's bank, would guarantee to reimburse Capital National against any losses up to $375,000 and that it would also leave on deposit in Capital National for at least one year the amount of $1 million. Reo's directors, with the interests of their chairman's and their president's banks at stake, agreed to the proposal on December 28, 1931. The cash loss that they thereby averted by preventing City National from going under was only postponed until the even greater loss the company sustained with the collapse of Capital National fifteen months later.[30]

This new setback, plus the continuation of the operational losses Reo had been suffering since 1929, stirred up the fires of internal dissension once again. Despite what would have seemed the all-important need for retrenchment, Scott had not entirely abandoned his expansion program. He pushed ahead with the costly development of an automatic transmission system. This invention by Horace Thomas was introduced in some 1934 Reo cars that were displayed at the auto shows early that year, and placed the company years ahead of most automakers in providing the kind of increased ease in driving that motorists would before long come to demand in most of the cars they bought. However, Thomas' pioneering innovation, coming when it did, failed to have the impact on Reo sales that it might have, had it come in the more favorable market conditions of the previous decade. Its result only seemed to add to Reo's financial woes.[31]

The climactic battle for the control of Reo began on December 15, 1933, when Olds submitted his resignation from the board of directors, explaining that since he was "not in sympathy with the policy of the present management," he felt it his "duty to take this action rather than have the world blame me for what I am in no way responsible." This action had the effect Olds no doubt intended. A special meeting of the board was convened on December 18. Olds was prevailed upon to withdraw his resignation and to assume the chairmanship of a special Executive Committee that was invested with complete control over managerial policy until these matters could be finally decided at the annual stockholders meeting on April 17, 1934. Scott was stripped of his managerial duties, although he was allowed to save face by retaining his post as president. Charles W. Avery, chairman and president of the Murray Corporation of Detroit, which had supplied bodies to Reo, was brought in to replace Scott as general manager, and also to serve on the executive committee with Olds and two Olds supporters, Donald Bates and George Smith.

Olds and his committee moved quickly to gain a firm control of the situation. For whatever reason, Avery resigned almost immediately and was replaced early in January 1934 by Ray A. DeVlieg, a recent import from the Chrysler organization. DeVlieg not only became general manager and a member of the executive committee, but his additional title of works manager left Harry Teel, Scott's brother-in-law, with little or no authority, despite his retention of the title of factory superintendent. The following month, another former Chrysler executive, Ray J. Fitness, was named to replace Horace Thomas as chief engineer. Thomas was not fired, but his new responsibilities as "chief research engineer" could not disguise the fact that Thomas, who was a Scott supporter, had been—like Teel and Scott himself—demoted.

In March, a proxy committee mailed out notices of the annual stockholders' meeting and solicited the support of the stockholders at that time for the new course that Olds and the executive committee were following. The fact that Scott was a member of the proxy committee and that he signed the letter, along with Olds, Smith, and DeVlieg, seemed to indicate that he was not fighting the changes. But in April, news of Reo's internal conflicts (which, despite their long duration, had generally been kept from the public) burst into the press. The revelation came shortly after an "Independent Stockholders' Committee," composed of three New Yorkers, headed by W. S. Diamond, sent a letter to Reo stockholders on April 3, charging that Reo's decline was attributable more to mismanagement than it was to the Depression. Responsibility for these managerial mistakes and failures was laid at the doorstep of Ransom Olds, who, the letter said, "dominated" the board of directors. Stockholders were urged to support a return to power of Richard Scott and his associates, who, because they owned 150,000 shares of Reo stock, had a personal stake in what happened to the company. It was revealed that Olds, on the other hand, had retained only 600 shares of stock. The committee said they found something sinister in the way Olds had been able to remove the stock he had had on deposit at his Capital National Bank after the closure of that bank in 1933 and then sell the approximately 25,000 shares. It was implied that Olds had been able to do this only because he had inside knowledge, not readily available to the public, of the impact that the bank's closing would have on Reo's cash reserves and hence on the value of that stock, once this information became known. Olds had thus accomplished the same thing that he had in the twenties, when he had sold most of his stock at the high prices then available. Thus Olds was depicted as one who had had his own welfare, not that of his company, in mind, and had thereby forfeited his right to be trusted with that company's destinies.

Ransom Olds now came out fighting to retain his new-found authority in the company with a vigor that surprised many and belied the fact that he was only two months shy of his seventieth birthday. The charges of Diamond's group were effectively answered by the "New Management Committee." Regarding the sale of Olds' stock in 1933, evidence was presented to indicate that there was nothing underhanded or illegal in the way Olds had removed the stock from the closed bank. He had replaced that stock with municipal bonds of an equivalent value, a procedure approved by the bank conservator. As for the contention that his sale of this stock had left him with no real interest in what happened to Reo, Olds declared that the supporters of the Scott faction had failed to mention that both Scott and Thomas had signed an option to sell their stock.

The credibility and motivation of W. S. Diamond and his associates were called into question with the publication of a letter from a stockholder, Hugh R. Baker of the American Bank Note Company, who informed Olds that his investigations convinced him that Diamond was "nothing more than a professional proxy seeker" whose interest in Reo's future was the least important reason behind the actions he was taking. Baker was sure that other stockholders, given the opportunity, would reach the same conclusion and would, as he was doing, turn their proxies over to Olds, who, Baker believed, could "rebuild the business which you so remarkably developed during those many years."

The main battle lines in the proxy fight were drawn, however, between Olds and Richard Scott. These two associates, who had worked together since 1898 and whose homes in Lansing had faced each other on opposite sides of South Main Street for nearly as long a time, had differed in the past; but this was the first time that differences were aired so publicly and, unfortunately, in a manner that left no possibility of any reconciliation between the two men. Scott had indicated his support of the Diamond committee in a letter to the stockholders on April 5. Only by supporting this group with their proxies, Scott said, could the stockholders be assured of having "proper representation in the management of the Company." Only then would harmony within the company be established and would Reo be able to regain "its former position in the automotive industry."

Scott's subsequent contention that prior to April 5 he had had no connection with the Independent Stockholders' Committee was undermined by the Olds group, which was able to cite letters that Scott had written in March, while he was still officially aligned with the company's own proxy committee, in which Scott aided the Diamond committee in organizing its proxy campaign. The larger issue at stake, however, had to do with fixing the blame for the fall of Reo from its once respected position in the industry. Scott, who had been general manager during most of the past twenty years, took credit for the profits that the company had earned during that period; but he sought to shift the blame for the losses of the recent years to the board, and especially to Olds, who, he said, dominated the board. Scott maintained that the general manager was, after all, subject to the authority of the directors, and thus if the company had been mismanaged, the final responsibility for such mismanagement must rest with the board. It was "distasteful," Scott confessed, to speak out against his associates, but he was forced to defend himself "against the odious and untrue statements" of the Olds faction.

Olds' response to this attack, which he termed "the most vicious thing I have ever seen printed," was to lay the blame for Reo's troubles "squarely" on the shoulders of Richard Scott, the president of the company for the past decade and general manager for all but two years since 1915. As general manager, the Olds committee pointed out, Scott was granted by the company's by-laws "the full power and authority to manage the business." Since the executive committee's removal of Scott, his brother-in-law, and other members of what was termed a "family clique" from authority, the New Management Committee asserted, Reo had made "real progress" and had restored the public's interest in the company to its "highest point in years."[32]

The outcome of the hotly contested proxy fight was still uncertain up to the eve of the April 17 annual meeting. However, on April 16, W. S. Diamond's faction lost its main support when first Horace Thomas, and then Richard Scott, unexpectedly switched their votes to Olds. Thomas expressed his "regret" that he had had "anything to do with the Independent Reo Proxy Committee." He had been with Olds "for over thirty years and must say I consider you the most honorable man it has been my lot to be associated with." Diamond's group might have retained some hope of success with the stockholders, despite Thomas' defection, until they lost their "ace of trumps," as one of them called Scott.

It must have been an especially bitter pill for this proud and powerful citizen of Lansing to swallow to have his statement of surrender to Olds appear in the columns of the local newspaper. Announcing that he was resigning as president and director of Reo, Scott, like Thomas, expressed his "regret" that the differences over policy matters that had developed between himself and Olds were being used by a group that sought to take advantage of the company's misfortunes. "Mr. Olds and I have been friends for over 30 years. I believe he has at all times sought to do whatever he thought best for the interest of the company. It would be a great misfortune if any personal differences should adversely affect the company." Scott had decided, therefore, to give his proxy to Olds and "to whole-heartedly support the new management." It was a courageous statement, reflecting great honor on a man who was bowing out of the company he had served for thirty years. No one can say what pressures were exerted on him to abandon the fight to get back his power. Years later his wife told Glenn Niemeyer that he apparently had decided there was no way he could win that fight, and that under the circumstances his loyalty to the company convinced him that Reo would be better off under Olds than it would be under Diamond's group. Scott had come to believe that the latter did not have the best interests of Reo at heart. But Scott's statement of April 16 signaled no change in the resentment and bitterness that had built up in him over what he regarded as his unjust treatment by Olds and Olds' supporters. Until his death in March 1944, Scott remained alienated from the man who had brought him up from Toledo, forty-six years earlier, to handle the first of many crises the two would face in the years that followed.

For Olds, the results of the vote at the annual meeting on April 17, 1934, were a foregone conclusion. A spokesman for the opposing Diamond group admitted before the meeting that it now had only a small fraction of the votes it would need to overturn Olds' management committee. After the meeting, Olds, whose successful defense of his control of the company won him the admiration of national business writers, said that it had been "an interesting fight," which he had "enjoyed . . . from start to finish." He professed to "hold no bitterness toward anyone involved." His interest now was only to continue the effort to enable Reo to "grow and prosper" once again.

However, Olds' triumph turned out to be short-lived. Brim full of ideas, now that he was exerting more authority over the management of the company than he had since its very early days, he began making suggestions to the other members of the executive committee as soon as it was organized at the beginning of 1934. He proposed that Reo look into the possibility of producing a four-cylinder car to sell for only $400. This proposal was based on the assumption that such a car might attract more sales during a depressed period, just as Olds' original idea of producing an inexpensive horseless carriage back in the nineties may have been partly a reaction to the hard times of that decade. Another of Olds' ideas was for the company to produce a "gasifier," a device he is said to have invented but which he never patented. It was claimed that the gasifier would be capable of reducing automobile gasoline consumption by some seventy per cent. Olds was convinced that an announcement regarding this cost-saving attachment would create much favorable publicity for Reo and "would let the people know that Reo was alive instead of asleep." Of course, Olds said, the company could take its time in actually putting this accessory on its cars, but in the meantime "everybody would have been talking about it, which would have been an ad worth many times its cost."

Still another of Olds' ideas was for Reo to adopt the engine produced by his Hill Diesel Engine Company. The Independent Stockholders Committee had charged that Olds would try to get Reo to take over that company, in exchange for 200,000 shares of Reo stock. Olds denied the charge at the time, but at the end of the year his statement that he "would favor the Reo considering taking on the Diesel Engine busi-

One of the last ads for a Reo automobile appeared in the May 23, 1936 issue of the *Saturday Evening Post*. Despite its Depression-born emphasis on economy in operation, and the immensely popular medium in which it appeared, the ad was promoting a lost cause, a car with only weeks remaining before the company gave it the axe.

ness" seemed to substantiate the Diamond group's statement. From Olds' standpoint, however, the deal he was proposing would have been an advantageous one for Reo. "I feel that my new engine recently invented has great possibilities and will make the most ideal engine for bus, truck, marine and direct connected generator service." As Olds pointed out, Alexander Winton's diesel engine company, which General Motors had acquired in 1930, had proved to be a profitable addition to that great automaker's roster of divisions.[33]

To his dismay, Olds found his associates unwilling to go along with any of his ideas. Although W. S. Diamond's committee had gone down to an overwhelming defeat at the annual meeting in April, it had not disbanded, and it continued to criticize the new management. Olds' associates on the Executive Committee apparently reacted to his suggestions as they did partly as a means of showing their independence, so that there would be no grounds for charging them with being mere puppets of the chairman. Furthermore, at a time when any company move had to be made with an eye to its effect on the company's ever-weakening financial situation, Olds' proposals may well have seemed too costly and the prospects of profitability to Reo not at all assured.

On December 17, 1934, therefore, Olds resigned from the Executive Committee. He declared that he had "reached a point where I cannot sleep nights and unless I do something I may find myself a nervous wreck, so that I believe I owe it to myself to take steps to relieve myself." He had the highest respect for the members of the committee and for the other directors, but they were simply not thinking "along the same line." He said that he had been reluctant to resume an active role in the company's management but had taken on the job because it seemed necessary, and he felt that the suggestions he had made were feasible. He believed it would have been possible to put the $400 car on the market by June or July of 1934, and that it would have drawn the customers back into the Reo dealers' showrooms in great numbers. Instead, the company had not only turned down this idea but had proceeded with a costly revamping of the existing Reo's body style, at a time when the passenger-car division was suffering a loss of over $600,000 during the first eight months of the year. This was, Olds said, "in my opinion, very poor judgment." He regretted having to make these criticisms, but he felt it his "duty" to do so. He also felt, because of concern for his physical well-being, "that I owe it to myself to retire from any active management in the company."

Olds continued in his honorary capacity as chairman of the board of directors; but it now devolved upon Donald Bates, who had succeeded Richard Scott as president, to try to find a way of pulling Reo out of its prolonged decline. One approach being discussed in 1934, while Olds was still active, was a merger with other companies. In view of the fact that the companies mentioned—Auburn, Cord, Duesenberg, Graham-Paige, Hupp, and Pierce-Arrow—were for the most part in as bad or worse shape than Reo, Olds was quite correct when he commented that summer that he saw little value in this suggestion. Bates and the other directors shared Olds' pessimism, and in this case it would be difficult to fault their judgment. Being part of a combination that would have produced the prestigious but prohibitively expensive Duesenberg, Pierce-Arrow, and Cord would have ticketed Reo for certain oblivion during those Depression years. Although Reo did enter into some cooperative arrangements with Graham-Paige and Mack Trucks in 1935, the directors again refused to consider any suggestion of an outright merger with these or any other firms.

The decision that should have been made years before was finally made in 1936. With the Reo passenger-car sales continuing to be a drain on the company's resources, and with sales showing no signs of improving, Donald Bates announced on September 3 that Reo was halting any further production of cars. Since truck sales were rebounding from the lows reached in 1932 and 1933, the company was going to concentrate entirely on this side of the business which showed prospects for success. Bates sought to put the best face on this announcement by stating that "the day has passed when trucks and buses can be considered as sidelines. The truck and bus and trailer engineer has nothing

REO ENTERS LOWEST-PRICE FIELD

with Brilliant New ½ and ¾ Ton Truck!

★100% TRUCK CONSTRUCTION

Built by Truck Engineers ★★ Powered with Sturdy Truck Engine ★★
Balanced Load Distribution ★★ Exceptional Economy and Flexibility

$555

SPEED DELIVERY—COMPLETE
F. O. B. Lansing, Michigan

Price includes all-steel top cab with safety glass and option of 4-cylinder or 6-cylinder Silver Crown truck engine. Panel units, on short or long wheelbases, at correspondingly low prices.

Reo Speed Wagons and Trucks range from ½ to 4-6 tons including Tractor Trailers and Buses. All models feature new streamlined styling with V-type windshields. Prices start at $555 f.o.b. Lansing, Michigan, plus tax. Special equipment extra.

America's Toughest Truck!

NOW see the new Reo Speed Delivery—America's fine quality truck in the lowest price class and Reo's ringing answer to "the challenge of a new day".

Brand new truck engineering makes scientific load distribution possible in this new low-priced Reo. Easier handling and greater operating economy result. New engine and axle locations permit the use of longer bodies.

Bulkier loads can be carried than in conventional trucks of corresponding size.

Typically Reo in every detail — the new Speed Delivery is built by truck engineers to do a real truck job. Avail-

able in ½ or ¾ ton models of 114 and 120 inch wheelbase, it introduces a new conception of value in the low-price truck field.

Two Silver Crown Engines are optional—6 cylinders for fast highway transport and 4 cylinders for economical multi-stop work. Both handle capacity loads at high speed with remarkably low gas and oil consumption.

All-steel cabs of roomier construction provide greater driver comfort. V-type safety glass windshields assure unobstructed vision and better ventilation. These features are standard equipment on all cab models.

Check the new Reo Speed Delivery feature by feature. Compare it with other trucks at or near its low price. See for yourself that Reo's Speed Delivery is America's highest quality low-priced truck!

REO MOTOR CAR COMPANY, LANSING, MICHIGAN

REO SPEEDWAGONS TRUCKS AND BUSES

Courtesy of Eastern Michigan University Library

In late 1936, when this advertisement came out, the Reo company name appeared only on trucks, as it would for the remaining troubled decades of its existence. The emphasis here is reminiscent of Olds' approach with the runabout thirty-five years earlier, but the long-term results for the ailing Reo firm were unfortunately not the same.

more to learn from the passenger car." As the demand for buses and trucks grew, therefore, it was necessary for Reo to devote its full attention to taking advantage of this market. What Bates did not say, however, was that the decision to concentrate their efforts entirely on commercial vehicles was by no means a voluntary action. Reo, like nearly all other small producers of automobiles that had survived into the thirties, had found that the competition from the Big Three, combined with the enormous drop in sales resulting from the Depression, made it impossible for them to stay in business. Reo's decision to stop producing automobiles undoubtedly saved it at that time and enabled it to survive, after a fashion, for thirty-nine more years. By the forties it was enjoying something like the prosperity of its earlier days, but only for a time; eventually the stiff competition among the independent truck manufacturers began to take its toll. Finally, on May 30, 1975, Diamond Reo Trucks, Inc., the latest of several permutations through which the original Reo company had passed during its last years, was declared bankrupt. That October the assets at the old-fashioned, seventy-year-old red-brick factory on South Washington Avenue in Lansing were auctioned off.[34]

Fortunately, Ransom Olds did not live to witness the final painful years in Reo's corporate history. However, the decision in 1936 to concentrate solely on trucks must have saddened him. For the first time in forty years he was not involved with the manufacturing of automobiles. This was, Olds apparently concluded, as good a time as any to cut all remaining ties with Reo. On December 28, 1936, therefore, he notified Donald Bates that he was tendering his resignation as a member of the board of directors because of his "desire to retire from as many obligations as possible. . . . It is with a great deal of regret that I take this step as my long association with you and the Board has been very pleasant and I have felt that I had your full cooperation at all times."[35]

Thus, twenty-five years after Claude Hopkins mounted his advertising campaign for what he called Ransom Olds' "Farewell Car," Olds bade farewell to the industry that he had helped to found. Nor was this a Sarah Bernhardt farewell—subject, as Hopkins had explained, to reconsideration. Olds did not reconsider his decision, nor did the other Reo directors apparently make any special effort to persuade him to reconsider. Ransom Eli Olds' retirement would be permanent.

CHAPTER FOURTEEN

Olds' Last Years

It SEEMS LIKELY that Ransom Olds' lack of success in 1934 with his plans to restore Reo to a more important position in the industry had little bearing on his decision to retire. That announcement in December 1936 came at a time when he was cutting most of his remaining ties with the more active business life of his earlier years. Olds was now in his seventies and white-haired, the once dark mustache now so light as to be hardly noticeable. But his posture was still erect and his mental faculties sharp, while his general physical condition was good enough to allow him to go off on a trip to the West Coast during the month following his retirement from Reo. In fact, in the latter part of 1937 he took an ocean cruise all around South America. But, though health problems were not an obvious matter of concern, Olds told Arthur Lauder a few years later that his doctor had advised him that he must slow down.[1]

Olds took this medical advice to heart, as Hugo Lundberg, Jr. and Ransom Able, a nephew of Olds, had discovered. Sometime around 1933, Able had suggested to Lundberg that they discuss with his uncle the possibility of getting his help to put Driggs Aircraft, which had been closed down by the Depression, back on its feet. Lundberg agreed to accompany Olds' nephew, even though he was not optimistic about the success of their mission. Olds received the two younger men in his office and listened to their proposal with the same courtesy and sympathy Samuel Smith had displayed when Olds had appealed to him for funds to save his automobile venture nearly forty years earlier. After hearing them out,

369

however, Olds smiled and said to Able and Lundberg, "Fellows, I'm starting to get my stuff together. I'm not interested in new enterprises."[2]

Shortly before this, in 1932, Hugo Lundberg, Sr. had had much the same experience when he too approached Olds about an investment in a new screw company that the former was trying to organize. Instead of showing interest in becoming involved in a new business venture, Olds had turned the tables on Lundberg and tried to interest him in taking over the direction of his Ideal Lawn Mower, Hill-Diesel, and Kold-Hold companies, which Olds proposed to merge into one organization under Lundberg's management. This was no doubt the first step towards a complete withdrawal by Olds from these lesser manufacturing interests. Lundberg declined Olds' offer and went ahead with the development of Lundberg Screw, which his sons continued to operate over forty years later. In June 1937, Olds succeeded in selling Kold-Hold and five years later his lawnmower interests. He retained an interest in Hill-Diesel and in the last years of his life, after World War II, he still was doing some experimenting with diesels in the company's plant. However, aside from maintaining this connection with his first business love—engines—he had severed all other connections with the manufacturing activities that had brought him fame and wealth.

It was also in the mid-thirties that Olds disposed of the Bellerive Hotel in Kansas City, which he had acquired the previous decade when liquidating his Oldsmar land holdings. However, he continued to head up the companies that owned and managed Clearwater's Fort Harrison Hotel and the Olds Hotel in Lansing, to which he added in 1942 the development and management of Olds Hall in Daytona Beach. When he was in Lansing, Olds regularly checked into his office at the R. E. Olds Company in the Olds Tower to keep an eye on his other real estate holdings, now largely concentrated in Lansing, Detroit, and St. Louis, Missouri.[3]

One reason that Olds gave for his retirement from most of his business interests was the unfavorable political climate of the thirties and forties. His view of these developments reflected both his continuing interest in politics and the radical shift that that interest had taken since the early 1890s, when he had been identified with the Populist party and had held elected public office as a member of the Lansing Board of Education. A few years after that he had become a Republican and would remain one throughout the rest of his life, but at no time, apparently, with any thought of again seeking a public office. His most active involvement in Republican party politics came in 1908, at the height of his fame as a businessman: a year after he drove Theodore Roosevelt out to the campus of Michigan State University, he helped to nominate Roosevelt's designated successor as president, William Howard Taft. On May 6, 1908, the Ingham County Republican Convention, upon the motion of William H. Porter, Lansing businessman and friend of Olds, recommended to the upcoming district convention that Olds be named as a delegate to the national convention. Olds was present and accepted the convention's endorsement "with a few words." Five days later, the district convention, which Olds' associates Richard Scott and Edward Peer also attended as delegates, elected Olds to be one of the two delegates from the district to the national convention. Olds, whose name again was placed in nomination by William Porter, was identified as "a prominent Taft supporter" in a front-page story in the Lansing *Journal*. That Democratic newspaper commented that nearly everyone in Lansing, regardless of party, was pleased with Olds' selection "because a citizen has been honored who has done much to promote the growth and prominence of the city."

Although it seems likely that Olds would have had to exert himself to some degree in order to obtain his delegate's position, he showed no more desire here than he did in other interest areas outside of his own companies to use this position to push himself forward. When Chase S. Osborn of Sault Ste. Marie wrote Olds, asking his support for the chairmanship of the Michigan delegation—a position that Osborn would use to project himself forward in his successful drive to become governor of Michigan in 1910—Olds answered that he would "gladly support Osborn." Unless Olds had retained some of his earlier Populist inclinations, his support of the aggressively progressive Osborn would seem to indicate either his naiveté or indifference toward political philosophies, since there were certainly others in the party who would have been far more in tune with the conservative political views that Olds expressed later, to whom he could have thrown his support. Similarly, Olds seems to have been little more than an interested spectator to the proceedings at the national convention in Chicago in mid-June. On June 15, the day after Olds and his wife arrived in Chicago, he attended the meeting of the Michigan delegation in the afternoon. In his customarily cryptic fashion, Olds noted in his diary his presence on the floor of the convention during the following four days. On June 18 he attended another state delegation caucus at nine in the morning, before going to the convention floor, where his only comment on that day's major event was: "Nominated Wm. H. Taft." The next day's proceedings he summarized as follows: "Nominated Sherman V Pres. left 3 p. m. for home."[4]

One national political convention seems to have been enough for Olds, and the fact that Taft would be frequently photographed campaigning in a Reo suggests that Olds' main interest in the 1908 convention may have been more related to business than to politics. In any event, during the rest of his life his active politicking seems to have been confined to making money contributions and to a certain amount of socializing. In June 1936, he invited the Republican gubernatorial candidate, Frank D. Fitzgerald, to be a guest on his yacht during a portion of the upcoming Chicago-to-Mackinac yacht races. Fitzgerald asked to be given "a rain check," saying that his heavy campaign schedule would not permit such a pleasant diversion at that time. Olds responded that he realized "that you, as well as every other good Republican, have a good job on your hands." Nevertheless, there is no indication that Olds felt an inclination to curtail his customary summer-long vacation in the north in order to join his fellow Republicans in battling the Democrats in that presidential election year. In the midst of the financial and political crisis of 1932, the state banking commissioner likewise declined an invitation from the vacationing bank president Olds to a boating excursion.[5]

Politically inactive though he may have been, Olds shared with most businessmen of his generation the same feelings of intense dislike for the path down which the country was being led in the 1930s and 1940s. He disapproved of most, if not all, of the domestic policies of Franklin Roosevelt and his New Deal, and in an interview in 1949 blamed these policies for his withdrawal from further business ventures. "Too uncertain," he said, "to invest money. There has been no incentive, considering the high taxes, labor difficulties and the other problems." On the subject of taxes, Olds could become almost livid. On one occasion he told of having invested in a company that made a new type of razor. The first year, he said, the company made a million dollars, but the government took $999,000 of that. On another occasion, when he and some guests drove over a new bridge near his summer home at Charlevoix, he declared that the sounds they heard were "the groans of the taxpayers."

The increasing power that labor unions gained during the New Deal was not felt at Reo until several weeks after Olds' final retirement from the company. In the spring of 1937 the Reo plant was closed for a month by a sit-down strike, which was finally concluded with the company's recognition of the United Automobile Workers union. Although Olds was not personally involved, he fumed that it was impossible to "run the business the way you want to with a union shop. When agitators come in and try to dictate policy—that's bad business." Olds, who had fought and beaten down union moves in earlier days, declared that "it was the free hand to run our business the way we wanted to" during that period "that made the industry great."

In a more general criticism of what was happening in the country, Olds maintained that there were simply "too many laws"—laws that placed more and more restrictions on the freedom of business and industry to operate as they once had done. He proposed an original solution: "If Congress and the state Legislature would adjourn for 10 years, the country wouldn't be hurt at all." Toward the end of his life, Olds saw some hopes of better times ahead. He foresaw the defeat of Truman's "spending administration" in 1952 and felt that the threat of war with Russia had receded. The Russians, he told a reporter a few weeks before the outbreak of the Korean War, had "bitten off too much to handle. . . . The Reds won't win, because they aren't right, in my belief." But pessimism was more typical of Olds' political outlook in these last years. "My doctor has asked me to slow up," he said at the time of his eighty-fifth birthday. "He wants to stretch me to 100, but I'm not sure I want to live that long the way things are today."[6]

* * * * *

Olds never became widely known for his philanthropic activities, at least not to the same degree that was true of such Michigan business contemporaries as Henry Ford, W. K. Kellogg, and S. S. Kresge. In fact, some critics charged Olds with being stingy—even miserly—in the spending of his money, and there seems no doubt that Olds was careful with his wealth. His fortune, of course, never approached that of Ford, C. S. Mott, or a good many others of his generation of automotive pioneers. His taxable estate at the time of his death was reported to be about $4.5 million; but the bulk of his fortune, as much as $60 million by some estimates, had long since been divided up among the members of Olds' family, with the R. E. Olds Company acting as the holding corporation for these family funds. Thus, by most standards, Olds was exceedingly well off; but perhaps Fred Smith was right in 1939, when he said that Olds had always had a great fear of being poor again. Such a feeling would help explain some of the stories that are told, such as the report that Olds would argue with his eye-doctor over the price of his spectacles.

Olds was convinced—probably with some reason—that people tried to take advantage of him because of his wealth, and he sometimes resorted to subterfuge to outwit them. On one occasion, Charles M. Taylor, property manager for the R. E. Olds Company, came into the office to find Olds talking on the phone to a local car dealer. "This is Charlie Taylor," Olds was saying. "How much do you want for that limousine you have on display?" After he hung up, Olds explained to Taylor that he had used the latter's name "because if I gave my own they'd double the price on that limousine." Similarly, when the pastor of the First Baptist Church in Lansing discussed with Olds the church's need for a place where young people could meet, Olds agreed to solve the problem by buying a private residence that was located next to the church, but only if someone else were made to appear to be purchasing the property. "If I buy it," Olds said, "they will charge two or three times as much."

Olds obviously enjoyed playing the role of the tightwad. He would joke about the alleged age and cheapness of his suits, although it was clear from looking at them that neither charge was true. When he stayed at his summer home on Grosse Ile, the young daughter of one of his estate employees would sometimes ride with him to Lansing to visit friends. In those pre-expressway years, the trip from Grosse Ile to Lansing took much of the day to complete, and they would stop at a restaurant for lunch. When it came time to pay for the meal, the girl would make a move to take out the money that her mother always gave her for these trips. But finally the millionaire manufacturer would pick up the check and with a twinkle say, "I think I have enough to pay for both of us." Of course, there was never any doubt that Olds would pay the bill, but he seemed to want to retain the common touch of the person who does not always have the assurance that he can buy almost anything he sees or wants.[7]

Any charge that Olds was in fact miserly, however, was disproved by his actions. In general, he did not like to deal with national charitable organizations, believing, he said, that too much of their income went to pay for staff salaries and fancy offices. He wanted to know what the money he was being asked to give was going to be used for, and when he made a donation, he wanted a strict accounting of its use. If the money was not used as he thought it should have been used, he would cease to support that charity. On the other hand, charities and philanthropic groups that measured up to his standards could count on continued support, which, after 1915, was sometimes channeled through the Ransom Fidelity Company, a nonprofit charitable foundation that Olds set up and provided with over a million dollars in working capital.

In Lansing, Olds' benefactions and service to the community were many. In April 1910, he recorded in his diary that three times in six days he met with Edward W. Sparrow regarding the new hospital building that Olds' long-time business acquaintance was promoting. For twenty years Sparrow had been active in the effort to provide Lansing with better medical facilities and had drawn others in the community into the movement. One of these was Metta Olds, who served on the women's hospital board that—among other things—directed the nurses' training program. Graduation services for the 1908 nurses' class had been held in the Olds home before an assembled gathering of one hundred guests. On April 28, 1910, Ransom Olds was appointed to the all-male board of trustees of the Edward W. Sparrow Hospital Association, a post that he continued to fill until his death in 1950. When the new Sparrow Hospital was opened in 1912, Olds and his wife purchased the former hospital building for use as a day nursery for the children of working mothers, long before day-care centers had become fashionable. This action in turn was consistent with the interest which Olds had always had in children and young people, an interest that was also shown by his service as an officer in the Michigan Children's Aid Society.

In 1914, Olds and his wife provided the land and building for the Ladies' Library and Literary Club in Lansing, and when the clubhouse later burned, Olds aided in its replacement. This project was also in keeping with an active interest that Metta Olds had in women's club work. Both she and her husband were also active supporters of the YWCA and YMCA, both at the local and national levels. In 1908 they donated their summer home on Pine Lake as a summer camp site for the Lansing YWCA, and in later years they contributed to the building programs of the two organizations in Lansing. Toward the end of Olds' life, when the local YMCA was seeking support for a new building, Hugo Lundberg, Jr. conferred with Olds, who held a mortgage on the existing YMCA building. Olds agreed to cancel the mortgage and to make a substantial contribution to a new building fund, provided the organization built the new facilities "like a box." Olds had definite ideas about what was practical and what was not practical in building styles. His admonitions were heeded in this instance, and Lundberg has said that when he sees the problems other organizations have had with the more elaborate buildings they have constructed, he constantly blesses R. E. Olds for insisting that the Lansing YMCA adopt a design that is admittedly plain but has resulted in a minimum of maintenance problems in the quarter of a century since its completion.[8]

The educational programs of the YMCA organizations were certainly one aspect of their work that attracted the attention of Olds, for whom education had remained an important interest—at least since his days on the Lansing school board—and a major beneficiary of his philanthropies. Briefly, from 1905 to 1907, Olds served as president, along with Ray Owen, who served as treasurer, of the Correspondence School of Automobile Engineering, before it was absorbed by the New School of Automobile Engineers. Olds, like many of his contemporaries in the auto industry, was well aware of the critical shortage of trained personnel created by the industry's overnight growth. Beyond lending his name to the organization, however, the extent to which he was involved in the operations of the correspondence school, which was managed by Victor Lougheed, was probably of a very limited nature, as was his later involvement with the training and educational programs of the Reo Company.

In a more traditional educational vein, in 1909, Olds was appointed to the board of trustees of Kalamazoo College, a Baptist-affiliated school, and he continued to hold this position until his death forty-one years later. During part of this time, from 1920 to 1937, he was also a member of the governing board of Hillsdale College, another Michigan school with Baptist connections. Olds and his wife shared this interest in education, not only in Kalamazoo and Hillsdale, but also in Storer College for Negroes in Virginia, on whose governing board Metta Olds served. And occasionally they entertained officials of the two Michigan colleges at their home in Lansing. However, records of the colleges indicate that Olds, despite his long tenure on their governing boards, took little direct part in board meetings and the policy decisions that were established on those occasions. Such matters, of course, had nothing to do with Olds' appointment to either of these boards. As a wealthy Baptist who had never graduated from high school, Olds, it was hoped, would contribute not time and advice, but money; and he did. In 1925, a year after Kalamazoo College conferred upon him the honorary degree of Doctor of Science, Olds provided $130,000 to construct the R. E. Olds Science Hall, a vitally important step in securing the full accreditation of the science programs for which the Kalamazoo school has become famous since the dedication of the new facilities in 1928. At that time, Olds' fellow trustees formally thanked him for "this projection of his life and labor as a gift to both present and future generations." A bequest of $80,000 was also provided at the time of Olds' death to aid in the construction of an addition to Olds Science Hall. At the same time, a bequest of $25,000 was made to Hillsdale College. In addition to such large donations—and no doubt a number of smaller contributions to these colleges—Olds and his wife financed the college education of numerous young people.[9]

Closer to home, Olds had an interest in Michigan Agricultural College, as Michigan State University in East Lansing was known during most of his lifetime. This interest went back to the 1880s, when P. F. Olds & Son did some repair work for the college and when Professor Robert C. Kedzie's timely loan saved the Olds firm from collapse. Although Olds was never an avid sports enthusiast, he did develop an interest in the agricultural college's football team. As early as 1910 he traveled to Ann Arbor to attend the annual gridiron contest between the East Lansing school and the University of Michigan. In his later years he was reported to have taken "keen enjoyment" in serving as part of a delegation that welcomed visiting teams to the Lansing area. He seldom missed the annual alumni reunions, which he attended as an honorary member of the college's Patriarch's Alumni Club. Olds' ties with the college were further strengthened in 1939, when it conferred upon him the honorary degree of Doctor of Engineering. The college's citation, in awarding Olds this degree, declared that Olds' "first runabout presaged economical transportation which has relieved rural life of dread isolation and provided facilities for a new economic standard for the peoples of the United States and the world." These are strong words, but not really an exaggerated statement of the impact of Olds' pioneering automotive work.

The honors bestowed by Michigan State on this high school dropout were more than earned by the actions Olds had taken in 1916 at a particularly critical juncture in the school's history. On a Sunday morning in March of that year, fire destroyed the classroom building and shops of the engineering division. For some years there had been strong pressure from various quarters to transfer these engineering activities to the University of Michigan. This, it was argued, would be less costly to the state than it would be to provide the added facilities that the engineering faculty and students at East Lansing needed. The destruction of the existing facilities seemed certain to strengthen the hand of the legislators who favored shutting down this engineering division. There were even suggestions that this would be an appropriate time to consider annexing the entire college to the University of Michigan.

President Frank A. Kedzie, son of the beloved Robert Kedzie, returned to the campus from an out-of-town meeting later on that fateful March Sunday. He refused to listen to the voices of doom. He immediately located temporary quarters on campus and in nearby business establishments, where, he announced, engineering classes would resume the following day as usual. That same day, however, he dispatched a telegram to Ransom Olds, who was spending the winter in Florida, as usual. Kedzie had earlier proposed to Olds that he donate funds for a building on a campus that to this time had depended entirely on public funds for its facilities. Olds had taken no action on that proposal. But now the wire from President Kedzie, which no doubt recalled to Olds the debt he would always owe Kedzie's father, as well as the similar crisis with which Olds himself had been confronted by another fire on a March weekend fifteen years earlier, led him to donate $100,000. With certain surplus funds available to the college, this enabled the engineering building, with three flanking shops, to be reconstructed, and it relieved the college of the necessity of going to the legislature, where the prospects of obtaining the necessary appropriation were viewed as most unpromising.

Olds' gift thus may have saved the engineering division at Michigan State, while the source of the money was itself an impressive endorsement of this program. "Coming from a man who holds a position of acknowledged leadership in a great industry," the college faculty declared, Olds' gift "is

R. E. Olds Hall of Engineering at what is now Michigan State University, an impressive monument to Olds' memory and an impressive indication of what $100,000 could buy in 1916

Courtesy of Michigan State University Archives and Historical Collections

substantial evidence that he believes in the Engineering Division of the College." In addition, President Kedzie observed, the R. E. Olds Hall of Engineering established the precedent that the college, "as a state and national institution, is not beyond the pale of private bequest." Kedzie's efforts to get others to follow Olds' example met with little success, but eventually additional buildings on the campus, such as the Kellogg Center, which was made possible by a grant from the W. K. Kellogg Foundation, bore testimony to the extent to which Olds' pioneering donation in 1916 enabled private funding to become an increasingly important supplement to state appropriations in aiding the school's expansion.[10]

Honorary degrees (in addition to those from Kalamazoo and Michigan State, Olds received a Doctor of Engineering degree in 1941 from Michigan College of Mining and Technology) were not the only awards given to Olds in recognition of his philanthropies. In 1926, the patriarch of the Greek Orthodox Church in Jerusalem appointed Olds a Grand Knight of the Order of the Orthodox Knights of the Holy Sepulchre. Ten years later King George II of Greece bestowed on Olds the Cross of the Redeemer, while the Russian Veterans Society awarded him the Cross of the Compassionate Heart. These honors were the outgrowth of a trip Olds and his wife took in 1922, during which they visited the Near East, including stops in Constantinople and the Holy Lands. Here Olds' name had been well known for many years as one whose factory doors were open to immigrants, providing them with jobs and security in a new land. Rajee Tobia, whose father was one of these immigrants who went to work for Olds and was to be nicknamed "Reo Joe," declares that the term "AR-REO" became a common one in the Holy Lands; it was variously used to refer to the man, the rather mysterious contrivance he had developed, and the opportunities that were offered from its manufacture. By World War I, according to Tobia, there were more than two hundred Holy Landers working for Reo. They sent letters home to relatives and friends with money and reports of "their

Benefactor—now known as Mr. Olds to some and still 'AR-REO' to new-comers—" whom they had met when he visited with them during lunchtime at the plant or at social gatherings in the Reo Club House.

These contacts may have added to Olds' distress in 1922 at the sight of thousands of refugees, many of them war orphans, uprooted by the war and its violent aftermath in the Near East. The result was his decision to pay the expenses of an American relief program in Constantinople to assist these refugees in finding their families or in getting new homes. Olds maintained the program for seven years. Among the expressions of appreciation that he received from those he had helped was one signed by Prince Shalikoff and thirty other individuals, a document which Olds hung in his Olds Tower office, along with other mementoes of his activities. It read:

> Dear Mr. and Mrs. Olds:
> We, the undersigned men, women and children of all nationalities in Constantinople, wish to express to you our eternal gratitude for saving our lives in our most difficult position. Thousands of miles distant, you have opened the door for us when other doors were closed. You have fed us, clothed us, and given us hope and courage to regain health and work. How great has been your aid, we alone can realize. We wish you to feel, dear Mr. and Mrs. Olds, that each day our hearts hold the thankful knowledge of your great goodness.[11]

* * * * *

During the last half of his life, perhaps none of Olds' nonbusiness interests received as much consistent attention as that which he devoted to church work. Within six months after this one-time religious skeptic officially joined the First Baptist Church of Lansing in July 1912, he had been named to the church's board of trustees. Eventually, he was made an honorary lifetime member of the board; and despite the honorary status, he attended board meetings regularly when he was in Lansing. If he was not notified of meetings, he wanted to know why. "That's my responsibility and I want to be there," he declared. Olds and his family could be counted on to be in church on Sunday when they were in town and to observe the Sabbath by attending other churches when they were away from Lansing. During the years that he spent summers on Grosse Ile, where there was no Baptist church, Olds would load up the car on Sunday mornings and go off to attend services at the island's Episcopal church.

At church functions Olds liked to be treated as an ordinary person. And yet he obviously enjoyed the special status that his wealth and business positions could not help but bestow on him in the church. Once, during the Depression of the thirties, the First Baptist Church was faced with a substantial deficit of several thousand dollars as the year drew to an end. When the pastor, who was new to the church, discussed the matter with the trustees, they assured him that the problem could be taken care of simply by contacting Olds, who was in Florida at the time. He would make up the deficit. The pastor insisted, however, that this was the responsibility of the entire church, whose members could not afford always to rely on the generosity of one member to bail them out. As a result, the debt was cleared without Olds' help. When Olds was informed of how the matter had been taken care of, he did not like it. He enjoyed being the church's principal financial benefactor, though later he agreed with the logic of the pastor's position when it was explained to him in more detail.

As a general rule, Olds' advice and assistance were welcomed by his church. As trustee, he took an experienced businessman's special interest in seeing that the church was operated in an efficient manner. He was particularly insistent that the church building be properly maintained and that any repairs that became necessary be taken care of at once and not put off to some future date. In addition, of course, Olds' regular financial contributions were of vital importance to the maintenance of the church's programs, and his special gifts made possible a number of improvements and additions to the church facilities. Olds also contributed large amounts to the American Baptist Convention, the national denominational organization to which his Lansing church belonged. This organization recognized Olds' long-time support in 1946 by naming him co-chairman of the Baptist World Mission Crusade, which raised $14 million, though Olds' function in the fund-raising work was largely an honorary one.[12]

In his church giving Olds maintained the same close watch on what happened to his money that he did on his other charitable and philanthropic donations. He had a set policy of contributing a thousand dollars to every Lansing church-building project, regardless of denomination. On one occasion, when two fund-raisers came to the Olds home and asked him for a large contribution to a national Baptist project, Olds called his pastor, who assured him that the two men were what they said they were, and that they were working on behalf of the American Baptist Convention. However, the men had obviously not been well briefed for their mission to Lansing, since Olds reported that in their interview with him they kept calling him Kraft, apparently under the impression that they were after part of a cheese fortune, instead of one in automobiles.

Despite the fact that Olds took on the co-chairmanship of the world mission drive in 1946, he did not like foreign missions and would not support them—though he did support home mission work. On the other hand, foreign missions was one of Metta Olds' particular interests, and she always matched her husband's gifts to home missions with her own contributions to the foreign mission cause.[13] The differing views that Ransom and Metta Olds held toward church missionary work constituted but one example of differences— some of a more serious character—that developed between the two. Indeed, if one is to believe frequently heard local gossip in Lansing, some of these differences appear to have placed some very severe strains on their marriage. The marital problems of Metta and Ransom Olds may well have stemmed from their contrasting personalities. Ransom, while scarcely the typical back-slapping, extroverted American businessman, was a warm, friendly, outgoing person who enjoyed a good time and had a well-developed sense of humor. Metta, on the other hand, was of a more serious nature, and as she grew older she became more retiring and withdrawn, devoting herself increasingly to nothing but her family and her church, giving up the club work and other outside interests of her younger days.

Although the couple may well have grown farther apart as the years passed in terms of such personality traits, they did retain certain strong common interests. Regarding their family, for example, there could certainly have been little on which they disagreed, Ransom Olds being as devoted to his family as was his wife. One of the great sorrows of their life together was the death of their last two children, Mildred and Ralph, shortly after birth. The fact that Ransom Olds never had a son to carry on the family name was particularly distressing to him and led him to lavish extra attention on his sons-in-law and especially his grandsons.

Ransom Olds also shared with his wife a common devotion to the strictest interpretation of Baptist standards of individual conduct. In April 1912, for example, Olds copied into his diary a resolution stating the intention of Lansing manufacturers not to employ any worker who did not attend church regularly, or who frequented saloons or other places of "bad moral influence"—as rigid a hiring policy as any of those for which Henry Ford would become notorious. Olds' name, like Ford's, W. C. Durant's, and Henry Leland's, was always associated with the forces of prohibition, and it was Olds' influence that is said to have kept Lansing dry until after his death. Like Ford also, Olds was strongly opposed to smoking and did his best to discourage such practices among employees and members of his family.[14] However, Olds seems to have been more tolerant of those who did not conform to his standards than was his associate Richard Scott or Metta Olds. Those who knew Olds and Scott blamed the latter for Reo's antismoking policy, which was not only enforced in the plant, where spies were employed to report anyone who smoked—the offender being fired immediately—but even on the sidewalks outside the factory. (The chewing of tobacco, on the other hand, was not actively prohibited and was a habit almost universally enjoyed by the workers; even Scott's brother-in-law, Harry Teel, was known to "bum a chew" from any worker that he encountered in the course of his supervisory tours of the shop.)

It would appear that Olds preferred more subtle techniques in attacking the evils of smoking. In the case of his grandsons, he sought to persuade them not to take up smoking by promising each a speedboat on their twenty-first birthday if they had remained nonsmokers. When R. E. Olds Anderson attained that age, he confessed to his grandfather that he smoked a pipe and thus could not accept the proffered gift. Olds, rather than showing anger or disappointment, praised the young man for his honesty and asked him what he would like in place of the speedboat. Anderson, who had become involved with farming, said he could use a barn. Olds promptly had the barn built, and it was not until several years later that the grandson learned that his foxy grandfather had paid for the building out of the grandson's own share of the family fortune.

The hard-nosed prohibitionist Richard Scott reportedly would fire any Reo employee who was seen entering or leaving a speakeasy. Olds would ask job applicants whether they smoked or drank or saved money, and he gave preference in his hiring practices to the nondrinking, nonsmoking, thrifty applicant. But he was flexible enough to see the necessity to make exceptions in some cases. Around the time of the First World War, the sales manager for Reo, Robert C. Rueschaw, quit his job when he refused to abide by orders from Olds and Richard Scott to stop drinking. Rueschaw, one of the most talented auto sales executives of his day, went to work for the Mitchell Motor Company in Racine, Wisconsin. Shortly afterward, when Rueschaw's value to Reo became apparent, Olds and Scott persuaded him to return to his job at an increased salary and, according to Rueschaw's daughter-in-law, with the assurance that he could drink if he wanted to. One suspects that it was Ransom Olds who relaxed the rules in this case and not Scott, whose opposition to alcohol was so strong that he refused to authorize sales of Reo trucks to beer companies after the end of prohibition, in spite of the dire financial straits in which Reo was then struggling.[15]

Not only did Olds have to contend with the formidable

Courtesy of Gladys Olds Anderson

Elbamar as seen from the riverside entrance to Olds' Grosse Ile mansion

Richard Scott in trying to implement his more lenient ideas in business relationships; he also had to face his wife's views. On the liquor question, Metta Olds remained adamantly committed to the Baptist position and was an active member of the Lansing chapter of the Women's Christian Temperance Union. As much as she might appear to be in the background, her views carried weight in the Olds household. In his later years, Olds was advised by his doctor that an occasional drink would be beneficial to his health. However, such an act could not help but incur the wrath of Metta. Thus Ransom was careful to have his medicinal Scotch and soda without his wife's knowing about it. When the family was at its northern Michigan retreat, for example, Olds would duck over to the separate quarters of one of his daughters so that he would be out of sight of his wife when he imbibed. What her reaction might have been had she known of her husband's clandestine activity is suggested by an incident involving the two of them and their grandson, Olds Anderson. As they were returning by car from Detroit to Lansing, they passed a combination bowling alley and beer garden, and Olds revealed to his grandson that this was one of his

Detroit properties, and, he observed, "We make a nice little income off that place." The following day Olds called Anderson to one side and confessed that he had been indiscreet in saying what he had the previous day. Mrs. Olds had overheard his remarks and had insisted that he sell the profitable Detroit property immediately. This incident would also suggest that Olds' well-known refusal to allow his hotel in Lansing to sell alcoholic beverages was less the result of any deep-seated commitment on his part to the dry point of view than it was of his desire to avoid the irate disapproval of his wife and hometown church groups.[16]

The alcohol question was not the only one that created problems between Olds and his wife. Olds loved to play games, including card games. In 1911, he began to take part in regular sessions at which, from his diary entries, it would appear that a variety of bridge was played. As a good Baptist, Olds did not engage in such frivolous activities on Sunday, and Metta Olds apparently tolerated such card-playing activity by her husband at other times. But there were occasions when, in her view, he went too far. Once, when the Oldses

Ransom Olds (extreme left) entertains a group of his old Lansing friends at his Charlevoix summer home. The laughing Metta Olds is seated second from right.

were on their yacht in northern Michigan, Olds shocked his wife when he came into the cabin and asked their pastor and his wife, who were aboard, "How about a game of cards?" Metta rebuked him, saying, "Why, Ransom, this is the preacher and his wife you're talking to." Olds, who had perhaps suggested the game as a way of getting his guests' minds off the sailing conditions, which were quite rough, replied, "Well, they ought to have something to do."[17]

This remark was typical of Olds' entire approach to the spending of leisure time. From the day he began to take a less active role in the operations of his businesses, Olds devoted the same kind of energy to the task of enjoying himself as he had earlier to the manufacture of engines and automobiles. The vigorous pace he set was tiring to his wife and others, but her frequently heard admonition, "Now, Ransom, calm down," had no noticeable effect on her husband. The simple logistics involved in carrying out Olds' leisure-time plans were wearying enough in a lifetime that was spent before the advances that have made travel in the last half of the twentieth century increasingly faster, more convenient, and comfortable. In addition to the heavy itinerary of special trips to distant places, the Olds family continued right through the winter preceding the parents' death to travel south to winter at Daytona Beach. In the summer, the excursions out of Lansing to the family cottage at nearby Pine Lake, which had begun in the 1880s, were dropped in the twentieth century in favor of more extended stays at summer homes on the Great Lakes.

First there was Elbamar, which Olds built about the time of World War I on Grosse Ile, downriver from Detroit. This elaborate white-stuccoed mansion was far bigger and costlier than the Olds home in Lansing. The Oldses used it primarily during the summer and early fall. They had little or no social contact with the island residents, but they used the home to entertain friends and business acquaintances on a lavish scale. Olds was proud of Elbamar. He may well have felt that he had proved to his fellow industrialists that he could have everything they had. But Elbamar also had its practical side. The extensive grounds provided a good opportunity for tests of Olds' Ideal Lawn Mower. In addition, he employed a farm manager to handle the poultry, livestock, and truck garden operation that was in part designed to supply the needs of Elbamar but was also tied to the agricultural development planned for Oldsmar in Florida. About the same time that the latter project folded, Olds gave up Elbamar; it served as a USO center for servicemen during World War II and survives today as a structure divided into several apartments.[18]

From Grosse Ile, Olds went north to Charlevoix. There, in the fall of 1926, he began the construction of a huge lodge on a 150-acre tract of land he had acquired on Lake Charlevoix, from which he had direct access to Lake Michigan. Called Oldswood—with an "e" sometimes added at the end in keeping with the English half-timber architectural style—this seventeen-bedroom structure remained the permanent summer home of Ransom and Metta Olds up to the last few weeks of their lives. In these later years the couple's friends from Lansing and elsewhere would come here, as many as thirty or forty at a time, for a long weekend or a week. The guests were subjected to the rigorous entertainment schedule that Olds had planned for them. He himself would be up by 6 a. m. and, weather permitting, would soon be in for a swim. Later, after breakfast, he rang a bell and announced that activities would commence in half an hour. These would include darts, bowling on the green, and some of the other rather genteel games that Olds enjoyed. One or more trips on the Olds yacht would be scheduled sometime during the guests' stay. In the evening there would likely be a song fest, which Olds would lead until it was time for bed. There were also special events, as when Olds had the male guests surprise the women one evening by painting themselves up like Indians. "The girls doll up," Olds pointed out. "Why shouldn't we?" Then there was Olds' Demi Tasse Club, a kind of Baptist version of chug-a-lug, in which Olds placed a quart mug of coffee before a guest, who, if he succeeded in quaffing the entire contents in one sitting, would have his name inscribed on the wall at Oldswoode as a member of this club.[19]

Olds, one of his guests recalled, was "a tremendous host,"

but he always wanted some activity going on. The idea that his guests might enjoy relaxing and doing nothing was as difficult a concept for Olds to grasp in these later leisure years as was his father's desire to stop and pass the time talking with the workers in the shop when he was a youth. Ransom Olds was apparently always an impatient man, in this respect fully in tune with the fast-paced way of life his automobiles would help to usher in. The story is told of the time he went fishing with a friend. After five minutes had elapsed and they had not had a nibble on their lines, Olds said, "That's all, let's go." This same impatient streak showed up in his driving habits, where he did not always see the need to observe all the traffic laws. When old age forced him to give up driving his own car, he would fret when the person with whom he was riding would pause at an intersection. "Go ahead," he told a grandson on one such occasion. "They won't hurt you. He who hesitates is lost."[20]

Similarly, sailing vessels never interested Olds; they were too slow for his tastes. As a result, save for one sailing craft in his early days (and it had an auxiliary power unit), the yachts that became Olds' favorite source of recreation were mechanically driven, as one would expect from a man who spent over a half-century directly involved in the manufacture of engines and mechanically driven vehicles. While Olds was still in high school he reportedly built a twenty-five-foot steamboat, which he named the *Mary Ann* and operated on the Grand River in Lansing on Sunday afternoons, carrying passengers for a fee. Later, he and his father provided the engine for a larger boat, appropriately dubbed the *Jumbo.* When the builder was unable to pay for the engine, P. F. Olds and his son took over the boat and ran it on the Grand for several years. During this period, Olds also had a couple of motorized boats that he used on Pine Lake. When he and his family moved to Detroit at the end of the nineties, he acquired a 35-foot cruiser, the *East Wind,* which he used during the brief period the family lived in that city.

All this, however, was but a preliminary to the far greater yachting days that lay ahead as Olds became wealthier. When he was in Florida for the winter of 1906, he chartered

Courtesy of Gladys Olds Anderson

Olds' original *Reomar*, Florida-based yacht

a houseboat. He liked it so much that he had the forty-seven-foot *Reo Pastime* built in Muskegon and shipped to Florida, where Olds and his family used the boat for three years before he traded it for an unspecified number of bonds. He then proceeded to have a ninety-foot boat built in New York, which he named the *Reomar I;* he would later trade it in also for the first in a series of crafts he called *Reola.*

In the summer of 1912, Olds, who had previously had to confine his yachting activities to Florida and the East Coast during the winter, shipped the *Reomar II* north and began to sail the Great Lakes in the summer. He spent nearly the entire following summer aboard the *Reomar,* with the new facilities he was developing at Elbamar on Grosse Ile as the vessel's home base. By World War II, with his Charlevoix summer home now serving as his base, he was aboard the *Reomar IV,* at 134 feet the largest of all the numerous yachts he would own. The boat was taken over by the navy during the war and was used for coast patrol duty. Subsequently, Olds returned to smaller boats. At the time of his last birthday, in June 1950, Olds was eagerly awaiting the delivery of a 58-foot boat that he was having built in Manitowoc, Wisconsin, and that he planned to call the *Reola IV*.[21]

Although Olds seems to have inherited some of his father's knack for trading one piece of property for another and was thus able to reduce to some extent the cost of his yachts through similar trading activities, his yachting obsession was an expensive hobby. At least by the time he had moved up to the larger vessels he was using in Florida and on the Great Lakes by the second decade of the twentieth century Olds had to hire a crew to run the boats for him, although he always maintained a keen interest in the details of the boats' construction, their operation, and the courses that were charted. Residents of Grosse Ile recall that one of the early yachts that Olds docked at Elbamar had a crew of six. The big *Reomar IV* required a crew of fourteen, under the command of Captain Alfred Brow, who served as Olds' skipper for a quarter of a century. Besides the wages of the crew, there was the expense of running the boats, which was considerable. An officer in one of Olds' companies found this out when he was in Florida visiting Olds. With the best of intentions, he told Olds that he wanted to buy the fuel for Olds' yacht. Olds reportedly told his associate that the fuel cost $600, at which news the official said, "Well, I'll be damned," and hastily put his checkbook back in his pocket.[22]

* * * * *

In spite of his constant traveling and his long absences from Lansing, Olds, in response to one inquiry about what he enjoyed most about traveling, replied: "Coming home." The sight of the flag flying at the home on South Washington Avenue was the signal that the Olds family was back in town. Lansing had been his home, except for two years, since 1880; he had grown to love it and with good reason. Lansing had been good to Olds, and he had been good to it. Here in Lansing the hectic round of social functions that Olds doted on continued. At Christmas time the Oldses and their friends would have a "snow ball," or progressive, party, going from house to house, but always ending up at the Olds home where there would be music and dancing, the love for which Olds did not lose with the passing of the years, and which he indulged in with his accustomed vigor until shortly before his death. On New Year's Day, Olds and his wife frequently held open house for their friends, with the numbers attending these receptions sometimes exceeding 250.

In Lansing there were special functions to honor the city's most famous couple. The Oldses' fiftieth wedding anniversary celebration in June 1939 was an event long remembered. The guests, among whom were the Henry Fords, arrived late in the afternoon at Woldumar, Gladys Olds Anderson's home. "An elaborate supper was served," one of the guests recalled. "The guests ate al-fresco on the spacious porches facing the river, on the broad steps leading from these porches, and a few in the dining room. An unusual feature was the myriad of waitresses, serving food to the many guests. They were dressed in pastel colored uniforms and perky caps—a real departure, at that time, from the conventional black with white organdy aprons and caps." Later in the evening there was dancing in a specially built pavilion.

Five years later, on Olds' eightieth birthday, there was a great community celebration, with five hundred people filling the Hotel Olds' ballroom for a luncheon sponsored by the Rotary Club, to which Olds had long belonged. Messages of congratulations had been received from such a diverse and unlikely group of famous people as Herbert Hoover, who could "well remember that you served me at one time with an Oldsmobile [it is more likely the car was a Reo]," Henry A. Wallace, a symbol of the New Deal policies Olds found so objectionable, Thomas E. Dewey, J. Edgar Hoover, Pierre S. duPont, William Green of the AFL, Henry Ford, and Dwight D. Eisenhower, about to lead the invasion of Europe. Present for the luncheon were such national dignitaries as Charles Nash, A. B. C. Hardy, one of Olds' successors as head of Oldsmobile, and Alfred Reeves; from the local area, Governor Harry Kelly, Lansing Mayor Ralph Crego, the executive brass from the Reo, Oldsmobile, and Motor Wheel organizations, and such one-time associates of Olds as Horace

Courtesy of Gladys Olds Anderson

Ransom and Metta Olds surrounded by their family at their golden wedding anniversary celebration. In the front row, to the left of the Oldses, are grandson Armin Sage Roe and daughter Gladys Olds Anderson; to their right are daughter Bernice Olds Roe and grandson J. Woodward Roe. Standing, from left to right, are Bernice's son, Edward Olds Roe; Gladys' daughter, Peggy Anderson Wortz; Bernice's husband, Clarence S. Roe; the Roes' daughter, Bernice Olds Roe; and Gladys' daughter-in-law and son, Barbara Piatt Anderson and R. E. Olds Anderson, who were married at the time.

Thomas and Arthur C. Stebbins. C. W. Otto, head of the local chamber of commerce, served as master of ceremonies, introducing, among others, Mayor Crego, who hailed Olds as the "first citizen of Lansing," and Alfred Reeves, who referred to Olds as the "father of mass production in the motor industry."

In the course of these proceedings, or perhaps later in the day, Olds announced that while he hoped everyone stayed and had a good time, he was leaving to attend a wedding. A few days earlier he had noted in the newspaper that the daughter of his business associate Charles Taylor was getting married. Olds, who had once complained to Taylor that he wished "people wouldn't think I am sitting on a throne," asked Taylor why he and Mrs. Olds had not been invited to the wedding. Taylor had not really thought the event would interest his employer, especially since it was scheduled for the night of the Olds birthday celebration. The oversight was hastily corrected and an invitation extended, which Olds not only accepted and used, but which he accompanied with a check for a thousand dollars to the bride.[23]

As this incident illustrates, Olds liked people and wanted greatly to be liked. In his business relationships he was a man with certain definite ideas, and when these clashed with those held by others with whom he came into contact, the result could be undying enmity toward Olds on the part of those individuals who crossed him. The attitudes of Fred Smith, Reuben Shettler, and Richard Scott, after their breaks with Olds, are examples of his ability, in spite of himself, to make enemies. Nearly two decades after Olds' death and more than forty years after the Blackstone Theater affair, LeRoy Brown was still mailing his latest anti-Olds diatribe to every Oldsmobile dealer in the country as part of an effort on his part to get the Oldsmobile Division to adopt a new name, divorcing itself from any association with the man whom Brown hated. But such hostility, although regrettable, is to be expected toward anyone who had the kind of power and influence Olds had been able to exert. In general, however, it would appear that Olds was successful in retaining the respect and friendship of most of those with whom he had dealings as a businessman, while on the social level the number of his friends and acquaintances was legion.[24]

No matter what else he did, in Lansing Olds still meant cars. Though he was retired from any connection with the manufacturing of automobiles for the last fourteen years of his life, Olds could not easily escape from his past. Reporters inevitably got around to asking him his views on the new cars, and he was quick to respond. He was firmly convinced in his last years that the industry could produce perfectly good cars at much lower prices than those being asked. "Prices are much too high," he declared in 1949. "More people should have the benefit of this fine equipment." He blamed what he called gadgets for some of the inflated cost of the car. "The public wants transportation, not gadgets," he said. "Take a windshield washer for instance. I wouldn't have one on my car. Maybe I'm old-fashioned. But the gasoline station attendant will wipe off your window anyway." More fundamental as a cause of the car's high cost, Olds maintained, was the constant emphasis on restyling the new models. The cost simply of retooling for the annual model change was "enormous," observed the man who had encountered heavy criticism decades earlier for his tendency to stick too long with the same car designs.[25]

Of course, though he was no longer directly connected with either, R. E. Olds continued to be associated by the public with the two Lansing motor vehicle manufacturers that bore his name or initials. At a dinner given by the Reo company in May 1945, this continuing link between Olds and the Reo trucks was given some publicity when Olds, an honorary member of the employees' service club, and 274 Reo workers were given gold rings in recognition of twenty-five years or more of service to the firm. But in these last years of Olds' life, there was also what must have been for him a most gratifying reconciliation with his first automobile venture.

Once Olds' managerial connection with Reo came to an end in 1936, the Oldsmobile management openly sought to re-establish that division's connection with this automotive pioneer. The Smiths had been gone from the company for almost three decades, and for the new generation of staff officials who had taken over since that time, the issues that had caused so much bitterness between the Smiths and Olds had long since ceased to have any meaning. This was evident in 1939 by the reaction of some of these officers to Fred Smith's

Courtesy of Motor Vehicle Manufacturers Association

This 1938 publicity shot of Olds and C. L. McCuen, Oldsmobile's general manager from 1933 to 1940, previewing the 1939 Oldsmobiles symbolized the reconciliation of the seventy-four-year-old industrialist and his namesake manufacturing firm.

attempts to rekindle those ancient fires through a prolonged letter campaign, in which he pointed out the errors that were being perpetuated by referring to the 1897 Olds motor vehicle—now on display in the Smithsonian Institution—as the first or the "original" Oldsmobile. This was, of course, an anachronistic use of a trade name that had not been coined and employed until 1900; but more important, Smith stated, the application of the name to what Smith claimed was a decidedly inferior vehicle served to discredit the quality of the legitimate Oldsmobiles. But the Oldsmobile publicists were not interested in the fine points of historical accuracy that Smith was raising, and they politely ignored his nit-picking arguments. The name of Fred Smith, after all, meant nothing to the car-buying public of the thirties; but Ransom

Olds' name still carried an instant and obvious association with the cars these publicists were promoting.

At least as early as October 1938, Olds attended a special preview showing of the 1939 Oldsmobile models, at which time he was identified as the "creator of the original Olds-mobile car back in 1897." He was quoted as saying of the new models: "Unquestionably they are the most beautiful and most scientifically correct cars that Oldsmobile has ever built in its 42 years of manufacturing." To have the founder of the firm and the designer of the "original Oldsmobile" present on such occasions was a publicity coup—and Olds loved it. He maintained a close interest in the mechanical development of the Oldsmobile. In fact, for several years he had included two Oldsmobiles, along with two Reos, in the stable of cars he maintained for his personal use. When Olds-mobile introduced its Hydra-Matic Drive, an automatic transmission, on its 1939 models, Olds may well have taken pride in the fact that the engineering staff was pioneering an approach that would become universally adopted in the future. Oldsmobile was not the first car to have automatic transmission (Horace Thomas' Reo, among others, had pre-ceded Oldsmobile in this regard by a half decade), any more than Olds' curved-dash runabout was the first mass-produced, lightweight, inexpensive car on the market. But in both cases it was Oldsmobile that had the first real success with these new approaches.

Thus the 1939 Oldsmobile strengthened that image of a car which Olds had first established as the most innovative of the popular American automobiles. Olds was so intrigued by Oldsmobile's Hydra-Matic Drive that he insisted on pay-ing to have it installed in the new Oldsmobile which Dr. Julius Fischbach, pastor of Lansing's First Baptist Church, had bought for a trip he and his family were taking to the West. Olds assured them that it would give them a more pleasant trip, although the system was so new that the fac-tory was not certain that any garages would know how to repair the transmission if something went wrong on the trip. Like Roy Chapin many years before, the Fischbachs, with much trepidation, tested out the new Oldsmobile, and their experiences on their western trip testified to the general soundness of Olds' judgment in such matters. However, on their return, despite the fact that the Hydra-Matic transmission had worked perfectly, they had the car converted back to the more familiar manual transmission system.[26]

Early in June 1950, around the time of his eighty-sixth birthday, Ransom Olds was interviewed by Carlisle Carver of the Lansing *State Journal*. Carver reported that Olds was confident that if he were younger he could successfully manufacture and sell a small car that would sell for $500, well below the going rate for cars of any size by that time. But such a goal was now obviously out of the question for Olds. An attack of pneumonia in 1947 had noticeably slowed him down. He suddenly seemed to age more rapidly, his once erect body now becoming stooped by an octogenarian's infirmities. Nevertheless, his voice, as recorded around this time, though somewhat weak, was still very much alert and showed a vital interest in life. He recalled those distant days, over a half-century before, when he had been the only motorist on the road, in and around Lansing, and contrasted those days with the congested traffic conditions of the mid-twentieth century. But, though Olds did a great deal of reflecting on the past in his last years, he was still looking to the future as well, telling Carlisle Carver in that interview of his eagerness to break in his new boat, the *Reola IV*, when he took up his annual summer residence at Oldswoode.[27]

Olds went north that summer, but for this indefatigable traveler it was to be his last trip. On July 28 he complained of not feeling well. He was driven from Charlevoix back to Lansing, where he underwent tests in the hospital, the results of which led his doctors to report that he was suffering the "complications of old age." He returned to his Lansing residence of the past forty-six years, but his condition did not improve in these familiar surroundings. On August 20, the news services sent word to the nation's papers that Olds was "critically ill and weakening." One of his physicians declared that Olds put up "a game fight" until August 25, when he lapsed into a coma. The following day Ransom Olds was dead. The funeral was held three days later, and his remains were placed in the family mausoleum, along with those of Pliny and Sarah Olds. Metta Olds, who had been in failing health for several years, died a week after her husband. She had attended Olds' funeral in a wheelchair; but she fell afterwards, breaking a hip. Pneumonia set in, and she died on September 2, 1950.[28]

*　*　*　*　*

The comments that appeared at the time of the death of Ransom Eli Olds were what would be expected on the occasion of the death of an individual of obvious importance. The attention, quite naturally, was focused on his automotive career. All work at the Oldsmobile and Reo plants was halted for two minutes at the moment the funeral was scheduled to begin. George W. Mason, chairman of the Nash-Kelvinator Corporation, speaking on behalf of the Automobile Manufacturers Association which he headed, described Olds—not too accurately—"as the first volume producer of automobiles," and as one who had "displayed the initiative, courage and vision of the truly great of our times."[29] It had indeed taken such qualities for Olds to surrender the security of a safe, established engine-manufacturing business in the late 1890s to tackle the potentially far more profitable but also far riskier prospect of manufacturing and marketing automobiles. There Olds had spotted the proper course to take almost at once, and his success would inspire a multitude of others to improve and perfect the approaches, methods, and techniques which he pioneered, bringing to fruition the greatest industrial boom in American history.

However, it had also taken great insight on the part of Ransom Olds to realize his own limitations. He must have recognized that he had no real aptitude for the tedious administrative tasks that were required to run a large automobile firm once it had been firmly established. Thus he stepped to one side, leaving these tasks to others, while he devoted himself to the things that interested him. With occasional interludes, such as his involvement in the unpleasant internal fighting in the Reo organization during the thirties, the last forty years of Olds' life seem rather placid; but they are also largely devoid of the tragic elements that were to mar the last decades of the careers of Olds' great contemporaries Henry Ford and W. C. Durant. Unlike Olds, those two leaders in the industry did not know their limitations and when to quit, and their reputations, which were based on astounding earlier achievements, have suffered greatly as a result.

Those last forty years of Olds' life, if relatively peaceful and uneventful, are not unimportant years. A knowledge of them, as well as of his early years, is essential to an understanding of the personality of the man who, for a ten-year period in the middle of a long life, sketched the outlines of America's greatest industry and thereby influenced the future development of his city, his state, his country, and his world to an extent that was equalled or surpassed by few of his contemporaries.

Appendix

The Patents of Ransom E. Olds

THE FOLLOWING information on what is believed to be all of the patents that were issued to Ransom Olds is based first on an examination of the weekly *Official Gazette* of the United States Patent Office from 1880 to 1950, followed by an examination of the unpublished application files for those patents that were indicated in the *Gazette* as having been issued to Olds. This material is found in the Patent Application Files of the Records of the Patent Office (Record Group 241) in the General Archives Division, National Archives and Records Center, Washington National Records Center, Suitland, Maryland. The microfilming of these Olds application files was paid for by R. E. Olds Anderson, and the microfilm copies are in the R. E. Olds Collection, Historical Collections, Michigan State University. In addition to the patents that Olds had issued to him, he undoubtedly applied for a number of other patents which were not issued to him, either because the Patent Office rejected his claim or because he withdrew the application. Information about these unsuccessful applications, however, is almost totally lacking.

In the following list, the number of the patent is followed by the name of the invention, device, or design for which the patent was sought, the date on which Olds signed the application statement and swore to the truthfulness of its contents, and the date that the patent was officially issued by the Patent Office.

No. 456,837: Governor for Steam Engines. Subscribed and sworn to by R. E. Olds, Mar. 6, 1890; issued July 28, 1891.

No. 521,622: Multiplex Vapor Burner. Subscribed and sworn to by R. E. and W. S. Olds, Jan. 9, 1894; issued June 19, 1894.

No. 557,219: Elevator Gate. Subscribed and sworn to by Olds and George E. DeVore, July 2, 1895; issued Mar. 31, 1896.

No. 565,786: Gas or Vapor Engine. Subscribed and sworn to by Olds and Madison F. Bates, Aug. 13, 1895; issued Aug. 11, 1896.

No. 570,263: Combined Gas and Steam Engine. Subscribed and sworn to by Olds, July 31, 1895; issued Oct. 27, 1896.

No. 594,338: Motor Carriage. Subscribed and sworn to by Olds, Sept. 5, 1896; issued Nov. 23, 1897.

No. 635,506: Electrical Ignition for Gas or Hydrocarbon Engine. Subscribed and sworn to by Olds, Feb. 26, 1898; issued Oct. 24, 1899.

No. 658,461: Vehicle Tire. Subscribed and sworn to by Olds, Nov. 1, 1899; issued Sept. 25, 1900.

No. 661,070: Clutch Mechanism. Subscribed and sworn to by Olds, Nov. 10, 1899; issued Nov. 6, 1900.

No. 670,921: Carburetor. Subscribed and sworn to by Olds, June 26, 1900; issued Mar. 26, 1901.

No. 679,263: Mixing and Controlling Device for Gas Engine. Subscribed and sworn to by Olds, April 13, 1899; issued July 23, 1901.

No. 689,511: Motor Vehicle. Subscribed and sworn to by Olds, Feb. 5, 1901; issued Dec. 24, 1901.

No. 698,131: Motor and Frame therefor for Motor Vehicle. Subscribed and sworn to by Olds, Sept. 30, 1901; issued April 22, 1902.

No. 704,911: Friction Clutch. Subscribed and sworn to by Olds, Feb. 18, 1902; issued July 15, 1902.

No. 745,654: Cooler for Motor Vehicles. Subscribed and sworn to by Olds, Sept. 30, 1901; assigned to Olds Motor Works; issued Dec. 1, 1903.

No. 749,903: Brake Mechanism. Subscribed and sworn to by Olds, Feb. 18, 1902; assigned to Olds Motor Works; issued Jan. 19, 1904.

No. 750,684: Valve-gear for Explosion Engines. Subscribed and sworn to by Olds, Oct. 10, 1901; assigned to Olds Motor Works; issued Jan. 26, 1904.

No. 761,392: Carburetor for Explosion Engines. Subscribed and sworn to by Olds, June 12, 1902; assigned to Olds Motor Works; issued May 31, 1904.

No. 792,158: Vaporizing Device for Explosive Engines. Subscribed and sworn to by Olds, Sept. 30, 1901; assigned to Olds Motor Works; issued June 13, 1905.

No. 807,958: Motor Vehicle Running Gear. Subscribed and sworn to by Olds, Oct. 24, 1904; issued Dec. 19, 1905.

No. 890,571: Gas Engine. Subscribed and sworn to by Olds and Horace T. Thomas, July 1, 1907; assigned to Reo Motor Car Company; issued June 9, 1908.

No. 952,575: Convertible Automobile Body. Subscribed and sworn to by Olds, Nov. 27, 1905; assigned to Reo Motor Car Company; issued Mar. 22, 1910.

No. 1,008,051: Tire. Subscribed and sworn to by Olds, May 25, 1910; issued Nov. 7, 1911.

No. 1,105,686: Tractor. Subscribed and sworn to by Olds, Dec. 4, 1913; issued Aug. 4, 1914.

No. 1,131,156: Power Lawn Mower. Subscribed and sworn to by Olds, May 12, 1914; issued Mar. 9, 1915.

No. 1,368,283: Tractor. Subscribed and sworn to by Olds, Jan. 23, 1920; issued Feb. 15, 1921.

No. 1,443,033: Detachable Propulsion Unit for Railway Vehicles. Subscribed and sworn to by Olds, Mar. 22, 1919; issued Jan. 23, 1923.

No. 1,443,034: Root Extractor. Subscribed and sworn to by Olds, Jan. 23, 1920; issued Jan. 23, 1923.

No. 1,477,661: Auxiliary Tread for Pneumatic Tires. Subscribed and sworn to by Olds, May 8, 1919; issued Dec. 18, 1923.

No. 2,099,371: Diesel Engine. Subscribed and sworn to by Olds, Aug. 20, 1934; assigned to Hill-Diesel Engine Co.; issued Nov. 16, 1937.

No. 2,230,308: Internal Combustion Engine. Subscribed and sworn to by Olds, Jan. 4, 1939; issued Feb. 4, 1941.

Design Patents:

No. 34,831: Vehicle Body. Subscribed and sworn to by Olds, May 1, 1901; issued July 23, 1901.

No. 35,076: Vehicle-body Frame. Subscribed and sworn to by Olds, May 1, 1901; issued Sept. 10, 1901.

No. 35,540: Engine Cylinder Head and Chest. Subscribed and sworn to by Olds, Oct. 10, 1901; issued Dec. 31, 1901.

Bibliography
and Acknowledgments

RATHER THAN repeating the bibliographical information cited in the footnotes, the following is simply an assessment of some of the more important of these sources and an acknowledgment of the help that many people generously provided during the preparation of this book.

The present biography is, as noted in the Prologue, the third such full-length look at Ransom E. Olds to appear in print. Although the published material relating to Olds is not extensive, a careful examination of this material is basic to any study of his life. Duane Yarnell's *Auto Pioneering: A Remarkable Story of Ransom E. Olds, father of Oldsmobile and Reo* (Lansing, 1949) has considerable value, despite its innumerable errors and inaccuracies, because it provides the most complete account of the way in which Olds himself in his last years wished his activities to be viewed. Significant biographical sketches that appeared earlier and were likewise essentially conduits for Olds' own view of his work include chapters in B. C. Forbes and O. D. Foster, *Automotive Giants of America* ... (New York, 1926) and Arthur Russell Lauder, *Lansing Unlimited* (n. p., 1947), and the Olds biography in that great compendium of valuable—but totally uncritical—biographical information, the *National Cyclopaedia of American Biography*, XXXIX, 480–481.

In refreshing contrast to the uniformly adulatory character of these accounts of Olds' life is Glenn E. Niemeyer's *The Automotive Career of Ransom E. Olds* (East Lansing, 1963), the first attempt to present an objective view of Olds, based not on what Olds told the author but on a scholarly examination and evaluation of some of the available historical resources. Despite its inadequacies, Niemeyer's work has lasting value, particularly in its treatment of Olds' less controversial later business career.

In a more popular vein, [Beverly Rae Kimes and Richard M. Langworth], *Oldsmobile: The First Seventy-five Years* (New York, 1972) is disappointingly traditional in its treatment of Olds' years with this corporate manufacturing giant. Many will continue to prefer the treatment of Olds and Oldsmobile provided by Arthur Pound in his classic—but regrettably undocumented—*The Turning Wheel: The Story of General Motors through Twenty-five Years, 1908–1933* (Garden City, N. Y., 1934). On the other hand, another work by Beverly Rae Kimes, "Reo Remembered: A History," *Automobile Quarterly*, XIV (First Quarter, 1976), 4–35, supplements in admirable fashion the account of Olds' role in this company that is provided in Niemeyer's biography.

Among the numerous general histories of the American automobile industry, those that were most useful in providing the background for assessing Olds' importance in the overall development of the industry were John B. Rae's two books: *American Automobile Manufacturers: The First Forty Years* (Philadelphia, 1959) and *The American Automobile: A Brief History* (Chicago, 1965). Of course, my own views on this subject are foreshadowed in my earlier study, *A Most Unique Machine: The Michigan Origins of the American Automobile Industry* (Grand Rapids, 1975).

Among unpublished sources relating to Olds, the most important by far is the R. E. Olds Collection of the Historical Collections at Michigan State University. The Olds Collection includes Olds' correspondence and his diaries. Although the collection is obviously incomplete—materials for the years before 1900, particularly, are almost nonexistent—it does provide invaluable insights into Olds' activities in the last fifty years of his life. Important supplementary material on Olds' career with Reo is found in the Reo Collection, also located in Michigan State's Historical Collections. Dr. William S. Combs, director of the collections, and his staff, especially Suzann P. Jude, were helpful and cooperative, as always, in making these materials readily available.

The family of Ransom Olds has cooperated in all stages of this project. Interviews with Olds' daughters, Gladys Olds Anderson and Bernice Olds Roe, and his grandsons, R. E. Olds Anderson and Woodward Roe, were sources of valuable insights into Olds' personality and of certain details of his career. In addition, R. E. Olds Anderson patiently answered numerous questions that were raised during an extended correspondence, and he made available certain materials at the office of the R. E. Olds Company, including the unpublished memoir "That Boy Ranny" and his mother's extensive family photographic collection.

I was able to obtain important information regarding Olds in interviews with a number of other individuals who had known Olds. These persons included Hugo Lundberg, Jr., and his brother Theodore Lundberg, Dr. and Mrs. Julius Fischbach, Mrs. Cecelia Rueschaw, Herman Staebler, Mrs. Violet Oldani, and Miss Isabella Swan.

Dennis Casteele, although not personally acquainted with Olds, provided information concerning Olds and Oldsmobile that grew out of his former position on the Oldsmobile public relations staff. More important, Mr. Casteele made available to me the minute books of the Olds Motor Works board of directors and certain other manuscript materials that are part of his private historical collection, which no previous researcher has used.

L. Gaylord Hulbert related his personal experiences with Olds in his role as a patent law firm official; but he was especially helpful in the development of the entire subject of Olds' patents, opening the files in the office of his firm, Whittemore, Hulbert & Belknap in Detroit. The resulting research on Olds' patents led not only to a thorough examination of the published reports of the United States Patent Office but to the unpublished files of application for these patents, which are found in the Records of the Patent Office (Record Group 241) in the General Archives Division, National Archives and Records Center, a group located in the

Washington National Records Center, Suitland, Maryland. The assistance of Jerome Finster, William B. Fraley, David Crowe, and Mrs. Mary Barton of the staff of the National Archives is gratefully acknowledged for the use of these materials, which have been completely overlooked by previous researchers. R. E. Olds Anderson generously took care of the cost of microfilming the Olds application files, and the microfilm was then deposited in the R. E. Olds Collection at Michigan State University.

Records of the state of Michigan that concerned Olds' business activities included the Articles of Association of P. F. Olds & Son and the Olds Motor Works, filed in the Corporation and Securities Bureau of the Michigan Department of Commerce, copies of which were supplied to me by Mrs. Pauline Guy of that department. In the State Archives, Michigan History Division, Michigan Department of State, the annual reports of Olds' various companies are filed in the Corporation and Securities Commission Records. Special appreciation is due to the staff of the archives for making these and other materials available, especially to past and present staff members Dennis Bodem, Geneva Kebler Wiskemann, Beth Rademacher, and Rosalie Clarez.

A state agency whose services were indispensable was the Michigan State Library. Richard J. Hathaway, head of the library's Michigan Section, was helpful in directing me to some of the various materials concerning Olds, particularly city directories and the library's clipping file. But it is the Michigan newspaper microfilming project, which Mr. Hathaway directs in cooperation with several Michigan institutions (including Eastern Michigan University), that has put this researcher and all others working in the field of Michigan history in this library's debt. Newspaper files that were previously unavailable or could be used only at great inconvenience and expense can now be obtained through interlibrary loan. The new information on Olds that I was able to glean through a search of the issues of Lansing newspapers for selected periods suggests how much more complete our knowledge of Olds would be if time permitted a day-by-day search of all pertinent newspapers published during his entire lifetime. Ronda Glikin and Donnetta Noland of the Eastern Michigan University library handled my requests for these and other interlibrary loans promptly and efficiently. (In addition to newspaper microfilms borrowed from the State Library, I also used certain newspapers filed in the Graduate Library of the University of Michigan and the Michigan Historical Collections at that university.)

Another major source of information on Olds' business activities are the trade journals. I consulted the files of such publications as *Horseless Age, Motor Age, Automobile,* a number of other automotive journals, and the carriage industry publication, *The Hub,* which has not received the attention from automotive historians that it deserves, in the University of Michigan's Transportation Library, together with much other material housed in that special library. Mrs. Sharon Balius, head of the library, was most helpful in facilitating the use of these resources.

The collection of trade journals and publications housed in the National Automotive History Collection of the Detroit Public Library, which I also consulted in the course of research for this book, makes it one of the great centers for automotive research. In addition, however, its manuscript collections, especially the Charles B. King Papers, and its copy of the transcript of the Selden patent trial, were especially valuable for their information about Olds. James J. Bradley, head of the collection, and his assistant, George Risley, were gracious and unfailingly helpful, as always.

The library of the Motor Vehicle Manufacturers Association in Detroit contains important information regarding the Olds Motor Works in its collection of advertising brochures, many of which were not found in other collections. For making these materials available and also for opening up the association's vast photographic holdings, I gratefully acknowledge the assistance of James Wren, the librarian, and Bernice Huffman.

The advantages of working on the Olds biography after having completed a general history of the early development of the auto industry in Michigan are the insights into the work of Olds' contemporaries and the greater understanding this provides about the conditions under which Olds labored. The William Maybury Papers in the Burton Historical Collection at the Detroit Public Library, for example, contain some important material relating to Henry Ford's early automotive activities; however, some of this material also throws important light on the developing interest among some businessmen in the emerging auto industry during the period when Olds was moving toward the formation of the Olds Motor Works. The Henry B. Joy Papers in the Michigan Historical Collections at the University of Michigan, along with additional Joy Papers in the Burton Historical Collection, reveal important similarities and differences between the approach Joy took in the management of the Packard company and the approach followed by Olds. Among published works, the three-volume biography of Henry Ford by Allan Nevins and associates, Lawrence R. Gustin's *Billy Durant: Creator of General Motors* (Grand Rapids, 1973), Clarence H. Young and William A. Quinn, *Foundation for Living: The Story of Charles Stewart Mott and Flint* (New York, 1963), and Mrs. Wilfred C. Leland, with Minnie Dubbs Millbrook, *Master of Precision: Henry M. Leland* (Detroit, 1966) would have to rank as among the most useful biographies of Olds' automotive contemporaries.

Mott and Leland were closely tied to Olds since they were among the early suppliers for the Oldsmobile. Among manuscript collections of Olds' business associates, the most important is the Roy D. Chapin Papers at the Michigan Historical Collections, University of Michigan, though the bulk of the coverage of this collection is that aspect of Chapin's career that followed both his and Olds' departure from the Olds Motor Works. The Michigan Historical Collections also has a small collection of the papers of Eugene Cooley, which contain a few items concerning Cooley's business activities. The typed memoir which Reuben Shettler prepared in 1936 is also found in the Michigan Historical Collections, as well as at the Historical Collections at Michigan State University. As always, I owe a debt of gratitude to Dr. Robert M. Warner, director of the Michigan Historical Collections, and to his staff, especially Mary Jo Pugh, for making my research visits to that depository so pleasant and productive.

One would hope that in the future papers of some of the other associates of R. E. Olds will turn up. The lack of the Samuel Smith/Fred Smith papers is the most obvious gap in the available sources, which is only partially filled by Fred Smith's brief memoir *Motoring Down a Quarter of a Century* (Detroit, 1928). Dennis Casteele's copies of the board minutes of the Olds Motor Works also suggest how valuable it would be to the researcher into Olds' career to have access to any business records of that early period which the Oldsmobile Division may still possess. As yet, however, Oldsmobile—along with the entire General Motors organization—has shown little interest in opening any of its records to scholars.

In addition to the individuals whose help has already been acknowledged, and others whose assistance has been noted in the footnotes, a special word of appreciation is due Charles E. Hulse of Flint, Michigan, who generously shared information that he has gathered in the course of some forty years of research on Oldsmobile and R. E. Olds, and who gave my wife, my grandson, and myself a memorable ride in his 1902 Oldsmobile runabout at the 1976 Old Car Festival at Greenfield Village.

Larry Gustin, automotive editor of the *Flint Journal* and biographer of William C. Durant; Richard P. Scharchburg, director of the Alumni Historical Collection, General Motors Institute; and Jerry T. Robbins, public relations administrator at Oldsmobile, provided valuable advice. Richard G. Oltmanns and his staff in Media Services at Eastern Michigan University excelled in the work they performed in reproducing the majority of the photographs for this book, as did John Gant, head of the photo duplication service at the University of Michigan Graduate Library.

My colleagues at Eastern Michigan University, especially Ira M. Wheatley, head of the history department, and the members of that department were always helpful in answering questions and providing advice.

Again, it is my pleasure as well as obligation to point out

that this book would not have appeared in print without the support that William B. Eerdmans, Jr. provided by agreeing that there would be a market for a biography of Olds; and the quality of the resulting publication was immeasurably improved by the work of Reinder Van Til, editor of Eerdmans' American History Series, and the other members of Eerdmans' editorial and production staff.

Finally, it is not possible to express the thanks I owe my wife Tish for the help and support and encouragement that she gave to me in this project, as she has to all such projects in which we have been involved over the past twenty years.

Notes

Prologue

1. For the origins of the Automotive Golden Jubilee, see Tom Mahoney, *The Story of George Romney* ... (New York, 1960), pp. 122–127. Seven years before this jubilee celebration was held, the Automotive Old Timers organization, formed in 1939, had established as one of its three objectives the construction of a permanent Hall of Fame to honor the leaders of the auto industry. The Automobile Manufacturers Association's 1946 Hall of Fame was in no way connected with this earlier proposal. In the 1970s the Automotive Old Timers, reorganized as the Automotive Organization Team, Inc., constructed a building for its Hall of Fame at a site made available to it in Midland, Michigan, on the campus of the business school, Northwood Institute. Dedication of the building and of the exhibits took place in October 1976. By 1976, forty deceased individuals had been named to the AOT's Hall of Fame, including Ransom Olds, Henry Ford, Charles Nash, and Barney Oldfield, among those who had been inducted into the AMA's hall in 1946, but not including such notables as Charles King, Frank Duryea, or Edgar Apperson, who had also been honored during the Golden Jubilee. See letter of Dorothy M. Ross, executive vice-president of the AOT, to the author, June 2, 1976; *AOT News,* IX (July–Sept. 1975), 26–27 and X (April–June 1976), 16–17.
2. *Detroit News,* May 29, 1946.
3. *Detroit News,* Aug. 27, 1950; Ransom Olds to John M. Hammond, May 9, 1946, copy furnished to the author by Dr. William S. Combs, director of the Historical Collections, Michigan State University.
4. Yarnell's previous publications, *Polo Boys, The Winning Basket,* and *Through Forest and Stream,* all first published in 1940, were part of a series of books for boys. On the origins of Yarnell's biography of Olds, see Glenn Niemeyer, *The Automotive Career of Ransom E. Olds* (East Lansing, 1963), p. 215 (hereafter cited as Niemeyer); Daytona Beach (Fla.) *Journal and News,* Apr. 17, 1949, a copy of which was furnished the author by the paper's publisher.
5. Review of Niemeyer's book, *Michigan History,* XLVIII (September 1964), 281.

Chapter One

1. Edson B. Olds, ed., *The Olds (Old, Ould) Family in England and America* (Washington, D.C., 1915), pp. 172, 195; author's interview with Gladys Olds Anderson and Bernice Olds Roe, June 28, 1973; letters of Emory Olds to R. E. Olds (MSS in R. E. Olds Collection, Historical Collection, Michigan State University). Unless otherwise noted, all correspondence cited in this work is from the Olds Collection.

2. Details of Pliny Olds' ancestry in Edson B. Olds, *op. cit.;* see also Gladys Olds Anderson, *For My Grandchildren,* privately published by Mrs. Anderson (copy in the Michigan State University Library). Sketchy details of Pliny Olds' career are found in Duane Yarnell, *Auto Pioneering: A Remarkable Story of Ransom E. Olds, Father of Oldsmobile and Reo* (Lansing, 1949), pp. 8–9 (hereafter cited as Yarnell); Arthur Russell Lauder, *Lansing Unlimited* (n. p., 1947), pp. 123–124; Niemeyer, pp. 4–5; *Men of Progress* (Detroit, 1900), p. 94; B. C. Forbes and O. D. Foster, *Automotive Giants of America* (New York, 1926), p. 226; and especially "That Boy Ranny," a typewritten account possibly written by R. E. Olds himself (MS in the files of the R. E. Olds Company, Lansing, Michigan).

3. "That Boy Ranny"; Yarnell, pp. 8–11; Lauder, *Lansing Unlimited,* pp. 123–124; Henry Ford, with Samuel Crowther, *My Life and Work* (Garden City, N. Y., 1923), p. 22; author's interview with Gladys Olds Anderson and Bernice Olds Roe, June 28, 1973; George S. May, *A Most Unique Machine: The Michigan Origins of the American Automobile Industry* (Grand Rapids, 1975), pp. 180–183; Anne Jardim, *The First Henry Ford: A Study in Personality and Business Leadership* (Cambridge, Mass., 1970), *passim.*

4. Ford, *My Life and Work,* p. 22; David J. Wilkie, *Esquire's American Autos and Their Makers* (New York, 1963), p. 25.

5. Gladys Olds Anderson, as reported in a letter from R. E. Olds Anderson to the author, July 31, 1972; Lauder, *Lansing Unlimited,* p. 124; Yarnell, p. 8.

6. *Michigan State Gazetteer and Business Directory, 1881,* p. 742; Albert E. Cowles, *Past and Present of the City of Lansing and Ingham County, Michigan* (Lansing, 1904), pp. 68–96; "That Boy Ranny"; Mrs. Franc L. Adams, comp., *Pioneer History of Ingham County* (Lansing, 1923), pp. 511–515.

7. *Michigan State Gazetteer and Business Directory, 1883,* p. 1003; *ibid., 1885,* p. 1057.

8. Forbes and Foster, *Automotive Giants,* pp. 226–227; Kenneth J. Mead, Department of Child Accounting, Lansing School District, to the author, July 18, 1973; Ford Ceasar to the author, Nov. 8, 1973; Bernice Olds Roe, as reported in a letter from R. E. Olds Anderson to the author, May 20, 1974.

9. Samuel W. Durant, *History of Ingham and Eaton Counties, Michigan* (Philadelphia, 1880), p. 167; Forbes and Foster, *Automotive Giants,* pp. 226–227; Yarnell, p. 13; James L. LaParl, Director of Education, Lansing Business University, reported that the records of this school, the former Lansing Business College, have not survived for the period

in which Olds is reported to have attended the institution, in a letter to the author, Aug. 17, 1973.

10. Forbes and Foster, *Automotive Giants,* p. 227.

11. Edson B. Olds, ed., *The Olds (Old, Ould) Family in England and America,* p. 195; *Lansing City Directory,* 1887.

12. Physical characteristics such as height and weight were noted by Olds in his pocket diaries, which have survived in an almost unbroken run for the years from 1906 to the late 1940s (MSS in the R. E. Olds Collection); Olds' voice, recorded a few weeks before his death in 1950, is on a tape of the twenty-fourth program in the series *A Name to Remember,* broadcast by the University of Michigan's radio station WUOM on July 15, 1965 (now filed in the Michigan Historical Collections at the Bentley Historical Library, University of Michigan).

13. Niemeyer, pp. 6-7; Ransom E. Olds, "Revolution of the World for Good," an article originally published in the *Bankers Home Magazine,* March, 1921, and reprinted as a separate leaflet (without pagination), a copy of which was furnished the author by Mrs. Kay Stratton, Kalamazoo College; "That Boy Ranny"; Yarnell, p. 201, where the claim is made that it was R. E. Olds, not his father, who negotiated the loan from Kedzie, and that the amount of the loan was only $1,000.

14. "That Boy Ranny"; Forbes and Foster, *Automotive Giants,* pp. 227–228; *Michigan State Gazetteer, 1889,* p. 1235; *Lansing City Directory, 1894.*

15. Lansing *State Republican,* Aug. 2, 1890 and Mar. 31, 1897; *Columbia Motor Car Company and George B. Selden vs. C. A. Duerr and Company and the Ford Motor Company,* U.S. Circuit Court of Appeals, Second Circuit, Transcript of Record on Appeal, XVIII, 887 (copy in the Automotive History Collection, Detroit Public Library, and cited hereafter as Selden Case Record); Lansing *Journal,* Sept. 10, 1891; *Scientific American,* LXX (June 9, 1894), 357. Sales figures for the Olds business interests for the period from 1891 to 1904 are given on a typed sheet, not dated, but probably prepared by or for Olds early in 1904 (MS in Box 1 of the R. E. Olds Collection). Employment figures from 1893 on are to be found in the annual reports of *Inspection of Factories in Michigan.*

16. Articles of Association in P. F. Olds & Son, Corporation and Securities Bureau, Michigan Department of Commerce (copy furnished to the author by Mrs. Pauline Guy of that department); Niemeyer, pp. 11–12; Arthur Pound, *The Turning Wheel: The Story of General Motors through Twenty-Five Years, 1908-1933* (Garden City, N. Y., 1934), p. 46 (hereafter cited as Pound) mentions only Smith as investing in the Olds company, which Pound incorrectly identifies as the Olds Gasoline Engine Works, with the incorporation date listed as 1892—also incorrect; Yarnell, p. 45, is likewise confused and incorrect; Lansing *State Republican,* Aug. 2, 1890; annual reports of P. F. Olds & Son, 1892-98, Corporation and Securities Commission Records, State Archives, Michigan History Division, Michigan Department of State, Lansing, Michigan (hereafter cited as Corporation and Securities Records).

17. R. E. Olds to Dr. Tappey, Sept. 6, 1904; Yarnell, pp. 44-45; annual

reports of P. F. Olds & Son, 1892–98, in Corporation and Securities Records; Lansing *State Republican,* Nov. 15, 1898; R. E. Olds Anderson to the author, Oct. 17, 1972; author's interview with Gladys Olds Anderson and Bernice Olds Roe, June 28, 1973; Olds diary for June 21, July 1, 2, and 3, 1908; obituary of P. F. Olds in Lansing *Journal,* July 1, 1908.

18. *Ibid.;* Selden Case Record, XVIII, 887; information on Olds' patents, summarized in the appendix to this volume, is found in the published volumes of the *Official Gazette* of the United States Patent Office and in the Patent Application Files of the Records of the Patent Office (Record Group 241) in the General Archives Division, National Archives and Records Center, Washington National Records Center, Suitland, Maryland.

19. Lauder, *Lansing Unlimited,* p. 124; undated clipping from the Charlotte *Republican-Tribune,* an article apparently published at the time of Olds' death in 1950, a copy of which was supplied to the author by David W. Dolson, Mt. Pleasant, Michigan.

20. Niemeyer, p. 24; Lansing *State Journal,* Sept. 2, 1950; interview with Gladys Olds Anderson and Bernice Olds Roe, June 28, 1973.

Chapter Two

1. Author's interview with Gladys Olds Anderson and Bernice Olds Roe, June 28, 1973.

2. Author's interview with R. E. Olds Anderson, June 28, 1973; obituaries of Metta and Ransom Olds, Lansing *State Journal,* Aug. 27 and Sept. 2, 1950; Miss Bernice C. Scott, First Baptist Church, Lansing, to the author, Aug. 18, 1976; Olds, "Revolution of the World for Good"; Evelyn Huber Raphael, *A History of the Haslett-Lake Lansing Area* (Haslett, Mich., 1958); Olds diaries; author's interview with Dr. and Mrs. Julius Fischbach, June 14, 1973; Lansing *Journal,* Nov. 17, 1891.

3. Lansing *Journal,* Mar. 22, Apr. 4 and 7, 1893; Oct. 26, 1897; Lansing *State Republican,* Jan. 28, Apr. 27, 1897; Frederick C. Aldinger, "History of the Lansing Public Schools, 1847–1944," I, 18–19 (unpublished work in the Lansing Public Library); *Catalogue of the Public Schools of the City of Lansing, 1893; Course of Study of Lansing City Schools, 1895–1896.*

4. See Appendix.

5. "That Boy Ranny."

6. Yarnell, p. 11.

7. Article from the Ohio Historical Society, reprinted in *Lake Front News* (Port Clinton, Ohio), Aug. 12, 1972; Ford, *My Life and Work,* p. 22.

8. Editors of *Automobile Quarterly, The American Car Since 1775* (New York, 1971), pp. 11–47; Smith Hempstone Oliver, *Automobiles and Motorcycles in the U. S. National Museum* (U. S. National Museum Bulletin 213, Washington, 1957), pp. 11–18; Selden Case Record, XVIII, 916.

9. Pound, pp. 31–33; Dorothy Marie Mitts, *That Noble Country: The Romance of the St. Clair River Region* (Philadelphia, 1968), pp. 246–247.

10. *Detroit Free Press,* May 28, 1946; Jackson *Citizen-Patriot,* July 7, 1929;

Yarnell, pp. 14–23; *Men of Progress,* p. 94; *Automobile Review,* X
(April 9, 1904), 581; Selden Case Record, XVIII, 889, 925; David Beecroft, "The History of the American Automobile Industry," *Automobile,* XXXIII (Dec. 9, 1915), 1055; Forbes and Foster, *Automotive
Giants,* p. 225.

11. Ransom E. Olds, "The Horseless Carriage," *Michigan Engineers'
Annual, Containing the Proceedings of the Michigan Engineering
Society for 1898* (Battle Creek, 1898), pp. 92–93. Published in 1898,
Olds' paper was given before the meeting of the engineers held at Port
Huron from December 28 to 30, 1897.

12. *Ibid.,* p. 93; Forbes and Foster, *Automotive Giants,* p. 225; Yarnell,
pp. 19–23.

13. *Detroit Free Press,* Aug. 27, 1950; Lansing *State Journal,* Aug. 27,
1950.

14. Olds, *op. cit.,* pp. 93–94; Frank N. Turner, ed., *An Account of Ingham
Country From Its Organization* (Vol. III in George N. Fuller, ed., *His-
toric Michigan* [n. p., *ca.* 1924]), p. 341; Yarnell, pp. 14–22, 27–31;
Forbes and Foster, *Automotive Giants,* p. 226.

15. Olds, *op. cit.,* pp. 92–93; Lauder, *Lansing Unlimited,* p. 124; *Scientific
American,* LXVI (May 21, 1892), 329.

16. *Scientific American,* LXVI (May 21, 1892), 329; *The Hub,* XXXIV
(July, 1892), 145; Yarnell, p. 36. P. F. Olds & Son had been running
occasional ads in *Scientific American* at least since that magazine's
issue of May 2, 1891 (LXIV: 285).

17. *Scientific American,* LXVI (May 21, 1892), 329; Olds, *op. cit.,* p. 94.

18. Niemeyer, p. 9; Yarnell, p. 37; *Automobile Review and Automobile
News,* VII (Dec. 15, 1902), 321; IX (July 15, 1903), 36; *Automobile
Trade Journal,* XXIX (Dec. 1924), 36.

19. Among those who have given some credence to the exaggerated claims
made regarding the sale of Olds' steam vehicle are Pound, p. 47;
Niemeyer, p. 9; and James J. Flink, *America Adopts the Automobile,
1895–1910* (Cambridge, Mass., 1970), p. 17.

20. Olds, *op. cit.,* p. 94; Charles E. Hulse to the author, Apr. 1, 1976;
Merrill Denison, *The Power to Go* (Garden City, N. Y., 1956), pp. 54,
71.

21. May, *A Most Unique Machine,* pp. 18–21; Selden Case Record, XVIII,
897, 920; see patent information in Appendix.

22. *Scientific American,* LXXIV (Mar. 14, 1896), 167; LXXIV (Mar. 28,
1896), 206; LXXVI (May 1, 1897), 285; *Horseless Age,* I (Mar. 1896),
26; Lansing *State Republican,* Mar. 31, 1897; sales figures from typed
notes of sales from 1891 to 1904 in R. E. Olds Collection; Niemeyer,
p. 13.

23. Yarnell, p. 54; Selden Case Record, XVIII, 889–90, 925; Forbes and
Foster, *Automotive Giants,* p. 229; Olds, *op. cit.,* p. 94; Niemeyer, p. 12.

24. Selden Case Record, XVIII, 897, 916, 920; Pound, p. 49; May, *op. cit.,*
pp. 15–16, 25–31, 40–44.

25. Forbes and Foster, *Automotive Giants,* pp. 228–229.

26. Olds, *op. cit.,* p. 92.

27. Lansing *State Republican,* Aug. 12, 1896; Birt Darling, *City in the
Forest: The Story of Lansing* (New York, 1950), pp. 159–162; *The Hub,*
XXXVIII (Apr. 1896), 8; XL (July 1898), 300.

28. Yarnell, pp. 52–53; *Motocycle,* I (Nov. 1895), 20–21; patent application

signed by Olds on Sept. 5, 1896, for Patent No. 594,338, awarded to him on Nov. 23, 1897, in Patent Application Files; Olds, *op. cit.,* p. 94; Lauder, *Lansing Unlimited,* p. 126; Selden Case Record, XVIII, 918.

29. Lansing *State Republican,* Aug. 12, 1896; *Detroit News,* Aug. 13, 1896; Olds, *op. cit.,* pp. 95–96; May, *op. cit.,* p. 127.
30. *Detroit News,* Aug. 13, 1896; *Detroit Free Press,* quoted in *The Hub,* XXXVIII (Oct. 1896), 474; *Grand Rapids Democrat,* Aug. 14, 1896; Charles B. King to W. G. Walton, Aug. 20, 1896, in the Public Library; *Motocycle,* I (Sept. 1896), 16; *Horseless Age,* I (Oct. 1896), 18; *Scientific American,* LXXV (Nov. 21, 1896), 380.
31. Pound, pp. 49–50.
32. File for Olds' Patent No. 594,338, in Patent Application Files; Casebook 3 in the offices of Whittemore, Hulbert & Belknap, Penobscot Building, Detroit; reminiscences of Prescott Hulbert, copy supplied to the author by L. Gaylord Hulbert; see patent information in Appendix.
33. File for Olds' Patent No. 594,338, in Patent Application Files.
34. *Ibid.;* the specifications for Olds' motor carriage were published by the U. S. Patent Office in 1897 and were subsequently reprinted in James T. Allen, *Digest of United States Automobile Patents from 1789 to July 1, 1899,* 501 (Washington, 1900). In the published version, besides minor punctuation changes from the original specifications submitted by Olds in his application, his—or his attorneys'—spelling of gasoline was changed to the more archaic "gasolene."
35. Olds, *op. cit.,* pp. 94–97; Olds interview on *A Name to Remember* tape.
36. Lansing *State Republican,* Aug. 2 and 23, 1897.

Chapter Three

1. Lansing *State Republican,* Aug. 12, 1896.
2. Niemeyer, p. 17. Niemeyer states that he found a copy of what he takes to be an 1896 Olds advertisement in the Roy D. Chapin Papers at the Michigan Historical Collections, University of Michigan. My own search of these papers failed to turn up this item.
3. *The Hub,* XXXIX (Aug. 1897), 304; XXXIX (Oct. 1897), 451; G. N. Georgano, ed., *Encyclopedia of American Automobiles* (New York, 1971), p. 209; *Automobile Review,* X (Apr. 9, 1904), 581.
4. Lansing *State Republican,* Jan. 13, Mar. 31, 1897; *Horseless Age,* II (Jan. 1897), 3; *The Hub,* XXXIX (Aug. 1897), 304.
5. Selden Case Record, XVIII, 914; Charles King to Oscar Mueller, Aug. 22, 1896, in the King Papers.
6. Lansing *State Republican,* Nov. 10, 1897.
7. *Ibid.,* Aug. 22, 1897.
8. *National Cyclopaedia of American Biography,* XLIX, 198.
9. Lansing *State Republican,* Aug. 10 and 23, Sept. 15 and 16, Dec. 22, 1897.
10. Yarnell, pp. 57–59; Lansing *Journal,* Dec. 2, 1891; Lansing *State Republican,* Aug. 23, 1897.
11. *Ibid.;* Charles King to Charles Duryea, Apr. 7, 1896, in the King Papers.
12. John K. Barnes, "The Romance of Our Automobile Makers," *World's Work,* XLI (Apr. 1921), 561.

13. Lansing *State Republican,* Aug. 23, 1897.
14. George N. Fuller, ed., *Michigan: A Centennial History of the State and Its People,* V (Chicago, 1939), 491; Lansing *Journal,* Sept. 3, 1891; Eugene Cooley letters for May and June, 1884, and a typed sheet, dated Oct. 3, 1932, on the formation of the City National Bank of Lansing, in the Eugene F. Cooley Papers, Michigan Historical Collections, University of Michigan.
15. *Lansing City Directory, 1899;* Lansing *State Republican,* Dec. 15, 1898, May 27, 1899.
16. Lansing *Journal,* Feb. 14, Apr. 10 and 26, 1893; C. M. Burton, ed., *The City of Detroit, Michigan, 1701–1922* (Detroit, 1922), IV, 647; C. M. Burton, *History of Wayne County and the City of Detroit* (Chicago, 1930), IV, 9; Samuel L. Smith, "Pre-Historic and Modern Copper Mines of Lake Superior," *Michigan Pioneer and Historical Collections,* XXXIX,137n; Michigan Historical Commission, *Michigan Biographies,* II (Lansing, 1924), 306.
17. Lansing *State Republican,* Feb. 18, 1897; Turner, ed., *An Account of Ingham County From Its Organization,* p. 342.
18. *Ibid.,* pp. 342–343; Niemeyer, pp. 18–20.
19. Yarnell, pp. 60–61; Turner, ed., *An Account of Ingham County From Its Organization,* p. 343.
20. Lansing *State Republican,* Sept. 15 and 16, 1897; Oct. 1, 1898. Helen Grant Sparrow died less than two years later, a few weeks after giving birth to a son. *Ibid.,* June 17, 1899.
21. *Ibid.,* Aug. 23, 1897.
22. Olds interview on *A Name to Remember* tape; Barnes, "The Romance of Our Automobile Makers," *World's Work,* XLI, 561; Lansing *State Republican,* June 24 and 25, 1897; June 1, July 26, Aug. 12, 21, and 24, 1899.
23. Charlotte *Tribune,* Oct. 13, 1897; Hastings *Banner,* Sept. 30, Oct. 7, 1897; clipping from Charlotte *Republican-Tribune (ca.* Sept. 1950); Selden Case Record, XVIII, 929; Lansing *State Republican,* Oct. 2, 1897; Aug. 5, 1899.
24. *The Hub,* XXXVIII (Jan. 1897), 651; XXXIX (Oct. 1897), 451; Lansing *State Republican,* Aug. 23, 1897.
25. *The Hub,* XXXIX (Oct. 1897), 451; Lansing *State Republican,* Oct. 2, Nov. 11, 1897; Selden Case Record, XVIII, 914; Olds obituary in Daytona Beach (Fla.) *Journal and News,* Aug. 27, 1950.
27. *Detroit News,* April 8, 1899; Niemeyer, p. 22; J. P. Edmonds, *Development of the Automobile and Gasoline Engine in Michigan* (Lansing, 1942), p. 12.
28. Niemeyer, p. 17; Selden Case Record, XVIII, 930; Oliver, *Automobiles and Motorcycles in the U. S. National Museum,* pp. 57–58.
29. Lansing *State Republican,* Aug. 23, Nov. 11, 1897; Olds, "The Horseless Carriage," *Michigan Engineers' Annual,* p. 96; *The Hub,* XL (May 1898), 127.
30. Hastings *Banner,* Sept. 30, 1897; undated clipping from the Charlotte *Republican-Tribune (ca.* Sept. 1950); Turner, ed., *An Acccount of Ingham County From Its Organization,* p. 343.
31. Niemeyer, p. 55; Lansing *State Republican,* Dec. 27, 1897.
32. *Ibid.,* May 8 and 22, 1897; U. S. Patent Office *Official Gazette,* XCII (July 31, 1900), 1023; Fred Smith to Olds, undated letter (*ca.* July 1902);

Lansing *Journal,* July 1, 1908; Olds diary memoranda for July 1928. On Sept. 6, 1929, Olds noted in his diary: "Wallace died. 10:30 p.m."
33. Typed sheet listing Olds' sales from 1891 to 1904 (in Olds Collection).
34. Fred L. Smith, *Motoring Down a Quarter of a Century* (Detroit, 1928), p. 16.
35. Niemeyer, pp. 24–25; *Michigan State Gazetteer, 1899,* 610, 652; *Detroit News,* Oct. 1, 1898; Apr. 8, 1899.
36. "That Boy Ranny"; *Detroit News,* Oct. 1, 1898; Lansing *State Republican,* Oct. 1, 1898; annual report of the Olds Gasoline Engine Works for 1899 (in Corporation and Securities Records).
37. *Ibid.; Detroit News,* Oct. 1, 1898; *Detroit Free Press,* May 7, 1905.
38. Lansing *State Republican,* Oct. 1, 1898.
39. *Ibid.*
40. *The Hub,* XL (Nov. 1898), 589; annual reports of the Olds Motor Vehicle Company for 1899 (in Corporation and Securities Records).

Chapter Four

1. Lansing *State Republican,* Nov. 23, 1898; Pound, p. 51; Ellery I. Garfield to William Maybury, Jan. 21, 1899 (in the William Maybury Papers, Burton Historical Collection, Detroit Public Library); Ray Stannard Baker, "The Automobile in Common Use," *McClure's Magazine,* XIII (July 1899), 195.
2. Lansing *State Republican,* Mar. 28, 1899; Pound, p. 51; Niemeyer, p. 25.
3. *Ibid.,* pp. 25–26; Barnes, "The Romance of Our Automobile Makers," *World's Work,* XLI, 562.
4. *Ibid.; Detroit Free Press,* May 7, 1905; obituaries of Samuel Smith in *Detroit Free Press,* May 9, 1917, and *Automobile,* XXXVI (May 10, 1917), 894.
5. Lansing *State Republican,* Apr. 6 and 8, 1899; *Detroit News,* Apr. 8, 1899; *Detroit Free Press,* Apr. 9, 1899.
6. Articles for Association of the Olds Motor Works (in Corporation and Securities Bureau, Michigan Department of Commerce), copy supplied to the author by Mrs. Pauline Guy of that department; Pound, p. 51; Smith, *Motoring Down a Quarter of a Century,* p. 16.
7. *Men of Progress,* p. 220.
8. Fred Smith, *op. cit.,* p. 16; annual report of the Olds Motor Works for 1900 (in Corporation and Securities Records).
9. Melvin G. Holli, *Reform in Detroit: Hazen S. Pingree and Urban Politics* (New York, 1969), pp. 200–210; *National Cyclopaedia of American Biography,* XIX, 249.
10. Lansing *State Republican,* June 12, 1897; *Compendium of History and Biography of the City of Detroit and Wayne County, Michigan* (Chicago, 1909), pp. 253, 271, 388, 390.
11. Annual report of the Olds Motor Works, 1900 (in Corporation and Securities Records); Lansing *State Republican,* Apr. 8, 1899; *The Hub,* XLI (May 1899), 69; Niemeyer, p. 27; minutes of meeting of board of directors of the Olds Motor Works, Jan. 9, 1900 (MS in the private collection of Dennis Casteele, Lansing, Michigan; hereafter referred to as Olds Motor Works minutes).
12. *Detroit Free Press,* Apr. 9, May 14, 1899; May 7, 1905; *Detroit News,*

May 13, 1899; Lansing *State Republican,* Apr. 8, 1899; Niemeyer, pp. 27–28; *The Hub,* XLI (June 1899), 116; XLI (July 1899), 161.

13. Lansing *State Republican,* Apr. 8, May 12, Sept. 1, 1899.
14. Articles of Association of the Olds Motor Works; *The Hub,* XLI (June, 1899), 116; Lansing *State Republican,* May 12, 1899.
15. Articles of Association of the Olds Motor Works; Lansing *State Republican,* Apr. 8, 1899; *Detroit Free Press,* Apr. 9, May 14, 1899.
16. Pound, p. 51; "That Boy Ranny."
17. *The Hub,* XXXIX (July, 1897), 239; Barnes, "The Romance of Our Automobile Makers," *World's Work,* XLI, 560.
18. Lansing *State Republican,* Apr. 8 and 13, Sept. 12, Nov. 1, 1899; author's interview with Bernice Olds Roe, June 28, 1973.
19. Lansing *State Republican,* Nov. 9, 1899; Richard Crabb, *Birth of a Giant: The Men and Incidents that Gave America the Motorcar* (Philadelphia, 1969), viii.

Chapter Five

1. *Detroit News,* Mar. 9, July 26, 1901.
2. For early automobile developments in Detroit, see May, *A Most Unique Machine,* pp. 83–87.
3. *Motor Age,* I (Sept. 26, 1899), 44–45.
4. Stephen B. McCracken, ed., *Detroit in Nineteen Hundred* (Detroit, 1901), p. 102.
5. *Detroit News,* May 13, June 25, 1899; Mar. 9 and 10, 1901; Lansing *State Republican,* May 15, June 10 and 17, July 8, Oct. 5, 1899; *Detroit Free Press,* May 14, 1899; Mar. 10, 1901; *The Hub,* XLI (June 1899), 116; *Horseless Age,* IV (May 24, 1899), 6; V (Jan. 10, 1900), 8; *Motor Age,* II (Mar. 22, 1900), 58.
6. Norman Beasley and George W. Stark, *Made in Detroit* (New York, 1957), p. 16; *Horseless Age,* V (Feb. 14, 1900), 13; Forbes and Foster, *Automotive Giants,* p. 230; Smith, *Motoring Down a Quarter of a Century,* p. 16.
7. Niemeyer, p. 29; Floyd Clymer, *Treasury of Early American Automobiles, 1877–1925* (New York, 1950), p. 11; *The Hub,* XLI (May 1899), 69.
8. See Appendix for Olds' patents; Forbes and Foster, p. 230.
9. *Horseless Age,* VIII (Nov. 20, 1901), 727–728.
10. Forbes and Foster, p. 230.
11. U. S. Patent Office, *Official Gazette,* CI (Dec. 2, 1902), 2071.
12. *Horseless Age,* IV (Sept. 13, 1899), 7; *Automobile Review,* V (Nov. 1901), 84; *The Hub,* XXXIX (Jan. 1898), 721.
13. *Automobile Review,* IV (May 1901), 98–99; John B. Rae, *American Automobile Manufacturers; The First Forty Years* (Philadelphia, 1959), pp. 68–69; *Detroit News,* Nov. 16, 1900; *Horseless Age,* VIII (Apr. 3, 1901), 20; Allan Nevins, with Frank E. Hill, *Ford: The Times, the Man, the Company* (New York, 1954), p. 198; *Detroit Free Press,* May 4, 1902.
14. *The Hub,* XXXIX (Sept. 1897), 369; May, *op. cit.,* p. 331.
15. *Motor Age,* II (July 19, 1900), 652; *Horseless Age,* VI (Sept. 26, 1900), 11.

16. *Motor Age,* III (Sept. 27, 1900), 13; Clymer, *Treasury of Early American Automobiles,* p. 11; see Appendix.

17. E. D. Kennedy, *The Automobile Industry* (New York, 1941), p. 19; *The Hub,* XLI (May 1899), 19, 69; XLI (June 1899), 116; *Horseless Age,* VII (Oct. 17, 1900), 11; *Automobile Review,* X (Apr. 9, 1904), 581.

18. Niemeyer, p. 30; Lansing *State Republican,* June 27, 1899; Forbes and Foster, *Automotive Giants,* pp. 230–31; *Cycle and Automobile Trade Journal,* IX (Oct. 1, 1904), 33, 102.

19. C. F. Caunter, *The Light Car* (London, 1970), pp. 18–19; T. R. Nicholson, *Passenger Cars, 1863–1904* (New York, 1970), p. 124; *Horseless Age,* IV (June 28, 1899), 13; IV (July 5, 1899), 8; IV (July 28, 1899), 5–6; VII (Nov. 14, 1900), 18; *Motor Age,* III (Nov. 1, 1900), 366.

20. *Horseless Age,* IV (July 28, 1899), 5–6.

21. *The Hub,* XXXIX (Oct. 1897), 433.

22. *Horseless Age,* IV (June 7, 1899), 11; V (Dec. 6, 1899), 18.

23. *Motor Age,* I (Jan. 11, 1900), 373.

24. Nicholson, *Passenger Cars, 1863–1904,* color plate 74, and pp. 142–143; *Horseless Age,* VII (Nov. 7, 1900), 52; *Motor Age,* III (Sept. 20, 1900), 78; IV (Mar. 13, 1901), n. p.; applications for Olds' Patent No. 745,654 and Design Patent No. 34,831 in Patent Application Files; see Appendix; *Automobile Review,* V (Aug. 1901), 6; V (Nov. 1901), 6; *Horseless Age,* IX (Mar. 12, 1902), 331.

25. Willis F. Dunbar, *Michigan: A History of the Wolverine State* (Grand Rapids, 1970), p. 556, in calling the Oldsmobile "the first cheap car," simply echoed what others—some of them authorities on automobile history—had been saying in the past; *Horseless Age,* XVIII (Feb. 28, 1906), 355; *Outing,* XXXVI (Sept. 1900), 703.

26. *Horseless Age,* IV (June 28, 1899), 4; V (Dec. 6, 1899), 8; *Cycle and Automobile Trade Journal,* IV (Oct. 1, 1901), 56; VII (Feb. 1, 1903), 225; *Automobile Review,* IV (Jan. 1901), 17–18; Georgano, ed., *Encyclopaedia of American Automobiles,* p. 61; *Scientific American,* LXXXIX (Aug. 8, 1903), 112; also the author's analysis of the automobile advertisements in general for the period 1899 to 1903.

27. For the financial troubles of the People's and DeDion-Bouton Motorette companies, see *Horseless Age,* VIII (Dec. 18, 1901), 814; IX (Jan. 8, 1902), 54.

28. Olds to W. B. Chenoweth, Nov. 28, 1900; Olds Motor Works catalog, *ca.* Jan. 1901 (in the library of the Motor Vehicle Maufacturers Association, Detroit); *Horseless Age,* V (Feb. 14, 1900), 12; VII (Nov. 7, 1900), 97; VIII (July 17, 1901), 354; VIII (Dec. 18, 1901), 814; IX (Jan. 1, 1902), 16; X (Sept. 3, 1902), 259; *Automobile,* IV (Jan. 1902), 23; *Motor World,* V (Oct. 23, 1902), 103.

29. *Horseless Age,* VII (Jan. 23, 1901), 32; VII (Feb. 20, 1901), 13–14; *Motor World,* I (Feb. 28, 1901), 368.

30. *Motor Age,* III (Mar. 6, 1901), 1197; *Motor World,* I (Feb. 7, 1901), 316; *Automobile Review,* IV (Feb. 1901), 36; *Horseless Age,* VII (Feb. 20, 1901), 13–14.

31. *Automobile Review,* IV (Feb. 1901), 5; *Motor World,* I (Feb. 28, 1901), 368; *Motor Age,* III (Mar. 6, 1901), 1212.

32. *Automobile Review,* IV (Mar. 1901), 66; *Motor Age,* IV (Mar. 21, 1901), n.p.; Alfred P. Sloan, Jr., with Boyden Sparkes, *Adventures of a White*

Collar Man (New York, 1941), pp. 27–32. C. B. Wilson, an original member of the Olds Motor Works production staff, still had in his possession in 1924 the order that Olds had issued calling for the building of 1,000 runabouts in 1901. *Automobile Trade Journal,* XXIX (Dec. 1924), 239; Mott's recollection in 1968, as reported in the *Detroit Free Press,* Feb. 21, 1973, was that Olds' initial tire order was for five hundred sets, which is consistent with the number of wheels Mott earlier reported that Olds ordered from the Weston-Mott company in 1900. See Clarence H. Young and William A. Quinn, *Foundation for Living: The Story of Charles Stewart Mott and Flint* (New York, 1963), p. 21.

33. Author's interviews with Bernice Olds Roe and Gladys Olds Anderson, June 28, 1973.

34. *Detroit Free Press,* Mar. 10, 1901; *Detroit News,* Mar. 9 and 10, Apr. 4, 1901.

35. *Detroit Free Press,* Mar. 10 and 17, 1901; *Detroit News,* Mar. 11 and Apr. 4, 1901; Bob Huxtable to the author, Mar. 7, 1976; Charles E. Hulse to the author, Apr. 1, 1976.

36. Motor Vehicle Manufacturers Association, *Automobiles of America: Milestones, Pioneers, Roll Call, Highlights,* 4th ed., revised (Detroit, 1974), pp. 24–25 (the same account appeared in earlier editions of the book). For examples of works of widely varying quality that accepted the Olds fire story, see Rae, *American Automobile Manufacturers,* p. 31; Pound, p. 53; and Reginald M. Cleveland and S. T. Williamson, *The Road is Yours . . .* (New York, 1951), p. 178.

37. *Detroit Free Press,* Mar. 10, 1901; *Horseless Age,* VIII (Apr. 3, 1901), 20.

38. *Detroit Free Press,* Mar. 10, 1901; Smith, *Motoring Down a Quarter of a Century,* p. 16; *Motor Age,* IV (Mar. 21, 1901), n.p.

39. *Ibid.,* II (Mar. 15, 1900), 3; May, *op. cit.,* p. 117; *Cycle and Automobile Trade Journal,* IX (Oct. 1, 1904), 86.

40. Lansing *State Republican,* Aug. 12, 1896; *Detroit News,* Mar. 9, 1901; Young and Quinn, *Foundation for Living,* p. 21; Sloan, *Adventures of a White Collar Man,* pp. 27–32; *Horseless Age,* XI (Jan. 28, 1903), 169.

41. Typed sheet listing Olds sales from 1891 to 1904 (MS in Olds Collection); Samuel Smith to Olds, July 19, 1901; *22nd Annual Report of the* [Michigan] *Bureau of Labor,* p. 138.

42. Niemeyer, pp. 36–38; Mrs. Wilfred C. Leland, with Minnie Dubbs Millbrook, *Master of Precision: Henry M. Leland* (Detroit, 1966), pp. 61–62.

43. Charles B. King, *A Golden Anniversary, 1895–1945* (Larchmont, N.Y., 1945), p. 15; notice to stockholders of Olds Gasoline Engine Works, June 22, 1903, and F. L. Smith to Olds, June 22, 1903 (MS in Olds Collection); manuscript volume containing minutes of special meetings of stockholders and directors of Olds Gasoline Engine Works, June 2–July 1, 1903, and Olds Motor Works minutes for the same period (MSS in private collection of Dennis Casteele).

44. Forbes and Foster, *Automotive Giants,* pp. 17–18; H. Jay Hayes Papers, Automotive History Collection, Detroit Public Library; Benjamin Briscoe, "The Inside Story of General Motors," *Detroit Saturday Night,* XV (Jan. 15, 1921), 9.

45. May, *A Most Unique Machine, passim.*

Chapter Six

1. Statement included on a dues notice from the Fellowcraft Club, sent to Olds, Aug. 26, 1901 (MS in Olds Collection); *Bi-Centenary of the Founding of the City of Detroit, 1701–1901* ... (Detroit, 1901), p. 85.
2. Pound, p. 53; Samuel Smith to Olds, July 19, 1901; Reuben Shettler to Olds, Nov. 27, 1901.
3. *Motor Age,* IV (June 13, 1901), no pagination.
4. *Ibid.,* IV (July 31, 1901), no pagination; Dwight S. Cole to Olds, Dec. 3, 1901.
5. Olds Motor Works catalog, *ca.* Jan. 1901 (in Motor Vehicle Manufacturers Association library); for the de-emphasis on the Olds engines in Olds ads, compare ads in *Automobile Review,* V (July 1901), 6 and V (Aug. 1901), 6; Joseph P. Fried, "The Merry, Merry Oldsmobile," *American History Illustrated,* I (Apr. 1966), 60.
6. Frank Presbrey, *The History and Development of Advertising* (Garden City, N. Y., 1929), pp. 557–559.
7. *Ibid.,* p. 559; *The Hub,* XLI (May, 1899), 19.
8. Presbrey, pp. 557–559; Henry B. Joy to James W. Packard, Mar. 28, 1903, in Joy's letterbook (MS in Henry B. Joy Papers, Michigan Historical Collections, University of Michigan).
9. Edmonds, *Development of the Automobile and Gasoline Engine in Michigan,* p. 26; *Saturday Evening Post,* CLXXIII (Feb. 23, 1901), 24; CLXXIV (Dec. 14, 1901), 19; CLXXIV (Feb. 8, 1902), 12; CLXXIV (Feb. 15, 1902), 16; Presbrey, p. 557.
10. *Horseless Age,* XV (May 3, 1905), 500; Jackson *Daily Citizen,* July 14, 1902; Jan. 10, 17, 24, 31, 1903; Presbrey, p. 560.
11. Pound, p. 61; announcement concerning the Oldsmobile Club of America (leaflet in the Motor Vehicle Manufacturers Association library); Lawrence H. Seltzer, *A Financial History of the American Automobile Industry* ... (Boston and New York, 1928), p. 156.
12. *Ladies Home Journal,* XIX (Feb. 1902), 34; XX (Apr. 1903), 43; XX (May 1903), 34; XX (June, 1903), 50. The claim that Olds was the first automaker to advertise in a woman's magazine appears in Beasley and Stark, *Made in Detroit,* p. 53; Pound, p. 61, simply states that Oldsmobile was the first automobile to be advertised in the *Journal.*
13. The last-mentioned ad is reproduced in Yarnell, facing p. 100.
14. Leland and Millbrook, *Master of Precision,* p. 65; author's interview with Mrs. Violet Oldani, May 8, 1975; author's interview with R. E. Olds Anderson, June 28, 1973.
15. Olds obituary in Daytona Beach (Fla.) *Journal and News,* Aug. 27, 1950.
16. Author's interview with Gladys Olds Anderson, June 28, 1973; *Motor,* I (Dec. 1903), 6 and *Automobile Review,* XI (Sept. 3, 1904), 220 mention motoring exploits of three children, ages nine to eleven.
17. Yarnell, pp. 80–81; Charles Hulse, "The Day Henry Put Detroit on the Map," *Antique Automobile,* XXXVII (May-June, 1973), 33; *Detroit News,* Mar. 27, 1901.
18. The importance of Detroit's flat surfaces to that city's development as an automobile center was first suggested to the author by Professor Madison Kuhn of Michigan State University several years ago; George

S. May, "The Detroit-New York Odyssey of Roy D. Chapin," *Detroit in Perspective,* II (Autumn 1973), 9–10; *Scientific American,* XC (Jan. 4, 1904), 29; author's interview with L. Gaylord Hulbert, Feb. 27, 1974; Don Lochbiler, *Detroit's Coming of Age, 1873 to 1973* (Detroit, 1973), pp. 168–169.

19. May, "The Detroit-New York Odyssey of Roy D. Chapin," pp. 7–8.
20. *Ibid.,* pp. 8–12; Hulse, "The Day Henry Put Detroit on the Map," p. 33.
21. The material in this paragraph and the six paragraphs that follow is based largely on May, "The Detroit-New York Odyssey of Roy D. Chapin," *passim.*
22. Olds to Alvan Macauley, May 22, 1941 (MS in the Roy D. Chapin Papers).
23. *Motor Age,* IV (Apr. 4, 1901), no pagination; see the advance reports of registrations for the New York auto show in the issues of *Horseless Age* in Oct. 1901.
24. Chapin's telegram to the Olds Motor Works, Nov. 5, 1901 (MS in the Chapin Papers), reprinted in a number of works, including Niemeyer, p. 46.
25. Chris Sinsabaugh, *Who, Me? Forty Years of Automobile History* (Detroit, 1940), p. 325. Crabb, *Birth of a Giant,* p. 66, and Cleveland and Williamson, *The Road is Yours,* p. 75, are examples of other writers who have exaggerated the record-setting character of Chapin's trip.
26. *Motor World,* III (Nov. 7, 1901), 164c.
27. *Horseless Age,* VIII (Nov. 13, 1901), 696, 711; *New York Times,* Nov. 3, 1901; hand-written, undated sheet (*ca.* autumn 1901) listing Oldsmobile dealers in the country (MS in the R. E. Olds Collection); Lou [?] Baker to Olds, May 3, 1901; Niemeyer, pp. 46–47; *Automobile Review,* V (Nov. 1901), 95; *Horseless Age,* VIII (Nov. 13, 1901), 711.
28. *National Cyclopaedia of American Biography,* XXXII, 109; *Horseless Age,* IV (May 31, 1899), 10; VIII (May 1, 1901), 113; XI (Jan. 7, 1903), 77. Booth, in the last cited article in *Horseless Age,* was quoted as saying that he sold his car to the Owen brothers in 1897, but the biography of Ray Owen in the *National Cyclopaedia of American Biography,* based on information supplied by Owen, claimed the earlier date of 1896.
29. Forbes and Foster, *Automotive Giants,* pp. 232–233; Niemeyer, pp. 46–47; *Horseless Age,* VIII (Dec. 4, 1901), 786; IX (Jan. 29, 1902), 153–154; XI (Jan. 14, 1903), 95.
30. *Harper's Weekly,* XLVI (July 26, 1902), 1004; *Horseless Age,* IX (Feb. 12, 1902), 218; IX (June 4, 1902), 689; XII (July 8, 1903), 47; Floyd Clymer, *Treasury of Foreign Cars, Old and New* (New York, 1957), p. 3.
31. Pound, pp. 58–59; Flint *Journal,* Dec. 10, 1976; *Automobile Review and Automobile News,* VII (Dec. 15, 1902), 327; *Automobile Review,* XI (Oct. 1, 1904), 328; *Motor Way,* XIII (Dec. 28, 1905), 14; *Motor Age,* III (May 7, 1903), 18. The Oldsmobile which Richard Whittaker purchased in 1901 still survives and is presently owned by Charles E. Hulse of Flint, who purchased it in 1963 and restored it to its original condition and working order.
32. Editors of *Automobile Quarterly, The American Car Since 1775,* p. 139; [Beverly Rae Kimes and Richard M. Langworth], *Oldsmobile: The*

First Seventy-five Years (New York, 1972), p. 70; Pound, p. 54; Yarnell, p. 101; *Horseless Age,* VIII (Dec. 4, 1901), 787; X (Dec. 24, 1902), 708; Jackson *Daily Citizen,* Jan. 17, 1903; *Detroit News,* Feb. 10, 1903; *Automobile Review and Automobile News,* VIII (May 1, 1903), 171; IX (ad section, Dec. 19, 1903), 8.

33. Typed sheet listing Olds sales from 1891 to 1904 (MS in Olds Collection).
34. Barnes, "The Romance of Our Automobile Makers," *World's Work,* XLI, 567; Seltzer, *Financial History of the American Automobile Industry,* p. 21.
35. Lansing *State Republican,* Aug. 14, 1897; Niemeyer, p. 49; James J. Flink, *The Car Culture* (Cambridge, Mass., 1975), p. 148.
36. Motor Vehicle Manufacturers Association, *Automobiles of America,* p. 283.
37. Georgano, *Encyclopedia of American Automobiles,* pp. 22, 135; Nicholson, *Passenger Cars, 1863–1904,* p. 124; T. R. Nicholson, *Passenger Cars, 1905–1912* (New York, 1971), pp. 6–7; Rae, *American Automobile Manufacturers,* p. 69; *Horseless Age,* VIII (Nov. 13, 1901), 709; IX (May 21, 1902), 612; Editors of *Automobile Quarterly, The American Car Since 1775,* p. 139. Olds and his staff were apparently aware of some, if not all, of the production achievements of other companies in these years. In the fall of 1902, at the time that Oldsmobile production for that year had equalled the record of 2,000 vehicles in one year that the Electric Vehicle Company had achieved in 1899, Olds' workers reportedly presented him with a gold watch charm—in the shape of a curved-dash runabout—in honor of the occasion: Crabb, *Birth of a Giant,* p. 70.
38. *Horseless Age,* XII (July 29, 1903), 111; XII (Dec. 9, 1903), 591; *Scientific American,* XC (Jan. 9, 1904), 29–30; May, *A Most Unique Machine,* p. 172.
39. *Detroit Free Press,* Mar. 17, 1901; *Motor Age,* IV (Mar. 28, 1901), no pagination; May, *op. cit.,* pp. 212–213.
40. *Motor Age,* IV (Mar. 28, 1901), no pagination; IV (Apr. 4, 1901), no pagination.
41. Lauder, *Lansing Unlimited,* pp. 36–37; Lansing *State Republican,* July 2, 1898; July 29, 1899; Edmonds, *Development of the Automobile and Gasoline Engine in Michigan,* pp. 14–15.
42. Olds Motor Works minutes for June 30, 1901; Samuel Smith to Olds, July 19, 1901.
43. Beverly Rae Kimes, "Reo Remembered: A History," *Automobile Quarterly,* XIV (1st qtr. 1976), 4; Lansing *Journal,* Oct. 3, 1891; Lansing *State Republican,* June 3, Sept. 29, 1897; Nov. 19, 1898; May 8, Nov. 6, 1899.
44. "R. Shettler's Efforts—The Growth of Lansing" (typescript copies in the Historical Collections, Michigan State University, and the Michigan Historical Collections, University of Michigan); annual report of the Olds Gasoline Engine Works for 1899 (in Corporation and Securities Records).
45. "R. Shettler's Efforts"; *Detroit News,* Oct. 1, 1898; Lansing *State Republican,* June 17, 1899.
46. "R. Shettler's Efforts"; Shettler to Olds Motor Works, Aug. 14, 1901.

47. Olds Motor Works minutes for Aug. 12, 1901, Aug. 14, 1902, July 1, 1903; *Motor Age,* V (Sept. 12, 1901), no pagination; "R. Shettler's Efforts"; undated fragment of a letter from Fred Smith to Olds, apparently from the latter part of 1901. According to the Olds Motor Works minutes, the directors were initially informed that the amount paid for the property was $4,750; but in July 1903 the amount that was actually paid by the company to the Lansing Business Men's Association and the subscribers to its purchase fund was $5,118, which is still less than the figure of $5,200, which has always been the published figure for the price of the fairgrounds site.

48. *Motor Age,* IV (Aug. 21, 1901), no pagination.

49. *18th Annual Report of the* [Michigan] *Bureau of Labor,* pp. 23, 64; *19th Annual Report of the* [Michigan] *Bureau of Labor,* pp. 248–249, 292–293.

50. May, *op. cit.,* p. 123.

51. *Horseless Age,* VIII (Nov. 13, 1901), 715; *Motor Age,* V (Nov. 14, 1901), no pagination; Olds Motor Works minutes for Aug. 14, 1902.

Chapter Seven

1. Application for Patent No. 761,392 (in Patent Application Files); *Lansing City Directory for 1902;* James P. Edmonds, *Early Lansing History* (Lansing, 1944), p. 32.

2. For D. B. Moon's earlier work, see Lansing *State Republican,* May 22 and Sept. 25, 1899. Harley J. McKee, "Glimpses of Architecture in Michigan," *Michigan History,* L (Mar. 1966), 22; R. E. Olds Anderson to the author, May 20, 1974.

3. Lansing *Journal,* Nov. 17, 1891; F. J. Schwankovsky Music House to Olds, Apr. 15, 1901; R. E. Olds Anderson to the author, May 20, 1974 and Sept. 4, 1976; Olds Diaries, including Dec. 1945 news clipping inserted in the December section of the Olds diary for that year; Lansing *State Journal,* May 31, 1964.

4. Lansing *State Journal,* May 31, 1964; Apr. 2, 1911 entry in Olds diary. For Ford's dancing interests, see David L. Lewis, *The Public Image of Henry Ford: An American Folk Hero and His Company* (Detroit, 1976), pp. 226–228.

5. *Detroit Free Press,* June 5, 1904; *Automobile,* X (Feb. 27, 1904), 250; Lansing *State Journal,* May 31, 1964.

6. *Detroit Free Press,* June 5, 1904; May, *A Most Unique Machine,* p. 237.

7. *Horseless Age,* X (Nov. 12, 1902), 541; letterhead of American Motor League, used in a letter from the league's president, Isaac B. Potter, to Olds, Dec. 4, 1903.

8. Olds Motor Works minutes, Jan. 8, 1901; *Motor Age,* IV (Mar. 21, 1901), no pagination; Samuel Smith to Olds, July 19, 1901; R. Shettler to Olds Motor Works, Aug. 14, 1901.

9. Among the more respected writers who have cited the disagreement over the kind of car they should produce as the cause of the break between Olds and the Smiths are Pound, p. 62, and Rae, *American Automobile Manufacturers,* p. 31. Niemeyer, pp. 54–55, also emphasizes

this point but indicates that there were additional issues involved in the dispute.

10. Fred Smith to Olds, May 17 and Nov. 27, 1902; *Horseless Age,* X (Aug. 13, 1902), 179; X (Sept. 10, 1902), 285; X (Sept. 17, 1902), 308; X (Nov. 12, 1902), 540.

11. *Automobile Review and Automobile News,* VIII (Feb. 1, 1903), 42; VIII (Feb. 15, 1903), 66; *Cycle and Automobile Trade Journal,* VII (Feb. 1, 1903), 101–103.

12. Eugene W. Lewis, *Motor Memories, A Saga of Whirling Gears* (Detroit, 1947), pp. 40–41; *Detroit News,* Feb. 8, 1903; Fred Smith to Olds, Apr. 22, 1903; Reuben Shettler to Olds, Dec. 14, 1903.

13. *Detroit News,* Feb. 8, 1903.

14. Olds' claim that he had accepted the necessity of the larger touring car as a production model by the fall of 1903 is made in a letter to Reuben Shettler, May 23, 1904.

15. Fred Smith to Olds, Apr. 22 and Sept. 3, 1903.

16. John Bohnet, Lansing, Michigan, to Olds, Aug. 16, 1901; Maxwell biography in *National Cyclopaedia of American Biography,* XXV, 28; Milton Beck's Canadian background in Lansing *State Republican,* June 27, 1899; T. L. Elliott, Wheeling, W. Va., to Olds Motor Works, Sept. 21, 1901; Fred L. White, Gambier, Ohio, to Olds Motor Works, Aug. 31, 1901; Henry W. Purcell, Chicago, to Olds Motor Works, Mar. 31, 1901; Albert Ross, Toronto, to Olds Motor Works, Oct. 23, 1901.

17. Donald Wilhelm, "The Evolution of American Industry: The Automobile," *Harper's,* CLXXV (Nov. 1937), vi; Davis & Deyo, Binghamton, N. Y., to Olds Motor Works, Sept. 1, 1902; Fred Smith to Mrs. E. C. Chapin, June 6, 1902 (in the Chapin Papers); Fred Smith to Olds, July 9, 1902.

18. May, pp. 282–288; Olds Motor Works minutes for June 27, 1902; Mar. 2 and Apr. 9, 1903; Olds to Dr. Tappey, Sept. 6, 1904.

19. Fred Smith to Olds, May 17, 1902, undated letter (*ca.* July 1902), and Aug. 1902; Samuel Smith to Olds, Aug. 8, 1902.

20. James B. Seager to Fred Smith (undated, *ca.* July 1902); Reuben Shettler to Olds, Nov. 27 and Dec. 23, 1901; Olds Motor Works minutes for Aug. 14, 1902; Jan. 6, 1903; Henry Russel to Olds, Apr. 19, 1903.

21. H. H. Westinghouse to M. F. Loomis, April 19, 1902 (in the Chapin Papers); *Horseless Age,* XII (Oct. 14, 1903), 402; author's interviews with Gladys Olds Anderson and Bernice Olds Roe, June 28, 1973; Sinsabaugh, *Who, Me?,* p. 222; *Story of the Automobile from the First Toy Car to the Present Perfect Self Propelled Vehicle* (published by Sports of the Times [New York, 1903]), p. 123.

22. *Motor World,* V (Dec. 4, 1902), 302.

23. *Automobile Review and Automobile News,* VI (May, 1902), 101; VII (Oct. 15, 1902), 257, 261; *Horseless Age,* X (Aug. 6, 1902), 136–139.

24. *Automobile Review and Automobile News,* VIII (Apr. 1, 1903), 127–128.

25. *Horseless Age,* XII (Oct. 14, 1903), 405–406; *Automobile Review and Automobile News,* IX (Nov. 1, 1903), 168.

26. Motor Vehicle Manufacturers Association, *Automobiles of America,* pp. 31, 36.

27. W. Worley Beaumont, *Motor Vehicles and Motors* ... (London, 1906), II, 278; *Automobile Review,* XI (Dec. 31, 1904), 620.
28. Niemeyer, p. 51; *Scientific American,* LXXXVIII (Apr. 18, 1903), 295; *Automobile Review and Automobile News,* IX (Sept. 15, 1903),121–122.
29. Henry Russel to Olds, Apr. 19, 1903.
30. Pound, p. 56; Yarnell, pp. 74–75, 116; Kimes, "Reo Remembered," *Automobile Quarterly,* XIV, 18.
31. *Horseless Age,* X (Nov. 6, 1902), 516; Pound, p. 60; [Arthur Jerome Eddy], *Two Thousand Miles on an Automobile* ... (Philadelphia, 1902), 81.
32. Leland and Millbrook, *Master of Precision,* p. 62.
33. Fred Smith to Olds, May 17, 1902; undated letter (*ca.* July 1902); Apr. 22, 1903.
34. Olds to Fred Smith, May 1, 1903; Patent application for Patent No. 743,402 (in Patent Application Files); U. S. Patent Office *Official Gazette,* CVII (Nov. 3, 1903), 245.
35. Olds to Fred Smith, May 1, 1903; author's interview with Mrs. Violet Oldani, May 8, 1975; author's interviews with Hugo Lundberg, Jr. and Theodore Lundberg, Mar. 14, 1975.
36. Olds Motor Works minutes, Dec. 7, 1903; Jan. 11, 1904; Olds to Fred Smith, Jan. 29, 1904; Olds to Dr. Tappey, Sept. 6, 1904.
37. Olds to Dr. Tappey, Sept. 6, 1904; Olds Motor Works minutes, Oct. 21, 1902; annual report of Olds Motor Works for year ending Dec. 31, 1902 (in Corporation and Securities Records); Niemeyer, p. 54; Henry Russel to Olds, Apr. 19, May 9, and Aug. 20, 1903; Olds to F. M. Delano, Jan. 28, 1904.
38. Minutes of special meetings of stockholders of Olds Gasoline Engine Works, June 2–July 1, 1903 (in private collection of Dennis Casteele); Olds Motor Works minutes for the same period and for July 14, 1903; amendments to articles of association of Olds Motor Works, Aug. 1, 1903, recorded Aug. 7, 1903 (in Corporation and Securities Bureau, Michigan Department of Commerce).
39. See Appendix and Patent Application Files.
40. Niemeyer, pp. 58–65, provides many details on the sale of Olds' stock, but Niemeyer was apparently unaware of the stock split voted in 1903 and the decisive impact that that action would have had on the market price for stock in the Olds Motor Works; J. L. Carleton to Eugene Cooley, Apr. 10, 1907 (in the Cooley Papers).
41. *Detroit Free Press,* Aug. 29, 1950.
42. May, pp. 315–316, 320–322.
43. Introductory statement by Chapin in Smith, *Motoring Down a Quarter of a Century.*
44. Author's interview with Gladys Olds Anderson and Bernice Olds Roe, June 28, 1973. The incident involving Smith and Olds late in their lives may well be the letter campaign waged by Smith in 1939 against the labelling of the Olds gasoline vehicle, vintage 1897–98, in the Smithsonian Institution as the first Oldsmobile. In the course of this campaign Smith, in letters to Olds as well as to the Smithsonian and to the Oldsmobile Division of General Motors, used some rather harsh

language in referring to his one-time business associate (correspondence in the private collection of Dennis Casteele).

Chapter Eight

1. Lansing *State Journal*, Aug. 30, 1950.
2. Lansing *State Republican*, Sept. 25, Nov. 1, 1899; Niemeyer, p. 62; information on Emory Olds in correspondence in the Olds Collection, and in author's interviews with Gladys Olds Anderson and Bernice Olds Roe, June 28, 1973.
3. *Horseless Age*, XIII (Jan. 13, 1904), 51; XIII (Jan. 27, 1904), 113, 115; XIII (Feb. 3, 1904), 149; XIII (Mar. 9, 1904), 292; Olds to F. M. Delano, Jan. 15, 1904; Olds to W. J. Morgan, July 5, 1904. The statistics on the production of the Michigan carriage and wagon industry in 1898 are found in the *17th Annual Report of the* [Michigan] *Bureau of Labor*, p. 65.
4. May, *A Most Unique Machine*, pp. 222–224.
5. Yarnell, p. 139.
6. Olds to Ray Owen, Aug. 4, 1904; Yarnell, p. 139; R. Carlyle Buley, *The Equitable Life Assurance Society of the United States, 1859–1964* (New York, 1967), I, 567–572.
7. *Automobile Review*, XI (Aug. 27, 1904), 201.
8. Olds to F. M. Delano, Jan. 28, 1904; "R. Shettler's Efforts"; *Automobile Review, loc. cit.*
9. Niemeyer, pp. 66–68.
10. *Ibid.; Automobile Review*, X (Apr. 30, 1904), 647; for Edward Peer's career, see *Lansing City Directory*, where his name and position are listed in each edition from 1892 to 1910.
11. Benjamin F. Davis to Eugene Cooley, Aug. 5, 1904 (in the Cooley Papers); Niemeyer, pp. 70–71; see Olds' patents listed in Appendix.
12. Olds to Ray Owen, Aug. 4, 1904.
13. Forbes and Foster, *Automotive Giants*, p. 235; Yarnell, pp. 145–147.
14. *Automobile Review*, XI (Aug. 27, 1904), 201; Turner, *An Account of Ingham County . . .* , p. 590.
15. *Automobile*, XI (Aug. 27, 1904), 246; *Horseless Age*, XIV (Aug. 24, 1904), 192; *Detroit Free Press*, Aug. 18, 1904. See also *Detroit News*, Aug. 17, 1904.
16. Names of the Reo stockholders are given in the reports of the company (in Corporation and Securities Records); for biographical data, see Turner, *An Account of Ingham County . . .* , pp. 349–350, 356–357, 402, 456, 569–570, 607–608, 634–635, 677–678, 681, 764.
17. *Automobile*, XI (Aug. 27, 1904), 246; *Automobile Review*, XI (Aug. 27, 1904), 201.
18. Kimes, "Reo Remembered," *Automobile Quarterly*, XIV, 4; Olds Motor Works to Olds, Aug. 18, 1904.
19. Olds to Olds Motor Works, Aug. 19, 1904; Olds to Henry Russel, Sept. 19, 1904.
20. Kimes, *op. cit.*, p. 9; Olds Motor Works to Benjamin Davis, Aug. 18, 1904 (in the Cooley Papers); Olds to Henry Russel, Sept. 19, 1904; R. M. Owen to Olds, Sept. 27, 1904; Niemeyer, pp. 73–74.

21. *Horseless Age,* XIV (Aug. 31, 1904), 219.
22. Niemeyer, pp. 73–75.
23. "R. Shettler's Efforts."
24. Olds to Owen, Aug. 4, 1904; Lansing *Journal,* Aug. 19, 22, 23, and Sept. 3, 1904; Yarnell, p. 154.
25. Lansing *Journal,* Sept. 6, 1904.
26. May, pp. 227–228.
27. *Scientific American,* XCII (June 24, 1905), 508; *Horseless Age,* XIV (Nov. 2, 1904), 458; *Motor,* III (Jan. 1905), 12; Niemeyer, p. 77; Yarnell, p. 151.
28. Lansing *State Journal,* June 3, 1949; June 3, 1950.
29. Yarnell, p. 158.
30. Lansing *State Journal,* June 3, 1949; *Motor,* III (Feb. 1905), 16.
31. Forbes and Foster, *Automotive Giants,* p. 235; Yarnell, pp. 158–159.
32. Olds to Owen, Aug. 4 and 19, 1904; Owen to Olds, Aug. 8 and 30, 1904; Niemeyer, p. 79.
33. Owen to Olds, Sept. 1, 1904; Niemeyer, pp. 79–81; *Automobile Review,* XI (Oct. 29, 1904), 428; Yarnell, pp. 160–161.
34. *Motor Age,* VI (Dec. 29, 1904), 19.
35. *Motor,* III (Nov. 1904), 61; III (Dec. 1904), 6; III (Jan. 1905), 12; J. O. Powers to Olds, Nov. 9, 1904.
36. *Motor,* III (Dec. 1904), 6; III (Feb. 1905), 16; *Motor Age,* VI (Dec. 22, 1904), 37.

Chapter Nine

1. *Automobile Review,* XI (Dec. 31, 1904), 644; *Horseless Age,* XV (Jan. 25, 1905), 123.
2. *Automobile Review,* XI (Nov. 19, 1904), 496; XII (Jan. 21, 1905), 60; *Scientific American,* XCII (Jan. 28, 1905), 83.
3. *Automobile Review,* XI (Nov. 19, 1904), 496.
4. *Motor Way, Horseless Age,* and especially *Motor Age* carried frequent reports on the progress of the Reo Mountaineer. Motor Vehicle Manufacturers Association, *Automobiles of America,* p. 42, declares that another Reo performed the same round-trip cross-country feat in 1907.
5. *Automobile Review,* XII (May 25, 1905), 513; *Horseless Age,* XV (May 3, 1905), 516; XVI (July 5, 1905), xvi.
6. *Horseless Age,* XV (Apr. 19, 1905), 474; XV (May 31, 1905), 620; XV (June 14, 1905), 668; XVI (Sept. 20, 1905), 349; *Automobile Review,* XII (June 8, 1905), 558; *Motor Way,* XIII (Aug. 10, 1905), 9.
7. *Horseless Age,* XVI (July 19, 1905), 127–128; XVI (July 26, 1905), 151–152; XVI (Aug. 9, 1905), 206; *Motor Way,* XIII (July 20, 1905), 8; XIII (July 27, 1905), 4–7; Yarnell, pp. 175–177; Kimes, "Reo Remembered," *Automobile Quarterly,* XIV, 15.
8. *Horseless Age,* XVI (Aug. 16, 1905), xvii; XVI (Sept. 6, 1905), xxv.
9. *Automobile Review,* XI (Dec. 10, 1904), 556; *Motor Age,* VII (Jan. 5, 1905), 14; Niemeyer, pp. 91–93, 110–111; James Rood Doolittle, ed., *The Romance of the Automobile Industry* (New York, 1916), p. 290.
10. Niemeyer, pp. 94–95; Darling, *City in the Forest,* pp. 164–165.

11. *Horseless Age,* XIX (Feb. 6, 1907), 198; *Motor,* V (Jan. 1906), 73–88; Pound, pp. 63–64.
12. *Motor Age,* XI (June 6, 1907), 14; Yarnell, pp. 174–175.

Chapter Ten

1. For Hopkins' career, see his autobiography, *My Life in Advertising* (New York, 1927).
2. Reo production figures and the company's ranking among auto producers can be found in Niemeyer, p. 110, and Editors of *Automobile Quarterly, The American Car Since 1775,* pp. 138–139.
3. Hopkins, *My Life in Advertising,* pp. 110–111, 118; *Motor,* V (Nov. 1905), 97.
4. The statement by R. M. Owen & Company is found in "A reprint of thirty-six advertisements in *Collier's* special automobile supplement of January 6, 1912," a large brochure (no pagination) specially printed for the auto trade (copy in the University of Michigan Graduate Library); Niemeyer, pp. 108, 112.
5. Kimes, "Reo Remembered," *Automobile Quarterly,* XIV, 20; Hopkins, pp. 80–81.
6. Hopkins, p. 119.
7. Yarnell, p. 191; for production figures, see the sources cited in note 2 above.
8. Olds' diaries for the years from 1906 to about 1915; Yarnell, pp. 166–167.
9. See data on Olds' patents in Appendix.
10. Niemeyer, pp. 85–86.
11. *Ibid.,* p. 86.
12. *Motor,* II (Aug. 1904), 53; *Automobile Review,* X (Jan. 30, 1904), 350.
13. Owen to Olds, Sept. 27, 1904.
14. Rae, *American Automobile Manufacturers,* p. 77; Niemeyer, pp. 87–88; Olds to Ford Motor Company, Oct. 31, 1904; R. Shettler to J. B. Bartholomew, Nov. 3, 1904.
15. J. Couzens, Ford Motor Company, to Olds, Nov. 16, 1904; Niemeyer, pp. 88–91; *Horseless Age,* XV (Mar. 1, 1905), 289.
16. Niemeyer, pp. 95–96.
17. *Automobile,* XXII (Jan. 20, 1910), 171; Olds' diary entries for Jan. 12 and 13, 1910.
18. *Automobile,* XXII (Apr. 7, 1910), 690.
19. Actually, the disparity between Ford production figures and those of all others in the industry may well have been far greater than that indicated if one accepts the traditional estimate of under 40,000 as the Ford production for 1911. According to Editors of *Automobile Quarterly, The American Car Since 1775,* p. 139, Ford produced 69,762 cars in 1911, nearly two and a half times more than did the second largest manufacturer, Studebaker-EMF, and nearly thirteen times more than did Reo that year.

Chapter Eleven

1. *Horseless Age,* XX (Aug. 14, 1907), 203.
2. Yarnell, pp. 179–180.
3. For the origins of the merger talks, see May, *A Most Unique Machine,* pp. 298–300.
4. *Ibid.,* pp. 300–301.
5. *Ibid.,* pp. 301–302.
6. *Ibid.,* p. 302; Olds' diary for 1908.
7. May, pp. 302–303.
8. *Ibid.,* pp. 303–304; Yarnell, p. 182.
9. Lansing *State Journal,* June 4, 1944; June 3, 1949; May, pp. 303–304.
10. May, p. 304.
11. *Ibid.*
12. Niemeyer, p. 111; Harry Barnard, *Independent Man: The Life of Senator James Couzens* (New York, 1958), p. 66; the estimate of Mott's wealth has appeared in numerous publications, including such a distant one as the British newspaper *The Guardian,* where the information appeared as part of an article on Mott's son Stewart, in the issue of Mar. 9, 1973.
13. Lawrence R. Gustin, *Billy Durant: Creator of General Motors* (Grand Rapids, 1973), p. 131.
14. May, pp. 310–322; Olds' diary entry for Oct. 19, 1908.
15. May, pp. 323–328.
16. *Ibid.,* pp. 325–326.
17. *Ibid.,* p. 326.
18. Briscoe, "The Inside Story of General Motors," *Detroit Saturday Night,* XV (Feb. 5, 1921), 4 (section 2); Olds' diary entry for Sept. 27, 1909; Niemeyer, pp. 103–104.
19. Niemeyer, p. 104; *Motor Age,* XX (Aug. 3, 1911), 43; Olds' diary entry for Sept. 29, 1911.
20. Rae, *American Automobile Manufacturers,* pp. 48–49; Editors of *Automobile Quarterly, The American Car Since 1775,* p. 139.
21. Rae, *American Automobile Manufacturers,* p. 97; Olds' diary entries for Jan. 3, 7, 9, 16, 1912.
22. Niemeyer, p. 104.

Chapter Twelve

1. Niemeyer, p. 102.
2. *Ibid.,* pp. 104–106; *Scientific American,* XCII (June 24, 1905), 508; *Motor Age,* IX (Mar. 15, 1906), 27.
3. Advertisement in *Lansing City Directory, 1912,* facing p. 440.
4. "R. Shettler's Efforts"; author's interviews with Herman Staebler, July 28, 1971, and R. E. Olds Anderson, June 28, 1973.
5. Author's interview with R. E. Olds Anderson, June 28, 1973.
6. "R. Shettler's Efforts."
7. Olds' diary for period from Feb. 27 to Apr. 20, 1910; *Automobile,* XXII

(Apr. 21, 1910), 775; XXII (June 23, 1910), 1154; *Motor Age,* XVII (June 23, 1910), 36.

8. Agreement, dated Oct. 19, 1910, between Reo Motor Car Company and Owen Motor Car Company (Vol. 5 in Reo Collection, Historical Collections, Michigan State University); Niemeyer, pp. 106–107.

9. The evidence for Peer's departure from Lansing is based on an examination of the *Lansing City Directories* for the years jsut after 1910; Olds' diary entries for Mar. 31 and Apr. 2, 1915; "R. Shettler's Efforts."

10. Note in Olds' diary opposite entries for Apr. 29 to May 5, 1906; Reo board minutes for Dec. 26, 1913 (Vol. 1, Reo Collection). The board minutes beginning with April, 1913, showed a continuing concern among the directors about the slow sales of Reo vehicles and discussions of the degree to which Owen was responsible for these lagging sales.

11. Niemeyer, pp. 114, 130.

Chapter Thirteen

1. Author's interview with L. Gaylord Hulbert, Feb. 27, 1974.
2. See Appendix.
3. Lauder, *Lansing Unlimited,* p. 135.
4. Niemeyer, pp. 162–163.
5. Author's interview with Hugo Lundberg, Jr., Mar. 14, 1975. Beasley and Stark, *Made in Detroit,* pp. 296–297.
6. Lauder, *Lansing Unlimited,* pp. 217–218.
7. The most extensive discussion of Olds' Florida land development project is in Niemeyer, pp. 115–123, and is the basis for the account that follows.
8. Unidentified and undated news clipping folded into Olds' diary for 1918.
9. Olds' diary entry for Mar. 27, 1916; author's interview with Herman Staebler, July 28, 1971.
10. Copy of unidentified, undated magazine article, entitled "Auto Maker Olds Planned Dream City," supplied to the author by Woodward Roe.
11. *Ibid.*
12. *Ibid.*
13. The attempts to secure a shipyard are discussed in Niemeyer, pp. 120–122.
14. Rae, *American Automobile Manufacturers,* pp. 138–139.
15. Olds' diaries, 1927–1932; "Auto Maker Olds Planned Dream City"; federal census statistics for 1960 and 1970.
16. *National Cyclopaedia of American Biography,* XXXIX, 480; Yarnell, p. 196; R. E. Olds Anderson to the author, Sept. 4, 1976. Olds' estate sold his interests in the Fort Harrison Hotel in the early 1950s, and in 1960 Olds Anderson, who was then managing the Olds Hotel, sold that hotel to the Jack Tar Hotel chain. Subsequently Lansing-area businessmen purchased the hotel and restored the Olds name to the establishment's marquee.
17. Niemeyer, pp. 173–174.
18. Brown's published statements, filed in the R. E. Olds file (in the biographical file of the Michigan State Library, Lansing); author's inter-

views with Hugo Lundberg, Jr., and Theodore Lundberg, Mar. 14, 1975, and Dennis Casteele, Aug. 11, 1976.

19. Yarnell, pp. 185–186; author's interviews with Woodward Roe and R. E. Olds Anderson, June 28, 1973. The name of Olds' office building was in later years changed to the Michigan National Bank Tower, after the banking institution that succeeded to the quarters previously occupied by the defunct Capital National Bank.

20. A photograph of the 1925 event appears as the frontispiece to Epstein, *The Automobile Industry*.

21. Niemeyer, p. 130; interview with Hugo Lundberg, Jr., Mar. 14, 1975; Kimes, "Reo Remembered," *Automobile Quarterly*, XIV, 27.

22. Niemeyer, pp. 110–111, 137–138.

23. *Ibid.*, pp. 134–139; Kimes, *op. cit.*, p. 29.

24. Kimes, p. 29; Niemeyer, pp. 139–140.

25. Niemeyer, pp. 137–138.

26. *Ibid.*, pp. 110–111, 137–138.

27. *Ibid.*, pp. 143–144.

28. Kimes, p. 33; Niemeyer, pp. 145–146, 148.

29. *Ibid.*, pp. 146, 148–149.

30. *Ibid.*, pp. 151–152.

31. *Ibid.*, p. 153; Motor Vehicle Manufacturers Association, *Automobiles of America*, p. 95.

32. *Newsweek*, III (Apr. 28, 1934), 28.

33. Niemeyer, pp. 153–161.

34. Niemeyer, pp. 161–171; *Ann Arbor News*, Feb. 22, 1976. The Reo Speedwagon name has not vanished from the marketplace. A rock music group going by that name enjoyed increasing success in the 1970s, appearing in concert with a major rock figure, Bob Segar, at Detroit's Cobo Arena in September 1975, and recording several albums that were listed in recording industry catalogs in January 1977. Information supplied to the author by Arthur Timko, manager of WEMU-FM, Jan. 26, 1977.

Chapter Fourteen

1. Olds' diary for 1937; Lauder, *Lansing Unlimited*, p. 134.

2. Author's interview with Hugo Lundberg, Jr., Mar. 14, 1975.

3. *Ibid.; National Cyclopaedia of American Biography*, XXXIX, 480–481; author's interview with R. E. Olds Anderson, June 28, 1973; R. E. Olds Anderson to the author, Sept. 4, 1976; Lansing *State Journal*, June 3, 1949.

4. Lansing *Journal*, May 7, 11, 12, June 15, 1908; Chase S. Osborn to Olds, May 19, 1908, and Olds to Osborn, May 28, 1908 (MSS in the Chase S. Osborn Papers, Michigan Historical Collections, University of Michigan); Olds' diary entries for June 14–19, 1908.

5. Olds to Frank D. Fitzgerald, June 22 and 29, 1936, and Fitzgerald to Olds, June 23, 1936 (MSS in the Frank D. Fitzgerald Papers, Michigan Historical Collections, University of Michigan); Olds to Rudolph E. Reichert, July 6, 1932 (MSS in the Rudolph E. Reichert Papers, Michigan Historical Collections, University of Michigan).

6. Lansing *State Journal,* June 3, 1949; June 3, 1950; author's interview with Dr. Julius Fischbach, June 14, 1973; Niemeyer, p. 171.
7. Author's interviews with Dennis Casteele, Aug. 11, 1976, Dr. Julius Fischbach, and Mrs. Violet Oldani, May 8, 1975; Lansing *State Journal,* Aug. 31, 1950; May 31, 1964; Fred Smith letters for 1939 (MSS in private collection of Dennis Casteele).
8. Author's interviews with Dr. Julius Fischbach and Hugo Lundberg, Jr.; *National Cyclopaedia of American Biography,* XXXIX, 481; Olds' diary entries for Apr. 25, 28, 30, 1910; Turner, *An Account of Ingham County . . . ,* pp. 258–259; *Sparrow News,* July, Aug., Sept., 1976; F. Bioten Plasman, Edward W. Sparrow Hospital Association, to the author, Sept. 24, 1976.
9. *Motor Way,* XIII (Nov. 23, 1905), 20–21; *Horseless Age,* XVI (Nov. 29, 1905), 716; XIX (Feb. 6, 1907), 221; Mrs. Kay Stratton, secretary to the president, Kalamazoo College, to the author, May 25, 1973; Lillian A. Comar, archivist, Hillsdale College, to the author, May 15, 1973; Olds' diary entry for June 17, 1913; Lansing *State Journal,* Aug. 31, Sept. 2, 1950.
10. Olds' diary entry for Nov. 19, 1910; Lansing *State Journal,* June 4, 1944; Aug. 27, 1950; Madison Kuhn, *Michigan State: The First Hundred Years* (East Lansing, 1955), pp. 266–269.
11. *National Cyclopaedia of American Biography, loc. cit.;* Rajee Tobia, "R. E. Olds—Benefactor to the Holy Lands," address delivered at the Reo Club House to the Historical Society of Greater Lansing, May 19, 1965 (published by the society in 1966); Yarnell, pp. 202–203.
12. Lansing *State Journal,* Aug. 27, 1950; Olds' diary entry for Jan. 15, 1913, which reports he had gone to his "1st Trustee Meeting at Church"; author's interviews with Mrs. Violet Oldani and Dr. and Mrs. Julius Fischbach.
13. Author's interview with Dr. Julius Fischbach.
14. Author's interview with Mrs. Cecelia Rueschaw, Mar. 14, 1975; Theodore Lundberg and Hugo Lundberg, Jr., Mar. 14, 1975; and R. E. Olds Anderson, June 28, 1973; Olds' diary entry for April 21, 1912.
15. Author's interviews with Theodore Lundberg, R. E. Olds Anderson, and Mrs. Cecelia Rueschaw; Niemeyer, p. 128.
16. *History of Lansing Central Union WCTU, 1874–1949* (in the Ludwig Papers, Michigan Historical Collections, University of Michigan); author's interview with R. E. Olds Anderson.
17. Olds' diary entry for Nov. 13, 1911; author's interview with Dr. and Mrs. Julius Fischbach, June 28, 1973.
18. Author's interviews with Mrs. Violet Oldani and Miss Isabella Swan, May 8, 1975.
19. Olds' diaries from 1926 on; Lansing *State Journal,* May 31, 1964; author's interviews with Gladys Olds Anderson and Bernice Olds Roe, June 28, 1973; with Dr. and Mrs. Julius Fischbach.
20. Lansing *State Journal,* May 31, 1964; interview with Dr. Julius Fischbach.
21. Lansing *State Journal,* June 3, 1950; May 31, 1964; "That Boy Ranny."
22. Author's interviews with Mrs. Violet Oldani and Theodore Lundberg; Lansing *State Journal,* May 31, 1964.
23. Author's interview with Dr. and Mrs. Julius Fischbach; Olds' diary

entry for Jan. 1, 1912; Juliette Bartholomew Stucky, "To Lansing with Love," paper read to the Historical Society of Greater Lansing, April 30, 1959 (published by the society in 1960); Lansing *State Journal,* June 2 and 4, 1944; May 31, 1964; Lauder, *Lansing Unlimited,* p. 123. Taylor's recollections in 1964 would indicate that Olds' departure from the gathering that had assembled for his eightieth birthday occurred later in the day than would have been the case if he were referring to a luncheon.

24. Author's interviews with Dennis Casteele, Theodore Lundberg, and Hugo Lundberg, Jr.

25. *New York Times,* Aug. 27, 1950; Lansing *State Journal,* June 3, 1949; June 3, 1950.

26. Lauder, *Lansing Unlimited,* p. 213; publicity release, dated Oct. 1938 (in the photo collections of the Motor Vehicle Manufacturers Association); Olds' diary for 1936; author's interviews with Dennis Casteele and Dr. and Mrs. Julius Fischbach; Fred Smith letters for 1939 (in private collection of Dennis Casteele).

27. Lansing *State Journal,* June 3, Aug. 27, 1950; Olds interview on *A Name to Remember* tape.

28. Niemeyer, p. 174; *New York Times,* Aug. 21, 27, 1950; Lansing *State Journal,* Aug. 27, 30, Sept. 2, 1950.

29. *Detroit Free Press,* Aug. 29, 1950.

Index